Cycling "Complex" Conditioning

Istvan Javorek

Dedication

I dedicate my book to my daughter Henriette, who "survived" my strict educational rules, completed a PHD at age 29 and, beside her studies and university teaching, also became an aerobics instructor and personal trainer. She was my first student who learned to always smile and say: "Yes I love it".

To my wife Julia who "survived" all of those years I spent more time with my athletes than at home and still managed to pursue a successful medical career and be an incredible mother and wife.

Henriette inspires me to write and Julia fills me with the love of family and my grandkids give me strength and desire to enjoy life. They mean the world to me.

Dr. Henriette Andrea Javorek
Editor

Randy Breeden
Art Direction/Design

Select photos courtesy of **Brett Gustafson,** and **Bruce Klemens.**

ISBN: 9780977957408

Table of Contents

Acknowledgements

I express my gratitude to those who have helped me to be able to put together my first book: Doug Allen, Randy Breeden and for their hard work in the gym and on editing my book; Sumya Anani, Wesley Barnett, Randy Barnes, Dragomir Cioroslan, Jim Dice, Kareem Rush, Wayne Simien, Istvan Tasnadi, Dirk Yasko, and all of my athletes who were and are enduring my experiences with my dumbbell and barbell complex exercises, and older and new conditioning routines; to photographs Brett Gustafson, and Bruce Klemens for their great photos; to my former coach Ferenc Szathmari, who was teaching me hard and disciplined work; to University of Texas A&M, College Station, TX and Johnson County Community College, Overland Park, KS in supporting me to develop a new direction in sports conditioning.

Chapter 1
Introduction

Have you reached a sticking point in your training? Has your progress stagnated for ages? Are you bored with your program or exercises you have done for years? Maybe you are suffering from nagging overtraining injuries. Maybe you are a coach and you have run out of training exercises and ideas. Possibly you have read almost every book on strength exercises that you could lay your hands upon. Maybe you simply are looking to add some more interesting or novel exercises to your already extensive program. If any of these questions sound familiar to you, then this book is for you.

Objectives

This text is all about strength exercises and their almost infinite number of possible variations. More specifically, it shows you how to use and combine many different types of free weight training, be it with dumbbells or barbells. What you will read about in depth here is a compendium of strength exercises which have come from the fascinating history of the Iron Game and its many pioneers from the 19th century up to the present day, as well as from the many years of my practical coaching and competitive experience. Here you will learn about the idea of complex or combinations method of training which is now becoming popular in the West, even though it has been used in Eastern Europe for many decades.

You will learn about the thousands of exercises and complexes of exercises that I have been applying with eminent success, both in my earlier days in my native Romania and more recently in the USA, where I live now. You will learn old and new barbell exercises and their numerous variations drawn from Olympic style Weightlifting, from Powerlifting and bodybuilding, as well a huge collection of my unique collection of dumbbell and plyometric exercises. In addition, you will learn how to combine into a single exercise several different movements with barbells or dumbbells so as to create what often are called complexes. Consequently, you should never again run short of training ideas, and any tendency to training boredom should become a thing of the past.

My athletes at Johnson County Community College call me Coach Javorkian. At the University of Texas A&M my athletes called me Coach Pop, while several college and high school conditioning coaches are calling me "The DB King", for reasons which will become very obvious as you delve more deeply into this book. Back in Romania I was simply Coach Comrade, and for the more intimate athletes, Pista bacsi (or Uncle Pista, which is the Hungarian nickname for Istvan or Steven).

Almost paradoxically, I started my sporting career as a violin player. At 14 years of age my bodymass was 45 kilogram (99 lb). I was skinny and not even remotely the strongest child in the neighborhood. Then, one day while I was walking home from violin practice, my sister's, (who was a master level gymnast and capable of beating me in wrestling) friends ambushed me on the street and coerced me to press my violin bow overhead. Obviously I felt very embarrassed, but I recall that this apparently trivial event was the turning point in my life. I hurried home and to my mother's amazement, I officially announced that I wish to abandon my "bright violinist future" and become an athlete.

When I started sport, I was flat-footed, with very poor physical coordination and high blood pressure. At my request, my sister took me to the gymnasium where I practiced competitive gymnastics four times a week until the age of sixteen. At the same time, like many other Eastern European children, I was regularly ice skating, snow sliding, snow skiing, tree climbing, swimming, and playing daily informal soccer games on the streets of my hometown. These ordinary physical activities involved all youngsters in the Eastern European generation directly following World War II and provided a natural way of exercising and becoming seasonally fit. At school we had a very organized and mandatory physical education program, beginning with the first elementary classes, but especially from the fifth elementary class. I underwent all the basic preparation to become an athlete and my flair for explosive activities seemed to suggest a genetically high proportion of fast twitch muscle fibers. All that was missing was strength. After high school graduation and an unsuccessful attempt to become a student at the University of International Relations, I was not allowed by my parents to sit for the admission exams for the Theatrical Art University. Already being late September, with no other chances for admission to a College, I felt that it was definitely preferable to take the admission tests for the Physical Education department at the Pedagogical Institute from Cluj (Kolozsvar) in Romania instead of being drafted for the mandatory two years military program.

Always being a very optimistic lad, I loved my choice and from the very beginning I was very excited at the prospect of becoming a physical educator and coach. At my college in Cluj, I acquired a basic knowledge of almost all Olympic sports, and received a more advanced education in track and field, weightlifting and fitness conditioning. I started practicing weightlifting and, thanks to the detailed and multifaceted athletic preparation there, my performances improved tremendously. In a very short time, from being a weak, flatfooted child, I grew into a serious athlete who, at a bodymass of 75-78 kg (165-171 lbs.), could back squat 200 kg (440 lbs.), Clean & Jerk 155 kg (341 lbs.), Snatch 115 kg (253 lbs.), and Press 130 kg (286 lbs.) In addition I could do a 60 m (66 yard) sprint in 6.9 seconds, a five consecutive double leg jump-bound of 17.07m (56 feet) a 7.00 m (23.1 feet) long jump, and a 1.80 m (6 feet) high jump with a three step approach.

In 1964 I graduated from college, and in February 1968, I became a coach. Between these two dates I was using my own athletic preparation to experiment with different methods of preparation. I kept meticulous notes of all of my workouts, with detailed information about the effect of each method and my own personal conclusions. I read all possible relevant literature and tried to gather as much information as was available from any sources whatsoever. Then I analyzed them and tried to implement them in my own programs. As a young coach, I continued to apply this same analytical philosophy and experimented to establish safe and effective methods for my athletes, involving all of them with the club's physician together in a controlled research environment.

Coaching Romanian Athletes

Back in Romania I used my growing knowledge to start developing world-class athletes. One of these was Dragomir Cioroslan, bronze medallist in Weightlifting at the 1984 Los Angeles Summer Olympic Games in the 75 kg (164 lbs.) Bodyweight class. Dragomir was translating the latest Soviet coaching publications for me, which involved him from the very beginning in what may be called the triadic collaboration of coach-athlete-physician. Because it is my intention with this book to give practical information to coaches, I intentionally wish to relate a few words about this young athlete, who was between 1990 to 2003 the Head Coach of the USA Weightlifting residential program at the USA Olympic Training Center in Colorado Springs.

In July 1969, I was selecting group of children with natural abilities and inclinations for weightlifting to recruit for my Weightlifting Center. The best method of selection was to organize a neighborhood soccer street championship, with a special rule that every athlete from each team also had to participate in a high pull Snatch contest. After each contest I invited the selected youngsters to participate in my workouts held on the east side of the Iris district, in the city of Cluj-Napoca, the capital of Transylvania in Romania (with a population of approximately 300,000). During that summer I selected between others, four youths from Byron Street, but I did not select Dragomir Cioroslan, who did not physically meet the required weightlifting selection standards. However, at the insistence of Dragomir's teammates and friends, eventually I relented and admitted him into the gym. Dragomir at the time weighed all of 37 kg (81 lbs.)and was capable of 20 kg (44 lbs.) Snatch and 30 kg (66 lbs.)Clean & Jerk. He was born in 1954 in Cluj-Napoca, Romania, with visible signs of rickets, and at the age of seven, he was afflicted with rheumatic heart disease. Dragomir spent years in hospital and had a very hard time keeping up with the other children at school. He always was the shortest and the weakest among his classmates. Then he started gymnastics under Dr. Eugene Duma, a sport physician and gymnastics coach, which helped him to develop self-confidence and considerable spatial coordination. The summer of 1969 marked the turning point in his life.

After I admitted Dragomir to my program, I had a long serious talk with him, telling him that he had to work ten times harder than the others, and that he would involve him in a special experiment. In the beginning, I did not seriously think that Dragomir would be able to produce any noteworthy performances in Weightlifting. I remember that at his first official meet, the "August 23 Cup"-1969, where at a 37 kg (81 lb) bodymass, 148 cm (4.85 feet) tall, Dragomir squat snatched 37.5 kg (82 lb) and then clean-and-jerked, first 40 kg (88 lb), then 45 kg (99 lb). At his third attempt on 50 kg (110 lb), when he cleaned the weight, I felt compelled to turn my back to the platform, because I was afraid to see that tiny frame dropping under the bar into a very deep squat. I spun around just in time when I heard the crowd yelling at Dragomir to get up with the bar to witness that the jerk "was just a piece of cake for him." This was the day when I realized that I had some really great talent in my gym.

Dragomir was a wonderful and hard working youngster. He trained every day for four to five hours and at the same time he maintained a high-grade score at High School No. 14 of Cluj-Napoca, being consid-

ered a top student there. He respected all of my advice for his studies, private life, workouts and even his diet. In the beginning he seemed to be the most finicky kid in the world. In a very short time I effectively became his second parent and a very close friend. Being a very intelligent lad, I gave him special assignments, such as translating the Russian Weightlifting books of Lucikin and Roman. At the time, I was studying their methods and trying to implement them in Dragomir's training program and that of my whole Weightlifting club.

Dragomir's health and performance improved from day to day, and within the short space of three years he became a member of the Romanian Olympic hopes team. Dragomir's best performances were 158.5 kg (349 lb) in the Snatch and 202.5 kg (445 lb) in the Clean & Jerk in the 75 kg (165 lb) bodyweight class. I often make special mention about this wonderful youngster who loved literature, especially poems and classical music. I have to point out Dragomir's ability to speak several languages fluently, and his many other successes despite suffering from rheumatic heart disease. As the Head Coach of the USA Weightlifting Federation residents program, where he was implementing everything that he learned and experimented with in his life, from his early days in hospital right up to the Olympic platform at the 1984 Los Angeles Summer Olympic Games, where he finished third during the closing stages of a glittering sport career.

My other athlete, Istvan Tasnadi, was the silver medallist at the 1984 Los Angeles Summer Olympic games in 110 kg (242 lb) bodyweight class. His life's best performances were 180 kg (396 lb) Snatch and 225 kg (495 lb) Clean & Jerk and a member of the 400 kg (880 lb) total club. Tasnadi with his 110 kg (242 lb) bodyweight had a 5% body fat, could perform a 3.50 m (11.5 feet) standing long jump, run 60 m in 7.1 seconds, and do 10 consecutive box jumps onto a 1.50 m (4.9 feet) high box. I consider that Tasnadi could have been one of the biggest football stars in the USA, had he received the chance to live in this country.

Coaching American Athletes

What I must stress is that none of these performances were achieved in a short period of time, something that all young aspiring athletes should note. They were the results of continuous perseverance and scientific workouts, supervised and analyzed by all three players: the triad of coach, physician and athlete.

In April of 1982, I decided that for myself and my family the best move would be to escape from "the nonsensical totalitarian communist system". So I defected through West Germany, asking for political asylum in the United States of America. After a first year of struggling to secure a place in American society, in 1984, I became an all sports conditioning coach at University of Texas A&M, where I developed sports conditioning programs for tennis, softball, women's volleyball, women's basketball, track and field and also served as assistant coach for football conditioning. In the track and field program at Texas A & M, as well as being responsible for the whole conditioning program, I had to coach the jumpers and throwers. I recall with pride that I was the first coach at A&M to Randy Barnes, who became world shot put record holder. and Olympic champion. During that time I noted that Randy's technical and strength improvement probably was the most impressive of his illustrious career. When I started working out with Randy, his bodymass was around 136 kg (300 lb) and he was able to power snatch 95 kg (209 lb) and power clean & jerk 125 kg (275 lb). Within the short period of four months working out four times a day his body weight dropped to 122 kg (268 lbs.), he improved to a 130 kg (286 lb) power Snatch, and a 160 kg (352 lb) power Clean & Jerk. Actually, Randy even ranked as the No 1 US junior superheavy bodymass class weightlifter of the year of 1985, without doing any specific

Weightlifting preparation.

I have to point out that, for any throwers, I am using Weightlifting lifts and their many variations as a conditioning system, and I do not teach any athlete unnecessary technical exercises. I like throwers to compete on a Weightlifting platform, because I consider that it offers a very similar atmosphere to a throwing ring. Randy Barnes lost in that intensive 4-month short period of time more than 14 kg (30 lb) in bodymass. This is what his interview with Sieg Lindstrom in the 1990 July issue of the Track & Field News said: "Barnes says he has worked harder in the past, particularly from 1986, when Steve Javorek, a Romanian strength coach at A&M, drove him through a regimen under which even mountains of greasy dorm food could not prevent him from losing weight" Randy improved from an 18 meters shot put to an impressive 21 meter with a 122 kg (268 lb) bodyweight.

At University of Texas A&M, I designed the whole conditioning program for the 1986 world fastest 200 m sprinter, Floyd Heard; former 10,000 m world record holder, Arturo Barrios; javelin thrower Juan de la Garza, former Canadian long jump record holder; Ian James, Mexican record holder triple jumper; Francisco Olivares, and several other top athletes

Moving to Johnson County Community College (JCCC) in Kansas, starting from the ground level, I began to develop a new sports conditioning program. Coaches at JCCC have recognized that my conditioning program has greatly contributed to their athletes' success. Thus, in a short period of time Eduard Kaminski became a recognized name in javelin throwing, while Wesley Barnett, (I was his personal coach between 1989-91) finished sixth, the best among U.S. Weightlifting competitors, with new U.S. National records set at the 1996 Atlanta Summer Olympic Games and won one silver and two bronze medals

at the 1997 World Weightlifting Championships. I also coached U.S. Nationals silver medallist and U.S. collegiate National champion Jim Dice, U.S. National champion Dirk Yasko, U.S. Collegiate National champion Larry Scott and U.S. Junior National champion Larry Dice in Weightlifting; Gaskin Wendell, Scott Vanwyngarden and Robert Jones in sprinting; Ann Golubski and Valerie Spencer in cross country, professional baseball player Kit Pellow (KC Royals and Colorado Rockies), L.A. Lakers basketball player Kareem Rush (he completed between several of my programs, two times Javorek's "Big Fun" program), and University of Kansas McDonald All American basketball player Wayne Simien (he completed several Javorek's conditioning and the "Big Fun" program also) and several other track athletes, baseball, basketball and soccer players who were offered NCAA schools scholarships while they were students at JCCC performing my conditioning programs.

This book is my first in English and draws on various previous articles written by me for the National Strength and Conditioning Journal, Best of Coaching Volleyball, T&C Training and Conditioning Journal, Muscle & Fitness, Men's Health as well as other more consumer-oriented magazines, many of my professional experiences in weightlifting, and the application of many weightlifting derived exercises in all sports conditioning. At the same time, it covers several general and specific sports conditioning programs, practical exercise applications and considerable information on plyometrics, general conditioning, weightlifting and weight training in general, developed by me during my 40 years of active coaching career

Istvan Javorek – violin player.

Coaching at an outdoor sport clinics.

Istvan Javorek – Mr. Triceps, 1965.

Istvan Javorek – 110 kg split snatch.

Istvan Javorek – the aggie violinist.

Istvan Javorek – body building at age 22 and 21.

Istvan Javorek – high jump 180 cm.

Istvan Javorek – 125 kg press.

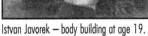

Istvan Javorek – body building at age 19.

Istvan Javorek – at the first Romanian body building nationals in 1966.

Istvan Javorek – shot putting 12 m.

Istvan Javorek – 130 kg clean and jerk.

Istvan Javorek - 140 kg clean.

Istvan Tasnadi — barbell squat clean.

Kareem Rush and me on May 31, 2003.

USA College Strength and Conditioning Coaches 2003 Hall of Famer.

Istvan Javorek — 147.5 kg split clean.

Javelin conditioning with rubber tube.

Istvan Javorek — 110 kg split snatch.

Randy Barnes and me in the Texas A&M new conditioning center.

Wayne Simien and me.

Istvan Javorek with Stiinta Cluj weightlifting team in 1963.

Randy Barnes shrugs.

Wayne Simien, the body builder.

Dragomir's first body building champion title as a 18 years old.

Randy Barnes and me at Texas A&M September 1985.

Muscle & Fitness, May 2002 photo session for an article.

Chapter 1

Chapter 2
Weightlifter or Weight Trainer?

I n the USA, the terms "weightlifting", "weightlifter", and "weight training" are seriously misused by the general public. These combinations of words themselves generally are confused with ordinary training with weights and machines. Just because someone is exercising with weights does not mean that the person is a weightlifter. He is an athlete or person who practices a noncompetitive form of fitness with weights to achieve certain personal goals.

According to correct terminology, Weightlifting is a competitive sport, currently the only Olympic sport in the weights family comprising weightlifting, powerlifting and bodybuilding. Weightlifting comprises the Snatch and Clean & Jerk lifts, but during the preparation phases, several other assistance and auxiliary exercises with barbells (BB) and dumbbells (DB) may also be employed. Weightlifting is a very demanding dynamic sport, which develops the integrity of all basic physical qualities necessary in modern sports. Speed, power, strength, special, general and cardiovascular endurance, explosiveness, velocity, acceleration, and flexibility are the most important qualities which should be found in an athlete and many aspects of weightlifting training can enhance most or all of these fitness qualities.

There are some who believe that weightlifting is ineffective or dangerous as a form of strength training, but such criticism ignores the fact that the same comments apply to all forms of sports conditioning. Selection of any exercise depends upon the specificity of each sport, individual needs, the phase of the training period and several other general and specific factors relating to the sport, the athlete and the facilities available. Only once an intelligent selection of suitable exercises has been made on this basis, can these exercises be organized into a long-term training program, which varies exercises, repetitions, sets and intensities according to the specific needs and goals of the athlete.

Weightlifting Conditioning Terminology

Weight training must not be confused with the sport of Weightlifting. Weightlifting, as mentioned before, is an Olympic sport, whereas weight training is a method of fitness, physique and strength development. The weight training exercises may include assistance exercises from the sport of Weightlifting, exercises on different machines, or even calisthenics exercises with and without free weights.

Powerlifting is really a grandchild of Olympic style Weightlifting, and its main characteristic is the absence of explosive and ballistic movements because the great loads being raised prevents this type of action. The powerlifting competition exercises are the back squat, bench press, and deadlift. Actually, it has often been pointed out that the name, "powerlifting", is more appropriate for the sport of weightlifting, because the power (rate of doing work) involved in this sport is very large. Accordingly, the popular strength sport of powerlifting would then more logically change its name to something like "Strength Lifting".

Bodybuilding, the last of the "Iron Game" family, is another fitness and muscular development method whose main goals are muscular hyper-trophy, physique competition and general fitness. Bodybuilding like its 'brother', powerlifting, usually omits from its arsenal any kind of explosive exercise. However, back in Romania, I trained many bodybuilders, and successfully included several explosive exercises in their programs. All of my bodybuilders possessed harmonious musculature and had a very athletic physical appearance. Besides employing appropriate explosive and ballistic movements, which can increase neural drive, soft tissue strength, peak strength and power enormously, bodybuilding could also gain from the use of many weightlifting exercises and principles, including scientific periodization of the overall plan of preparation. After all, if one increases peak strength and power, one generally can do more repetitions with heavier loads, which is something that is well known to enhance muscle and connective tissue hypertrophy.

Bodybuilding, muscle development, or whatever one wishes to call it, carries different descriptions in different nations. The Germans call it Kraftsport or strength sport. The French call Culturistique or "body culture." I think that the term, "body sculpture" could also be added to the Iron Game dictionary.

A wonderful aspect of bodybuilding, even without going to the excessively demanding competitive levels or relying on anabolic steroids, is that with will power and perseverance, everyone can build or reshape the body. The discipline of bodybuilding has a very long past, with the ancient Greeks and Romans having practiced different forms of physical exercises to "culture" the body to achieve various goals. The Latin idiom of "Mens sana in corpore sano" or "Sound mind in a sound body" offers further evidence of the huge emphasis placed by Romans on daily physical activities.

In our time Eugene Sandow was the first who became famous by practicing physical exercises with free weights. As a youth Eugene Sandow had several health problems. He decided to study medicine and parallel with his study to practice and experiment physical education exercises. After several years of hard work he no longer showed any sign of illness, but developed an harmonious and "steel hard" physique. Sandow was enthusiastic about his achievement and very soon he instituted a program called Physical Culture. Later on he wrote a book, entitled "Body Building." Eugene Sandow developed new methods of exercising and athletes still look back on him as the father of modern bodybuilding. He was convinced that with his methods, besides increasing strength, could also develop a very athletic and balanced musculature.

Bodybuilding, as a sport, first gained tremendous popularity in the United States, but gradually became more popular all around the world. If we put aside any prejudices, we should consider some of the methods of bodybuilding to be very important for the general conditioning of young athletes, and in any athlete's year-round conditioning during certain stages of the overall program.

The goal of physical education is to take care of general health of the population. Bodybuilding as a method, if applied gradually, could be a part of this goal, developing harmonious musculature, and as Eugene Sandow stated, already has a positive stimulatory effect on the human body. Just as I have stated several times before, bodybuilding programs must be combined with different dynamic programs.

Many years ago sports scientists showed that exercising with light weights stimulates growth and contributes to the development of a healthy, well-proportioned body, which could be a good starting point for any young athlete. We can start practicing with light weights as early as nine years of age without any negative effect on the musculoskeletal system. What is very important is to respect the regularity of exercising, and not to overload a physically underdeveloped youth's body.

With suitable exercises we can produce a great increase in muscle strength, and even though the bones of the skeleton are very much inherited, we still can make tremendous improvement in a young athlete's physical appearance, developing the right musculature and the right posture. This approach I call body sculpting or body building.

Exercising with weights at a young age must be unconditionally combined with different dynamic movements, games, running, skiing and swimming exercises. I believe that every youth who starts with multifaceted preparation later on in life will achieve greater success in any given sport, because they have developed a solid foundation, with enhanced neuromuscular coordination, reflexes, posture and musculature.

Knowing that any form of physical activity has a stimulating effect on circulatory, hormonal and nervous system, exercising your physique is important at every age and for both sexes. Increased physical activity increases heart and lung capacity, while developing the heart and the intercostal musculature. Balanced physical exercise stimulates the vital functions of the body, and fortifies the body immune system, protecting it from different illnesses and pathological deformations. This activity shapes new muscle-nerve relationships, which contribute to newly conditioning reflexes, and encourages balanced and graceful body movements. Exercise also has a significant effect on the neuro-

muscular system, on orientation in space and one's sense of balance.

Continuous and systematic physical activities extend the age of youthful vitality, develop physical harmony and beauty, and everyone who practices them generally will display a more positive disposition, greater self-confidence and other qualities that can make you happy, satisfied and healthy.

The old and false theory that sport, exercise or body building have a detrimental effect on a woman's body, stating that physical activities make a lady look more like a man, lost their credibility long time ago, and it has become obvious that organized physical activities can enable women to achieve the same fitness goals as males, besides making them more attractive, better balanced and highly energetic.

The concept of beauty is very relative and complex. Over the centuries and across cultures large differences have always been evident. Mona Lisa of Leonardo da Vinci would not have been considered a beauty in the second part of the 20th century. Similarly, the emaciated models in many fashion magazines are regarded in many non-Western countries as ugly and ill. Actresses who may have been regarded as beautiful during one era may not be considered attractive in another era. However, during any age, these beautiful women have demonstrated that the idea of beauty is determined not only by facial appearance and bodily proportions, but also by posture, deportment, overall freshness, vitality of body, and grace of movement, qualities that can all be enhanced by regular physical training.

While I am on the topic of movement, it is interesting to recall that old people once told me that to maintain your health everyone should walk a minimum of twelve thousand steps a day. Be entirely honest and ask yourself this question: how many steps have you taken today, yesterday, the day before? In this sedentary lifetime we spend less and less time using our legs. The heart needs to pump the blood more than a meter up the legs and well-developed leg muscles can contribute significantly in this regard.

Fitness and wellness do not necessarily require practicing a sport, nor achieving any elite performance, although we need to stress that programs and exercises derived from sport and strength training can help anyone to achieve their physical and mental goals in life.

JCCC dumbbell bench press.

Jim Dice-dumbbell bent over fly.

Perfect posture for a dumbbell lunge walk demonstrated by Sumya Anani.

Barbell 130 kg overhead press by Javorek.

Barbell squat by Dirk Yasko.

Dragomir 202.5 kg clean and jerk.

Dumbbell press by Wayne Simien.

Chapter 3

Chapter 3
A Brief History of Weightlifting and Sports Conditioning

Title he sport of Weightlifting was born with the emergence of the human species. Since time immemorial, man has been compelled to lift heavy objects for survival and for a better life. Later with the evolution of civilization, strength, this main physical characteristic of human

beings became a virtue, and for millennia the "Strongman" was the idol and a very respected person in different societies and eras. Hercules, Spartacus, Odysseus, are typical examples. Milo of Crotona, the first athlete who practiced and pioneered progressive overload training, is the classical example, and his name soon became a symbol of strength and power

Weightlifting is one of the privileged sports to be represented at the Olympics right since the start of modern Summer Olympic Games in 1896. Until 1920 it involved no weight class limits and only two separate events: the one handed lift and two handed lift, both lifts being very close to today's clean & jerk. The 1920 Summer Olympic Games in Antwerp, Belgium, marked the beginning of modern Weightlifting as a sport. There were three different lifts: one-hand Snatch, one-hand Clean & Jerk, and two hand Clean & Jerk. The athletes competed in five bodyweight classes of: up to 60 kg (132 lb) up to 67.5 kg (148 lb.) up to 75 kg (165 lb) up to 82.5 kg (181.5 lb) and over 82.5 kg, which became the famous super-heavy weight class division.

At the 1924 Olympic Games in Paris, France, the two hand Snatch and two hand Clean & Press were added, with an uniformed rule system: one-hand Snatch, one-hand Clean & Jerk, two hand clean & press, two hand Snatch, two hand Clean & Jerk, and Total. From the 1928 Summer Olympics from Amsterdam, Holland, the competition was reduced to two-hand clean & press, two hands Snatch, two-hand clean & jerk, and Total. The sport of Weightlifting was increasing in popularity and it became necessary to add the new bodyweight class of 56 kg (123 lb) then, but the interest in this exciting sport was growing so keenly that the 90 kg (198 lb) bodyweight class was added at the 1952 Summer Olympic Games in Helsinki, Finland, thereby creating a fairer battle between the world's heavier men.

That age especially favored the popularity of Weightlifting. The athletes became bigger and stronger, more and more nations sent representatives to the Olympic Games and World Weightlifting Championships. In the two extreme bodyweight classes of 56 kg (123 lb) and over 90 kg (198 lb) the number of competitors grew rapidly. The scientific training methods, and nutrition programs developed bigger and better athletes. However, competition became very unfair for athletes lighter than 52 kg (114 lb) to compete against four kg heavier athletes, and more difficult for lighter athletes to challenge over-120 kg (264 lb) behemoths in the over 90 kg (198 lb) bodyweight class.

This is why new bodyweight classes of 52 kg (114 lb), up to 110 kg (242 lb) and over 110 kg (+242 lb) were introduced at the Munich 1972 Summer Olympics. At the same Olympics, Weightlifting competition for the last time included the three different lifts (Press, Snatch and Clean & Jerk), and was reduced to only two exercises, namely the

Snatch, and Clean & Jerk. Two Olympic Games later, at the 1980 Summer Olympic Games in Moscow, the last new bodyweight class of up to 100 kg was born, which made competition between the heavier athletes even more balanced.

The 10-bodyweight classes were:

52 kg (114.61 lb) Flyweight class

56 kg (123 lb)   Bantamweight class

60 kg (132 lb)   Featherweight class

67.5 kg (148.75 lb) Lightweight class

75 kg (165 lb) Light Middleweight class

82.5 kg (181.5 lb) Middleweight class

90 kg (198.25 lb) Light Heavyweight class

100 kg (220.25 lb) Middle Heavyweight class

110 kg (242.5 lb) Heavyweight class

+ 110 kg (+242 lb) Super heavyweight-Unlimited

In the meantime, women's Weightlifting started to establish deeper roots in the USA and around the world. It did not take too long to be recognized by the International Weightlifting Federation and to see the first Women's World Weightlifting Championship organized in 1989 for the following bodyweight classes:

44 kg, 48 kg, 52 kg, 56 kg, 60 kg, 67.5 kg, 75 kg, 82.5 kg, + 82.5 kg

At its November 16, 1992, Congress meeting the IWF, in Tenerife (Canary Islands) announced a change for the men and women's bodyweight categories, which did not really change anything in the world Weightlifting hierarchy, and offered no special advantage or disadvantage to any athlete. Then, in 1997 a new IWF decision was made which once again changed the bodyweight classes, ostensibly to give a chance for women's Weightlifting to be introduced at a future Summer Olympic Games

The former and the new weight classes are:

Men		Women	
54 kg	56 kg	46 kg	48 kg
59 kg	62 kg	50 kg	53 kg
64 kg	69 kg	54 kg	58 kg
70 kg	77 kg	59 kg	63 kg
76 kg	85 kg	64 kg	69 kg
83 kg	94 kg	70 kg	75 kg
91 kg	105 kg	76 kg	+ 75 kg
99 kg	+ 105 kg	83 kg	
108 kg		+ 83 kg	
+ 108 kg			

I trust that we can keep up with the new changes in the definition of bodyweight classes, which in the last decades has shown a very fast rate of change and a minimal range of benefits.

The most important international events in Weightlifting are considered: the Olympic Games, the annual World Senior (Men), Junior and Women Championships, Pan-American Games, Asian Games, European Men, Junior and Women Championships, and several World Cup events.

The governing body of international Weightlifting activities is the International Weightlifting Federation (IWF), which was founded in 1920 and is responsible for all major international competitions. Today there are over 150 IWF member countries around the world. The number is increasing, with recognition of more and more new independent countries, making the IWF one of the most extensive international sport federations in the world.

Weightlifting, the only Olympic 'strength' sport and its competitive exercises of the Snatch and Clean & Jerk, and its many auxiliary or assistance exercises, became the basis for all sports conditioning, though not without considerable confusion and misuse.

It is now difficult to imagine modern conditioning without the huge repertoire of exercise variations made possible by Weightlifting, but it is inappropriate to use its methods strictly as they are used in competitive lifting, because we do need to adapt and adjust its various exercises to satisfy the specific requirements of each given sport, according to:

Forty-five to fifty years ago in many countries, Weightlifting was considered as being very detrimental to athletic performances in general, especially regarding its alleged negative effects on reaction time, flexibility, power, speed and cardiovascular endurance. Then gradually with the publication of research into the physiology of strength, explosive movement, and so-called 'plyometrics' and stretch-shortening processes, the whole attitude towards Weightlifting and general sports conditioning changed dramatically.

In the USA, Powerlifting became the dominant exercise method in sports conditioning. In the earliest days of strength training for sport, virtually the only sport, which did formal conditioning, was American football, which used the barbell bench press, deadlift and back squat as the basic and best exercises to achieve its goals. It took a while, but gradually Olympic style Weightlifting gained more inroads into general athletic conditioning, especially through increasing contact with translated Eastern European material and coaches. More and more coaches from high schools to colleges were learning about Weightlifting exercises and introducing them into their conditioning programs. Gary Gubner, the first really well known US track athlete, who was both a shot-put and Weightlifting world record holder, and Randy Barnes, (Olympic gold and silver medallist, indoor and outdoor world record holder), were among the first American athletes who broke the magical psychological barrier, thereby giving a green light for Weightlifting as a suitable conditioning method for all sports.

Despite our very strong Weightlifting background (both as athletes and later as coaches), I do not consider it appropriate to apply Weightlifting with great specificity to all sport conditioning. What is good for a weightlifter could be detrimental to or not helpful for another athlete. For example, except during the early period of preparation, or in recuperation, rehabilitation after an injury, a sprinter never needs to deep squat, squat Snatch, squat clean and split jerk. However, one certainly can use squat variations such as wave squats, quarter squats, squat jump, split jumps, lunges, step-ups, alternate leg split snatches with DB or BB, and alternate leg split cleans.

A defensive or offensive lineman should do power snatches and alternate leg split snatches with DB or BB, power cleans, push presses, push and power jerks with DB and BB, but he would not necessarily benefit much more from using a split or so-called "classical jerk". We do not need to rigidly apply Weightlifting methods word by word, but rather we need to determine the most specific and beneficial variations of the classical Snatch and Clean & Jerk and the other Weightlifting assistance exercises for each individual sport.

Sports, which require an "explosive first step", can benefit from the use of phases of the weightlifting movements, which also enhance this quality. In this respect, this "first step" does not just apply to foot speed, but also to an explosive midsection and arms. Sports such as football, basketball, baseball, tennis, track and field, volleyball, wrestling, boxing, and rugby can benefit enormously from the use of exercises derived from the weightlifting movements and their training variations. At the same time, we consider that any given sport also can benefit tremendously from the astute and well-planned use of these same exercises.

What is the particularly advantageous about Weightlifting is that we can monitor with complete quantitative accuracy the number of repetitions, sets, volume, load average and intensity, and we can easily adapt the training to suit a given sport's goals during a given period of preparation.

It is difficult to find any other conditioning regime, which seriously rivals the weightlifting compendium of exercises in conditioning a wide range of all athletes, especially if it is combined properly with various plyometrics, ballistic or stretch-shortening exercises. Such a remarkable conditioning compendium can profoundly enhance an athlete's power, acceleration, velocity, muscle endurance, muscular strength and size (if necessary), flexibility, orientation in space, ligament and tendon strength, resistance to injury, recuperation, mental drive and injury rehabilitation.

Barbell 110 kg split snatch by Javorek.

Pavel Kuznetzov world record.

Barbell split clean by Colette Kibler.

Pavel Kuznetzov world record.

Nicu Vlad 1984 LA Olympic Record clean and jerk.

Nicu Vlad 1984 L.A. Olympic record clean and jerk.

Barbell split snatch by Andreas Heckel.

Pavel Kuznetzov world record clean & jerk.

Nicu Vlad 1984 L.A. Olympic record clean & jerk.

Dumbbell from squat overhead press by Wesley Barnett

Dumbbell from squat overhead press by Wesley Barnett.

Dumbbell press from squat by Wesley Barnett.

Dumbbell overhead triceps curls by Wesley Barnett.

Wesley Barnett.225 kg clean & jerk.

A Brief History of Weightlifting and Sports Conditioning   13

Chapter 4
Physical Appearance of the Weightlifter

I f we ask one hundred people at random about a weightlifter's typical physical appearance, the vast majority probably would answer: something like "big", "fat", behemoth like the Russian Alexeev, or the ex-Bulgarian, Turkish wonder mini-Hercules, World and Olympic champion,

Naim Suleymanoglu, or even like a powerlifter appareled in an extra-tight lifting suit, double sized belt, and yards of knee wraps.

Fortunately, the truth is very different. First, there are several body-weight classes, which include tiny lifters right up to superheavy gargantuans. The second reason is, that after 1972 Summer Olympic Games in Munich, the very strength-dominant exercise, the two-hand barbell Clean & Press, was eliminated from competition, making the sport of Weightlifting more dynamic and athletic, qualities that are the basic elements of all sports conditioning.

This book pays special attention to the fact that Weightlifting with its assistance exercises together can develop the most important fundamental qualities of power, explosiveness, flexibility, balance, spatial orientation, and different types of muscular endurance.

After eliminating the "Olympic" Press from its competitive arsenal, the methodology of weightlifting changed dramatically, due to the specific explosive character of the Snatch and Clean & Jerk, which led to coaches recruiting far more athletic youths instead of the shorter more robust athletes of yesteryear. Consequently, the athlete's mean height has grown over the years, and is now it is much more rare to see a preponderance of gigantic or fatter lifters.

Today's weightlifters (except in the heaviest division) are muscularly slim, flexible, very explosive athletes, who with some specific preparation, could perform well in a wide variety of sports. It is not by chance that my weightlifters from Romania were complete athletes. At Johnson County Community College, the situation is the same; the weightlifters in the sports conditioning class are achieving the best physical test performances among the college's 200 athletes, which give a general view of physical preparation.

It is not an accident that Wesley Barnett, was a Missouri High School All American basketball player, became the best USA weightlifter, who could dunk easily at 200 lb. bodyweight and 6 feet height. I will list a few former JCCC weightlifters' test performances only to underline my claims of the tremendous benefit of Weightlifting exercises in all sports conditioning, and to show that weightlifters frequently are versatile and well-conditioned athletes.

	Standing Long Jump	30 m Sprint	Standing Vertical. Jump	10 lb Med. Ball.Over-Head Throw
Wesley Barnett	10.4 feet	3.98 sec.	36 inch	64 feet
Jim Dice	10.0 feet	4.20 sec.	34 inch	68 feet
Brian Higginbotham	10.1 feet	3.89 sec.	35 inch	55 feet
Carla Prewitt	9.1 feet	4.55 sec.	29 inch	46 feet

A primary concern in Weightlifting is the starting age of the athlete. My personal experience, starting in one case with a child as young as three years of age, is that a well-designed scientific Weightlifting program will not harm a youth's structural-functional development, but can even stimulate it. Of course, I do not recommend bringing three year old children into the weight room, but consider that choosing a special general conditioning program and concurrently teaching Weightlifting technique with very light weight does not harm any youth, but actually helps them to improve their general physical and psychological development. In Romania I kept statistics of siblings who practiced Weightlifting. The conclusion was that younger they started, the taller they grew, because with no exception, all of the younger brothers grew taller than their older brothers by an average of 2-3 inches. In their program I integrated general sports conditioning, body posture exercises, technical Weightlifting exercises, and swimming, basketball, volleyball, acrobatics and basic plyometrics.

The rules which I respected with those youths, and which I still apply with all of my athletes are:

1. Do not hurry; be patient.

2. Emphasize strengthening of the tendons and ligaments first, then after that the muscles.

3. Under no circumstances allow an athlete to rebound from a deep back squat, and never squat heavier than 75-80% of their maximum potentials.

4. Before starting any plyometrics exercises, teach proper walking, running, sprinting (sprint mechanics), and jumping techniques; do not perform any form of depth jump with young athletes. Always prefer the use of stair jumps, which eliminates the great impact in the landing phase on the ankle-knee-back chain.

5. Teach perfection of lifting technique for each individual exercise. Never accept from any athlete just a superficial knowledge of technique. It is not acceptable for a coach to consider a lift good just because the weight is overhead. Do not forget if a youngster does not have the right muscular development, you as a coach cannot insist on anyone performing movements, which the musculature does not support.

6. Respect the rules of periodization of preparation, which for the most part of the year should focus on general conditioning and gradually introduce more sport specific preparation.

7. Do not peak youngsters for every competition. They recover very rapidly and, as a coach, you do not need to waste time with peaking for a meet. Probably once or twice a year is most adequate to devote to specific preparation for a meet and here the period of time involved should not be longer than a week.

8. Use many variations of exercises, as well as many games, different sports and fun in their preparation.

9. Do not consider Weightlifting to be the only method of conditioning.

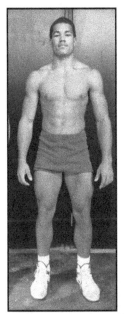

Wesley Barnett as a 83 kg weightlifter.

Wesley Barnett dunks the basketball.

Barbell clean pull by Wes Barnett.

Barbell Power Jerk by Wesley Barnett.

Dumbbell Press From Squat by Wesley Barnett proves that a weightlifter is a very flexible athlete.

Three time Olympian Wesley Barnett.

Barbell shrugs by shot put Olympic Champion Randy Barnes.

Barbell clean and jerk 202.5 kg by Dragomir Cioroslan.

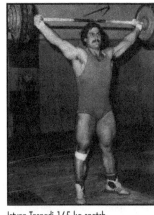

Istvan Tasnadi 165 kg snatch.

Wesley Barnett. Three time Olympian.

Physical Appearance of the Weightlifter

Chapter 5

Weightlifting as a Conditioning Tool

Any conditioning coach or individual athlete can benefit from the use of Weightlifting exercises on a year-round basis. As I stated earlier, when considering the use of weightlifting in all sports conditioning, it is a mistake to try applying the entire list of classical exercises

word by word for without keeping the specificity of sport in mind. In daily practice, I must ascertain which exercises are biomechanically the most appropriate for a respective sport. I thus can apply weightlifting to the respective sport's specificity, rather than trying to fit a certain sport into a weightlifting workout. I object to the idea, for example, that tennis or golf automatically need the bench press, squat or power clean. Instead, I look in depth at a certain sport's physiology and kinesiology, analyze the most important movements, and try to figure out which fundamental ("core") and supplemental exercises would be the best for that respective sport.

Many sports, such as baseball, softball, soccer, football, basketball, volleyball, wrestling, swimming, track and field, tennis, cross country, ice hockey, skiing, figure skating, boxing often need more training with dumbbells (DB), which develop overall balance and dynamic strength qualities closer to that of the actual sport. In addition, we should not exclude sports such as American football and rugby from the preceding list, but should just add a greater percentage of barbell (BB) exercises in their exercise programs. It can be a mistake to force a swimmer to learn the power clean or a tennis player to squat snatch, but, on the other hand, it can be most appropriate for a shot-putter, discuss thrower or hammer thrower to learn both classical exercises (the snatch and clean & jerk). Additionally, they also should compete in official Weightlifting competition during the off-season and pre-season phases of preparation, because the competitive platform provides the same psychological training as that of the throwing ring, and the exercises can serve as an effective physical test of the athlete.

I believe in complete and varied athletic preparation and am opposed to the extensive use of specialized, limited exercise preparation programs. By profiting from the benefit of several exercises, and a vast programs variation, I can eliminate the monotony, develop different muscle qualities (including power, endurance, explosiveness, hypertrophy, strength) and give the necessary "color" to the workout, which helps to motivate the athlete to improve performance.

It is very important to respect the principles of sensible periodization. In off-season, general conditioning is most important. Injury rehabilitation, and improvement of certain specific physical qualities like strength and power are also at the top of this list.

Usually I start with a two week introduction program, during which time athletes learn the whole arsenal of exercises and prepare their musculotendinous systems for the real conditioning program which follows. This preparatory period depends on each respective sport and on the athlete's existing level of preparation. At the beginning of a preparatory period I stress on general and then, later on specific conditioning. The length of the preparatory period depends on the relevant sport's characteristics.

In pre-season I do specific conditioning. In season I respect each sport's specificity and also monitor closely every individual athlete. In team sports like football, baseball, volleyball and basketball with long seasons and games every week or twice a week, I adapt the program to the respective sport coach's requirements, but usually I suggest that they perform short specific conditioning a day before the game, at an intensity of 70-80 % of maximum, covering 4-5 different exercises, using only 1-6 repetitions, for a total of 6 to 8 sets.

After a game I prefer a 30 minute-long "active-rest" type of conditioning workout, which is especially effective in helping the athlete to recover physically and mentally. With other sports and events like shot-put, discuss, javelin, hammer throw, wrestling, sprints, jump events, I still use, during the season, three conditioning sessions a week, where the length of each program is very individual. At the same time if an athlete already qualified for the nationals, I convince the coach to let athletes do certain preparatory period conditioning programs and just a week or two before the meet to return to a "peaking" conditioning program.

Finally, I favor the year-round use of weightlifting and its assistance exercises with the specification that one must change the intensity, repetitions, sets and exercises with respect to the goals and phase of preparation for the given individual in the given sport.

Barbell from squat behind the head press by Tim Hall.

Barbell wide grip overhead press from squat by Wes Barnett.

Dumbbell squat push press tennis conditioning.

Dumbbell squat push press tennis conditioning by Steve Nash.

Dumbbell lying on your back pull-over.

Barbell power snatch 130 kg by Randy Barnes.

Barbell power clean and jerk 160 kg by Randy Barnes.

Barbell power clean 205 lb by Wayne Simien.

Barbell back squat by Steve Nash.

Barbell back squat jump.

Special population conditioning.

Special population conditioning.

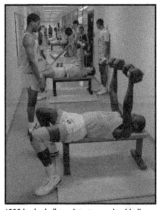

JCCC basketball conditioning — dumbbell bench press.

JCCC basketball conditioning — dumbbell upright row.

Weightlifting as a Conditioning Tool

Chapter 6
Planning the Training Program

Regardless of which aspect of life we are talking about, the planning of daily, weekly, monthly and yearly activities play a vital role in determining success or failure, psychological and physical fitness, the effects of stress accumulation, and the likelihood of psychological or physical burnout. Numerous experts in management theory and organizational behavior in business pay close attention to short- and long-term planning, so the case should not be different in sport, which is simply another type of structured human enterprise This is not simply necessary but even essential for every person who aspires to be a successful coach or athlete.

In my college years and as a young athlete, periodization and meticulous planning of training were integral parts of sports training and education. In Eastern European countries unfortunately everything was planned and centralized. All of us are now very familiar with the political and economic consequences of that sort of rigid regimentation. Nevertheless, if something positive emerged from the Eastern European system, it was the well-organized management of sport activities. Besides the so-called Eastern European "miracle method" of plyometrics, the concept of cyclically planned or periodized training was the other very important acquisition from this already dead, allegedly "utopian" society. To develop an elite athlete who can handle any kind of preparatory and competitional stress, one needs a well planned, scientific and detailed plan of preparation, where a well scheduled plan of preparation should have specific periods of preparation, such as the transitional or off-season, preparatory, pre-competitive and competitive phases.

Every plan of preparation should respect the rules of individualization; age and gender particularities; the school, job and workout schedule; the social, cultural and extracurricular activities; the athlete's physical, physiological and psychological characteristics; the quality and condition of the training facilities; and the competition schedule. By following these simple rules, everybody should be capable of developing a yearly plan of preparation by using the above-mentioned periods of preparation.

At this point, it is now up to the coach to decide what is needed. When a coach decides to devise a well planned, scientifically and experientially valid program, he/she will choose from the above criteria what appears to be necessary or capable of being managed by the athlete during each stage of preparation. Here is a short analysis of some of these criteria.

1. Individualization
A coach who works with a team should make a general team plan of preparation, as well as an individual plan for each athlete and especially for the most talented athletes. It is very professional to gather the necessary data and graphs of evolution and improvement of a young talented player and share them with any future coach who may take over. In this way, the coach will look very organized and professional, and at the same time will help future coaches to continue a well-planned program with the athlete.

What kind of data should a coach collect in order not to introduce excessive difficulty and complexity? Well, it can be helpful to take some anthropometrical measurements like body weight, height, length of the arms, legs, trunk, hands, chest circumference (if they are necessary for the given sport), as well as flexibility of the ankle, knee, hip, wrist, elbow and shoulder (relevant to the given sport). It can also be informative to include some simple physical tests like standing vertical jump, vertical jump with an approach, standing long jump, 10 alternate leg bounding, and 5-10 one leg (right and left) bounding. Tests of bounding need good physical preparation and a coach must be very careful before deciding to use a given test with any athlete. A 20 to 40 m sprint from a standing start, timing of specific athletic movements or drills, a standing double leg high jump, jack-knife or conventional sit-ups, conventional push-ups or "plyometric" (clapping) push-ups, chin-ups, and some form of different weight medicine ball throwing also could be taken into consideration.

It may sound a little complicated, but it is also often very important to conduct some basic medical-biological tests also such as resting and recovery heart rate, blood pressure, body fat, and lung vital capacity (using a spirometer). The inclusion of popular isokinetic tests generally are redundant because their relevance to performance in actual sporting movements is very dubious.

2. Age and Gender peculiarities:
When a coach decides to make an individual or overall team plan of preparation, the most important factor in deciding the intensity, specificity, and complexity of a program are the age and gender peculiarities. The yearly plan of preparation for young children, juniors or for adults is not the same, nor is it the same for females or males.

3. Physical, Physiological and Mental Qualities of the Athlete
As I mentioned before, the coach should carry out certain physical measurements, since this is important for a follow-up of ongoing physical development. Here, resting and recovery heart rate, body weight, vital capacity, body-fat and blood pressure constitute the basic biological data. Assessment of the psychological characteristics of a given athlete relies heavily on the coach and involves the long-term accumulation of observations made during practice and competition. In this regard it is most important to observe an athlete's reaction to different stress situations and to ascertain how the athlete is affected in given situations by negative and positive emotions. This is often made to sound very scientific in sport psychology, but it is not. It is usually very simple for any experienced coach. If an athlete achieves better results in practice than in a competition, it usually means that the coach should be pay more careful attention to the given athlete's psychological preparation. The finest and most fastidious physical training can be wasted in any competition if the athlete mentally is unable to cope with the situation.

Chapter 7
Overtraining and Restoration

I n modern athletics and general fitness, the concept of conditioning has changed enormously during the last few decades, but the basic rule of improvement has remained the same, namely the imposition of optimal stimulation, and the avoidance of overloading. Without stimulating the

neuromuscular and musculoskeletal systems correctly, the intended improvements and anticipated results will not show up at all or will do so at a lower level. At the same time working out at excessive intensity could fatigue the athlete and lead to different degrees of overtraining.

In modern scientific conditioning we like talking about a year-round preparation, but we make the biggest mistake if we ignore varying long-term organization or periodization of the loading. What I now refer to, as periodization of the yearly plan of preparation is fundamental to all sport and even many daily activities. It does not matter if I am talking about Weightlifting preparation or conditioning for all sports; the concept of a varying cyclical preparation is necessary and very important. The huge load of today's workouts and the year-round preparation of course produces its own consequences. Well-planned preparation optimizes adaptation and produces good results, whereas poorly planned or haphazard preparation leads to inadequate performance or overtraining.

What is recovery and why is it so important?
I might state that recovery means to quickly regain one hundred percent of physical, intellectual and psychological capacity, so that the athlete can begin a new workout or other activity with complete power, full capabilities and skillfulness. The other very similar word used in athletics is restoration, where the Webster Dictionary defines restorative as "capable of restoring one's health or strength", although in competitive sport, one would say that health and strength both need to be restored. Thus, restoration should be an important part of the overall program and intimately associated with functioning of the neuropsychological, neuromuscular, metabolic and cardio-respiratory systems of the body. Restoration can be general, but at the same time individualized. It has particularities in concordance with each workout, the periodization of preparation and adaptation to the progressively increasing effort. Restoration is a natural process dependent on the neuro-endocrine system, and it has to form an integral part of preparation, regardless of the different phases of training. Less work needs less restoration, which of course results in poor athletic performances.

In accordance with the rules of organized conditioning, we have to follow up our athletes' preparation level and health and personal problems, which can positively or negatively influence their restoration. Furthermore, you cannot use the same methods of restoration during the preparatory, competition and transitory phases, nor even the same methods between workouts. In the preparatory phase, one needs to concentrate more on physical restoration; and in the competition phase more on psychological restoration (though not neglecting physical restoration). The transition phases should offer complete physical and psychological restoration.

I would like to accentuate my idea of recovery and restoration with a very simple example. One two-hour workout per day, 3-4 times a week is not the same as working out 2-3 times a day, six days per week. Assuming 100% recovery in both cases, it would take a month's worth of once-a-day workouts to equal the load generated in just a week of working out 2-3 times per day. This means that in an Olympic cycle (4 years of 36 hours weekly preparation), the multi-workout per day athlete is doing as much in a single year as the other is doing in all four! You can achieve this goal by proper use of restoration and recovery, while at the same time avoiding overtraining and fatigue. This approach allows one to execute very demanding workloads without any physical or psychological ill effects.

The recovery and restoration process is the most important factor of any up-to-date athletic conditioning program. It may be designed not only for the healthy athlete's body but also for the recuperation and rehabilitation of the athlete who may be physically and/or psychologically handicapped as a result of an accident or illness. The recovery exercises should be part of the daily workout routine, and due to their importance, should demand adequate time for their successful implementation. Recovery must be a daily ritual for all athletes and the coach must convince all athletes of its great importance. Daily restoration has various phases and possibilities that can be used in concordance with the gym or club circumstances.

The most important point about recovery is that it is more crucial to prevent overtraining or injury than to treat it. Another point of view is the big difference between daily recovery exercises during the preparatory, transitory or competition periods, and its variations for different age groups. The recovery and restoration time is not the same for a child who is practically untiring, as it is for an older athlete. We have to take into consideration not just the age indicators, but the athlete's working, cultural and social life, as well as the scheduled workout length and intensity.

A coach's most important daily activity should be writing a precise, detailed plan, i.e., a four-year, yearly, monthly, weekly, and daily plan of preparation which integrates both training and restoration every step along the way. Following a well-organized program with dedication is a sure way to avoid overtraining and obtain full recovery.

Designing a workout schedule
There are four important factors for designing a workout schedule: make the schedule enjoyable, avoid monotony, use plenty of exercise variations, and individualize the schedule. All of these factors are very important, but monotony is one of the biggest enemies of good restoration, and contributes to overtraining and fatigue. Individualization of

the daily workout to make the program enjoyable and employment of adequate exercise variability are also of the same importance, especially because everybody has their personal manner of adaptation and reaction to a given workout schedule. When a coach realizes something is going wrong, he/she must change the athlete's plan of preparation by analyzing very carefully with the athlete the reason and circumstances, which contributed to the fatigue.

The use of several appropriate natural supplements, effective recovery, and a scientific training program combined with well-planned activities can yield very impressive results. The first aspect of a daily ritual is a routine including:

(a) Meals used for supplying energy and all necessary materials for losing, gaining or maintaining weight and increasing strength

(b) A balanced ratio of workouts, sleep, active rest, and social-cultural activity

(c) Well-organized hygienic activity.

Rest and Relaxation

An important aspect of the daily ritual is a mandatory twice-daily pulse and bodyweight check, and weekly blood pressure check. Former Eastern European coaches considered these checks as some of their most important daily duties. A daily pulse and bodyweight check can be a very effective mirror of an athlete's level of preparation and the influence of daily employment and informal social-cultural activities. Daily pulse and bodyweight must be taken at the same time and under the same conditions. (e.g., before or long after meals, standing, sitting or lying supine. To ensure greater accuracy, there should be at least one minute's rest in a fixed position before the pulse is taken.

When the resting pulse increases and lean bodyweight decreases over time, the restoration process is not complete and overtraining may well occur. One must analyze all the factors that contribute to this and take the necessary measures immediately to enhance the recovery process and to avoid the possibility of fatigue from overtraining. Back in Romania and later with my American athletes, I did not and still I do not check what time they were going to bed. The daily morning heart rate (occasionally blood pressure) was and is still my "secret eye-witness", which is more trust-worthy than one hundred private detectives. No secret methods exist which can help any athlete to hide tiredness after a sleepless night, if you as the coach keep a daily long-term record of their heart rate and bodyweight.

During the workout, a pulse and a blood pressure check (before and after a maximum attempt, exercise or drill) should be taken. The result could either indicate effective restoration or fatigue due to informal daily activities. Serious signs of overtraining could indicate a health problem, which may need immediate medical attention, or something amiss with the athlete's informal social life style. Insufficient restoration limits the physical performance of the muscles, resulting in hypoglycemia, very increased post activity oxygen needs, metabolical acidosis, inadequate metabolism of blood lactate and accumulation of tiredness. Insufficient restoration is manifested in different ways in each individual athlete, but in the long run, the result will be the same: burnout and overtraining.

Another aspect of a daily recovery is the enhancement of recovery during and following a workout. This involves allowing the athlete's joints, tendons, muscles and nerves adequate time to recover and adapt to the stresses of training. Dividing a long workout into two or three separate divisions follows the same philosophy. If an athlete works out several times a day, he/she needs to warm up several times a day, thereby preparing the tendons and ligaments, in particular, for the load-

ing to follow. At the start of a workout, or any kind of hard physical activities, testosterone levels automatically increase and stay elevated for almost an hour, and then drop rapidly. After a break of more than a half hour, the same autonomic reaction will occur. As we know, testosterone is one of the most important hormone, which supports physical activities for maintaining muscle strength, and stimulating muscle and bone growth. So, by dividing a daily workout program into several 60 - 90 minute sessions, every athlete can benefit from an advantageous testosterone response. Executing a well-organized warm-up contributes to active rest and thorough recovery. Sometimes it may not be possible to do this, but at the same time it can become possible via the use of little more professional management and dedicated attention.

There are several methods and types of restoration that are available for every coach: psychotherapy, psychosomatic training methods (like Schultz's Autogenic Training), different forms of massage, hydrotherapy, natural products such as herbs, bee products, minerals, vitamins, glucose, passive and active rest, nutrition and medication, if necessary (though under strict medical supervision).

Between sets, it can be useful to use dynamic stretching, mental relaxation and preparation for the next set, stimulating massage of the specific muscles involved in that respective exercise, and the drinking of water or special herbal teas. Between exercises, if the program is longer than an hour and it is possible to fit in at least a thirty-minute break, one should consider breaking the workout into two halves.

In my coaching practice in Romania, then at Texas A&M University and now at Johnson County Community College, Overland Park, Kansas, I tried and still try to divide the athletes' preparation with typical Weightlifting exercises into two or three separate sessions during the day, if necessary, with no single session being longer than one hour. Actually the same philosophy I apply in the general sports conditioning stage: in the morning, weight training or plyometrics; in the afternoon before practice, weight training and then practice. A longer break between the sessions would be better, but this depends upon the individual's personal schedule.

Restoration after workout is most important, and has to be as complete as possible. The weekly restoration must be closely coordinated with the weekly schedule, which has to follow an athlete's psychological and physiological rhythms. For example: Monday - warm up for the new weekly cycle; Tuesday - Wednesday - increased effort; Thursday - decreased effort; Friday - Saturday - peak effort.

An 80% intensity week, which means that the average intensity of the week is 80% , should look like the following:

Monday: 70 % intensity and 10 % of the week's load;

Tuesday: 75 % intensity and 20 % of the week's load;

Wednesday: 80 % intensity and 15 % of the week's load;

Thursday: 75 % intensity and 15 % of the week's load;

Friday: 90 % intensity and 25 % of the week's load;

Saturday: 90 % intensity and 15 % of the week's load;

I believe in periodization of a yearly plan of preparation and in restoration after each phase of preparation. The periodization of preparation can be the biggest challenge to restoration. The coach has to be flexible and to correct the slightest signs of overtraining. We should never forget that this is better and easier to prevent than treating overtraining. The time devoted to it depends on the degree of tiredness, general health and overall time available to do it.

If the daily restoration is of a high quality, then the year-round restoration will also be very complete. Unfortunately the majority of the ath-

Day of Month :	1	2	3	4	5	6	7	8	9	10	11	12	13	14	15	16	17	18	19	20	21	22	23	24	25	26	27	28	29	30	31	Observation...
# Hours																																
Restless																																
Poor																																
Fair																																
Good																																
V.Good																																
Excell.																																

letes' lack of a theoretical knowledge about the great importance of restoration, as well as impatience and different excuses not to implement restoration (job, class, dating, etc.) can also interfere with proper recovery.

Individual and group lectures with athletes about the value and role of preparation and restoration are very beneficial. On an individual basis, a coach should finalize the most rational daily plan of preparation, and then follow up closely to see if all of the prescribed recommendations are being respected or not. I believe that, within the limitations of their privacy, a coach still can control the athletes' rest activity to workout ratio and daily habits.

Daily restoration can be strongly facilitated by means of several herbs and other natural products. One does not want to sound like a promoter of any kind of herb products or health food store chain, but it is relevant to mention that there are several herbs, which can accelerate the restoration process and in the form of a tea can be useful in the adaptogenic and restorative process. Certainly, the effectiveness of herbal teas for enhancing the recovery process is not scientifically fully supported, but we note nowadays a far greater interest by scientists in the possible benefit of different natural products. Apparently the National Institute of Health has even opened a new department, the Office for the Study of Unconventional Medical Practices.

We have to note that some herbal teas and products may contain substances banned by the International Olympic Committee; therefore their use can result in a positive doping test and of course in a suspension. Several manufacturers add various stimulants to different natural products, and it is highly recommendable for everyone who wants to benefit from herb teas and products to contact the U.S. Olympic Committee Drug Hotline (1-800-233-0393) to obtain more information.

Instead of drinking cold water or some stimulating colas, these herbal teas taken during workout may help an athlete recover. My personal recovery ritual with herbs involves a tea drinking session during and after the workout. This is the most important time for rapid and complete restoration. Many coaches consider this a waste of time, and so do many athletes, but I have observed on many occasions the benefit of this practice in workouts. These thirty minutes of the additional cheerful time are worth the effort.

What could be done in these thirty minutes?: First of all, East German research has shown that running 1,500 m in eight to nine minutes after a workout significantly accelerates the recovery and relaxation processes. After this running, one follows with a 6-10 minute sauna, drinking the aforementioned tea very slowly. This 6-10 minute sauna enables the athlete to stretch more effectively than in an air-conditioned gym. The sauna apparently stimulates and speeds up the metabolic process, the vital organs and glands; accelerates the body's healing and restorative capacities; eliminates the metabolic waste; detoxifies and cleanses the body due to the stimulatory action of the sweat glands; rejuvenates the body; inhibits the growth of viruses or bacteria; is an ideal relaxant; and eliminates muscular pain and insomnia. If possible, after the sauna, an ice cold-hot-cold-hot-cold contrast bath ritual which stimulates and reactivates the adrenal and other endocrine glands' activities is recommended as follows: 1-2 minutes in a hot pool and 30 seconds in the cold pool. If it is not possible to install a cold and hot pool, a hot-cold-hot-cold shower will have a similar result. The result is much better if an athlete can stay longer than two minutes in hot water. Usually an athlete cannot extend the time longer and the coach or the trainer must decide on the time to be devoted to this type of hydro restoration. If a coach considers that this type of recovery is more essential than the others, or is too difficult to do together with the others, the best result will be achieved taking 4-5 minutes hot and 30-second cold and repeating several times.

After a sauna and hot-cold water massage, the next step of a recovery is to relax in a quiet place, lying on the back and continuing to drink a suitable herbal tea. This is a key point in physical and mental restoration. I would like to elaborate more on the issue of relaxation. As a college student in Romania I heard that in U.S. gyms you would find posters bearing the following text: "Remember the ones who succeed in sports are those who know the art of relaxation." When I came to the USA, I was very surprised not to see any of these alleged posters in the gyms. Self-relaxation, especially the Schultz Autogenic Training Method, is a very successful and active component of the daily workout routine in Romania and other East European countries. The method favored by me is the Schultz Autogenic Training Method, which I consider to be very important for all sports during certain periods of preparation. Therefore we have to take into consideration very serious mental preparation because success in sporting competition usually depends more upon coping with the psychological demands than the physical demands of the event alone. After all, the body of the well-trained athlete usually is extremely well conditioned and eminently capable of overcoming most of the physical challenges of competition, but the mind certainly may not be able to cope with the special stresses of a given task.

Complete restoration involves complete relaxation. If an athlete's muscles are still stiff, this means that recovery has not been complete. There also tends to be an equal ratio between relaxation and concentration. Thus, the degree to which you can relax, you generally will be capable to concentrate as well, and vice versa.

The human body was designed to always be in an expectant state and to respond to every outside stimulus with fight, flight or freezing in order to enhance survival and growth. As we can train our muscles to be faster, stronger, bigger or more resistant, so we can train our nervous system and will power to contribute more to our physical development and minimize the limitations of psychological inhibition.

This inhibition level can be minimized by special different psychological training methods, which are methodologically similar to physical training methods. In the sports selection process, psychological factors can be among the most important to be considered. To take as an example the Greek method of selection for the Ancient Olympics: athletes who turned pale in response to stress were not selected. Today we call it by various names such as negative emotion or "choking", processes that are detrimental to any effective physical or intellectual performance. Of course, we do not need to reject every athlete who shows signs of negative emotion, because there is always room for improvement and with proper educational methods it is often possible to turn a timid young athlete into a tenacious competitor. But at the same time, we should give careful extra thought if the athlete is older. Getting older and making more negative experiences part of one's nature can create a situation that is very hard or impossible to improve.

We can develop and improve our will power just as we develop our muscles. We can condition our minds to cope effectively with more and more demanding physical and psychological activities. Every time when I have a chance to talk about these themes to my athletes I mention one of my favorite mottos of anonymous origin, namely: "Everybody has unlimited potential to be the person that they want to be". Yes, we can certainly determine our destinies and profoundly influence how we wish our futures to be.

One of the biggest benefits of this kind of mental preparation is to speed up the recovery process. An athlete in a stressful situation such as a workout, competition, or an uncontrolled activity expends a great deal of energy, with nervous energy being the most difficult to recover. With well-designed and consciously practiced self-relaxation methods

an athlete will be able to diminish stress and accelerate recovery.

We need to educate athletes about the great importance of a well-balanced life, including its social and personal aspects. In this domain there has to be a very close and sincere coach-athlete relationship. Coaches have to implant in their athlete's mind the 'fanaticism' of sport; the desire to win, to be the best and to be a fighter under all circumstances; and to enjoy workout sessions which sometimes may look like torture.

The coach should play a major role in the athlete's restoration. Firstly, there must be an educational role: a coach should learn various restoration methods, and suggest to the athletes that several different variations of restoration give the best results. The second role should be to follow up on a daily basis their school-practice-workout-extracurricular activities. From the aforementioned three daily activities the practice session or workout is one that the coach should monitor in detail. The coach's main duties should be providing an effective warm-up and cool-down, designing a scientific workout schedule and implementing restoration into the program.

Another important factor of recovery is a massage, auto-massage or vibro-massage that could be partial or complete. Its effect can be great and is a very important part of implementing the concept of the cumulative effect of using several small factors together.

The athlete's individual biological rhythms could be another factor that needs to be followed closely. Every individual has a daily psychological, intellectual and physical proficiency, which is influenced by conditioned reflexes. These biological rhythms can be disrupted by different factors and consequently, physical performance can be diminished. When we have signs of fatigue or lack of enthusiasm for workouts, this could be the result of disruptions of one's physical and psychological rhythms. In this situation we need to change the workout schedule to avoid possible injuries or overtraining. Indicators, which that can be monitored without much difficulty, are changes in the daily pulse rate, bodyweight and blood pressure.

A gym with fresh air, good lighting, pleasant music, plants and flowers, and refreshing pastel colored walls and floor can contribute to a better restoration.

If we attempt to apply what has been discussed here, the combination of small and large restorative measures will produce better results in our athletes. With a well-recovered athlete, the load and intensity can be increased, while avoiding the risk of overtraining or fatigue.

To remedy overtraining, medical examination and assistance can be invaluable. If overtraining becomes evident, the coach should first require a complete break from the given sport, which does not totally exclude some form of active rest, such as participation in some other sport or exercise that will facilitate restoration.

The second step, which a coach could apply in an overtraining situation, is to start an active and gradually more intensive general conditioning program. When an athlete has all the necessary positive signs (the physical and mental desire of practicing), then he/she is ready to start. One begins with special conditioning and then follows step-by-step training for complete specific preparation.

However, the better remedy for overtraining is to prevent the occurrence of insufficient restoration. In this regard, systematic, carefully planned year-round preparation, respecting the rules of yearly periodization, will eliminate even the smallest chance of overtraining.

In this same chapter I feel necessary to talk about several other methods of preventing overtraining and facilitating restoration, which would contribute to a complete athlete development, the most important of which I call "Body Hardening." According to the Webster Dictionary, "hardy" refers to "the ability to withstand fatigue, privation, robust, vigorous, able to withstand adverse conditions". Body hardening is the capacity to adaptation to the environment, including changes in temperature and humidity, without suffering any functional or psychological deregulation that could create detrimental conditioned reflexes in response to the external factors. To achieve an ideal robust and vigorous body, those methods must exert repeated and prolonged actions on the body. This body hardening is so important because it improves the work capacity under all types of environmental conditions.

The most important principles of body hardening are to respect the gradualness of its applications, to practice systematically, to take into consideration of the variation of intensity of different meteorological factors, to respect the diversity of body hardening methods, and the last but not the least important, to respect the principle of individualization.

Body hardening can be practiced by exposure to air, by sun or by water. The most important effect of body hardening by the air method is that it intensifies the metabolism, fortifies the neural system, increases cardiovascular activity and solicits the body's thermoregulatory systems. The best result can be achieved if an athlete can be exposed for a maximum of thirty to forty minute session, of course getting into it gradually from a five minute starting session. As a precaution, only a hundred percent healthy athlete should practice exercising in warm or cold air, and on the first cold or uncomfortably hot feeling must stop the session. Everyone who wants to practice this method should consult a physician.

Solar radiation has different effects: biological effects, increased metabolism, hematopoetic and thermoregulatory functions, as well as bactericidal effects and prevention and healing of rickets. The infrared rays have a thermic, curing effect and intensifies the functions of locomotor apparatus. Ultraviolet radiation strengthens the connective tissues, and increases the muscular tonicity and activity (see Hettinger The Physiology of Strength, 1961). The solar radiation influences the cardiovascular apparatus and the endocrine glands' activities, stimulating and invigorating them.

It is very important that everyone takes precautionary measures to respect the rules of sun exposure. Ignoring these warnings can be very harmful if someone does not respect the rules of height of the sun (sunbathing is safer between 8.00-11.00 a.m. or 4.00-6.00 p.m.); the atmospheric transparency and the angle of the radiation. A recommendation from a dermatologist could also be very valuable.

Body toughening with water is the most efficient and the most studied and practiced method. The medical science of curing and preventing sickness by bathing is the balneology, which has been very successful in Europe and Asia. Just I would like to mention the Finnish Saunas, the Japanese Furros. Balneology is used for a large variation of illnesses, among them arthritis, ligament and tendon problems, muscular problems, nerve problems like stress, fatigue, etc.

Water has at least thirty times larger thermo-conductivity than air, and can strongly influence the cardiovascular system, the respiratory organs, the thermoregulatory system and the metabolism. The biggest advantage of body toughening by water is that it does not need special and complicated installations. There are a great many variations of body toughening methods with water. In particular one may mention bathing which could be cold - under 68 F(20 Celsius), cool 70 - 91 F (21-33 Celsius), normal 93 - 95 F (34-35 Celsius), warm 93 - 104 F (34-40 Celsius), and hot over 104 - 113 F (40-45 Celsius). Time-wise the bathing could be short 10 minutes, medium 10 to 20 minutes, and long over 20 minutes. Bathing can be partial or general, and its effect depends on temperature and duration. Short periods generally have a stimulating effect and longer ones a relaxing effect.

The most important general rules, which should be respected, are to practice at least two to three hours after meals and not start while perspiring heavily. As a warning, one must respect the rules of body hardening by cold water. In the first phase the athlete will feel the water to be very cold because of peripheral vasoconstriction and central vasodilatation. This is the accommodation of the thermoregulatory system with the water temperature. Then in the second phase after the accommodation phase, the athlete would have a pleasant sensation due to a peripheral vasodilatation. If the athlete stays too long in the cold water, then the third phase will occur, which involves peripheral paralytic vasodilatation. The athlete starts to shiver; the skin becomes blue and looks like gooseflesh. The bathing should be stopped before this phase occurs, or on the first signal of cold sensation. In the bathing regime one includes showering, jacuzzi, steam bath, saunas, furro method and salt water treatment. As is the case with the other methods, these also require a medical supervision and recommendation.

Acclimatization is the result of effective body toughening and implicates all physiological modifications, which are produced in an athlete's body to adapt to certain unfamiliar environmental conditions. Acclimatization involves special adaptation to different meteorological factors like humidity, temperature, atmospheric pressure, air motion and solar radiation, as well as to the altitude, and hygienic and social-cultural differences of the new area where the competition will take place or where an athlete will stay and work out for an extended period.

Acclimatization is especially important for elite athletes. In this respect careful attention must be paid to personal body hygiene to prevent sickness, a rational diet, suitable clothing, adaptation to the climate where the competition or preparation takes place, respect for the rules of traveling (jet lag, general stiffness and diminished muscular tone). Any deficits here can exert a major impact on any daily physical condition and its expression in better performances during workouts and competitions. If coaches or anyone involved with athletic preparation ignore these aforementioned rules then they must bear major responsibility for any failures of their athletes relating to environmental stresses.

In the daily routine of an athlete's life one should pay attention to morning recreational gymnastics activity, individual hygiene, nutritional balance, well-planned workout programs, an optimal workout-rest ratio, respect for the daily peaks of an athlete's neuromuscular activities, passive rest and recovery, active rest and recovery, external social-cultural activities, medical supervision, and the influence of meteorological conditions.

In short, the basics of a successful workout program, should include the appropriate combination of multifaceted general physical preparation with specific preparation for a given sport; progressive increase in effort and overload; rational alternation of rest and workouts; enjoyable and challenging workouts to avoid monotony; use of plenty of exercise variability; and individualization of all programs.

Another effective method of recuperation in athletic preparation to consider is massage. Massage is an ensemble of the manual and mechanical procedures with the specific goal of stimulating, invigorating, recuperating or relaxing the athlete's body before and after any practice, workout or competition. Massage could be a very important component of athletic preparation and restoration.

Massage can be applied in the workout process during the preparatory, competitional and transitional periods. As in athletic preparation, massage also should respect the rules of individualization and apply the appropriate methods in concordance with the goals and the specific sport's particularities.

During transition periods a hygienic morning massage can be the most important, executed at a rapid tempo and for not longer than twenty minutes, covering as many muscles as possible.

During the preparatory and competition periods the most important aspect of a massage session is forming part of a general or partial warm-up, restoration, relaxation and preparation for rest and sleep, or helping an athlete to maintain peak form for a longer period.

Massage, like any other type of daily activity, has its own rules and regulations which every trainer, coach or athlete should respect. First of all, it is vital to have sufficient knowledge of massage and anatomy; to know about the different massage techniques and their influence on an athlete's body; to respect the rules of personal hygiene of both: of the masseur and the client (the masseur should be perfectly healthy and in good physical shape); to choose a suitable place for massage, which usually should be a spacious, adequately lit, fresh, but not cold. It is ideal if it is close to a shower, sauna, relaxation room, hot tub (hot and cold tubs) or jacuzzi, and the lockers.

During sporting events, massage can be applied directly on the skin or in some athletic situations, over the clothes.

A coach who practices partial or complete massage as part of the daily activities must know if the athlete who is a subject for a massage session is completely healthy or not, and suffers or not some form of skin disease, or the skin is clean or not, or if the patient has fever or any contraindication for massage. We believe that every coach should learn more about different massage procedures and their benefit and effect.

Probably several readers may already feel daunted by the number of rules and regulations, but I still need to add a few more regulations: do not apply any massage technique on a full stomach: start with easy, light procedures; be very calm because the masseur will transmit calmness or irritability to the client; properly warm up the athlete's skin; and apply gradually different procedures to prevent habituation of the client to the massage. Before a practice, game or competition finish with invigorating procedures, but after competition and practice or before sleep, finish with longer relaxation procedures. If the client complains of anxiety or pain or shows any sign of fever, the massage should be stopped immediately.

In conclusion, all of these ideas about Recovery and Restoration may be summarized in the form of two graphs.

Chapter 8
Specificity In Sports Conditioning

Modern athletic preparation and conditioning has become far more involved during recent years with free weight training exercises. Weightlifting with its numerous auxiliary exercises has emerged as the most important sports conditioning factor worldwide.

Exercise routines are unlimited, and with some imagination and knowledge every coach can devise an efficient workout program.

At the very outset, I should note that that use of more exercise variations generally avoids monotony, injury and stagnation, and excites higher level motor functioning, neuromuscular coordination, and more complete athletic preparation.

A coach since 1964, I have always gathered as much information as possible about strength and conditioning and even created an "ideas" notebook, which I still use all these years later. Before making a final judgment about any program, I test the program and experiment on my own. Only after I become convinced of the program's value, I decide if it was worth introducing into my training plan. And I stick with the following rules

1. Gather as much detailed information as possible about the program.

2. Select and classify the information.

3. Implement new ideas gradually into any program.

4. Make ongoing daily observations.

5. Ask the athletes for their reaction to the new exercises.

6. Try the new elements on your own, or on a small number of athletes, usually novices. Remember, it is harder to change the attitude of older athletes who already have confidence in a certain routine, than it is to influence novices.

7. Follow up. Positive feedback from the participants gives a coach the necessary peace of mind and confidence to proceed into a program with a larger number of athletes. Actually, the athletes determine the success or failure of a program.

8. Learn and master new exercise techniques. Never teach an exercise which you cannot demonstrate properly. (Heavy weights aren't necessary for a demonstration. A broomstick or light DB can also be adequate). It is very important to know the theoretical and biomechanical description of any new exercises, so that coaches can spot and correct improper exercise technique.

9. Explore and experiment with new programs, but never put the athlete at risk.

10. Discuss with athletes improvements in the program, the desired benefit of the improvements and related problems.

It is satisfying to receive positive feedback about a program. It is even more satisfying when other strength and conditioning coaches implement my techniques into their programs, especially when those coaches have success.

Scientifically based guidelines for selecting programs for all-sports conditioning may be summarized in the form of the following 15 points:

1. Regardless of the sport, the conditioning program must begin with general conditioning.

2. Make a list of the primary movements of a specific sport, including specificity of energy utilization and biomechanics.

3. Make a list of the exercises that are as mechanics close to a sport's primary movements, but do not imitate them exactly.

4. Combine the general conditioning exercises with specific conditioning exercises for each sport. Code and subdivide the exercises into groups according to motion and muscle group involvement.

5. Include all possible conditioning variations in the program: free weights, medicine ball exercises, stair work, sand stair boxes and court, up and down hill activities, other plyometrics exercises, acrobatics, etc., which supports my before mentioned statement about the importance of exercise variations.

6. Avoid the monotony in the conditioning program; make the program more enjoyable. Include general and individual exercises in the program, regardless of whether the program is designed for individual or team sports. In case of team sports, follow the group's main goal, but maintain the freedom for designing an individual part into the program, which must be modulated to suit a particular athlete's physical and psychological particularities.

7. Teach in detail the efficient and safe technique of all exercises.

8. Introduce the exercises gradually into the program.

9. Do not imitate a program because a world or Olympic champion has used it, as this could be detrimental to your athletes' preparation. Remember, your athletes are probably not world champions. Understand your team's physical and psychological capabilities and the limitations of the conditioning center. Gradually implement what you consider to be most appropriate at a given time for a given athlete.

10. Never be satisfied with your program. Observe all athletes carefully during the season and draw conclusions after the season is over. Try to improve your program continuously.

11. Respect the rules and guidelines of sporting organization and periodization.

12. Keep in mind that athletes are human beings like everyone else. Therefore we must not be influenced by technology and computers to become too mechanistic in all of our daily activities. The conditioning program is for emotional humans with senses, thoughts and feelings, and should not look like a machine-created daily menu.

13. Take into consideration the effects of gender and age on trainability and regeneration.

14. The training frequency depends on the athlete's age, technical knowledge, and level of preparation and phase of preparation. The result of the training load is reflected in how well the athlete accommodates to the given programs. The desired performance occurs if the training stimulus has been of adequate intensity and magnitude.

15. The athletes must accommodate to the program. This accommodation refers to the capability of the athlete's body to adapt to progressively increasing levels of physical and mental stress in order to produce better performance.

The method of selection of exercises for any given sport is very simple: respect the above criteria, and then in relationship with time constraints, sport equipment and the condition of the gym facilities (space, temperature, safety tips, etc.), make a list of exercises which you, as a conditioning coach, consider to be the most appropriate for a given sport. Try to organize the exercises in a certain order and groups. After defining these exercise groups, any coach can then easily select one or a maximum of two exercises from each group, depending on goals for a respective period of preparation, and to build up a schedule of preparation without any need for a computer. This is the part of the scheduling where the coach must introduce personal feelings, intuitions, experiences and sentiments into the program, which no computer is able to do. This will impart the flavor, character and style, which mirror the individual coach's unique philosophy.

Examples of Exercises
1. DB Raise to Armpit
2. DB Upright Row
3. BB medium grip Upright Row
4. DB Squat Raise To Armpit
5. DB Squat Under Upright Row
6. BB wide grip Upright Row
7. DB Supinated Curls
8. BB Supinated Curls
9. DB Pronated Curls
10. BB Pronated Curls
11. DB Parallel Curls
12. DB Parallel Overhead Press
13. BB behind the head Overhead Press
14. DB Parallel Overhead Push Press
15. BB behind the head Overhead Press
16. DB Parallel Overhead Squat Push Press
17. BB behind the head Overhead Squat Push Press
18. DB From Hip High Pull Snatch
19. BB medium grip From Hip High Pull Snatch
20. DB High Pull Snatch
21. BB medium grip High Pull Snatch
22. BB behind the head Good Morning
23. DB Parallel Bench Press
24. BB medium grip Bench Press
25. DB Lying on Bench Pullover
26. BB Incline Bench Press
27. BB Decline Bench Press
28. DB Lying on Bench Fly
29. DB Single Leg Step Back Lunges
30. DB Alternating Leg Step Back Lunges
31. DB Single Leg Step-up on Box
32. DB Alternating Leg Step-up on Box
33. DB Lunge Walk
34. BB Back Squat
35. BB Front Squat
36. BB Wave Squat
37. BB Squat Jump
38. BB Wave Squat+ Back Squat + Wave Squat
40. Regular Crunches
41. Parallel Knee Hug Sit-ups
42. Bent Knees Hooked Feet Sit-ups
43. Straight Knees Feet up Half Jack-knives
44. Double Leg Stair Jump-Bounding
45. Upstairs Run

Workout No 1
DB Raise to Armpit
DB Supinated Curls
DB Parallel Overhead Press
DB From Hip High Pull Snatch
DB Parallel Bench Press
BB Back Squat
Regular Crunches
Double Leg Stair Jump-Bounding
Workout No 2
BB medium grip up Right Row
BB Supinated Curls
BB behind the head Push Press
BB medium grip High Pull Snatch
BB Incline Bench Press
DB Lunge Walk
Parallel Knee Hug Sit-ups
Upstairs Run

. And so forth.

As a coach when I start to define a workout program I respect the importance of appropriate ratios of repetitions, sets, intensities and exercises. There are several possibilities of variations in intensity. A few examples follow:

50% 50% 55% 55% 60% 60% 70% 70% or
50% 60% 70% 80% 50% 60% 70% 80%
50% 55% 60% 65% 70% 75% 80%
50% 60% 55% 65% 60% 70% 65% 75%
50% 50% 70% 70% 60% 80% 70% 90% x , and so on.

The goals could be different: muscular endurance with 12-20 repetitions and 30-70% intensity; muscle hypertrophy with 6-10 repetitions and 70-80% intensity; muscle strength with three to six repetitions and 80-90% intensity and absolute strength with 1-3 repetitions and 95% to over 100% intensity. Of course I never rigidly distinguish between these limits in my programs because, regardless of sports and preparation phase, I need to closely monitor the athlete's response in order to overload and to stimulate the muscle fibers and the aerobic/anaerobic capacity of each athlete in order to best achieve the goals of preparation. As a general rule in my philosophy of program writing: I finish every exercise with the highest intensity of that day for a respective exercise, considering as wasteful all sets with lighter intensities after that.

Example: Hypertrophy Workout No 1

DB Quarter Squat & Up On Toes Raise To Armpit 60% 14, 70% 10, 65% 12, 75% 8, 70% 10, 80% 6, 80% 6

DB Supinated Curls 60% 14, 65% 12, 70% 10, 75% 10, 80% 6, 85% 5

DB Parallel Overhead Press 65% 10, 75% 8, 65% 10, 75% 8, 70% 8, 80% 6, 80% 6

DB From Hip High Pull Snatch 60% 14, 65% 12, 70% 10, 65% 12, 75% 8, 75% 8

DB Parallel Bench Press 70% 10, 70% 10, 75% 10, 75% 10, 80% 6, 80% 6, 85% 4

BB Back Squat 50% 12, 60% 10, 70% 8, 80% 6, 75% 8, 65% 10, 75% 8, 80% 6

Regular Crunches 6 sets x 20

Double Leg Stair Jump-Bounding 6 sets x 8

Example: Muscular Endurance Workout No 1

DB Raise to Armpit .40% 20, 20, 45% 18, 45% 18, 50% 16, 50% 16, 60% 12, 65% 10

DB Supinated Curls 40% 20, 50% 16, 45% 18, 55% 16, 50% 16, 65% 12

DB Parallel Overhead Press 40% 16, 40% 16, 50% 14, 50% 14, 45% 16, 55% 12, 50% 14, 60% 12

DB From Hip High Pull Snatch 35% 20, 35% 20, 45% 18, 45% 18, 40% 20, 50% 16, 45% 18, 60% 10

DB Parallel Bench Press 40% 20, 45% 20, 50% 18, 55% 16, 60% 14, 70% 10, 70% 10

BB Back Squat 40% 16, 45% 14, 50% 14, 55% 12, 60% 12, 65% 10, 50% 14, 65% 12

Regular Crunches 6 sets x 40

Upstairs Run 6 sets x 6 etc.

Example: Muscular Strength Workout No 1

DB Quarter Squat & Up On Toes Raise To Armpit 60% 10, 70% 8, 80% 6, 75% 8, 85% 5, 90% 3, 90% 3

DB Supinated Curls 60% 10, 75% 8, 70% 10, 80% 6, 75% 8, 85% 5, 95% 1, 95% 1

DB Parallel Overhead Press 60% 10, 65% 8, 70% 8, 75% 6, 80% 6, 85% 4, 90% 2, 90% 2

DB From Hip High Pull Snatch 70% 6, 70% 6, 80% 5, 80% 5, 85% 4, 85% 4, 90% 2, 90% 2

DB Parallel Bench Press 70% 10, 80% 6, 90% 3, 75% 6, 85% 5, 95% 1, 95% 1

BB Back Squat 60% 10, 70% 6, 80% 5, 80% 5, 90% 2, 80% 5, 90% 2, 80% 5, 90% 2

Regular Crunches with 20 lb DB on chest 6 sets x 10

Double Leg Stair Jump-Bounding 6 sets x 18

How many times should one work out? This depends on several factors, such as total time available, goals, rules, stage and period of preparation, and the specificity of a respective sport.

Every conditioning program I start with at least a two-week introductory program in which proper technique is emphasized. In addition, I determine each athlete's 1 RM (one repetition maximum) for each exercise. However, to avoid injuries, athletes do not perform an actual 1 RM test. Instead, they are tested for a 5 RM and 5 kg (11 lb) is added to that figure to determine the approximate 1 RM. That gives the coaches peace of mind while avoiding injuries. Of course, for DB exercises we divide this 5 kg (11 lb) weight in two equal parts or 2.5 kg (5 lb) for the right and 2.5 kg (5 lb) for the left hand. For combination or hybrid exercises like the Back Squat Push Press, DB or BB Javorek's Complex # 1 & 2, 3, 4, 5, etc., the intensity must always be determined from the most difficult part of the exercise in order to be able to perform the whole exercise properly.

After the approximate 1 RM is determined for each athlete, the remainder of the two-week introductory program is devoted to adapting the athletes to the increased effort necessary in the program, which is accomplished through vigorous programs emphasizing the respective cardiovascular and power benefits.

The next step is the preparatory phase of the conditioning program. The first goal of this phase is to prepare the athletes for competition, and not just to increase strength. Not until spring (or fall or winter in several sports) does the preparation begin for the next season, and increased strength then becomes a priority. However, during the two-week introductory period, and during the preparation period, athletes still achieve very good muscular development. Due to the negative effect of an increasing volume of training a coach must carefully select the exercises, repetitions, sets, rest periods and intensities. Some basic mathematical-statistic calculations (volume, load average, total reps, sets, intensities and repetitions in different intensity zones) may be used to indicate the degree of correlation between the desired goals and achieved performance, which reflects the effectiveness of the conditioning program.

At the Johnson County Community College Sports Conditioning Center (the wrongly so called weight room) enough DB are available allowing thirty athletes to workout with four sets of DB, all of different weight. Other equipment includes twelve squat racks and benches, sixteen BB and sufficient plates, ranging from 1.25 kg (2.5 lb) to 25 kg (55 lb) for each set of squat racks and benches.

In my conditioning programs I use DB for more than ninety percent of the time, because I consider them more practical for the majority of the sports compared with barbells or machines. My opinion is that exercising with DB is more dynamically challenging. The range of motion in all directions is large, and the range of exercise variations is almost unlimited. They tend to stimulate the stabilization role of muscles, which machines largely neglect, and which BB partially eliminate. DB exercises are easy to teach, and are very safe for exercising with. The specific arm and leg movements and coordination is also better achieved with DB. After these main arguments, my other motives for using DB are that they do not need a large and special practice area, and being cheap, are much more affordable for every team or individual.

However, all of these arguments do not eliminate the use of barbells from my programs. I use several squats, clean & jerk, and snatch assistant exercises, in different in-season, off-season, specific or general strength and conditioining programs.

Starting a program with DB and BB must begin with an inventory of the equipment, which must be in a good ratio to the number of athletes. The athletes line up with three or four pairs of DB, different weights. In case of limited number of DB the team must be organized in groups of two or three for each set of DB in order to workout in a rotational system. On command, the athletes begin and finish each exercise at the same time, allowing 20-30 seconds (for certain exercises up to 90 seconds) break between sets. Athletes take 20-90 second breaks between sets, depending of a specific exercise's difficulty or upon their level of conditioning and the goal of the workout. The last 5 seconds of each break are counted to ensure that the athlete is prepared for the next set. After each exercise is completed, athletes are informed of the next exercise. When the weight training session is completed, athletes perform the prescribed program of brief abdominal and plyometrics exercises, including medicine ball, stair, sand, stair boxes or uphill exercises. The program is very efficient and athletes perform a complete workout in fifty to sixty minutes.

In-season athletes perform maintenance work and harder workouts when the team needs a "shake-up" or during longer breaks between competitions. In case of physical or mental fatigue among athletes, the program shifts to "active rest" that emphasizes recovery while maintaining conditioning levels.

In contrast, off-season strength program is individualized, based on the athletes' individual strengths, weaknesses, conditioning levels and goals for the next season.

During the preparatory phase, regardless of the sport, dumbbells are used extensively because, as discussed earlier, I consider them to be more time efficient, and with the time constraints on athletes and conditioning programs, the efficiency of the program is critical. With some imagination, DB can be successfully incorporated into conditioning programs for every sport, including all professional and Olympic sports

Dumbbell step up on box for high jump.

Barbell shrug shot put conditioning shot put Olympic champion Randy Barnes.

Dumbbell incline bench press.

Barbell curl spring by Wayne Simien basketball conditioning.

Javelin conditioning medicine ball two hand overhead throw from a box by Colette Kibler.

Dumbbell press by Wayne Simien basketball conditioning.

Sand stair boxes left shoulder right leg side bounding tennis conditioning by Steve Nash.

Barbell power clean by Wayne Simien basketball conditioning.

Javelin conditioning pathway development exercise with a rubber tubing rope.

Sumya Anani professional womenboxing.world champion.

Dumbbell overhead triceps curls tennis conditioningm by Steve Nash.

Baseball conditioning medicine ball situps.

Barbell back squat tennis conditioning by Steve Nash.

Chapter 9
Drug-free Physical Preparation in Sport

I have always enjoyed studying the old time strong men and their athletic preparation. As a young athlete, I saw a photo of Richard Weisz of Hungary, the 1908 London Olympic Games super heavyweight Greco-Roman style wrestling champion. I was impressed with his impressive physique and muscular harmony.

In 1965, I met in Gherla-Szamosujvar, Romania, Jozsef Kovacs, a 60 year-old former circus wrestler and powerlifter. He impressed me with his well-proportioned body and his unusual amount of strength and power. This gentleman put an iron belt 2.5 cm (1 inch) wide, 2 mm (almost 1/8 inch) thick, on the back of his neck. He bent it around his neck into the shape of a tie, and then opened it easily. With the same ease, he wrapped a 5/8-inch thick iron bar around his forearm into the shape of a spring. Mr. Kovacs told me that he started working out as a young boy bending narrow iron wires, gradually increasing the length and thickness of the wires and belts. He worked out regularly, when he felt comfortable and when he had the desire. He said that he ate 'a lot of eggs, bacon, sausage and drink after meal a cup of good wines'. Kovacs regularly ate vegetables and seasonal fruits.

Most significantly, he motivated himself, without being pushed by someone or something other than the desire to be the strongest and the best. There are hundreds of other great old-time champions who were amazingly strong before the anabolic steroids craze began. I would like to mention a few of their accomplishments:

Louis Cyr, from Canada (1863-1912), lifted a 124 kg (272 lb). thick-handled DB overhead with one hand; Horace Barre, also from Canada(1872 - 1918), performed a 125 kg (275 lb) one arm lift, 157.5 kg (346 lb) jerk (taking the bar in two movements, first to waist, then to shoulders, and finally the jerk); and Henry Holtgrewe, from Cincinnati, Ohio (1872-1917) lifted 130 kg (286 lb) in one arm lifting.

There was also Eugene Sandow (actually Frederick Mueller) who was born in Konigsberg, Germany on April 2, 1867, but became successful in England after starting to exercise because of his poor health, and later becoming the father of modern bodybuilding. Among many other feats, he performed a 122.5 kg (269 lb) one arm bent style press.

Consider the following as well:

John Grunn Marx of Germany snatched overhead with one-hand a 70 kg (154 lb) dumbbell with a 7.5 cm (almost 3 inch) thick grip; Apollon of France, overhead snatched a 103 kg (226 lb) "unliftable" barbell with one hand. The BB diameter was 6 cm (2.3 inch). He did not fix it overhead, because the thickness of the BB caused him to lose balance; George Hackenschmidt of Russia right hand pressed 116 kg (252 lb), right hand snatched 89.5 kg (169 lb) and right hand jerked 105 kg (231 lb) at a slim 86 kg (189 lb) body weight.

G.W. Rolandow, of Switzerland, snatched 81.8 kg (180 lb) with his right hand and 77.2 kg (170 lb) with his left hand, bent pressed 135.5 kg (298 lb) from his shoulder with his right hand and 120.5 kg (265 lb) with his left hand. He was capable of jumping over a 92 cm (3 feet) high 64 cm (2.1 feet) wide table, while holding a 34 kg (75 lb) dumbbell in both hands. Rollandow performed several other explosive drills. He jumped forward backward over a 91 kg (200 lb.) BB that he held in his hands. He also performed a standing back somersault with 27 kg (60 lb) dumbbells in each hand, and did 15,000 consecutive rope skips without a miss.

Another German athlete Arthur Saxon, right hand snatched 90.5 kg (199 lb) and right hand clean & jerked 113.5 kg (250 lb).

The Hungarian national, Jozsef Grafl, who started weight training at age 25 in Vienna, Austria, won several super heavyweight world Weightlifting championships. Among those he defeated were famous names like Karl Swoboda and Berthold Tandler. Grafl was capable of right hand snatching 88 kg (193 lb), left hand snatching 82 kg (180 lb), two hand snatching 117 kg (257 lb), two hand Pressing 144 kg (316 lb), military pressing 100 kg (220 lb) 18 times in succession with feet together, and two hands DB jerking 150 kg (330 lb). Grafl probably was the first "ideal" type of super heavyweight athlete: he was 190 cm (6.2 feet) tall and weighed 122 kg (268 lb).

I collected this information about the strongmen from different sources back in Romania, Hungary, and later in the USA. My special thanks go to Dr. Tamas Ajan, Aniko Nemeth-Mora, Virgil Hodgea, Ferencz Szathmary, Terry Todd, Rudy Sablo, and Bill Clark for the information they provided to me about old time strong men.

We know that the old-time strong men built up their strength over a long time. We should do the same with our athletes. We have to start with them in kindergarten, giving them the necessary sporting culture and education, implanting in their minds the concept that success is possible without performance-enhancing drugs.

Children may face negative outcomes in the problems and situations that occur in their lives if we, (the parents and educators, including coaches) do not help them learn to make the right choice. From the youngest age, our children see on television, magazines and in newspapers thousands of commercials encouraging them to take drugs for everything, starting with the simple cold or headache. Several sport magazines inform youths about different "wonder" products and their so-called benefits. Today's modern society wants bigger, faster and stronger athletes in a short time, and the very seductive dream of "big bucks" in professional sports push the athletes to risk everything. Politics in sports, the fact that national prestige is decided on the basis of their athletes' results at the Olympics or World Championships, and the fact that their results directly influence their future professional careers, navigate athletes into very dangerous waters.

I consider being an athlete to be a privilege like driving a car. As car drivers must respect the rules related to safe driving or lose the privilege of driving if they do not, so athletes should also be in same situation.

I believe in complete and diverse athletic preparation. I am against a specialized, limited exercise preparation program. I cannot agree with some specialists who maintain that 6-8 exercises on a year-round basis for elite athletes is enough. In my personal, and several other specialists' opinion that approach is very questionable. An athlete with clean preparation needs, after each peak (competition period), to recover, to regenerate the whole structural-functional system and to start a new preparatory cycle to achieve a new and higher competitive level. In my opinion and experience, if we reduce an athlete's preparation using only 6-8 exercises on a year round basis, the results would be overtraining, burnout and stagnation. By profiting from the benefit of several exercises, we can eliminate the monotony, develop different muscle groups with a different approach, and give the necessary flavor to the workout, which helps motivate the athlete to improve performance. The preparation of elite athletes in the pre-competition and competitive periods could be different from several points of view and I will talk about it in the year-round preparation.

As I mentioned before, I put a tremendous accent on building and rebuilding an athlete's basic preparation level. I achieve these goals by different general and special conditioning programs, which I implement in the yearly athletic plan of preparation."

Richard Weisz, Olympic chapmion 1902. Courtesy of Hungarian Museum of Physical Education and Sports.

All-American McDonald, All-big 12 first team basketball player, Wayne Simien, barbell curls.

Dragomir recovering after rheumatic heart desease.

Istvan Tasnadi.

Chapter 10
Warming Up

In any kind of athletic preparation I devote a great deal of time to warming-up exercises. I consider a good warm-up to be the first step in preventing injuries, as well as providing very good mental and physical preparation for the practice or game. An effective warm-up should comprise a general and a specific component. The general component, which involves a preparatory cardiovascular warm-up, elevates the whole body's temperature, preparing the tendons and muscles for the subsequent specific warm-up program and for practice or for competition. The general warm-up's basic exercises consist of walking variations, running variations, and standing exercises starting with the neck, shoulders, arms, back, trunk, and legs. After the general warm-up, the most important part of a specific warm-up concerns the muscles and other soft tissues of the ankles, knees, hips, back and neck. This part of the program includes a mandatory specially designed ankle-knee-hip exercise program, complete with some essential specific static stretching. However, it should be noted that too much general static stretching could reduce one's ability to produce power.

Any kind of engine needs a certain amount of time for warm up. An insufficiently warmed up engine will function improperly, and sooner or later will break.

This rule applies very well to sport and human body.

In sport, warm up is the most important part of a workout or competition, because it influences the athlete's performance in the upcoming practice or contest. At the same time it helps to prevent injuries to muscles and connective tissues.

The warm-up's influences are mechanical, physiological and psychological:

Mechanical, because movement generates heat, raising the temperature of tissues and blood;

Physiological, because the warmer muscles are more flexible, faster to react, and more explosive, while neuromuscular coordination also improves after a good warm-up;

Psychological, because a properly warmed up musculature suggests through the body's hormonal and neurological channels readiness, a "thirst to perform", and general feelings of well-being.

The scientific research shows that insufficiently warmed up musculature results in an improperly functioning myotic or stretch reflex, causing injuries. A properly warmed up musculature prevents injuries. As a result of warm up, the muscles utilize oxygen more efficiently due to hemoglobin's property of elaborating more oxygen at higher temperature.

A good warm up influences the respiratory-cardiovascular system, and strengthens the heart, reducing ischemia ("local anemia produced by local obstacle to the arterial flow" Webster's New Universal Unabridged Dictionary, page 754) in the heart muscle itself.

A few reminders and suggestions:

A. The first part of a warm-up should contain walking, jogging, skipping, shuffling and running variations;

B. So-called "Dynamic stretching" (not rapid ballistic stretching) and easy calisthenics exercises should follow the running. "Dynamic stretching" suggests such movements as giant steps, arm circles, jumping jacks, and high stepping.

C. Static stretching should follow dynamic stretching, and to include traditional movements for the quadriceps, hamstrings, hips, shoulders, and back, followed by several sport-specific positions and exercises. Each static stretching position has to be held at least 20 seconds to be efficient. Occasionally PNF (proprioreceptive neuromuscular facilitation) stretching can be very useful, but should be closely supervised by experienced coaching staff or trainers.

D. In the warm-up, any kind of intense ballistic stretching movements should be eliminated which could cause over-stretching injuries, due to sudden contraction of the muscles.

E. A good stretching program should fulfill the goals of an efficient warm-up, namely to improve coordination, increase range of motion and prevent injuries, but should follow, never precede, a gradual warm-up.

There are different types of warm-up methods, such as the passive, general and active approaches. I recommend the general and active warm-up methods.

Passive stretching prior to warming up increases the likelihood of injury.

Examples of my Warm-up program variations:

Walking: walk with high knees, hands on the waist; walk on heels, walk on outside edges of feet; arms extended overhead; walk on toes;

Running: regular running for 30-60 seconds; high knees running for 15 seconds; high heels to butt running for 15 seconds; straight legs running for 15 seconds; skipping with straight arms for 15 seconds; skipping with arms rotating forward for 15 times, backward 15 times; crossover steps running with toes pointing inside for 15 seconds and with toes pointing outside for other 15 seconds; backward running for 15 seconds, then on the coach's clap changing the direction (forward, backward, cross-over, etc.)

Standing in place exercises: these I usually start from the neck - neck rotation, bending and twisting;

Shoulder exercises: Rotation with bent arms to the shoulders; same arm position but elbows raising up and down (chicken wings); straight arms rotation forward and backward; straight arms raising (up and down) side to side. All of the above exercises with 10 repetitions; in front of the chest scissors for one minute (small, wide-large, and up and downs); trunk bending (forward, side to side) for one minute; diagonal straight arms in front of the chest-right leg raise up to left hand and then alternate, 8-10 reps on both sides; straight arms overhead and trunk rotation (bending forward with straight knees, bodyweight back on heels, and hyper-extending backward, feet up on toes), with six to eight rotations both ways; sit-ups variation, 30-60 repetitions; windmill 12 times; split jumps 20 times with straight arms in front of the chest; flat foot deep squat 10 times; deep squat jumps, 10 times; lunges 10 times with both legs; some ankle exercises.

This is only a sample, and it is up to the coach's imagination to vary the warm-up. The warm-up should take no longer than 10-12 minutes, and I consider it to offer the best dynamic stretching for a plyometrics or general conditioning class or workout. While warm-ups tend to bore the athletes, the patient coach will see positive results in the form of dramatically reduced injuries to the ankles, knees and hips. My college trainer staff has confirmed this.

Several times is not enough space for walking, and running. In this situation the easiest to line the group up, and do a lot of in-place walking, running and ankle-knee-hip exercises.

After the general warm-up exercises I am sacrificing a few minutes on "every day conditioning programs" for the ankle, knee and hip joints. I heard several comments about my ankle exercises. Majority of them are positive, but I heard one comment, which was very negative. The reason was, the lack of documentation, and claiming that some of the ankle exercises could be harmful to an athlete's ankle joint. I am using these exercises for my whole life. First, I did on my own, after two very serious ankle sprain. Then, I did with my athletes, and I am using in all of my sports conditioning classes and workouts as a part of the warm-up. What is the most important for me as a conditioning coach is the positive feed back from the athletes, which I get on a daily basis. After we start these ankle exercises, I explain to my athletes the reason why I am doing them: to develop, to strengthen the ankle joint, to improve its flexibility, and to improve the body conditioning reflex reaction, in case of an ankle sprain, during practice or game.

How we know, during an injury, like in this case a sprained ankle, an athlete does not have time to think about protecting against injury. Developing by these exercises of a conditioning reflex, the athlete's neuromuscular system could react in time, protecting against a major injury. Developing the reflexes, at the same time, we develop the athlete's tendons, and muscles, which are directly involved with the ankle joint. Of course on these exercises also we need to respect the rule of teaching them gradually, and limiting or excluding from an ankle injured athlete's daily routine, till the trainer staff do not recommend them. Is very important also to strengthen the ankle, and do not over emphasize any ankle stretching exercise, which could loose the tendons. At the same time we should realize, that all of these ankle exercises are for athletes, who are exposed on a daily basis to ankle injuries, and we, the conditioning coaches must try preventing them. This is why I consider using my ankle routine exercises every day, before every conditioning class, and trying to be intercalated in every sport's warm-up routine before practice, as well.

1. Extend onto toes and hold for ten seconds

2. Apply bodyweight gradually to side of foot, alternating feet, six to eight times for each foot

3. Apply bodyweight to sides of both feet, then return to position with feet flat. Perform ten to fifteen reps

4. Extend to toe raise from position described on exercise # 3, rolling bodyweight from the heels to the little toes, then to all toes. Reverse order and return to start position. Perform ten repetitions.

5. With feet shoulder width, push the knees in front of the feet, keeping feet flat and balancing bodyweight between the heels and balls of both feet. Hold this position for five to eight seconds. Then extend to the toes for two to three seconds. Repeat three to four times.

6. Continue the same exercise in the following way: push the hips forward while arching the back, and looking upward; then arch the shoulders and move the head and arms back; the feet remain flat throughout the movement. Hold this position for ten to fifteen seconds.

7. This exercise just for athletes with healthy ankles, and in an advanced conditioning phase: Holding one-hand on the wall, for a good balance, standing with feet flat, roll one foot to the side while raising the other. Hold this position three to four seconds. Perform ten repetitions on each foot.

8. Standing on sides of both feet. Gradually roll the feet forward, shifting the bodyweight toward the balls of the feet, first touching the little toes. Jump when weight has shifted to the balls, then land on the inside edge of the foot. Roll to the outside edges until the balance of the body shifts toward the heels. Perform ten repetitions.

9. Assume a deep squat position. Shift bodyweight the left, then to the right foot, stretching each ankle for fifteen to twenty seconds; then extend sideways one of the knee. The bent knee's foot is flat. Stretch forward, then point the toes and stretch over your straight knee, with both hands touching the extended knee's ankle.

10. The next exercise is the wide lunge stretching. With the trunk vertical, press the waist forward with hands. The back leg is kept fairly straight, with the ankle face up and all toes on the floor. Keeping balance in the center of the body, press down to the deepest possible position without pressing the torso forward. Hold for eight to ten seconds, and then reverse leg position. Press the hip into the deepest possible position, keeping the back knee straight. Then, change the bodyweight to bear on the front knee and ankle, bending the back leg into a kneeling position. Extend the back knee again and hold for six to eight seconds. Gradually shift bodyweight to the back foot, extending the knee of the front leg and stretching the ankle and knee joints. Bend forward and, with both hands, grabs the toes of the extended leg, holding this position for ten seconds. Repeat this procedure on the other leg.

11. Assuming the previously illustrated deep lunge position press up with the front leg until both legs are straight. Repeat five to ten times. Then step up, bringing both feet to a parallel position. Repeat five to ten times. Then, perform the same routine, alternating the positions of each leg.

12. Split jump. Following the technique and body alignment of the wide lunge, the split jump should be started from a wide lunge position. Arms bend on waist, the bodyweight equally balanced on both feet. Shift the legs as fast as possible, keeping the trunk on a "always vertical" position. As a special mention: the front leg, must land on heel and flat foot, instead of on toes.

13. With one-hand extended to the wall for support; perform toe raises, one leg at a time, ten repetitions for each leg.

14. Standing on one foot, bounce in place, and performing ten double-count repetitions for each leg.

15. Standing on one foot, back and fourth bouncing. Perform ten double-count repetitions for each leg.

16. Standing on one foot, sideways bouncing. Perform ten double-count repetitions for each leg.

17. Standing on one foot, ankle twist bouncing. Perform ten double-count repetitions for each leg.

If the team or the group of athletes is in good physical condition, and if time permits, all of the one-leg ankle bouncing exercises should also be performed as a bounding movement, forward, backward and sideways, with the same number of repetitions.

Chapter 11
Plyometrics in Theory and Practice

If we examine the history of sports, we will notice that researchers, coaches and athletes have always searched for new methods and techniques to improve performance in general and, especially during the last three decades, to improve speed and explosive power. Among the

components for improving athletic performance are two prominent fitness characteristics, namely strength and power.

Strength is the muscular quality for developing force against a movable object, or in other words, of moving heavy objects over a certain distance. In the expression of strength, the time factor is not of primary importance. From experience, we know that the strongest muscles are not necessarily the most efficient ones in any athletic events. In different sports and athletic events, stronger athletes are often less successful than more powerful, explosive opponents who have less absolute strength.

Power, on the other hand, refers to an athlete's ability to quickly move objects over a certain distance, since it is defined as the amount of work done per unit time. This suggests that power is a combination of muscular strength and speed, which is why power is often called "speed-strength" in Eastern Europe. Actually I consider power to be a specific manifestation of strength, with special preparation being used to stimulate its relationship to speed and explosiveness.

Every strength scientist and coach relates the term "plyometrics" to exercises that are characterized by powerful contractions in response to quick and very dynamic loading and stretching of certain muscles. Plyometric training includes bounding, bouncing, hopping, skipping, jumping, throwing, pushing, thrusting, tossing, crunching and twisting activities involving the muscles of the upper body, lower body and midsection to develop explosive power. There are very fast muscle actions, which intensively stimulate the athlete's fast twitch muscle fibers.

Generally, in sport physiology one refers to fast and slow twitch skeletal muscle fibers The fast, or white muscle fibers are characteristic of explosive, anaerobic movements, while the slow, red muscle fibers are distinctive of the endurance, aerobic activities. The belief of sport physiology is that everybody is born with a certain proportion of fast and slow twitch muscle fibers and that it is not possible to change this ratio. What is possible is to emphasize the relative involvement of the fast or slow twitch skeletal muscle fibers by means of scientific training. This is why it is important to test the speed or endurance qualities of young athletes during the selection process.

Plyometrics training stimulates the production of fast or extremely fast linked eccentric-concentric muscle actions, especially due to facilitation by the stretch reflexes. When a stretch is applied to muscles, the muscle spindles send out signals, which, in turn, cause the muscle to contract. The strength of these contractions produced by the stretch depends on the intensity and rate of stretch. It is not the same doing box jumps onto a 30 cm (12 inch) or on a 125 cm (49 inch) height box, because height determines the intensity of a muscle contraction during a plyometric exercise. If an athlete's rebounding phase is slow, allow-

ing a longer time for taking off for the next jump, then that athlete does not achieve the same efficiency as another athlete who tries to leap upwards as fast as possible. This refers to the rate factor of the stretch.

The faster the stretch, the intensity of contraction is greater. In practicing and coaching plyometrics, the rate is the more important of the two factors (intensity and rate), although, if we neglect to gradually increase the intensity of training, the athlete will lose the benefit of muscle fibers' stimulation factor. In plyometrics, stimulation means increasing the height, the difficulty or the rate of an exercise or drill. Thus, the same stimulus is not provided if one jumps onto the same height of box twenty times or forty times within a 30 second time frame.

In athletics, acceleration and explosiveness are the forms of expressing power. Acceleration refers to the slower or faster increase in speed. In sport we usually are looking for the explosive manifestation of power, which is a very typical quality of this century of time and speed. Plyometrics explosive drills and exercises form a bridge between strength and power, and are able to produce the fastest and the most explosive muscle fibers.

I first encountered the use of the term "plyometrics" after I arrived in the USA. Back in Romania where these exercises were used for many decades we simply called them "explosive drills". In Russia, Dr Verkhoshansky who played a major role in analyzing and formalizing them as a system of training called them the "shock method."

All of these explosive drills can offer huge benefits in training programs, but everybody must meticulously respect the rules of their usage, especially since they can place great stress on the entire musculoskeletal system. Plyometrics drills subject the wrists, shoulders, hip, knees, the lower back and many other joints, as well as numerous muscles and bones to very powerful eccentric/concentric muscle action, with the final goal of improving the action/reaction time in a specific athletic movement. This is why injury prevention and supervised application by qualified personnel should be the mandatory first rule.

I spent much of my life studying and experimenting with explosive drills. First, this happened when I was a child, living in a post World War II, East European city, where jumping, bouncing, hopping were a part of our daily games. Later, as a student and an athlete, I consciously studied this subject, being very interested in speed development. It was not an accident that, after one year of my retirement from the sport of Weightlifting, but still competing in track and field at the local level, the 1966 Romanian National Team Weightlifting Champion, C.S.M. Cluj (Romania), asked me to compete again, this time not in mine, but in a higher weight class for the 1967 National Team Championship final. The event of Weightlifting was combined with the five double leg consecutive bounding-jump, a 60 m (65.5 yard) sprint, and the double hand shot put backwards.

I finished fifth in the Weightlifting events, competing at a bodyweight of 75.1 kg (165.4 lb), against 82.5 kg (181.5 lb) athletes, but after the athletic events I achieved a second place, even though the Romanian Weightlifting Federation, at the insistence of 1965 Romanian National Weightlifting Team Champion, Steaua Bucharest, cut the points for the explosive events in half. After the championship, I was awarded the Outstanding Athletic Performance Award for my performances in the three athletic events: I ran 60m (66 yd) in 6.9 seconds, jumped 17.07 m (56 feet) in the double leg five consecutive jump-bounding and threw the shot double handed backward a distance of 14.00 m (46 feet), as well as for promoting the use of plyometrics among weightlifters.

In working as a coach in Romania up until 1982, at Texas A&M from 1984 and at Johnson County Community College since 1987, I implemented an extensive variety of explosive drills in my conditioning and athletic programs.

Plyometric exercises can be very monotonous and wearisome, and even boring, so that everyone should take this into consideration when implementing them into a program. Its exercises must be combined with speed, flexibility, coordination and spatial orientation exercises, practical and recreational games, and other activities, which are enjoyable and challenging for every athlete. There are a few questions, which we need to answer before we become more involved with the application of plyometrics.

Plyometrics Terminology?

At the outset, I consider that I am not the most qualified person to make precise definitions In English of all concepts used in plyometrics, because there is still a great deal of confusion out there among strength and conditioning coaches. However, I prefer to present some primary steps here to formalize the dictionary of plyometric terminology by examining the following methods:

1. Bounce
2. Jump
3. Hops
4. Bound
5. Skipping
6. Split Jumps
7. Medicine Ball Throw, Toss
8. Medicine Ball Pass, Scoop
9. Medicine Ball throw on target variations
10. Midsection Plyometrics exercises: Jack-Knives; Scissors Variations; Alternate Knee Bend Twisted Sit-ups; Arms under Hip Leg Raises; Feet hooked under a board, Medicine Ball Throw - Pass - Scoop Sit-ups; Roman Chair Sit-ups; Bench sit-ups, DB Overhead Press & Sit-ups; Bend Knees Fixed Feet DB on Chest Sit-ups.

Bounce: This involves a short separation from the floor with an energetic take off. The knees are relatively straight, just slightly bent. A bounce can be done:
- on two leg or on one leg
- in place up & down (ankle bounce)
- in place backward-forward
- in place sideways (left and right)
- in place in circle (left and right)
- in place in V shape backward-forward
- in place straddle bounce, or scissors bounce
- in lunge position with right or left leg forward.

Jump: A jump can be done with one or two foot landings, and one or two foot take offs, from standing or with a run-up. A jump is characterized by a sudden vertical or horizontal "spring type" motion into the air or onto, or over an object (like hurdle jump or box jump). Only one spring type movement in horizontal or vertical way is considered a jump. A jump could be executed forwards, backwards or sideways.

One technical observation is necessary here: the triple jump is actually is not a jump, but a technical event comprising a hop, step and jump.

When several jumps follow each other in a horizontal sequence, these may be called Jump-Bounding. A sequence of jumps onto or over one or more boxes, or over one or more hurdles, may simply be regarded as a series of box jumps or hurdle jumps.

Tuck Jumps: These are double-leg high knee bounces executed in place. In tuck jumps the athlete springs from the floor and brings the thighs at least parallel with the floor or higher, with the heels in front of the trunk. The athlete touches his knees with a gentle hugging movement, and then briskly extends his legs, touching the ground first with the balls of the feet. Several non-stop repetitions are referred to here as Multiple Tuck Jumps, Repetition Tuck Jumps or Series of Tuck Jumps. Repetition of a series of tuck jumps forward, backward, leftwards or rightwards is called Tuck Jump Bounding or High Knee Jump Bounding forward, backward, etc.

Pike Jump: The athlete springs from the floor, flexing the legs from the hip with straight knees and straddled legs (in gymnastics, this movement is known as straddle jump). During the jump the upper body should be erect, but with relaxed arms, which will touch the toes in the highest position of the jump. After the jump is performed, the athlete brings his legs back together at hip with or slightly wider, landing first on balls of the feet with flexed knees, to recoil the shock from the jump, and to prepare for the next pike jump. A non-stop sequence of of pike jumps are referred to here as Multiple Pike Jumps, Repetition Pike Jumps or Series of Pike Jumps.

Split Jump: This is a cycling movement, which involves shifting of the legs back and forward with the same speed and range of motion for both legs. Some important technical points of split jumps are:
- the heel of the front leg lands first with a continuous rolling motion on the flat foot.
- the heel of the front leg faces slightly outwards, providing better balance on landing
- the back foot's toes should touch the floor at the same time, and the heel should not strike the floor
- the trunk should keep perfectly vertical , during the split jump, with arms relaxed, but tight abdominal muscles
- take off of both feet should be at the same time
- the jump itself is much more a very quick shifting of the legs, without any great elevation from the floor

These can be done:
- with or without DB in the hands
- without arm movement, or with arms raised to armpit level

When these are done with arms raised to the armpits, one full arm raise and return should be done with each split jump movement.

Scissors Jump: This is a leg crossing exercise, involving most the lower leg's muscles. Start from a perfectly vertical standing position, with feet straddled at wider than shoulder width, and knees flexed. Bend the knees slightly, cross the feet in the air, then land with the feet in a crossed over position. Change foot position with each repetition: land during one jump with the right leg crossed in front of the left leg, and then, the next time, behind it.

Spin Jump: This is a 90, 180 degree, or a full 360-degree, rapid, rotational movement to the right or left. This plyometrics exercise requires a high level of general physical fitness and coordination. The most important injury prevention tip is: start gradually, doing first just a quarter spin; land on both feet with bent knees, or on one leg with knee bent.

There are different variations of spin jumps:

• on two legs

• on one leg

• with short 3-4 steps of run-up

• standing

• from a partial or full squat and finishing in a partial or full squat position

• from a partial or full squat and finishing with a spinning spiral movement in a standing position

• from standing and finishing with a spinning spiral movement in a partial or full squat

Squat Jump: This is an up and down springing movement. The starting position is standing on both feet or on one foot for the very advanced athlete. The squat jump can be practiced without added weight, or with a barbell on the shoulders (similar to the regular back squat position), or with DB in hand, holding them beside the hips. For the one-legged version it is not recommended to use a barbell on the back, although a well-conditioned athlete could perform this variant with DB in the hands. As a safety tip, the slow down in the squatting movement should take place with tight abdominal and shoulder muscles, head looking straight ahead, and the bodyweight balanced between the heels and the balls of the feet. In the jumping up phase the athlete should keep the above-mentioned body alignment, especially during the springing up phase. Squat jumps should never be practiced with weights, which do not allow the proper technical execution of at least five repetitions. Any athlete must first to be capable of properly performing a set of ten repetitions of squat jumps without weights, before considering doing squat jumps with weights. To learn the one legged squat jump, the athlete may first practice maintaining balance by touching a wall, grasping a ballet bar or a partner's hand.

Some sports which can benefit from one-leg squat jumps are: the pole vault, high jump, triple jump, diving, wrestling, gymnastics, figure skating, and skiing. Squat Jumps can be done in place, with or without a spin, forwards, sideways, backward, up stairs or sand boxes, in the form of squat jump bounding, or as a series of squat jumps.

Frog Jumps: Start from a squat position with the hips in an elevated position, trunk bent forward, and fingers touched to the toes. Jump up and forwards with full extension of the trunk and then regroup briskly in the starting position. This exercise can be done forwards, sideways (left or right), spinning (left or right) and also backwards by very skilled athletes.

Hops: These are executed in place on one leg with high knees using a series of repetitions done explosively

Bounding: This involves a continuous, linked series of jumps, hops, done in a straight line, or on a 15-25 degree incline or decline field, forwards, backwards or sideways. We can use a series of multiple hops, jumps, tuck jumps, frog jumps, box jumps or pike jumps and execute these with one leg, both legs together or alternating legs.

Hops Bounding: These may be executed on one leg, in a straight line or on a 15-25 degree incline or decline field, forwards, backwards, sideways, in a zig-zag pattern, high knees, as a series of multiple repetitions, or using explosive movements.

Double Leg Jump Bounding: These bounding movements are done forwards or backwards in a straight line, forwards or backwards in a zig-zag pattern, sideways in a straight line or zig-zag path, as bounding jumps, or as bounding tuck jumps. Note that a series of double-leg standing long jumps should not be confused with double leg bounding. In a series of standing long jumps the athlete must always stop after each individual jump and then take the next jump, whereas double-leg jump bounding is a continuous non-stop activity. All double-leg bounding can be executed on an horizontal plane, uphill, downhill, up stairs, or in sand boxes.

One Leg Jump Bounding: This refers to a series of one leg hops, jumps or bounces done in a non-stop, continuous manner. They can be executed forwards or backwards in a straight line or zig-zag pattern, with ankles rotating, with ankles rotating in a straight line, a zig-zag or sideways path. There are two sideways variations: same shoulder - same leg (right shoulder - right leg, or left shoulder - left leg), or opposite shoulder - opposite leg (left shoulder - right leg or right shoulder - left leg). All one leg bounding variations can be executed on an horizontal plane, uphill, downhill, up onto stairs, or up in

Alternate Leg Jump Bounding: This refers to a succession of left and right leg bounds, landing on alternating feet after a fast spring type "take off" motion. These exercises can be executed forwards in straight line or forwards in a zig-zag. Advanced athletes can also practice variations done backwards in a straight line or a zig-zag.

Skipping: This involves the alternate action of the arms and legs while leaping or bounding. In Hungary and Romania this exercise is also called Indian running. In skipping, the upward-moving arms should be relatively straight, the take-off leg extended with pointed toes. The downward moving arms are relatively straight and move backward next to the hip joint. The opposite leg bends at the same time as the take off leg, with the thigh reaching at least hip level with a very relaxed lower leg.

Medicine Ball Exercises
Description and Classification
Medicine Ball Throws and Toss: Here a medicine ball is thrown to another athlete at a certain speed, from different arm and trunk positions. Objects like medicine balls, weight plates, bags, DB or other heavy special sports objects may be used with the specific goal of improving throwing or tossing speed and explosiveness.

Medicine Ball Throw exercises can be done with or without a partner. With a partner, athletes face each other, or use other variations, but one of the athletes is always turned with the back towards the direction of the throw.

Drills with Partners are:

1. Forward or backward overhead throws, legs parallel

2. Throws over the left or right shoulder, legs parallel

3. The same exercises with a single step into the movement

4. Straight arm throws at shoulder level, from the left and right shoulder, with the twisted side's arm on top of the ball or with the twisted side's arm under the ball

5. Backward, bent-over overhead throws

6. Backward, bent-over throw between the legs, straddled legs (football hike imitation)

7. Forward, bent-over pass parallel to the floor

8. Forward, bent-over, scooping up pass

9. Throws from waist level standing face to face, feet straddled, feet flat, twisting the trunk to the right or left, covering the ball with the twisted side's hand on top, or with the twisted side's hand under the ball

10. One handed medicine ball push pass from shoulder level, standing face to face, twisting the trunk to left or right, holding the ball in balance with the twisted side's opposite hand

11. Overhead medicine ball throw, standing with the ball behind the back at hip level, knees bent and trunk bent forward

12. One-handed standing throws with football-shaped ball or small medicine ball

13. One-handed overhead throw with football-shaped, or small medicine ball

14. Two-handed throw over left or right shoulder with regular sized medicine ball.

These exercises may be practiced thus:

1. Standing with parallel feet

2. Standing with a forward step in motion, or with a short approach throws

3. Sitting on floor throws with bent knees

4. Sitting on floor with feet off from the floor, in suspension

5. Sitting on a Roman Chair, without or with body swing throws

6. Sitting throws on Incline Bench

7. Sitting on edge of a box or bench with legs on the floor or in suspension throws

8. Kneeling throws

9. Lying on back throws with a medicine ball under the lower back

10. Standing, kneeling, or on Roman Chair medicine ball throws to a target

11. Medicine ball chest pass with shuffle run across the gym or outdoors

12. Medicine ball chest pass with shuttle run

13. Medicine ball chest pass from running

14. Medicine ball chest pass from running with a full turn after passing the ball

15. Medicine ball chest pass in three men weaves

16. Medicine ball set (like in volleyball) or shooting imitation (like in basketball)

17. Medicine ball jumping set imitation, or jump shooting imitation

18. Kneeling, overhead throws

19. Kneeling throws, over left or right shoulder with bend elbows

20. Kneeling throws, over left or right shoulder with straight elbows, with the left or right side's hand on top or under the ball

21. Kneeling, chest pass

22. Kneeling, overhead set imitation (volleyball)

23. Kneeling, from left or right side of the hip, with the twisted side's hand on the top or on the bottom of the ball

24. Sitting, straddled legs, medicine ball chest pass

25. Sitting, straddled legs, medicine ball overhead throws

26. Sitting, straddled legs, medicine ball between the legs, upward scooping pass

27. Sitting, straddled legs, medicine ball between the legs, parallel pass

28. Sitting, straddled legs, twisted medicine ball pass: (a) with the twisted side hand on the top of the ball; (b) with the twisted side hand under the ball

29. Sitting, straddled legs, twisting the trunk to the left or right, holding the ball with the opposite hand to the twisted side, one-handed medicine ball push pass

30. Sitting, bent knees, rolling on back, with the medicine ball overhead, two hand throw and sit-up with the swing's inertia

31. Lying on your back, arms with the ball overhead, medicine ball (or a football shaped, or small sized medicine ball) one handed throw to a standing partner

32. Standing in a one handed gymnastic bridge position, throw with a football shaped or small sized medicine ball to a partner. (Only for javelin throwers and athletes who are capable of doing a stable gymnastic bridge).

Without a partner:

1. Standing or moving medicine ball overhead two handed setting, pushing, and shooting:

   (a) without body turning motion

   (b) with a half, or a full turn to the left or right

   (c) with forward, sideways, backward walking, shuffling or running

2. Standing or moving medicine ball overhead two handed scoop toss:

   (a) without body turning motion

   (b) with a half, or a full turn to the left or to the right

   (c) with forward, sideways, backward walking, shuffling or running

   (d) standing, after the scooping the ball overhead as high as possible, touch the floor with both palms and catch the ball

   (e) the same exercise, but instead of touching the floor, sitting down on the floor and very brisk stand up and catch the ball

3. Standing, medicine ball over left or right shoulder upward, one handed pushing.

There are several variations of overhead weight plates or DB toss, one handed throws, etc. which the conditioning coach can introduce into a program according to his knowledge and experience. From the outset, every conditioning coach must be very cautious with any metallic object throwing exercise. I recall a near accident back in Romania, when as an athlete I was practicing overhead backward throws with a 10kg iron plate. The grass was wet and after the scooping movement my feet slipped and I fell on my back with the plate diagonally above my head. Just my fast reactions saved me from being struck by the falling plate. Thus, when a coach practices with DB or weight plate throws exercises with his athletes, he first must warn his athletes about the danger of these exercises, and carefully organize the group, taking care to implement all safety precautions.

4. DB two hand twisted throw, for hammer throwers;

5. DB one-hand putting, for shot put;

6. DB, or weight plate one-hand twisted throw from the waist, for discuss throw;

7. Weight plate or DB backward, overhead throws for Olympic style weightlifters, gymnastics, and pole-vaulting, and high jump.

Building Up a Medicine Ball Exercise Program

1. Push-ups
2. Plyo Push-ups with clapping
3. Plyo Push-ups with Hands or One Hand onto a one foot tall Stable Box
4. Medicine Ball Standing in Front of Chest Pass
5. Medicine Ball Kneeling, in Front of Chest Pass
6. Medicine Ball Seated Straddled Legs in Front of Chest Pass
7. Medicine Ball Stepping forwards in Front of Chest Pass
8. Medicine Ball Standing Parallel Feet Overhead (Throw) Pass
9. Medicine Ball Kneeling Overhead (Throw) Pass
10. Medicine Ball Seated, Straddled Legs Overhead (Throw) Pass
11. Medicine Ball Stepping Forward Overhead (Throw) Pass
12. Medicine Ball Standing with a Slow Bent-Over Vertical Overhead Medicine Ball Toss
13. Medicine Ball Standing Sideways Twisted Toss
14. Medicine Ball Standing Pitching Imitation with Light Ball (1-4 lb)
15. Medicine Ball Standing Parallel Hand Overhead Medicine Ball Push
16. Medicine Ball Standing Overhead backward Throw
17. Medicine Ball Standing Overhead Pass
18. Medicine Ball Standing in Straddle, Bent-Over Forward Parallel Pass
19. Medicine Ball Standing in Straddle, Alternating Pass From L&R Side of The Hip
20. Medicine Ball Standing in Straddle Arms Straight down in Front of Trunk Parallel Pass
21. Medicine Ball Standing from the Hip's Left and Right Side Trunk Twisted Pass
22. Medicine Ball Standing from Right & Left Side of Hip Pass
23. Medicine Ball Standing backward Overhead Pass
24. Medicine Ball Standing back to the Partner Bent-Over between Legs Hike Pass
25. Medicine Ball Standing back to back Left and Right Side
26. Medicine Ball Seated Overhead rolling on back Throw The Ball and Sit-up
27. Medicine Ball Standing Bent-Over Between Legs backward Overhead Pass
28. Javorek's Throwers "Target Board" individual Exercises

Abdominal Exercise Routines

Javorek's GENERAL ABDOMINAL PROGRAM # 1

I consider the abdominal strength and fitness as the most important athletic quality for an athlete's vigorousity, vitality. I believe that athletic performance starts from abdominal strength and fitness.

I consider and I teach my students and athletes that there are two kinds of abdominal exercises:

1. With proper technique

2. With improper technique

I read and heard about dangerous and not dangerous abdominal exercises. In my long years of being a "practitioner coach" I learned that anything performed with improper technique could create potential health hazard.• Starting your mower with an elbow away from your waist could "blow up" your elbow; bending over on your toes with straight knees could create serious back problems; writing on your computer with an imperfect hand position creates severe hand/wrist problems; sitting in your car with very straight knees, away from the gas pedal could damage very seriously your lower back; even the so popular jogging can cause problems. Probably any daily activity could create serious injury and actually it does for thousands of people.

I could write pages about abdominal programs and concepts, but I do not want to develop this issue in a new chapter.

From my long experience I am convinced that if someone respects the basic rules of safety, performing from easy to more complicated and

from simple to more complex, and not trying to be an "over-achiever," anyone could enjoy great satisfaction and success.

Usually it takes month and months of patient work with the simplest abdominal exercises to be able to perform more difficult exercise.

I consider as not just very important but as "vital" for a prosperous health and athletic success. In order to stabilize the back, a well-developed abdominal musculature will contribute with great success.

I consider the following list as the most important to follow, in preventing injuries and achieving great abdominal strength and shape:

a) Does not matter what abdominal exercise your perform, you MUST hold your head bent to chest, back slightly curved, shoulders blades almost up from the floor

b) While performing crunches and sit-ups exercises keep the back curved and try touching the floor gradually with each vertebrate

c) Never perform sit-ups with straight back

d) To avoid misunderstanding about the hand position: never hold your neck or head with your hands. People trend to pull their neck forward, which actually strains their neck and also never stimulates their abdominal musculature. The best position is to hold your hands crossed on your chest with elbows pointed toward your knees.

e) For great and fast success: Don't rush! Those commercials about 6 weeks six packs, etc. are mostly for economical reasons. No "super pills, machines and exercises" helps anyone to develop a great abdominal strength and shape - just consistent hard exercising!

f) Rhythm: depending on speed of execution and rest between the exercises, the goals and achievements could be different. It is not the same trying to loose some extra pounds or trying to get ready for a competition.

g) Do not get confused about certain sports abdominal routines. Diving, gymnastics, wrestling probably performs several hard to perform abdominal routines. Those are not for wellness!! Those are performed for professional reason: to be an Olympian, etc.

h) My very personal general rule: after you master an exercise and want to gain general abdominal fitness do as many reps you are able plus three more! You will be surprised that after doing those extra three with "pain" and "crying" you will be able to perform several more without problem!

I developed several abdominal routines and I am always satisfied to receive letters from " before unknown" readers of my articles, considering my abdominal programs the most challenging but the most successful compared to their previous "abdominal challenger" programs.

The so called Javorek's Special Abdominal # 1, # 2 and # 3 I developed for performance athletes and for the regular moribund with the goals of achieving the highest quality of athletic abdominal shape.

The # 1 variation is the easiest and it is a "warm-up" variation for the # 2 and # 3 programs, and it is performed in a non-stop continuous order without any break between the exercises.

The # 2 program is performed combined with medicine ball and # 3 is the same concept and substitutes # 2 in case of not having medicine ball available.

Javorek's GENERAL ABDOMINAL PROGRAM #1

1. Simultaneous knee hugs	x 15
2. Crunches regular or in four sequences (two up + two down)	x 20
3. Parallel leg raise, arms under hip	x 14
4. Crunches	x 20
5. Legs up against the wall half jack knives	x 20
6. Crunches regular or in four sequences (2 up + 2 down)	x 10
7. Alternate knee bend, twisted sit-ups	x 10+10
8. Legs up against the wall or straight up crunches	x 10
9. Legs up against the wall half jack-knives	x 10
10. Bent knees feet hooked under a heavy DB sit-ups	x 20
11. Crunches regular or in four sequences (2 up + 2 down)	x 10
12. Alternate knee bend, twisted sit-ups	x 10+10
13. Twisted crunches	x 10
14. Legs up against the wall half jack-knives	x 10
15. Bent knees, feet on the floor, hold up in crunch up position	2 x 20 sec.
16. Legs up against the wall half jack-knives	x 20
17. Crunches	x 10
18. Bent knees, on your right or left side, arms overhead (left-right) side sit-ups	x 10+10
19. Legs up against the wall half jack-knives	x 10
20. Bent knees, feet on the floor, hold up in crunch-up position	2 x 30 sec.
21. Twisted crunches	x 15
22. Bent knees feet hooked under heavy DB different size DB on chest sit-ups	x 20
23. On stomach, arms close to the body, bent at chest level, holding the hips on the floor, gradually straighten the elbows, looking at the ceiling, and hyper extending the back, hold for	x 20 sec.

Depending on individual goals or the coach's prescription, repeat the program as many times as is prescribed. On an individual basis, other abdominal exercises may be added to the abdominal program. Do not take a longer break than 10-15 seconds between exercises. Do it slowly but with a dynamic and continuous rhythm. Do not exercise with improper technique.

Javorek's GENERAL ABDOMINAL PROGRAM #2

* FOR ADVANCED ATHLETES ONLY*

1. Lying down, arms overhead, simultaneous knee hugs	x 15
2. Crunches regular or in four sequences (two up + two down)	x 20
3. Parallel leg raise, arms under hip	x 20
4. Lying down, hands bent to head, alternate knee touch, bicycle	x 20+20
5. Lying down, straight legs up, half jack knives	x 20
6. Seated, hands behind, pointed toes, legs raised to 30 degrees up & down scissors	x 30+30
7. Alternate knee bend, twisted sit-ups	x 10+10
8. Lying with both shoulders on the floor, arms bent to shoulders, hip twisted to left or right side with the top foot crossed over, crunches	x 20+20
9. Jack-knives	x 15
10. Seated, hands behind, pointed toes, legs raised to 30 degrees side to side cross scissors	x 30+30
11. Crunches regular or in four sequences (two up + two down)	x 20
12. Lying down, bent knees, hands bent to head, alternate leg cross-over	x 20+20
13. Lying down, arms bent to head, bent knees, feet hooked under heavy DB or someone stepping on them, half & half sit-ups	x 15+15
14. Jack knives	x 10
15. Lying down, bent knees, feet on the floor, hold up in crunch up position	4 x 15 sec.
16. Lying down, straight legs up, half jack knives	x 20
17. Seated, hands behind, pointed straight legs, simultaneous knee pull to chest, kick out 30 degree, from the floor	x 15
18. Lying on right or left side, bent knees, top hand bent to head, bottom hand cross on side, (left-right) side crunches in four sequences (two up + two down)	x 20+20
19. Jack-knives	x 15
20. Seated, hands behind, pointed straight legs, simultaneous 30 deg leg raise, pull knees to chest, kick out close to the floor	x 15

21. Jack-knives	x 15
22. Straight legs up, hands on thighs, crunches	x 20
23. Lying down, arms bent to head, bent knees & straddled feet, twisted sit-ups	x 10+10
24. Bent knees feet hooked under heavy DB or someone stepping on them, different size DB on chest sit-ups	x 20
25. Bent knees, feet on the floor, hold up in crunch up position	4 x 15 sec.
26. Lying on stomach, arms close to the body, bent at chest level. Holding the hip on the floor, gradually straighten the elbows, looking up on the ceiling, and hyper extending the back. Hold this position for 15 sec, then raise to hands and knees, curve (round) & arch back for 20 sec. then with straight elbows sit back on heels for	x 20 sec.

Before starting this program, every individual athlete must be capable of performing with perfect body posture each of these exercises with at least 20 repetitions. Depending on individual goals, or the coach's prescription, repeat the program as many times is prescribed. On an individual basis, other abdominal exercises could be added to the abdominal program. Do not take a longer break than 10-15 seconds between exercises. Do it slowly but with a dynamic and continuous rhythm.

Javorek's SPECIAL ABDOMINAL PROGRAM # 1
* FOR ADVANCED ATHLETES ONLY*

Hooked feet arms cross on chest sit-ups	x 10
Hooked feet arms cross on chest half up & up + half down & down sit-ups	x 10+10
Half jack-knives Or Crunches	x 20
Hooked feet arms cross on chest half up & down sit-ups	x 10+10
Half jack-knives Or Crunches	x 20
Hooked feet arms cross on chest half down & up sit-ups	x 10+10
Jack-knives	x 10

Observation: if the routine becomes very comfortable and "easy-to-perform" add weight(DB on chest) for the hooked feet part of the program.

Javorek's SPECIAL "MEDICINE BALL" ABDOMINAL PROGRAM # 2
* FOR ADVANCED ATHLETES ONLY*

Hooked feet arms cross on chest sit-ups	x 10
Hooked feet arms cross on chest half up & up + half down & down sit-ups	x 10+10
Hooked feet medicine ball overhead pass & sit-up	x 10
Half jack-knives Or Crunches	x 10
Hooked feet arms cross on chest half up & down sit-ups	x 10+10
Hooked feet medicine ball chest pass & sit-up	x 10
Half jack-knives Or Crunches	x 10
Hooked feet arms cross on chest half down & up sit-ups	x 10+10
Hooked feet medicine ball overhead pass & sit-up	x 10
Hooked feet medicine ball chest pass & sit-up	x 10
Jack-knives	x 10

Javorek's SPECIAL ABDOMINAL PROGRAM # 3
* FOR ADVANCED ATHLETES ONLY*

Hooked feet arms cross on chest sit-ups	x 10
Hooked feet arms cross on chest half up & up + half down & down sit-ups	x 10+10
Jack-knives or Crunches	x 10
Half jack-knives or Crunches	x 10
Hooked feet arms cross on chest half up & down sit-ups	x 10+10
Jack-knives	x 10
Half jack-knives or Crunches	x 10
Hooked feet arms cross on chest half down & up sit-ups	x 10+10
Jack-knives	x 10
Hooked feet arms cross on chest half up & up+ half down & down sit-ups	x 10
Jack-knives	x 10

Classes of Plyometrics

The benefit of plyometrics would be classified as follows:

• Speed improvement

• Explosive improvement

The speed improvement plyometrics exercises develop maximum hopping speed (develop the legs for maximum hopping speed) and increase maximum running speed, which directly could increase the distance in a jump (vertical or horizontal)

Exercises for Improving Speed

(a) Bench jumps: forward, backward, side to side, in zig-zag, with 180 degree twist, or with a 360 deg (left, right) turn.

(b) hopping in place: double leg or one leg

(c) jump-bounding hops: double leg or one leg; sideways with same shoulder same leg, or opposite shoulder with opposite leg; forwards, backwards, or zig-zag; on an horizontal floor, uphill, upstairs or sand box, down hill;

(d) tuck jumps in place: double leg, one leg

(e) tuck jump bounding: double leg, one leg; forward, backward, in zig-zag; sideways double leg; sideways one leg, same leg same shoulder; sideways one leg, opposite leg opposite shoulder

(f) split jumps

(g) rope jumps

(h) hop jumps, or tuck jumps combined with sprint on a gym (horizontal) floor, uphill, downhill, up stairs or in sand boxes

(i) sprints uphill, downhill, upstairs, up stairs and on box

(j) abdominal exercises

2. Exercises for explosive improvements develop the neuromuscular system to be faster, more explosive, to shorten the execution time in running, jumping and throwing.

Exercises for Improving Explosiveness

(a) Frog jumps: in place, forward, sideways, backward, with right or left twist, with 180 degree right or left turn, with 360 degree right or left turn, without DB, with DB in hand

(b) Squat jumps: in place, forward, backward, side ward, with turns, without weight, with BB, with DB in hand; uphill, up stairs, up on sand boxes; up hill, up stairs, up on sand boxes 1, 2 or 3 squat jump & sprint up combinations

(c) Wave squats with barbells

(d) Step-up combinations on different height boxes: without weight forward, sideways; on one box step-up; on two, three or four (or if is possible more) higher and higher boxes walk or run up, with BB behind the neck, or with DB in hand. All of these step-up variations need adequate space, a high level of preparation, perfect technique of execution, and strict ongoing coaching supervision and spotting.

(e) Jumping exercises over a medicine ball: double leg, one leg, backwards, forwards, and sideways to the ball. If the height is not suitable for the athlete physical preparation level, the medicine ball may be replaced with a hump on the floor or with different height of hurdles, but in these situations coach spotting is mandatory.

(f) Hurdle jumps: double leg, one leg; forward, sideways or bounding hurdle jump, over several hurdles in sequence

(g) Giant (wide) split jump s: without or with DB in the hands

(h) Scissor jumps

(i) Jack-knives

(j) Medicine ball throwing variations

(k) Box jump variations:

• Jump up and step down: with double legs; with one leg

• Up and down jump without DB: with double leg; with one leg; up and down jump with DB in hand. [Note: This last variation needs a lot of attention and precautions. An athlete must control first the box jumps on a very high technical standard in order to be able of starting this variation. First on low box and light DB, then gradually the height and the weight could be increased. It is the coach's decision to use and when to start using this variation]

• Box jump sideways with double leg, box jumps side ways with one leg; box jumps bounding combination; depth jump, with rebounding on different height boxes.

An injury-free, perfectly executed depth jump must be learned in stages. The athlete should perfect the dropping, landing and rebounding techniques through progressive teaching. Beginning from a low box, first teach the dropping and landing without rebound and holding the landing phase for up to 3-5 seconds. Then, after this phase is perfected, add the rebounding phase after the landing. Finally, teach the athlete landing and rebounding (touch and go) by jumping from a low box. After this phase of preparation, it is time to progress to a higher box, and later on to continue with a longer series of combination boxes, medicine ball and hurdle jumps.

Never try to rebound without teaching the correct body position on landing and be absolutely certain that the athlete has well developed musculotendinous and ligamentous systems.

The body position for the dropping phase from the box should involve a generally relaxed musculature, with the exception of tight trunk muscles, and a relatively vertical body position. During the landing phase the hips and ankle joints should be kept in a vertical line, while the shoulders should be held in this same vertical line or slightly forward, with arms, shoulders and abdominal muscles contracted. During the landing phase the balls of the feet must touch the ground first, with the knees bending progressively to absorb the shock, and moving with a slight rotational movement down toward the heels. During the rebounding phase, the line of action of center of gravity moves toward the toes, the arms move backwards and the shoulders forward, with the a great deal of the trunk (especially abdominal) musculature being contracted.

Some exercises should be practiced from higher boxes, and depending on the athlete's preparation stage, the landing and rebounding phase should be emphasized. Never change to a higher box before excellent muscle and tendon development becomes evident. The soundest approach is to increase the height of the box by not more than 10-20 cm. (4 to 8 inch) at a time after perfecting each phase of the depth jump in turn.

The depth jump should always be started on lower boxes, regardless of the athlete's preparation level. Begin by warming up the tendons, ligaments and muscles. After achieving the maximum height needed to achieve one's specific goals, variations of the depth jump can be done. For example, you might want to have the athletes repeat the same height, up to a maximum of ten jumps, or to alternate different heights up to a maximum of twelve jumps. Always practice the jump from the new height without rebounding.

Progression for Teaching Depth Jumps

1. Depth Jump, no rebound. Gradually increase the height.

2. Depth Jump; stop 3-5 seconds with bent knees; no rebounds. Gradually increase height.

3. Depth Jump; stop 3-5 seconds with bent knees; rebound on the flat surface. Gradually increase box height.

4. Depth Jump and rebound on the flat surface. Gradually increase the height of the box.

5. Depth Jump and rebound onto a lower box. Gradually increase the height of the box.

6. Combination of jumps over medicine balls, hurdle jumps, box jumps (gradually increasing the height), and depth jumps. At the end of this series of jumps, the coach stands on a higher box, holds a ball or other object in the hand. After the last box depth jump rebounding, the athlete can spike, volley, dunk, heading the ball, pass it, sprint forward, sideways, or to do a 'faking' motion, depending on the specificity of each sport.

7. Series of combination jumps, sprints, shuffles, and depth jumps, onto or over boxes, hurdles and medicine balls. These exercises can be done forward or sideways several times consecutively, depending on goals and level of preparation. Here are two examples of these variations:

   (a) Combinations of increasing and decreasing height of medicine balls, hurdle, and boxes. After the last jump over a low hurdle or box, the athlete will practice the same exercises as Exercise 6.

   (b) Combination of high boxes, of decreasing and increasing height. According to the training objectives, the distance can be increased between certain boxes to allow one to do short distance sprints, shuffles, shuttle runs, double leg, alternate leg, and one leg bounding, tuck jumps, hops, etc., between jumps and depth jumps.

8. Series of combination of jumps, running variations and depth jumps over hurdles jumps. The athlete runs between the medicine balls going forwards, backwards, while turning, circling, etc. The coach should decide, depending on the training goals which variations of running and jumping will combine most effectively.

9. The athlete runs to a box, jumps onto it then off it, rebounds and returns to the starting point. The athlete may run in different patterns between medicine balls on the way to the box.

These are just a few examples and it is up to the coach to develop more and more variations. What is very important is not to over-complicate any drills and to ensure that all drills actually are useful in achieving the conditioning goals of a specific sport.

Everybody should realize that depth jumps are not used just to achieve great drop height, but more to benefit a certain sport by developing not just vertical explosive power, but also a combination of essential neuromuscular abilities, coordination, and skills. There certainly are sports, which would benefit from increasing the height of the box. In particular, weightlifters, hammer throwers, shot putters, gymnasts, figure skaters are among the athletes who benefit most from practicing depth jumps from progressively higher boxes. However, they also need to practice several variations and combinations of submaximal box and depth jumps.

Starting Age for Plyometrics
The starting age for plyometrics depends on several factors. They should be started in kindergarten in the form of a game. Frog jumps, rabbit jumps, stork steps, kangaroo jumps, jump rope and different dynamic games are some of the forms, which could be a part of a child's early informal athletic preparation. On the other hand, any kind of organized plyometrics activities must be supervised and carefully selected by a specialist. Certain sports, like women's gymnastics, ice hockey, skiing, figure skating, volleyball, basketball, soccer, football and wrestling need to develop explosive drills from the beginning, at a very young age. But any sport when practiced in an organized form

should be combined with a suitable volume and intensity of plyometrics exercises.

One initial remark needs to be made. Probably the biggest mistake in a young athlete's preparation is to start with the specificity of a particular sport. Instead, every child should begin with a general physical preparation (GPP) program and gradually progress to a special physical preparation (SPP) program, and finally move on to the chosen sport. Depending on the specificity of a certain sport, more or fewer explosive drills should be introduced into their preparation. After thorough general preparation a young athlete should then be ready to start the specific preparation. If all training were organized like this, there undoubtedly would be fewer burned-out and injured young athletes. It is surprising to note that many young athletes have never learned some of the most basic general skills. For example, there are often freshmen who do not know how to do a jack-knife, a tuck jump, not to mention alternate leg bounding, or box jumping. Unfortunately we, the college coaches, spend a very appreciable amount of time of rehabilitating athletes from high school athletic injuries, instead of preparing them for higher levels of competition. Thus, every sport should include a preventative-conditioning program, because it is much easier to prevent injuries than to heal them.

In conclusion, plyometrics should from the beginning, an active and essential part of athletic preparation.

When Plyometrics should be used

If we wish to decide when plyometrics should be used in training, we first need to appreciate that there are different variations and that all types of training depend on the preparatory period concerned. Plyometric drills can be used:

1. In a separate workout, when explosive drills must be combined with other general conditioning exercises

2. After each workout for no longer than five minutes per body part

3. After practice, 1-3 times per week in the competitive season. During this time of preparation, the explosive drills must have a character of maintaining, and not improving performance. The time sacrificed to it should be very short and the coach should decide the designated time, exercises and intensities.

4. Incorporated within a workout.

I have read a great deal about plyometrics. I have practiced it since the 1950s and cannot imagine how it is possible that even today there still are coaches who consider it appropriate to practice plyometrics twice a week for an hour at a time!

All explosive drills and exercises exert considerable stress on the entire musculoskeletal system and one should have great respect for the athlete's tendons, ligaments and muscles. When the tendons and ligaments become stressed and decrease their length or elasticity, severe injuries can occur. To minimize the chances of injuries, the plyometrics exercises should be practiced in various combinations such as middle section-legs-upper body, upper body-middle section-legs, or legs-middle section-upper body, with two to three minutes being devoted to each area. In this way the athlete's muscles and tendons become stressed or fatigued less quickly, and recuperation is much easier.

A few years ago, I read a college assistant conditioning coach's article about plyometrics being dangerous and was most surprised that someone involved in college athletic conditioning would make such a negative comment. He described in a half page a small encyclopedia of possible plyometrics-related injuries, yet I have not seen even one percent of them ever since I started my coaching career in 1964. Unfortunately, the young coach often considers any plyometrics exercise in a conditioning program as being inadvisable. All I can say is that his mistake probably comes from his background of not practicing any explosive drills in his life, or if so, of doing later in his life, without any proper preparation and without respecting the rules of gradualism and proper technique, thereby inevitably causing injury.

I have used plyometrics since the first day of my coaching career, and, "knock on wood", I never had any major debilitating injuries. The worst injuries which my athletes ever had were some shin splints, or the shins striking the box, but I have had and still have well-prepared athletes capable of doing depth jumps safely from 3 m (10 feet) height and rebounding onto a 1.20 m (48 inches) box, doing 35 m (38 yard) in ten consecutive alternate leg bounds, jumping 25 times in 30 seconds onto a 1.20 m (48 inches) high box, throwing a 5 kg (10 lb) medicine ball backwards overhead a distance of 20 m (22 yard), doing 24 clapping " plyo-push-ups" in 15 seconds, 29 jack-knives in 20 seconds, 3 m to 3.30 m (10 to 11 feet) standing long jumps, 30 m (33 yards) shuttle runs in 6.4 sec., 30 m sprints in 3.61 seconds (hand measured), a 91 cm (36 inches) standing vertical jump, a 105 cm (41 inches) three-step approach vertical jump, and other more sport specific explosive drill tests which I will discuss later in more detail in each sport conditioning program."

Preventing Plyometric Training Injuries
As I mentioned before, plyometric exercises need a very carefully prepared and gradually introduced approach.

1. Be patient in teaching or learning plyometrics

2. First develop the muscles, especially the tendons and ligaments

3. Implement the principles of specificity and gradual progression

4. Teach (as a coach) or learn (as an athlete) the proper techniques of execution and correct body positions.

5. Introduce all plyometrics exercises gradually, starting with the simplest and teaching just one exercise per workout

6. Respect the rules of age, gender, level of preparation, body weight, etc.

Note: The rule of age and gender stresses that it is not the same to practice plyometrics with an eleven-year-old youngster as with a mature athlete. The rule of preparation level means that there is a considerable difference doing explosive drills with a national level athlete or with a beginner. Bodyweight is one of the most important factors to be considered in preventing injuries. Before any group of athletes starts doing box jumps, stair jumps or any other plyometrics exercises, all necessary adjustments must be made for every individual athlete with respect to what quantity and in what form each exercise needs to be done. This step should never be forgotten, especially in team sports, because bodyweight alone makes a big difference to the individual execution of certain plyometrics drills.

Usually I have 2-3 female and 1-2 male athletes in every basketball team, who at the beginning of the year are not capable of doing a box jump, or bound - jumping up on stairs or in a sand box. Of course I do not force them to do so, but instead, if they are working in a group, I ask them to step-up on a box of appropriate height, or to run upstairs, instead of jumping. An easy variation, which usually I use with overweight or injured athletes, is jumping up onto a box and stepping down, instead of continuously jumping and rebounding. During the preparation, they usually improve very adequately, which enables them to keep up with the rest of the team. But it could happen that some of them never will be able to do certain drills. So, I just ask them to do as much as I consider them capable of doing properly and safely. I never allow the athletes alone to decide about their personal abilities, unless

I am fully convinced that they are capable of executing all drills competently.

7. Individualize the inclusion of plyometrics into any conditioning program.

8. Combine plyometric drills intelligently with other types of conditioning exercises

9. Start with a general warm-up followed by brief dynamic stretching, and by more specific, static stretching for each exercise, where this may be necessary

10. Finish the program with submaximal short sprints, relaxation, flexibility and cooling-down exercises

11. Use comfortable and safe equipment

12. Provide proper spotting, if necessary.

I believe that appropriate plyometrics of suitable intensity, volume and complexity should be an integral part of each workout. They should generally be done in the last part of a workout for a maximum period of 10-15 minutes. The comprehensive plyometrics program should be performed no more than twice a week, integrated into a general conditioning program.

Proper Technique of Plyometrics
In any kind of jumping, hopping or bouncing drills it is very important to hold perfect body alignment. Shoulders, hips, and ankle joints must be in a well balanced position, while the abdominal muscles must be tight, never allowing the lower back muscles to forcibly flex or hyperextend, especially during the rebounding and landing phases. The head always looks forward, with the spine held in a relatively neutral position.

Variations of plyometrics exercises hands behind the head, on the nape, or on the top of the head should be practiced only with advanced athletes who master the correct technique of execution of any jumping drills. It is important that the coach implements these variations gradually into the program, with a lower intensity and with a natural arm position.

Box jumps and depth jumps variations warrant special attention because these popular drills should be regarded as the Achilles tendon of plyometrics.

The rules of box jumping are :

1. Ensure that the athlete is in good general physical shape

2. Teach all of the basic landing, jumping, bounding, bouncing and hopping skills first

3. Start with very low box and progress only if skill does not deteriorate

4. Gradually increase the number of repetitions, noting that no set should last longer than 30 seconds

5. If the athlete executes two-legged box jumps perfectly, then one-legged box jumping can be started from a very low level; gradually increase the box height, with the number of repetitions lasting no more than 15 seconds

6. After these phases, gradually allow the athlete to learn other depth jump variations

Note that these phases could take 2-3 years of preparation for some athletes, but for others only a few months. As has been stressed before, it is up to the coach to decide when an athlete is ready to do more difficult exercises, whose benefits are potentially greater. But, in the meantime, it is better to reap smaller benefits from simpler exercises and avoid injury.

I do not want to scare away any coaches from using plyometrics exercises, especially because I use many of them personally in my conditioning classes. I am just trying to stress the point, which several coaches often forget: don't be impatient and don't try to imitate the plyometrics drills used by world-class athletes. What I learned in my coaching career is that coaches may read a lot about certain strength conditioning methods, but instead of adapting some of these to the preparation level of the athletes and to the specific conditions, several of them just copy some "wonder" program and force athletes to perform it, proclaiming that this is the best way to become a champion.

This often results in failure and injury. I hear in several gyms that they are "using the Russian squat routine", bench press plyometric dropping "secrets" or some other "secret" plyometric drills, but all too often they seem to be forgetting the basic principles of plyometric training. I think is much better to learn from the basics everything about plyometrics, start gradually with the novice athlete and then gain lot of practical experience, so that devising an integrated training program ultimately will become "child's play." What is the most important is that all of your athletes will improve tremendously. I know young coaches whom I was teaching from early 1984. They respected all of the rules and enjoyed great professional success as the years went by. We still communicate periodically and, believe it or not, I also learn from them a great deal about new applications of certain exercises, or they improve on my programs. This is the law of perfectionism. The student always will be better than the teacher, and it is not a shame to learn from your students or from others."

Plyometrics Exercise List

Note that this list includes exercises that are not necessarily "plyometric" or rebounding in nature (such as walking, shoulder rolling and neck rotations), but which form part of the whole compendium of movements which prepare one for plyometric drills.

1   Walking in place with high knees
2   Walking in place with heels high
3   Walking in place with straight Legs in front of trunk
4   Walking around the Gym or on different Field
5   Walking forwards with high knees
6   Walking backwards with high knees
7   Walking forwards on toes
8   Walking backward on toes
9   Walking forwards on toes with Arm Rotation
10 Walking sideways (L&R) on toes
11 Walking forwards with heels high
12 Walking backward with heels high
13 Walking forwards with straight Legs in front of trunk
14 Walking backward with straight Legs in front of trunk
15 Walking forwards (Military Parade Steps) with straight Legs & Excessive high Raise feet
16 Walking backward (Military Parade Steps) with straight Legs & Excessive high feet
16 Walking forwards on the exterior portion (side edge) of the feet
17 Walking backward on the exterior portion (side edge) of the feet
18 Walking forwards on the heels
19 Walking backward on the heels
20 Walking Sideways (L&R) on the heels
21 Walking forwards with Cross Steps
22 Standing Continuous Single Leg (L+R) Lunge
23 Standing Single Leg Continuous Step Back Lunge
24 Standing Alternating Leg Lunges
25 Walking forwards with Short Lunges
26 Walking forwards with wide Lunges (Giant Steps)
27 Standing Split Jump
28 Running in place

29 Running around the Gym or on different Field
30 Running in place with high knees
31 Running forwards with high knees
32 Running backward with high knees
33 Running Sideways (L&R) with high knees
34 Running in place with heels high
35 Running forwards with heels high
36 Running backward with heels high
37 Running Sideways (L&R) with heels high
38 Running in place with straight knees with feet in front of trunk
39 Running in place with straight knees with feet behind the trunk
40 Running forwards with straight knees, feet in front of trunk
41 Running backward with straight knees, feet in front of trunk
42 Running Sideways (L&R) with straight knees, feet in front of trunk
43 Running forwards with straight knees, feet behind the trunk
44 Running backward with straight knees, feet behind the trunk
45 Running Sideways (L&R) with straight knees, feet behind the trunk
46 Running forwards with forward arm rotation
47 Running forwards with backward arm rotation
48 Skipping with arms rotation forwards
49 Skipping with arm rotation backward
50 Skipping with opposite Arm Raise (Indian Steps)
51 Running with Cross Steps facing inside
52 Running with Cross Steps facing outside
53 Shuffle Steps Running Sideways (L&R)
54 Shuffle Steps Running forwards
55 Shuffle Steps Running backwards
56 Ankle Play in place
57 Ankle Play forwards
58 Ankle Play backwards
59 Ankle Play Sideways (L&R)
60 Standing up on toes & hold
61 Standing Continuous Heel Raise up on toes
62 Standing Continuous One Leg Heel Raise up on toes (Left + Right)
63 Standing Parallel feet Heel Raise Rolling on Side Edge and up on toes
64 Standing Double Leg in place Bouncing
65 Standing Double Leg forward & backward Bouncing
66 Standing Double Leg Sideways (L&R) Bouncing
67 Standing Double in V Shape Twisted Bouncing
68 Standing Single Leg Bouncing in place (L&R)
69 Standing Single Leg Bouncing forwards & backward (L&R)
70 Standing Single Leg (L&R) Sideways (L&R) Bouncing
71 Standing Single Leg (L&R) in V Shape Twisted Bouncing
72 Standing Continuous Single Leg Step-up on Box
73 Standing Alternating Leg Step-up on Box
74 Standing Combination of Single & Alternating Leg Step-up on Box
75 Standing Jump up and Step down Box Jump (different heights)
76 Standing Continuous up & down Box Jump (different heights)
77 Standing from (different height) Box, Depth Jump & No Rebound
78 Standing from (different height) Box Depth Jump & Rebound
79 Standing from (different height) Box, Depth Jump & Rebound on (different height) Box
80 Standing from (different height) Box Combination of Depth Jump and Box Jump
81 Standing from Series of different height Boxes, Combination, up & down Box Jumps
82 Uphill Running (different distances and speed)
83 Uphill backward Running (different distances and speed)
84 Uphill Single Leg forward Hop-Bounding (L&R) different distances or repetitions of Bounding
85 Uphill Single Leg (L&R), same shoulder same leg, sideways Hop Bounding (different distances or number of Hops)
86 Uphill Single Leg (L&R), opposite shoulder opposite leg, sideways Hop-Bounding (different distances or number of Hops)
87 Uphill Single Leg (L&R) backward Hop-Bounding (different distances or number of Hops)
88 Uphill Single Leg (L&R) forward Twisted Hop-Bounding (different distances)
89 Uphill Single Leg (L&R) backward Twisted Hop-Bounding (different distances)
90 Uphill Alternate Leg Bounding (different distances or number of Bounds)

Plyometrics in Theory and Practice

91 Uphill Frog Jumps (different distances or number of Jumps)

92 Uphill Squat Jumps (different distances or numbers of Jumps)

93 Upstairs Running (different distances, Speed & difficulty-Every Step, Every Second, etc)

94 Shredded Rubber Boxes or Sand Stair Box upward Running (different number of Shredded Rubber Boxes or Sand Stair Boxes, Speed & difficulty)

95 Upstairs Double Leg Jump-Bounding (different distances)

96 Shredded Rubber Boxes or Sand Stair Box upward Double Leg Jump-Bounding (different number of Shredded Rubber Boxes or Sand Stair Boxes)

97 Upstairs Double Leg Zig-Zag Jump-Bounding (different distances &difficulty)

98 Shredded Rubber Boxes or Sand Stair Boxes Double Leg upward Zig-Zag Jump-Bounding (different distances & difficulty)

99 Upstairs Single Leg (L&R) forward Hop-Bounding (different distances and difficulty-Every Step, Every Second Step, etc.)

100 Shredded Rubber Boxes or Sand Stair Box upward, Single Leg (L&R) forward Hop-Bounding (different number of Shredded Rubber Boxes or Sand Stair Boxes)

101 Upstairs Single Leg (L&R), Same Shoulder Same Leg, Sideways Hop-Bounding (different distances and difficulty)

102 Shredded Rubber Boxes or Sand Stair Box upward, Single Leg (L&R) Sideways Hop-Bounding (different number of Shredded Rubber Boxes or Sand Stair Boxes)

103 Upstairs Single Leg (L&R) opposite shoulder opposite leg, sideways Hop-Bounding (different distances & difficulty)

104 Shredded Rubber Boxes or Sand Stair Box upward, Single Leg (L&R) opposite shoulder opposite leg, Sideways Hop-Bounding

105 Upstairs Single Leg (L&R) forward, Twisted Hop-Bounding (different distances & difficulty)

106 Shredded Rubber Boxes or Sand Stair Box upward, Single Leg (L&R) forward Twisted Hop-Bounding

107 Upstairs Single Leg (L&R) backward Hop-Bounding (different distances & just every step)

108 Upstairs Run-Double Leg Take-off Jump & Sprint Combination (different distances, Speed, number of Combination & difficulty)

109 Shredded Rubber Boxes or Sand Stair Box Run-Double Leg Take-off Jump & Sprint (different difficulty)

110 Javorek's Stair Super Set Variations

111 Javorek's Shredded Rubber Boxes or Sand Stair Box Super Set Variations

112 Javorek's Uphill Super Set Variations

113 Standing Slow (L&R) Neck Rotations

114 Standing Neck Side Bends (L&R)

115 Standing Neck, backward and forward Bends

116 Standing Neck Side Twist (L&R)

117 Standing forward Shoulder Rotation with Bent Arms to the Shoulders

118 Standing backward Shoulder Rotation with Bent Arms to the Shoulders

119 Standing up & down Elbow Raise with Bent Arms to the Shoulders, and up on toes

120 Standing forward Shoulder Rotation with straight Arms on Flat Foot

121 Standing forward Shoulder Rotation with straight Arms & up on toes

122 Standing forward Shoulder Rotation with straight Arms and Double Leg Bouncing in place

123 Standing forward Rotation with straight Arms and Single Leg (L&R) Bouncing in place

124 Standing forward Arms Rotation with straight Arms, and Single Leg Bound-Hopping forwards

125 Standing forward Shoulder Rotation with straight Arms and Double Leg Bound-Hopping forwards

126 Standing forward Shoulder Rotation with straight Arms, and Single Leg Bound-Hopping backward

127 Standing forward Shoulder Rotation with straight Arms and Bound-Hopping backward

128 Standing backward Shoulder Rotation with straight Arms on Flat Foot

129 Standing backward Shoulder Rotation with straight Arms & up on toes

130 Standing backward Shoulder Rotation with straight Arms and Double Leg Bouncing in place

131 Standing backward Shoulder Rotation with straight Arms and Single Leg (R&L) Bouncing in place

132 Standing backward Shoulder Rotation with straight Arms and Double Leg Bound-Jumping forwards

133 Standing backward Shoulder Rotation with straight Arms, and Single Leg (L&R) Bound-Hoping forwards

134 Standing backward Shoulder Rotation with straight Arms and Double Leg Bound-Jumping backward

135 Standing backward Shoulder Rotation with straight Arms and Single Leg Bound-Hopping backward

136 Standing forward Shoulder Rotation with straight Arms, and Double Leg Bouncing to (L&R) Sideways

137 Pull-ups (Chin-ups)

138 Dips

139 Abdominal Exercises

140 Medicine Ball Exercises

Improving your Vertical Jump

There are several methods, which could help and improve an athlete's vertical jumping ability. In my over forty years of experiment as an athlete and then as a coach, I reached the conclusion that the safest and most efficient method to develop vertical jump ability is combining the overall body musculature with overall explosive capacities in a very patient and consistent way.

I read more and more advertising about different methods and equipment, which allegedly help young athletes to dramatically improve their vertical jump. I don't contest the fact that the use of different methods can overload the calf muscles and the Achilles tendon and how, one of the advertising brochure says: "Upon impact, the calf muscles are exercised with a force equal to six times body weight". However, my questions about this are as follows:

1. To prevent serious muscular and tendonal injuries, shouldn't you develop an athlete's muscles first to be able to overload the Achilles tendon with different methods and equipment or not? (I often see many youths exercising without supervision or any special musculotendinous preparation.)

2. How long is an athlete's Achilles tendon capable of supporting non-stop overloading without injury?

3. At what age is it recommended to begin using that miraculous equipment which supposedly increases an athlete's vertical leap so dramatically?

4. Are there any scientific studies, which compare the effects of normal methods of vertical, jump training and special equipment, and if so, what are the conclusions?

This is not to say that different types of specialized sports equipment may not be beneficial, but I want to stress that there is no magical system, which will make an athlete virtually fly over volleyball net. At the same time any equipment use should be combined with a thorough musculotendinous pre-strengthening program. In addition, its period of use should be limited, because of the risks associated with prolonged high levels of stress on the Achilles tendons. Personally I was a part of those "so called" East European Plyometrics programs, and benefiting from a great ratio of fast and slow twitch muscle fibers, after years and years of hard preparation I was able to perform a 105 cm (41 inches) standing vertical jump with a 75 kg (165 lb) body weight.

One of my favorite programs is the following:

Phase 1

• respect the age, preparation level and gender factors in prescribing any jumping exercises

• do not prescribe any kind of jumping exercises for injured or physically unfit athletes

• develop a good basic general strength

• develop good joint flexibility (especially of ankle, knee, hip and shoulder)

• teach the proper technique of every lifting exercise

• teach the proper technique of all abdominal exercises

• teach proper wave squat technique

• teach proper squat jump technique

• teach proper step-up technique

• teach proper box jump technique

- teach proper stair jumps and run variations technique

- teach proper standing long jump technique

- teach proper technique of the standing vertical jump and three-step approach vertical jump

- teach proper depth jumping technique

- practice deep squats 3 times a week (Note: squat as deep as possible without imposing excessive stress on ankles, knees and hip joints)

After teaching the proper technique of execution of the basic general lifting and conditioning exercises, which respect the rules of age, preparation level and gender factors, I prescribe different programs in terms of length and intensity. After concluding the above-mentioned scheme and after achieving an acceptable level of tendonal-muscular strength, athletes can now start several Javorek's conditioning programs, which are derived from my lifetime experience in developing vigorous, explosive athletes.

Phase 2

During this phase, the athlete should be ready to work on a more specific program improving vertical jump ability and performance. I do not renounce any ideas about continuing the general conditioning during this phase, but also consider that an athlete after working out more than a year should be ready to start working gradually on specific needs. After an athlete is ready to begin different types of specific conditioning programs I still like to work on vertical jump improvement, so I include the following exercises in the program:

Monday
All Intensities are relative to 1RM.

BB Back Squat

40% 10	50% 10	60% 10	65% 10	70% 8	75% 6

BB straight-knee Clean grip Deadlift Standing on a 20 cm height box

50% 10	55% 8	60% 8	65% 8	70% 6	70% 6

BB Power Clean from platform

50% 6	60% 6	70% 5	75% 5

Javorek's Special "Medicine Ball" Abdominal Program #2 x 1
Stair Run (30 stairs)   x 8

Wednesday

BB Front Squat

40% 10	50% 8	55% 8	60% 6	65% 5	70% 5

BB Power Snatch from platform

50% 8	60% 6	65% 5	70% 5	70% 5

Stair (30 stairs) Double Leg Bouncing x 8
Stair Run x 8

Javorek's Special "Medicine Ball" Abdominal Program # 2
x 1

Friday

BB Back Squat

50% 10	60% 10	70% 6	80% 4	85% 3

BB Straight Knee Clean Deadlift from platform

50% 10	60% 8	70% 6	80% 6

BB Alternate Leg Split Clean from platform

50% 6+6	60% 4+4	65% 4+4	70% 4+4

Stair Double Leg Bounding
x 6

Stair Double Leg Zig-Zag Bounding
x 6

Stair Run
x 6

Javorek's Special "Medicine Ball" Abdominal Program #2
x 1

Monday

BB Back Squat

50% 10	60% 10	65% 10	70% 8	75% 6	80% 3

BB Straight Knee Clean Deadlift from platform

50% 10	60% 10	70% 8	80% 6

BB Alternate Leg Split Snatch from platform

50% 6+6	60% 5+5	60% 5+5	65% 4+4
70% 3+3			

Squat Jumps without Weight
4 Sets x 8

Stair Double Leg Bounding
x 6

Stair Double Leg Zig-Zag Bounding
x 6

Stair Run
x 6

Javorek's Special "Medicine Ball" Abdominal Program #2.
x 1

Wednesday

BB Front Squat

50% 10	60% 8	65% 6	70% 5	75% 4	80% 2

BB Power Clean from Hang below the Knees

55% 6	60% 6	65% 6	70% 5	75% 4

Squat Jumps without Weight
6 Sets x 8

Stair Double Leg Bounding
x 4

Stair Zig-Zag Bounding
x 4

Stair Jump & Sprint
x 4

Stair Sprint
x 4

Javorek's Special "Medicine Ball" Abdominal Program #2
x 1

Friday

BB Back Squat

50% 10	70% 8	60% 10	80% 4	70% 6	90% 2	80% 3	90% 2

BB Straight Knee Clean Deadlift

60% 10	70% 8	80% 6	90% 6	90% 6

BB Power Snatch from Hang below the Knee

50% 6	55% 6	60% 5	65% 5	70% 4	75% 4

Squat Jumps Without Weight
6 Sets x 8

Box Jump (Individual height)
x 10 x 6

Stair Double Leg Bounding
x 6

Stair One Leg Bounding (if the athlete is capable of doing without any risk of ankle injuries)
R+L x 6

Stair Jump & Sprint
x 6

Stair Sprint
x 6

Javorek's Special "Medicine Ball" Abdominal Program #2
x 1

Monday

BB Back Squat

50% 10	60% 8	70% 6	60% 8	70% 6	80% 4	85% 2

BB Straight Knee Clean Deadlift from platform

60% 10	70% 8	80% 6	90% 6	90% 6

BB Alternate Leg Split Clean from Hang above the Knee

50% 5+5	60% 4+4	70% 3+3	75% 3+3

Squat Jumps without Weight
6 Sets x 10

Stair Double Leg Bounding
x 6

Stair One Leg Bounding (if the athlete is capable of doing without any risk of ankle injuries)
R+L x 6

Stair Double Leg Zig-Zag Bounding
x 6

Stair Sprint
x 6

Javorek's Special "Medicine Ball" Abdominal Program #2
x 1

Wednesday

BB Front Squat

50% 8	70% 5	60% 6	80% 3	75% 4	85% 3

BB Split Snatch from hang above the Knee

50% 5+5	55% 5+5	60% 4+4	65% 3+3	70% 3+3	75% 3+3

Box Jump (Individual height)
x 12 x 6

Stair Jump & Sprint
x 6

Stair Sprint
x 6

Javorek's Special "Medicine Ball" Abdominal Program #2
x 1

Friday

BB Back Squat

50% 8	60% 6	70% 4	80% 3	75% 5	85% 2	90% 1	95% 1
100% 1							

BB Straight Knee Deadlift from platform

70% 8	80% 8	90% 6	95% 6	100% 5

BB Power Clean from Hang above the Knee

50% 6	60% 5	65% 5	70% 4	75% 4

Squat Jumps without Weight
6 Sets x 8

Stair Double Leg Bounding
x 4

Stair One Leg Bounding (if the athlete is capable without any risk of ankle injuries)
(R+L) x 2

Stair One Leg, Right or Left Shoulder, Right or Left Leg Sideways Bounding
(R+L) x 2

Stair One Leg, Right or Left Shoulder, Left or Right Leg Sideways Bounding
(R+L) x 2

Stair Jump & Sprint
x 4

Stair Sprint
x 6

After such preparation, any athlete should be ready to gradually progress more to box jumps and depth jump exercise variations. Despite the fact that box jumps and depth jumps variations evidently improve vertical jumping ability, I would never give up any of the above mentioned exercises, because vertical jumping does not involve just the lower leg but all the muscles of the body. Upper leg, abdominal, back, arms, neck and torso muscles are involved in vertical jumping, and just as we improve the strength-explosive qualities of those muscles, so will we proportionately improve vertical jumping ability.

I have seen several intriguing vertical jump training devices, but I am still convinced that nothing can better improve an athlete's vertical jump abilities more than implementing the above-mentioned criteria provided at the beginning of this chapter.

Javorek's BB Explosive Squat Routines For Advanced Athletes

Combination Exercise # 1

(4 Sets: 25% 1 set	30% 1 set	35% 1 set	40% 1 set)

Intensity is relative to the maximum Barbell Back Squat -

BB Straight Knees Toe Raise -	15 reps
BB Quarter Squat & Up On Toes -	10 reps
BB Back Squat Jump -	4 reps
BB Back Squat & Up On Toes -	8 reps
BB Wave Squat (2+1 Jump +1 Squat Jump Combination)	24 reps (6 cycle x 4)
BB Straight Knees Toe Raise -	10 reps
BB Back Squat Jump -	4 reps
Suitable Height Box - Jump -	10 reps
Double Leg Stair Bounding or Tuck Jump -	10 reps

Perform in a non-stop continuous order

Combination Exercise #2
(45% 1 Set)

BB Straight Knees Toe Raise -	10 reps
BB Wave Squat (2+1 jump +1 Squat Jump Combination)	24 reps (6 cycle x 4)
BB Quarter Squat & Up On Toes -	10 reps
BB Back Squat Jump -	6 reps
Suitable Height Box - Jump -	10 reps
Double Leg Stair Bounding or Tuck Jump -	10 reps

Perform in a non-stop continuous order

Combination Exercise # 3
(50% 1 Set)

BB Straight Knees Toe Raise -	10 reps
BB Back Squat -	10 reps
BB Wave Squat (2+1 jump +1 Squat Jump Combination)	24 reps (6 cycle x 4)
BB Quarter Squat & Up On Toes -	10 reps
BB Back Squat Jump -	6 reps
Suitable Height Box - Jump -	10 reps
Double Leg Stair Bounding or Tuck Jump -	10 reps

Perform in a non-stop continuous order

Individual Exercises

BB Straight Knees Toe Raise

25% 20	30% 20	35% 20	40% 15	45% 10

BB Quarter Squat & Up On Toes

30% 10	35% 10	40% 10	50% 6	60% 5

BB Back Squat

40% 10	50% 10	60% 8	55% 10	65% 6	75% 4	70% 5	80% 3

BB Wave Squat (3+1 jump + 1 Squat Jump combination)

30% 30	40% 30	45% 25	50% 20	55% 20	60% 15	65% 10	70% 10

BB Toe Raises

25% 10	30% 10	35% 10	40% 8	45% 6

BB Back Squat Jump

30% 8	35% 7	40% 6	45% 6	50% 5	55% 4	60% 3

Double Leg Stair Bounding
6 Sets x 8 bounding

Suitable Height Box Jump
6 Sets x 10

Javorek's Barbell Squat + Squat Jump Combination

40% 10+6	50% 10+4	45% 10+5	55% 10+4	55% 10+4	60% 1+3	60% 1+2
60% 1+3	60% 1+2	70% 2+1	70% 1+1	70% 2+1;		
70% 2+1	65% 1+1	65% 1+1	65% 1+1	65% 1+1	75% 1+1	75% 1+1
75% 1+1	75% 1+1;					
50% 1+4	50% 1+4	50% 2+3	60% 1+3	60% 2+3	60% 1+3	55% 1+4
55% 1+5	55% 1+3	65% 1+3	65% 1+3	65% 1+3;		
80% 3+0	85% 3+0	80% 3+0	85% 3+0	40% 0+8	50% 3+3	40% 0+8
55% 3+3;						

Combining Horizontal and Vertical Actions

In modern athletics, one of the most important qualities an athlete can possess is the ability to transfer vertical motion to horizontal motion or vice-versa, through quick reaction time. Such situations occur, for example, in a missed jump shot in basketball, followed by a fast defensive move or new attack situation; or in soccer, running down the field to find the best position, heading the ball, followed by a quick slalom between opponents, then concluding with jumping up to chest stop the ball and passing or shooting the ball.

In most cases, a horizontal reaction is transferred into a vertical one, rather than a vertical reaction into a horizontal one. For example, these are some events that will benefit most from these exercises: in volleyball the recovery of a ball by diving, then setting or jumping for a spike; in tennis, the execution of sideways, forward or backward movements for a return, combined with vertical or sideways jumping-hitting combinations; and in track and field, the triple jump, long jump, high jump, hurdles, and steeple chase.

There are several plyometrics exercises, which will help to improve these qualities, but I have certain objections to using too many explosive drills on a horizontal surface. Plyometrics exercises on horizontal surfaces exert considerable stress on the ankle, leg, hip and lower back muscles, bones and tendons. The majority of sports cause stress in the lower leg bones and tendon-muscular system, which can cause very painful periostitis, shin splints or stress fractures. For these reasons, I combine, or in several situations, substitute the vertical-horizontal reaction transfer exercises from a horizontal surface to stairs or sand stair boxes. This transfers a big part of the stress during the exercise from the lower leg up to the thigh muscles, and at the same time activates, to a great degree, the fast twitch muscle fibers, improves the athlete's orientation in space, and enhances neuromuscular coordination. I do not wish to be misunderstood regarding this issue. I use horizontal plyometrics exercises on a daily basis in my programs, but for the specific goal of vertical-horizontal or horizontal-vertical transfer I prefer stairs or sand stair box activities for the above-mentioned reasons.

Teaching strategies:

- teach correct running up stairs, up shredded rubber boxes, uphill ramps and uphill

- teach the correct double leg jump bounding variations up stairs, up shredded rubber boxes, uphill ramps and uphill

- teach the correct one leg jump bounding variations up stairs, up shredded rubber boxes, uphill ramps and uphill

- teach the correct double leg jump bounding and sprint up variations up stairs, up shredded rubber boxes, uphill ramps and uphill

- combine the exercises in a certain order

Exercise # 1
Uphill 5m run (or approach) continued with a double leg take off-double leg forward uphill jumping and landing on both feet and sprinting up 5m. Repeat 2-3 times more, or as many times as possible.

Exercise # 2
Uphill 5m run (approach) continued with a one leg jump or two jumps (jump-jump) and sprint up 5m. Repeat 2-3 times more, or as many times as possible.

Exercise # 3
Uphill two squat jump and 5m sprint. Repeat uphill 2-3 times more, or as many times as possible.

Exercise # 4
Uphill two or more frog jumps and 5 m. sprint. Repeat uphill 2-3 or more times.

Exercise # 5
Practice Exercise # 1, # 2, # 3 up stairs, uphill ramps or uphill.

Exercise # 6
Uphill 5 m sprint (approach) continued with a double leg take off of 180 degree, and after several days of practice with 360 degree double leg rotational jumps (L&R), then sprint again. Repeat in a set as many times as possible. For a different variation this exercise can also be done with backward running.

Exercise # 7
Uphill 20m run continued with 5 alternate leg bounding;

Exercise # 8
Uphill 20m run continued with leg bounding (5R, 5L)

Exercise # 9
Uphill 10m sprint continued with a long jump;

Exercise # 10
Uphill 10m sprint continued with a one leg take off vertical jump, imitating a sport specific motion (spike, heading, jump shot, etc.)

Exercise # 11
Uphill 10m sprint continued with a double leg take off vertical jump, imitating a sport specific motion (spike, heading, jump shot, etc.)

Exercise # 12
Uphill double leg zig-zag jump bounding x 14.

Exercise # 13
Uphill alternate leg straight up jump bounding x 14 double steps.

Exercise # 14
Uphill one leg straight up jump bounding (12 R, 12 L).

Exercise # 15
Uphill one leg zig-zag bounding (12R, 12L).

Exercise # 16
Uphill same shoulder-same leg sideways jump bounding (10R, 10L).

Exercise # 17
Uphill five consecutive same shoulder-same leg sideways jump bounding (5R, 5L), continued with ten m. sprint. Repeat 2-3 times uphill.

Exercise # 18
Uphill opposite shoulder-opposite leg sideways jump bounding (10R, 10L).

Exercise # 19
Uphill opposite shoulder-opposite leg five consecutive sideways jump bounding (5R, 5L), continued with 10m sprint. Repeat 2-3 times uphill.

Exercise # 20
Five standing squat jump continued with 10m uphill sprint. Repeat 2-3 times uphill.

Exercise # 21
Exercises # 12, 13, 14, 15, 16, 18, 20 may be practiced on stairs or sand stair boxes.

Exercise # 22
With advanced athletes the exercises may be increased gradually by holding light DB in both hands next to the thighs.

Javorek's Conditioning Hill

Usually tearing down an old building or facility gives room and chances for rebuild a new and better one. This happened in the last two years with the JCCC sand stair boxes conditioning area.

The former sand boxes were a homemade series of sand-filled boxes arranged stair-like up a slope on campus, next to a stairway. It worked, but the sand in warm days was dirty and would quickly harden to feel like cement, so it had to be thoroughly broken up and raked each day before use. It also limited the types of drills and exercises I could use.

Giving room to a new modern Gym, the sand stair box-conditioning hill was demolished and with a new architectural concept rebuilt. Actually I did fulfill my previous ideas and dreams in building the first specific "conditioning hill" which we named "Javorek's Conditioning Hill". Behind my concept is the idea of giving a chance for any given sports to do a specific uphill conditioning.

Some sports requires cardio-vascular endurance but quick and explosive musculature, others short explosive movements, endurance or you specify what exactly your sport or your athletes need. The Conditioning Hill is a combination of stairs, shredded rubber boxes, (with a superior quality of absorbing the shock easy to maintain and at the same very hygienic) instead of sand boxes (which was more difficult to maintain), and an uphill running ramp, providing for any sports and to the most sophisticated coaching concept a chance to prescribe a sport specific conditioning program.

The training area stairs and ramp were constructed using concrete with steel reinforcing similar to normal exterior stair and sidewalk construction. The stair treads are 15" deep in lieu of 12", with 6" risers, the total rise is 13'-2" with an 8' long landing at the midpoint. The ramp is a continuous 3.5:1 slope, which is the grade on either side of the training area to allow for grass mowing. The third area for jumping was constructed using pressure treated wood risers bolted to galvanized steel angles

expansion anchored to the steel reinforced concrete walls that separate this area from the ramp on one side and the stairs on the other. The risers are 16" and the treads vary from 5' long at the bottom to 3' long at the top. The treads, which needed to be a soft surface for jumping and landing, were constructed of 8" deep rubber mulch over gravel and perforated drainpipe wrapped in filter fabric to allow storm water to drain from the "jumping boxes". The drainage system was run to daylight beyond the training area. The boxes get shorter to create an increased inclination from the bottom of the run to the top. This increased inclination makes the exercises progressively more difficult as athletes work their way up the jump boxes. The landing areas need to be soft enough to avoid overstressing to joints during the jumping exercises, but firm enough to hold up under repeated use. So, how I mentioned before, I filled the boxes with eight inches of rubber mulch and recycled tires similar to the material found at many playgrounds. The drains storm water from the boxes to an area well beyond the training area. As a result we are able to use the jump boxes on all but the worst days of our Kansas winters.

Maintenance is limited to occasional vacuuming of shredded rubber that spills out of the jump boxes, which we return to the boxes. We added some fence gates to keep out skateboarders who were attracted by the chance to work on their own programs.

I use this facility in the specific strength and conditioning programs I design for each team here at JCCC. Uphill training is a key part of our preseason strength and conditioning program, but it's not the only part. We do traditional weight work every day in addition to daily work on the uphill jump boxes.

The athletes have responded well to the uphill work and seem to enjoy it much more than simply running stairs and lifting weights. The uphill conditioning programs are hard work, though. The initial workouts often leave newcomers overwhelmed. In fact, returning athletes often explain to newcomers that we're doing this to make them better athletes, not to punish them. But the hard work has paid off. The basketball coaches, for example, say they can't run the team hard enough to affect their players. After going through our hill training program, the players laugh at the demands of running in the air-conditioned gym.

Because the hill training is so demanding, proper preparation is crucial. Regardless of the athletes' conditioning level before the preseason program begins, I work them into my superset programs gradually. First, I have them perform each exercise separately, focusing on technique instead of workload. It is imperative that athletes fully understand the proper way to complete each exercise before combining them into a program.

It is also important to not try to do too much too soon. For example, if I have a big, overweight basketball player, I prescribe more sprint up the slope or stairs until they are in good enough shape to begin leaping and bounding exercises. The prevention of injury must always be an overriding concern. Also as a general safety rule, I never let injured athletes perform any exercises that could aggravate their injuries. And once the athletic trainers clear athletes, I start them on sprints on the ramp and stairs before moving them on to jumps.

After everyone has fully mastered all the exercises, I begin to put them together into supersets. I start by having the athletes complete four repetitions of each exercise and work my way up to whatever final total I have determined for their specific teams. For some teams, I incorporate non-hill training activities, such as a mile run, into the hill workout.

The general conditioning level of the team and demands of the sport help determine the ultimate number of reps in the superset. I prefer to have athletes do all the of one exercise in a group before moving to the next, but sometimes for variety's sake, I have them complete one rep of each exercise in a series and then repeat that series a certain number of times.

I use most of the same exercises in each of my programs, but based on years of experience, combine them differently to meet the unique demands of each sport. As a general rule, jumping exercises are better used to develop explosive power, such as for sprinters, jumpers or track and field throwers. Endurance events are better prepared for using running exercises and easier jumping exercises on the stairs (not the shredded rubber boxes!) such as double leg jumps; zig-zag jumps; and run-jump & sprints. I like for everyone to use at least some jumping exercises to improve their fitness levels, but each coach should determine what works best for his or her athletes.

As with any strength and conditioning program, it is important to ensure that athletes are not "overworked" in some areas while being "underworked" in others. Backward runs up the ramp will work different group of muscles than forward sprints. The frog jumps are another effective way of spreading to load since they work to frontal lower leg muscles and quadriceps more than other exercises.

Although the hill conditioning programs are the focus of preseason training, I use them during the season as well. For example, we lead the women's and men's basketball teams through a shortened hill conditioning plan the day after each game and go through the full program when the coaches are feeling that teams' statistics are dropping. It is a well-known fact that if the team statistics drops it is a clear sign of a more mental tiredness than physical, which if is not taken care of it usually ends in catastrophic drop in the team's performance.

On the following samples, which I am using with my athletes, the number of reps listed reflects the maximum at the end of a training cycle. This is built up to gradually during the training cycle.

There is always room for improvement, so I am constantly adjusting my programs based on what I hear from the coaches and athletes. The athletes may tell me they want a little more variety or prefer doing one exercise more than another. Or a coach may say her team needs to work on its quickness this year more than its strength.

Although much of the effort is focused on the team supersets, they are not the only work we do on the hill facility. Motivated athletes who have shown they can easily and safely master the superset activities are offered the opportunity to do additional specialized individual work that is not practical for larger groups. These exercises require great care and concentration to avoid injury, so they must be done in smaller groups.

This is where I introduce outside weight to our hill training sessions. One of the favorites is a weighted wheelbarrow run up on ramp. This exercises is especially useful for pole vaulters, since it closely mimics the unique demands of their event. But sprinters, jumpers, American football players could benefit as well.

Another favorite is to have athletes perform exercises while carrying dumbbells, provided they are spaced far enough apart so a dropped dumbbell won't injure another athlete.

For the most part, I try to keep exercises basic and directly related to movements required for their sport. I do look to introduce as many variations to my exercises as I can, while at the same time keeping their necessity and usefulness in mind. It is easy to create new exercises that look good but don't help in athletic preparation. So I think twice before changing exercises or choosing new ones.

Most of the exercises listed in the Supersets samples are self-explanatory while others need a short description.

Run & Jump & Sprint:
Start with a three-four step run to first stair followed by double-leg jumps up two, three or four (or more) stairs. Sprint up through the midpoint landing and repeat again the same way: run, then jump and sprint to the top.

Single Leg Sideways Jumps
(same leg and shoulder; opposite leg and shoulder): The same leg and shoulder jump has the athlete jump using the same leg as his or her leading shoulder, such as jumping to his or her left using the left leg. The opposite leg and shoulder jump has the athlete jump using the leg opposite the leading shoulder, such as jumping to the left using the right leg. Repetition should typically be balanced so the athletes make the same number of jumps on each leg using each leading shoulder.

Frog Jumps:
Start bent over with a curved back, slightly bent knees, and ankles touching. Jump with arms swinging overhead, extending the whole body. Upon landing, return to start position and repeat to the top of the stairs or of the ramp or shredded rubber boxes.

Double Leg Zig-Zag Jumps:
Keeping feet parallel, jump from right side of step or box to the left side of the same box. Then jump up to the right side of the next step or box and repeat.

Javorek's Tennis "Hill Conditioning" Superset:
Since tennis involves a lot of lateral movements, I use more sideways jumps than in other programs. As with all my programs, athletes are introduced to the program slowly, mastering each exercise before I put the together into sets. The goal is to have them be able to complete the superset by the end of the preseason training session.

Exercise	Reps
Stair Double Leg Jump-Bounding	x 4
Stair Run-Jump & Sprint - Could Be Executed With One Jump & Sprint-Two Jumps & Sprint, Or Two Jumps In Zig-zag & Sprint-	x 4
Stair Double Leg Jump-Bounding	x 4
Stair Single Leg Jump-Bounding (Left And Right Alternating) Straight Up	x 4
Stair Run-Jump & Sprint (Same Way Like Before)	x 4
Stair Single Leg, Same Shoulder Same Leg Sideways Jump-Bounding (Right Leg Right Shoulder, Left Leg Left Shoulder)	x 4
Stair Run-Jump & Sprint (Same Way Like Before)	x 4
Stair Single Leg, Opposite Leg Opposite Shoulder (Right Leg Left Shoulder-Left Leg Right Shoulder) Sideways Jump- Bounding	x 4
Stair Run-Jump & Sprint (Same Way Like Before)	x 4
Shredded Rubber Boxes or Sand Stair Box Or Shredded Rubber Box Double Leg Jump-Bounding	x 4
Shredded Rubber Boxes or Sand Stair Box Or Shredded Rubber Box Single Leg Jump-Bounding	x 4
Shredded Rubber Boxes or Sand Stair Box Or Shredded Rubber Box Single Leg, Same Shoulder Same Leg Sideways Jump Bounding (Right Leg Right Shoulder, Left Leg Left Shoulder)	x 2
Shredded Rubber Boxes or Sand Stair Box Or Shredded Rubber Box Single Leg, Opposite Leg Opposite Shoulder (Right Leg Left Shoulder-Left Leg Right Shoulder) Sideways Bounding	x 2
Shredded Rubber Boxes or Sand Stair Box Or Shredded Rubber Box Single Leg (R+L) Jump-Bounding	x 4
Stairs Sprint Up	x 4
Shredded Rubber Boxes or Sand Stair Box Or Shredded Rubber Box Sprint	x 4
Up Hill Ramp, Backward Running	x 4
Up Hill Ramp Frog Jumps	x 2
Up Hill Ramps Sprint	x 4

Javorek's Basketball "Hill Conditioning" Superset:

The Stair-Sand Stair, or Shredded Rubber Boxes Combination Javorek's Super Set is the basic indicator about the team's cardio-vascular conditioning level. During the years of experiments with this Superset I got on a conclusion about the number of repetitions, which should indicate a team's readiness to be able of handling the most difficult practices. The players master each exercise before I combine them into small sets with the goal of being able to complete the full superset by the end of the training season. During the basketball season, players will complete a shortened version of this set whenever the coach feels they need the work.

1.	Shredded Rubber Box Double leg jump bounding	x 10
2.	Stairs Run-Jump & Sprint:	x 10
3.	Stairs Consecutive One leg bounding: - for right leg	x 5
	- for left leg in an alternating way	x 5
	And without break continue with # 4 (1 mile cross country)	
4.	1 mile cross country or on the track; return on the stairs and in order of arrival continue the	Superset:
5.	Stairs Consecutive One leg bounding: - for right leg	x 5
	- for left leg in an alternating way	x 5
6.	Shredded Rubber Box Running	x 10
7.	Stairs Double leg Zig-Zag jump bounding	x 10
9.	Up Hill Ramp 100 % intensity Sprint up	x 10

Javorek's "Hill Conditioning" Super Set for Sprinters:

The focus for sprinters is on explosive strength, so jumps are dominant exercise. Alternating the single-leg jumps and using frog jumps helps to keep training balanced throughout the lower body.

Stair Double Leg Jump-Bounding	x 2
Shredded Rubber Box Double Leg Jump-Bounding	x 2
Running Ramps Sprint	x 2
Shredded Rubber Box Double Leg Jump-Bounding	x 2
Stair Single Leg Jump-Bounding (Left And Right Alternating) Straight Up	x 2
Shredded Rubber Box Sprint	x 2
Running Ramp, Backward Running	x 2
Shredded Rubber Box Double Leg Squat-Jump	x 2
Shredded Rubber Box Sprint	x 2
Shredded Rubber Box Single Leg Jump-Bounding (Left And Right Alternating)	x 2
Running Ramp Frog Jumps	x 2
Shredded Rubber Box Sprint	x 2
Running Ramp, Backward Running	x 2
Stair Single Leg Jump-Bounding (Left And Right Alternating) Straight Up	x 2
Stairs Sprint Up	x 2
Shredded Rubber Box Single Leg Jump-Bounding (Left And Right Alternating)	x 2
Shredded Rubber Box Double Leg Squat-Jump	x 2
Stairs Sprint Up	x 2
Shredded Rubber Box Single Leg Jump-Bounding	x 2
Running Ramps Sprint	x 2
Shredded Rubber Box Sprint	x 2
Running Ramp, Backward Running	x 2
Shredded Rubber Box Sprint	x 2
Running Ramp Frog Jumps	x 2
Running Ramps Sprint	x 4

Medicine ball overhead jump pass.

Medicine ball overhead sideways pass.

Medicine ball overhead backward pass.

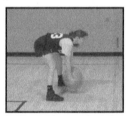

Medicine ball bent over forward pass.

Medicine ball bentover landing in push ups pass.

Medicine ball digging-pass from knees.

Medicine ball digging-pass from knees.

Medicine ball overhead jump pass.

Medicine ball squat or sqaut jump pass.

Medicine ball squat or sqaut jump pass.

Medicine ball overhead pass from kneeling.

Medicine ball two hand spiking.

Medicine ball exercise.

Medicine ball situps.

Situps with medicine ball.

Medicine ball two hand spiking.

Medicine ball exercise.

Situps with medicine ball chest pass.

Situps with weight on chest.

Organizing a plyomietrics class.

Basketball conditioning medicine ball chest pass.

Medicine ball exercise.

Situps with medicine ball chest pass.

situps with feet on box

Basketball conditioning medicine ball pass.

Medicine ball exercise.

Situps with medicine ball overhead pass.

Forward zig-zag alternate leg bounding.

Basketball conditioning medicine ball seated pass.

Medicine ball exercise.

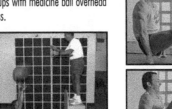

Situps with medicine ball overhead pass.

Sideways double leg box jump.

Medicine ball exercise.

Basketball conditioning medicine ball seated pass.

Sit-ups on three fingers at age 60.

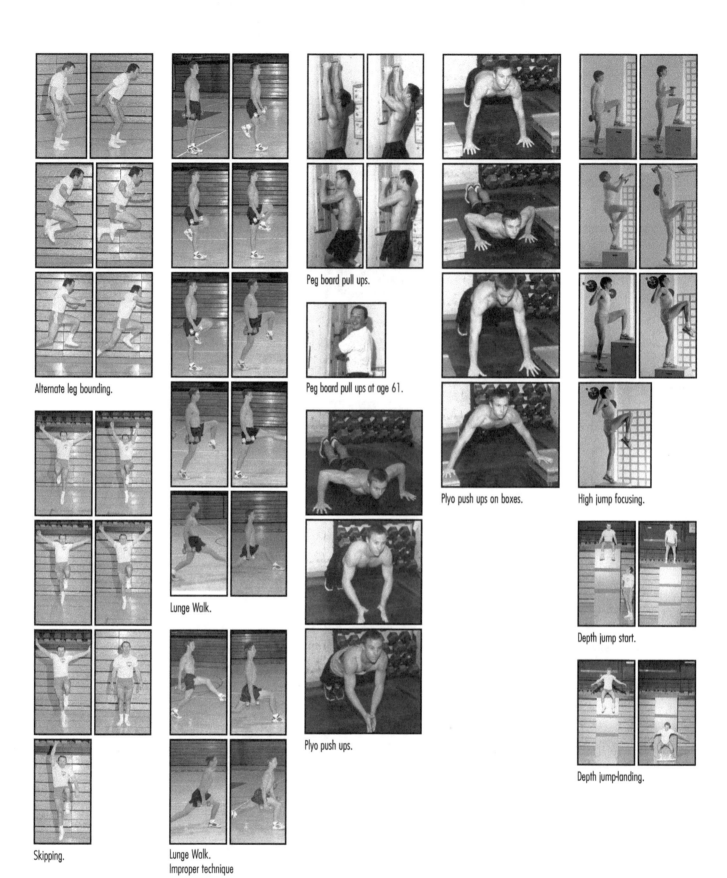

Alternate leg bounding.

Skipping.

Lunge Walk.

Lunge Walk.
Improper technique

Peg board pull ups.

Peg board pull ups at age 61.

Plyo push ups.

Plyo push ups on boxes.

High jump focusing.

Depth jump start.

Depth jump-landing.

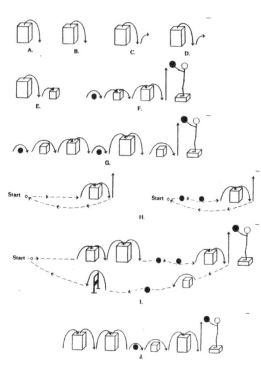

A. Depth jump, no rebound.
B. Depth jump; stop 3-5 seconds; on rebound.
C. Depth jump; stop 3-5 seconds; rebound.
D. Depth jump and rebound.
E. Depth jump and rebound on a lower box.
F. coach holds a ball or other object. the athlete can spike, volley, dunk or pass it, depending on the sport.
G. Exercise cam be done forward or sideways several times consecutively, depending on goals and preparation level.
H. Athlete runs to a box, jumps onto it then off it, rebounds and then returns to starting point. Athlete may run between medicine balls on the way to the box as shown in diagram.
I. Athlete runs between the medicine balls going forward, backward, while turning, circling, etc.
J. Athlete runs, bounds, shuffles, zig-zag bounds with both feet together and other variations depending on the sport.

Building the new Javorek's uphill complex.

Building the new Javorek's uphill complex.

High knees running on ramp.

Hill conditioning double leg stair bounding.

Hill conditioniong ramp backward running.

Hill conditioniong ramp backward running.

Hill conditioniong shredded rubber double leg bounding.

One leg, left shoulder — right leg sideways bounding.

Hill sprint on ramp.

Strides on ramp.

Wheel barrow up hill run on ramp.

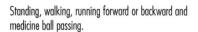

Standing, walking, running forward or backward and medicine ball passing.

With the ball on the floor, jumping over forward, backward, sideways.

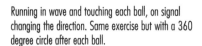

Running in wave and touching each ball, on signal changing the direction. Same exercise but with a 360 degree circle after each ball.

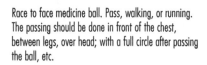

Race to face medicine ball. Pass, walking, or running. The passing should be done in front of the chest, between legs, over head; with a full circle after passing the ball, etc.

Up and down, forward or backward.

Side to side, up and down, or only right, or left side, or forward/backward.

Over the box, side to side, with right or left shoulder, after a proper preparation forward/backward. First practice over a medicine ball.

Plyometrics in Theory and Practice

Istvan Javorek — the hill conditioning inventor.

Indoor upstair Double leg bounding.

Indoor upstair running.

Sand stair boxes conditioning.

Uphill conditioning.

Chapter 11

Chapter 12
Dumbbells or Machines in General Sports Conditioning?

My answer and philosophy about the major issue of preferring the use of dumbbells rather than machines in all sports conditioning is as follows:

DB training

1. is generally safe

2. does not need a large practice area

3. is easy to teach

4. can be done simultaneously and very efficiently with a large number of athletes

5. is dynamic with a large range of motion (actually the range of motion is unlimited) and a large range of exercise variations

6. stimulates (very important in so many sports) the balance mechanisms powerfully (which much machine training does not adequately do).

7. enables one to develop unlimited muscular power, cardiovascular and muscular endurance, flexibility and strength; (most machine training develops muscles but not dynamic explosive strength)

8. is inexpensive to equip a gym with several sets of DB

9. can be very easily monitored with a 100 percent accuracy, because we have an exact number of repetitions, sets, volumes and rhythm of exercising

10. enables one to efficiently monitor the heart rate before and after each set, thus providing a very clear view of recovery time and the physical fitness level of the individual athlete.

Dumbbell Exercise

Classification and Description

A better system of dumbbell exercise classification has been needed for many years, so I have attempted to do in the following sections. DB exercise variations are unlimited and any experienced coach with a good knowledge of kinesiology should be able to figure out many novel variations of DB exercises. In order to be able to classify them, we need to follow certain rules and criteria, such as:

The Basic Body and Dumbbell Positions

A. Body position: standing; seated; bent-over; lying on your back on a bench(flat, incline, decline);

B. Dumbbell position:

1- simultaneous - performing with both hands at the same time

2 - alternating - performing with each hand individually in an alternating way

3 - one-hand - when we perform an exercise just with one hand

4- two hands - when we perform an exercise with both hands

5 - parallel - when both DB are in a parallel set

6 - linear - when both DB are forming a straight line:

    6(a) - linear Pronated - with palms down

    6(b)- linear Supinated - with palms up

7 - rotational - when we perform from:

    7(a) - linear pronated to parallel

    7(b) - linear pronated to linear supinated

    7(c) - linear supinated to parallel

    7(d) - linear supinated to linear pronated, etc. Rotational movement

8 - lateral arm raise with different hand position

9 - frontal arm raise with different hand position

10 - circle, in an alternating or simultaneous way perform a circling movement in different direction

11 - spiral movement, in a circling movement with the hand moving out or in, in a spiraling way

12 - oblique movements - exercises performed in an oblique direction instead of the standard position.

Dumbbell Exercise Variations

I developed more than 700 dumbbell exercises. I enclosed bellow the 220 most important variations of them.

1 **DB standing simultaneous quarter squat & up on toes two hands raise to armpit:** Standing with DB in hands at hip level. Bend your knees and simultaneously with knee extension, raise the DB up to your armpit, at the same time coming up onto your toes. Hold your body vertically upright and do not lean your trunk or your head forward. Keep your arms at your sides. Allow the DB to hang freely and do not reverse curl your wrist.

2 **DB standing alternate quarter squat & up on toes raise to armpit**

3 **DB standing one-hand quarter squat & up on toes raise to armpit**

4 **DB seated simultaneous two hands raise to armpit:** tight abdominal muscles. Look straight ahead.

5 **DB seated alternate raise to armpit**

6 **DB seated one-hand raise to armpit**

7 **DB standing simultaneous two hands raise to armpit and split jump**
Standing in a lunge, DB in hand next to the thighs, trunk in perfect vertical line. It is very important the perfect split jump technique. Do not jump up, just split the legs; keep the trunk in a vertical position; tighten the abdominal muscles; the front leg lands always first on heels and then rolls over on flat foot. There are three variations of it:

(a) regular split jump without any arm movement

(b) split jumps with simultaneous arms raises to the arm pit: on each leg split (changing leg position by splitting back and forth, but not jumping up), raise the arms up to the armpit (same technique as regular DB Raise to Armpit) and during the split let the arms down. Every leg split movement is connected with a DB raise to the armpit and repositioning of the arms, straight down to the initial position. Learning the exercise is best if the movement is sequenced, practicing each stage separately. After good arm-leg coordination is achieved, the different parts of the exercise can be connected and executed in a nonstop manner

(c) the split jump variations can be executed with short lunges or wide lunges, depending the goals. For example: sprinters, long and triple jumpers should practice both forms; long distance runners need to focus more on the short split jump with DB raises to the armpit.

8 DB standing alternate arm raise to armpit and walking in place Stand with DB next to the trunk at hip level, elbows slightly bent, regular walking. On each step raise one arm up to the armpit. Start slowly and try to synchronize arm-leg movement. Always raise the opposite arm to the front leg.

9 DB standing alternate raises to armpit and lateral bend: same position; instead of simultaneous arm raise one alternates an arm raise with a lateral bending movement. Keep the trunk in the same plane. Do not lean the trunk forwards or arch it backwards.

10 DB standing alternate raise to armpit and running in place: similar to the DB walk exercise, only one runs in place with high knees.

11 DB standing simultaneous raise to armpit and bouncing in place: this exercise is similar with the DB Raise to the armpit. The only difference is that on each DB raise during the toe rising movement we continue with a vertical bouncing movement and pay special attention to the rebounding phase. Keep the abdominal muscles tight and do not push the hips forward.

12 DB standing squat and raise to armpit: Standing, parallel DB next to your thighs. Go in comfortable deep squat and stand up raising up on toes and the DB under the armpit.

13 DB standing squat jump and raise to armpit

14 DB standing simultaneous two hands upright row: stand with DB in hand in front of your thighs in a linear position. Arms straight, elbows turned slightly outward, shoulders turned in, head looking straight ahead, with a firm chin position. Keep the chest in an upright position, with back straight and tight abdominal muscles. Raise the DB to neck level straight upward and point the elbows up as much as possible, and rise onto the toes.

15 DB seated simultaneous two hands upright row

16 DB standing alternate upright row: the same exercise, except the arms are raised alternately. At the same time the athlete may rise onto the toes for each upright rowing movement.

17 DB standing simultaneous two hands squat upright row. The start position is with parallel DB in front of the trunk slightly between the thighs. Squat, holding the parallel DB position, then standing up with a continuous arms rotation in pronated linear position and finish the movement with an up on toes, upright row.

18 DB standing two hand simultaneous squat under upright row. Concomitantly with the gradual knee bend perform a flatfooted upright row, and then with the knee extension finish the exercise in the original starting position of a DB upright row. It is very important to hold the bodyweight in balance from the balls of the feet toward to the heels.

19 DB standing simultaneous two hands From Hip High Pull Snatch: much the same exercise as # 22, the difference being that, instead of doing the full bend-over and then the overhead high pull snatch movement, the start from the hip will be continued into a high pull snatch, and one does not bend over. The first phase of the From Hip High Pull Snatch technically is similar to the upright row continued into snatching of the bar overhead. Remember to keep the elbow up as long as possible; accelerate the motion; turn the elbows upwards. It is incorrect to rotate the elbows suddenly downward when at shoulder level, so as to execute a pressing movement overhead. The correct return motion should be done, similar to the regular high pull snatch.

20 DB standing one-hand From Hip High Pull Snatch: this is similar to exercise # 19, the difference being that instead of two handed movement, the athlete will execute the same motion with one hand. The free DB hand should rest next to the trunk.

21 DB standing alternate From Hip High Pull Snatch: this is technically like the other high pull snatch exercises, the difference being that the arms are used alternately. It is a very important exercise for swimmers, long distance runners, and generally for endurance athletes.

22 DB standing simultaneous two hands high pull snatch. Hold DB in pronated hands at hip level. Bend over with head down, back extended, arms straight, knees slightly bent, and flatfooted, with the center of gravity shifted back from the balls of the feet toward the heels. Bring the dumbbells to the toes, and hold the dumbbells as close as possible to the body. Raise the DB in an upright row position, and without a stop, but with continued acceleration, raise the DB over your head, and at the same time rise up on toes. For competitive Weightlifting we need not rise up on toes After reaching the highest pulling position, do not let the elbows turn down to execute an overhead press, but keep the elbows up with the help of acceleration and turn the wrist overhead, locking elbows overhead. During the lift, the DB should be kept as close as possible to the body. After the overhead phase, lower the DB with the same technique in reverse order of execution.

23 DB standing simultaneous two hands high pull snatch with bounce up: the exercise is similar to exercise # 22, the difference being that the acceleration of the "high pull snatching" overhead movement is transferred into a vertical bounce. The overhead snatching movement must be executed upward with tight abdominal muscles, and without the arms moving backward in a ballistic manner.

24 DB standing one-hand high pull snatch

25 DB standing alternate high pull snatch

26 DB standing one hand (R+L) cross high pull snatch

27 DB standing simultaneous two hands squat under high pull snatch

28 DB standing one-hand (L, R) squat under high pull snatch

29 DB standing alternate hand squat under high pull snatch. Keep arms straight next to the trunk, DB in hand in front of the thighs. Simultaneously with a slowly squatting motion, pull one arm overhead. Arm movement is similar to that during an overhead high pull snatch. The deep squat should be reached at the same time as arm extension overhead. The feet remain shoulder width throughout the exercise. After recovering from the squat, let the hands meet at hip level. In this momentum the alternative

arm will execute the overhead snatch movement in connection with a squat. This exercise can also be done with simultaneous two-hand overhead squatting under a high pull snatch.

30 DB standing simultaneous two hands from platform power snatch. Start with DB in front of feet, bent knees, straight back, head looking down, and neck in a straight line with the back. Stop in this high hip starting position. Concomitantly raise the shoulders, extend the knees, then in the highest vertical body posture drive on flat feet with a brisk shrug of the trapezius muscles and thrust the body under the DB, with locked elbows, and reposition the feet in a quarter squat or higher position. This exercise is like the one-hand power snatch, although these times there are DB in both hands.

31 DB standing simultaneous two hands from hang below the knees power snatch

32 DB standing simultaneous two hands from hang above the knees power snatch

33 DB standing one-hand simultaneous from platform power snatch. The DB free hand is next to the trunk or bent at the waist. Bend over with an arched back, with the DB close to the shin. The head is in a straight line with the neck and back. The DB may be snatched from platform or a very deep hang position.

34 DB standing one-hand simultaneous from hang below the knees power snatch

35 DB standing one-hand simultaneous from hang above the knees power snatch

36 DB simultaneous two hands standing from hang below the knees split snatch

37 DB simultaneous two hands standing from hang above the knees split snatch

38 DB standing from platform and hang below the knees combined simultaneous two hands split snatch

39 DB standing from platform and hang above the knees combined simultaneous two hands split snatch

40 DB one-hand simultaneous standing from platform split snatch

41 DB standing simultaneous two hands from platform squat snatch. It is same like the DB two hands power snatch, just thrusting the body under the DB all the way down into a deep squat. See squat snatch technique in the chapter on Olympic Weightlifting.

42 DB standing from hang below the knees simultaneous two hands squat snatch

43 DB standing from hang above the knees simultaneous two hands squat snatch

44 DB standing from platform and hang below the knees combined simultaneous two hands squat snatch

45 DB standing from platform and hang above the knees combined simultaneous two hands squat snatch

46 DB standing from platform one-hand simultaneous squat snatch, like the DB one-hand power snatch, just pressing the body under the DB all the way down into a squat position. See squat snatch technique in the chapter on Olympic Weightlifting

47 DB standing one-hand simultaneous from hang below the knees squat snatch

48 DB standing one-hand simultaneous from hang above the knees squat snatch

49 DB standing from platform and hang below the knees combined one-hand simultaneous squat snatch

50 DB standing from platform and hang above the knees combined one-hand simultaneous squat snatch

51 DB standing simultaneous two hands bent-over row: palms parallel facing each other, standing in a bent-over position with knees relatively straight. Shift your weight back onto the heels, balancing the weight of the DB and your bodyweight between the balls of your feet and heels, with slightly more balance toward the heels. Your back may be either straight (or slightly concave) or curved. It is the coach's decision which back position is preferable, depending on the goals of the exercise. The DBs are hold in a parallel position, and slightly wider than the shoulder width. Without changing the body position (no swinging or raising the trunk), bend your elbows and raise the DB up to shoulder level. In this phase the elbows face sideways and not backward and you should feel a marked stress on your deltoids and trapezius. The arm raise must be done quickly and explosively. The down motion should be slow with a pause.

53 DB standing simultaneous two hands with parallel palms facing each other bent-over row

DB standing simultaneous two hands pronated bent-over row

54 DB standing simultaneous two hands supinated bent-over row

55 DB standing simultaneous two hands with rotation from pronation to supination bent-over row

56 **DB standing simultaneous two hands with rotation from supination to pronation bent-over row:** using the same starting position as in the bent-over row. It is the same exercise with a rotation during the exercise. First pull the arms up, rotating fully the DB from supination to pronation. Hold the hand position firmly as at the start. Continue the rotation, closing the DB in front of the neck with an accentuate shoulder muscles stretch and elbows parallel with the facing wall.

57 **DB standing alternate parallel palms facing each other bent-over row:** like a regular bent-over row, but done with alternate arms. This exercise is suited to long distance athletes and for rowing sports.

58 DB wrist exercise circuit: DB pronated wrist curls

59 DB wrist exercise circuit: DB supinated wrist curls

60 DB wrist exercise circuit: DB pronated sideways (L&R) wrist curls

61 DB wrist exercise circuit: DB supinated sideways (L&R) wrist curls

62 DB wrist exercise circuit: DB parallel inside & outside wrist curls

63 DB wrist exercise circuit: DB parallel up & down wrist curls

64 DB wrist exercise circuit: DB (L&R) wrist rotation

65 **DB standing simultaneous two hands regular (supinated) curls.** The hand is supinated, the elbows 1-2 inch apart from the hip. Curl the arms upward, bend the arms from the elbows without changing the elbow position relative to the trunk, and finish the curl up position in front of the chest. The exercise has several variations: (a) inward rotational movement, finishing in a pronated hands position, or (b) holding the elbows higher and doing an oblique curl.

66 DB seated simultaneous two hands regular (supinated) curls

67 DB standing alternate regular (supinated) curls

68 DB seated alternate regular (supinated) curls

69 **DB standing simultaneous two hands reverse (pronated) curls:** standing, with the hands pronated and DB in a linear position. The wrist must be in a stiff position and in continuation of forearms.

70 DB seated simultaneous two hands reverse (pronated) curls

71 DB standing alternate reverse (pronated) curls

72 DB seated alternate reverse (pronated) curls

73 DB standing simultaneous two hands from pronation to supination rotational curls

74 DB seated simultaneous two hands from pronation to supination rotational curls

75 DB standing simultaneous two hands from supination to pronation rotational curls

76 DB seated simultaneous two hands from supination to pronation rotational curls

77 DB standing simultaneous two hands parallel curls

78 DB standing simultaneous two hands from parallel to pronation rotational curls

79 DB seated simultaneous two hands from parallel to pronation rotational curls

80 DB standing simultaneous two hands from parallel to supination rotational curls

81 DB seated simultaneous two hands from parallel to supination rotational curls

82 **DB standing simultaneous two hands from pronation to parallel rotational curls:** and so on. It is up to your fantasy of developing new and new exercise variation

83 DB standing simultaneous two hands oblique reverse (pronated) curls

84 DB standing simultaneous two hands parallel curls in front of chest

85 DB seated simultaneous two hands parallel curls in front of chest

86 DB standing alternate in front of chest parallel curls

87 DB standing simultaneous two hands sideways at shoulder level regular (supinated) curls

88 DB seated simultaneous two hands sideways at shoulder level regular (supinated) curls

89 DB standing simultaneous two hands sideways at shoulder level parallel curls

90 DB seated simultaneous two hands sideways at shoulder level parallel curls

91 DB standing simultaneous two hands sideways at shoulder level, reverse (pronated) curls

92 DB standing simultaneous two hands, inward circle parallel curls

93 DB standing overhead simultaneous two hands supinated triceps curls

94 DB seated overhead simultaneous two hands supinated triceps curls

96 **DB standing alternate overhead supinated triceps curls:** stand with DB parallel in hands, arms overhead with bent elbows, the latter in as a high position as possible. Keep abdominal muscles tight, face forwards, with the body held upright. Extend the elbows without changing body and arm position.

97 DB seated overhead alternate supinated triceps curls

98 **DB standing bent-over two hands parallel "kick-back" triceps curls:** standing in a bend over position. DB in hand in a parallel position. Arms bent with elbows as high as possible. The back could be curved or straight. Without changing the elbows' position straighten the arms with a fast motion, continuing all the way possible, feeling the contraction in the triceps muscles. Never let the elbows lowering, swinging or moving sideways.

99 DB seated bent-over two hands parallel "kick-back" triceps curls

100 DB standing bent-over alternate parallel "kick-back" triceps curls

101 **DB standing frontal simultaneous parallel press** standing with DB in hands flatfooted. Bodyweight is balanced from the balls of the feet toward the heels, with contracted abdominal muscles. The vertical line of action of the center of gravity should pass through ankle, hip and shoulder joints. Press the DB forward, keeping the bodyweight in the same vertical line. The pressing may be simultaneous or alternating, inward or outward rotated, or straight forwards with parallel (vertical), linear (horizontal) DB position, with hands in a pronated or supinated position.

102 DB standing frontal simultaneous linear supinated press

103 DB standing frontal simultaneous linear pronated press

104 DB standing frontal alternate parallel press

105 DB standing frontal simultaneous from parallel to linear supinated rotational press

106 DB standing frontal simultaneous from parallel to linear pronated rotational press

107 DB standing frontal simultaneous from linear supinated to parallel rotational press

108 DB standing frontal simultaneous from linear pronated to parallel rotational press

109 **DB standing simultaneous sideways parallel press:** DB lateral at shoulders level. DB position may be vertical or horizontal. The lateral pressing may be done straight sideways with DB in a vertical or horizontal position with pronated or supinated hand position

110 **DB standing flatfooted simultaneous two hands overhead parallel press:** stand with feet at shoulder width, DB over the shoulders. The DB position can be parallel, or linear, depending on the goals. Keep tight abdominal muscles, head looking forward. Press overhead without bending the knees or changing the body position. There are several variations of DB position during press:

(a) start and finish with parallel DB
(b) start with parallel DB and finish up with linear (in line) DB, doing a rotational movement
(c) start and finish with linear (in line) DB
(d) start with linear DB and finish up with parallel DB, rotating the arms with the palms facing each other
(e) start with linear DB and finish up with parallel DB, rotating the arms with the forehands facing each other (useful for swimming, diving, volleyball, basketball)
(f) simultaneous or alternating pressing.

111 **DB seated simultaneous two hands overhead parallel press:** as above, but sitting on the edge of a bench. Sit on gluteus maximus, not on hamstrings. Hook the feet under the bench or have a spotter step on the toes.

112 DB standing flatfooted alternate overhead parallel press

113 DB seated alternate overhead press

114 DB standing simultaneous up on toes two hands parallel overhead press

115 DB standing simultaneous two hands up on toes, rotation from parallel to supination overhead press

116 DB standing high knees walking in place and alternate parallel overhead press: standing, arms at shoulders level, in a parallel position. Regular walk. On each step press the opposite arm overhead, with head looking forward and complete arm extension on each step.

117 DB standing high knees running in place and alternate parallel overhead press

118 DB standing in quarter squat overhead parallel press

119 DB standing in full squat overhead parallel press

120 DB standing in half squat overhead parallel press: take the same standing position as in the military press, then bend the knees approximately to a half squat level. Balance between the heels and balls of the feet. Press overhead without changing your balance or head position, which should be looking straightforward with a very firm neck. If it is too difficult pressing overhead and there is a tendency to change the head position, use lighter DB and do not descend into a half squat but assume a higher position.

121 DB standing flatfooted simultaneous two hands overhead parallel push press. Stand with DB in each hand at shoulder level. During the exercise you must tight the neck and abdominal muscles. The head is looking straight ahead. Bend the knees less than a quarter squat, balance between the balls of the feet and the heels. Keep the shoulder-hip-ankle alignment in a perfect vertical line. A continuous pressing overhead movement follows the knee bend. Depending on one's goals, this exercise may be done flatfooted or up onto the toes. The DB position could be varied, as in the DB military press.

122 DB standing simultaneous up onto toes two hands parallel overhead push press

123 DB standing alternate up on toes parallel overhead push press

124 DB standing simultaneous two hands up on toes from parallel to pronated rotational overhead push press

125 DB standing simultaneous two hand overhead parallel jump push press. Like the Push Press, it can be connected with a jump, for different goals or sports (volleyball, basketball). Do not catch the load on straight knees in the recovery phase. The arm and knee bending must be very well synchronized.

126 DB standing flatfooted simultaneous two hands overhead parallel squat push press: standing with DB in each hand at shoulder level. Same body position as in DB push press. Squat with the DB at the shoulders, without changing the body's verticality. The flatfooted position should be kept. The knees must be pointed outward in the squat position, allowing to the hip's joint to be pushed between the heels. The back should be concave (arched), head looking forwards. Raise up from the squat, maintaining the trunk's relatively vertical position and pushing the DB overhead with a dynamic, explosive motion, flatfooted or coming up on toes (depending on coach's indication) and then recover again with bending the knees and getting in the squat position

127 DB standing flatfooted alternate overhead parallel squat push press

128 DB standing simultaneous overhead up on toes two hands parallel squat push press

129 DB standing alternate overhead up on toes parallel squat push press

130 DB standing simultaneous two hands parallel overhead squat jump push press

131 DB standing alternate parallel overhead squat jump push press

132 DB standing simultaneous two hands linear (pronated) overhead squat jump push press

133 DB standing simultaneous two hands from parallel to pronation rotational overhead squat jump push press

134 DB seated parallel incline bench press

135 DB seated linear (supinated) incline bench press

136 DB seated linear (pronated) incline bench press

137 DB seated rotational from parallel to linear (supinated) incline bench press

138 DB seated rotational from parallel to linear (pronated) incline bench press

139 DB standing parallel incline board press

140 DB standing linear (supinated) incline board press

141 DB hooked feet head down parallel decline bench press

142 DB hooked feet head down linear (supinated) decline bench press

143 DB lying on back parallel simultaneous bench press: With DB in the hands, stand in front of the bench on its edge with your back towards it. Set the DB at the thighs close to the hip joint with a curling or swinging motion. DB may be parallel, or linear (in the same line) position. With a curved back, lie on the back, holding the DB on the thighs. After finishing the lying on back phase, set the arms on or next to the trunk, or at different angles, depending on your goals. The press overhead could be, regular (up and down) in a parallel or linear DB position, or with inward or outward rotation.

144 DB standing two hands from platform power clean

145 DB one-hand (R+L) standing from platform power clean

146 DB standing two hands from hang below the knee power clean

147 DB standing one-hand (R+L) from hang below the knee power) clean

148 DB standing from hang two hands above the knee power clean

149 DB standing one-hand (R+L) from hang above the knee power clean

150 DB standing from platform: two hands power clean & push jerk: same technique as one-hand power clean and push jerk. In both, one and two hand power cleans, the push jerk may be replaced by push press or split jerk, depending on the workout goals.

151 DB standing from platform one-hand (R+L) power clean and push jerk: a DB in one-hand and the other arm next to the trunk or bent at the waist. Bend over with straight back, DB close to the shin. The head is in a straight line with the neck and back, looking forwards 1-2 yards. The DB may be set on platform or held in a hang position. The power clean and push jerk technique is like for the regular power clean and push jerk with BB. See the Olympic Weightlifting technique chapter.

152 DB standing from hang below the knee two hands power clean and push jerk

153 DB standing from hang below the knee one-hand (R+L) power clean and push jerk

154 DB standing from hang above the knee two hands power clean and push jerk

155 DB standing from hang above the knee one-hand (R+L) power clean and push jerk

156 DB standing from platform two hands power clean and split jerk

157 DB standing one-hand (R+L) power clean from platform and split jerk

158 DB standing from hang below the knee two hands power clean and split jerk

159 DB standing from hang below the knee one-hand (R+L) power clean and split jerk

160 DB standing from hang above the knee two hands power clean and split jerk

161 DB standing from hang above the knee one-hand (R+L) power clean and split jerk

162 DB standing simultaneous straight supinated frontal arm raise:
(a) DB in hand at the hip level in parallel or linear position. With tight abdominal muscles, bodyweight on flat feet, balancing between the balls of the feet and heels, raise the arms straight up in front of the chest. The hand position may be held the same (parallel, or linear) or changed during the movement (from parallel in linear, or from linear in parallel); may also be executed with alternating or simultaneous DB movement.

(b) DB held in a parallel or linear position, bent-over, in a vertical line at shoulder level. Balance the body between the balls of the feet and hells. The back may be straight or curved. Head looking down 3-4 feet ahead of the toes. Raise the arms straight up and forwards, in front of the chest, as high as possible without straining the muscles and tendons of the shoulders. The hand position may be parallel or linear; one may also change the start position (linear or parallel) during the exercise to one in the opposite position (parallel or linear). The exercise may be executed in an alternating or simultaneous way.

163 DB standing simultaneous straight frontal arm raise, rotating from pronation to supination

164 DB standing alternate straight pronated frontal arm raise

165 DB standing simultaneous horizontal arms cross-scissors: Straight arms in front of the chest with DB in line. Abdominal and chest muscles tight, bodyweight balanced between the balls of the feet and heels. Cross the arms in front of chest repeatedly. The scissors may be short or wide arc. The wide variation may be executed with same DB position (linear) or during adduction of the arms, one may change the hand pronated position to supination. Pay special attention to coordination, to avoid DB collision during the crossing movements. Another variation is to do this exercise overhead.

166 DB standing alternate straight frontal arm raise, DB rotation from pronation to supination

167 DB standing simultaneous straight pronated lateral arm raise: Raise the pronated arms from hip level, straight up, sideways with shoulder abduction. As a variation, the hands in the start position may be held supine. One may start in a pronated and finish up in a supinated position, or start in a supinated position and finish up in a pronated one. The exercise may also be done finishing on flatfeet, or up on the toes. Keep abdominal muscles tight and vertical shoulder-hip-ankle alignment.

168 DB standing simultaneous straight supinated lateral arm raise

169 DB lying on stomach on a bench forward parallel straight arm raise: same exercise just lying on a bench. The head should be in front of the bench.

170 DB lying on stomach on a bench forward pronated straight-arm raise

171 DB lying on stomach on a bench forward supinated straight-arm raise

172 DB standing overhead in front of chest simultaneous inside circle: DB in hand at the shoulder level, but wider than the shoulders, in a parallel position. Press the DB upward in an incline-oblique adduction direction. After the arms reach the straight elbow position, use abduction to pull the arms close to each other. Then keeping the elbows outside, bend the arms and continue the exercise. Breathe in when the arms meet in front of the chest and start the outside-upward circular movement, and breathe out on the arms downward movement. Hold the DB continuously in a parallel position. As a variation, after the overhead arm extension, flex the pronated wrists, push down the arms close to each other and to the chest, (holding the elbows higher than the wrist), then supinate the wrist and continue the exercise as an oblique overhead press.

173 DB standing overhead in front of chest simultaneous outside circle: the same as above, only in a reverse direction. As a variation, after the DB is pressed overhead in front of the chest, rotate the wrists outwards, and press down in a circular movement, holding the elbows higher than the wrist, and keep the hands pronated. When the hands move close to each other in front of the stomach in a curled supinated position, press the arms up in front of the chest and continue the exercise.

174 DB standing, in front of chest horizontal parallel outward rotation.

175 DB standing in front of chest horizontal parallel inward rotation: DB in hands parallel to one another, bent at chest level. Start the rotation by moving the hands sideways from the trunk. When the elbows are relatively straight, continue the motion horizontally forwards, with DB meeting in front of the chest. Before touching the DB, pull the arms toward the chest and continue the exercise as described above. As a variation, at the moment when the arms move close to the chest, pronate the fist; finish the arms extension with pronated hands. Then rotate back the hands in a face-to-face position, holding the DB parallel.

176 DB up and down shrugs: standing with DB in hands, straight elbows, in front of thighs, in a linear pronated hand position, with the fingers touching the thighs. Elbows are turned out and shoulders turned in. The head looks straight ahead with a firm chin position. Perform the up and down shrugging action as many times as prescribed, without bending the elbows.

177 DB standing lateral frontal arms rotation

178 DB standing lateral backward arms rotation

179 DB standing bent-over parallel outside rotation: same exercise like standing, just now bend over. It looks almost as a bent over row Shoulders at same level with the hip, back straight, head looking forward, holding the bodyweight from balls of the feet toward the heels.

180 DB standing bent-over parallel inside rotation: like the standing version of this exercise, with the back held as straight as possible. The shoulders should be at same height as the hips, head looking forwards, and the body balanced from balls of feet toward the heels.

181 DB lying on stomach on bench frontal arms raise

182 DB lying on back on bench overhead pull-over: lie on back on a bench, with shoulders at the back edge of the bench with parallel dumbbell position in each hand. Press arms overhead like in a bench press, then bending your elbows gradually let the dumbbells backward behind the head. Holding your elbows parallel, stretch your shoulder slowly and when you feel a comfortable shoulder stretch, with an energetic movement extend your elbows and bring the arms with a parabolic motion up to the start position Pay big attention to a continuous movement. Never stop while you are in the parabolic arm extension phase

183 DB standing bent-over fly: standing with light DB in hand. Bend over, hold the body balance toward the heels, feel more pressure in the hamstrings instead of the lower back. The back should be curved (not straight or hyper-extended) the DB are held in a parallel position straight down, but never straighten the elbows completely. Stay flatfooted, but balance toward the heels, raise your arms laterally upwards as far as is possible without excessive strain.

184 DB lying on stomach, bench fly:

185 DB lying on back, bench fly:

(a) the DB could be in parallel or linear position. The flying movement must be executed sideways with straight elbows.

(b) perform with light weights. Elbows almost straight and stretch the shoulders as far as you feel comfortable, but never extend your elbows completely. Do not consider it as a variation of the bench press, with wide hand position.

186 DB Javorek's shoulder routine. Perform with alternate hand: curl your forearm to your chest all the way up to your chin. Press your hand up next to your chin, with palm looking backward. When you are reaching the straight-arm position overhead (close to your ear) turn your palm downward and let sideways your "slightly bent" arm down Continue the exercise with the other arm.

187 DB standing swimming breaststroke imitation in a quart bent-over position. Keep your chin up. Imagine that the water is up to your lips.

188 DB standing overhead swimming crawl imitation: standing, with DB in line at shoulder level. Imitate the full range of motion of the crawl swimming movement. The trunk should be in a rigid position. Attention on alternating and relaxed arms coordination.

189 DB standing frontal-horizontal swimming crawl imitation: same exercise, just the arms are hold in front of the chest, executing the same motion.

190 DB standing in a quart bent-over position swimming crawl imitation: same exercise, just in a bent-over position. The shoulders should be at the same horizontal line with the hip, bodyweight balanced from balls of the feet toward the heels, and the head looking down in front of the body, three-four feet ahead of toes.

191 DB seated swimming crawl imitation

192 DB seated bent-over swimming crawl imitation

193 DB lying on stomach on bench crawl imitation: same exercise, just lying on stomach on a bench, high enough to be safe for the rotational arms movements. The whole trunk from the collarbones and legs should be on the bench, and the head in front of it.

194 DB standing, swimming backstroke imitation: DB in hand at the hip level, with full range of motion, imitate the back stroke motions. Hold the trunk straight, with tight abdominal muscles.

195 DB seated swimming backstroke imitation

196 DB standing bent-over swimming backstroke imitation: DB in hand, bent-over, holding the bodyweight between balls of the feet and heels, with full range of motion, imitates the backstroke motions.

197 DB lying on back on bench swimming backstroke imitation

198 DB standing single leg continuous (L, R) lunge: standing, DB in hands, at hip level. Holding body weight on one leg, step forward with the opposite leg. The forward leg should land first on the heels and then continue the amortization phase on flat foot, by a rolling movement of the foot. There are four variations : (a) short step, and the back knee is bent accentuated; (b) large step, with relatively straight back knee; (c) simultaneous leg lunges; (d) alternating leg lunges. It is very important to hold the trunk upright. Do not lean the trunk forwards on the thigh of the front leg, or backward.

199 DB standing alternate leg (R+L) lunge

200 DB standing single leg continuous step back lunge

201 DB standing alternate leg step back lunge

202 DB lunge walk: standing, DB in hand at hip level. Step forward with high knees, push the leading leg forward, landing on heels and gradually roll onto the flat foot. Hold the trunk vertically, back knee as straight as possible, with all toes on the floor. Without slowing the stepping motion, push the back foot forward; bend the knee of the back leg, raising it as high as possible, continuing the lunge walk with the next giant step.

203 DB split jump

204 DB standing, on different height box, single leg continuous step-ups: standing, with DB in hand, at hip level. There are several variations possible:

(a) the height of the step-up box could be different, depending on goals

(b) different arms movements: i) arms raise overhead on each step-up (simultaneous, or alternating) depending on goals; ii) overhead press (alternating or simultaneous) on each step-up; iii) alternating arm swing forward or in front of the chest; iv) alternating or simultaneous arms rotation, forward or backward, on each step-up.

(c) single (simultaneous) leg step-up

(d) alternating leg step-up

(e) combination of alternating and simultaneous leg step-ups.

As general safety rules: step-up with full foot on the box, not just the toes, hold the trunk straight, do not lean forwards, tighten the abdominal muscles; increase the weight gradually, do not try too heavy DB for the different variations.

205 DB standing, on different height box, alternate leg (R+L) step-ups

206 DB standing, on different height box-single (R+L) plus alternate leg step-up on box

207 DB with arms upward swings alternating or single leg step-ups

208 DB with From Hip High Pull Snatch step-up on box

209 DB with one-hand overhead press step-up on box

210 DB Javorek's step-ups cardiovascular program

211 DB standing squat jumps: DB in hand at hip level, feet shoulders width. Hold the arms sideways, use a regular squat (flatfoot, straight back, looking forward) and jump up. On the recovery phase, land on the balls of the feet and roll back onto the flat foot.

212 DB standing long jump: DB in hand, in parallel position, with bent elbows, slightly forward. Swing the arms backward, roll bodyweight back on heels, then roll through flat foot forwards onto the toes, swing the arms, but not higher than head level, jump forwards, land on heels and roll onto the flat foot. During this exercise the shoulders and the abdominal muscles are tight. Do not land with exaggerated knee bend. The knee joint angle should be not less than 115-120 degree.

213 DB frog jumps: standing, DB in hand, next to the hip, in parallel position. Bent-Over, bending the knees, and touching the floor with the DB in front of the feet. Without stopping in this squatting position, jump up and forwards, swinging the arms forwards up to the eyes level, then continue the exercise with a fast regrouping of the trunk on the initial squatting position. Do not hyperextend the back. Keep the abdominal muscles contracted during the jump phase.

214 DB stair, sand stair or shredded rubber box run

215 DB stair, sand stair or shredded rubber box double leg jump bounding

216 DB Javorek's Complex exercise # 1.

217 DB Javorek's Complex exercise #2.

218 DB Javorek's Complex exercise # 3.

219 DB Javorek's Complex exercise # 4.

220 DB Javorek's Complex exercise # 5. and so on. Actually I already developed 16 Dumbbell Complex exercises.(See chapter 13.)

Dumbbells or Machines in Genral Sports Conditioning

Dumbbell quarter squat & up on toes raise to armpit.

Dumbbell raise to Armpit & split jump.

Dumbbell split jump - proper technique.

Dumbbell split jump-improper technique.

Dumbbell Quarter squat & up on toes raise to armpit.

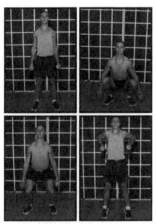

Dumbbell squat & up on toes raise to armpit.

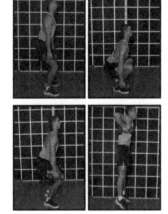

Dumbbell squat jump raise to armpit.

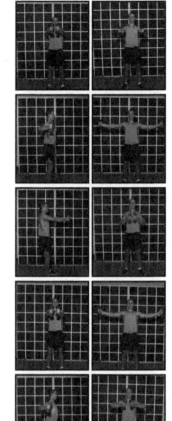

Dumbbell in front of chest inward-outward rotation.

Dumbbell in front of chest alternate horizontal forward press.

Dumbbell in front of chest arm cross.

Dumbbell lateral arm raise.

Dumbbell oblique pronated curls.

Dumbbell overhead triceps curls.

Dumbbell lying on your back pull over.

Chapter 12

Dumbbell bent over fly.

Dumbbell bent over kick back triceps curls.

Dumbbell squat under upright row.

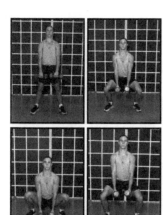

Dumbbell squat upright row.

Dumbbell press from squat.

Dumbbell seated bench press.

Dumbbell overhead flat footed press.

Dumbbell overhead final phase of squat jump or jump push press.

Dumbbell squat push press start.

Dumbbell overhead up on toes press, or final phase of squat or push press.

Dumbbell seated incline bench press.

Dumbbell upright row.

Dumbbell two hand power jerk.

Dumbbell squat jump.

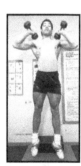

Dumbbell squat jump.

Dumbbell step up on box.

Dumbbell step-back lunges.

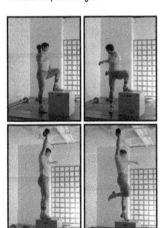

Dumbbell step up for throwers.

Dumbbell running in place & overhead press.

Dumbbell running in place & raise to armpit.

Dumbbell one hand high pull snatch.

Dumbbell one hand power clean & push jerk.

Dumbbell one hand power snatch.

Dumbbell one hand squat snatch.

Dumbbell complex 1 upright row.

Dumbbell complex 1 high pull snatch.

Dumbbell complex 1 squat push press.

Dumbbell complex 1 bent over row.

Dumbbell complex 1 high pull snatch.

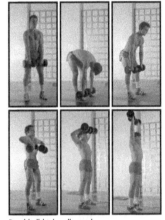

Dumbbell high pull snatch.

Dumbbell special exercises :standing long jump. Proper and improper technique.

Chapter 12

Chapter 13
Combined Dumbbell and Barbell Training

Dumbbell and Barbell Complex Exercises

In recent years, I have seen the term "combination lifts" used more and more in sports conditioning circles, and I published an article about combination lifts, "General Conditioning with Complex # 1 and #2", in 1988 in the NSCA Journal (volume 10, No. 1, 1988, pages 34-37).

First, a definition: combination lifts comprise two or more free weight exercises that are combined in a non-stop, continuous movement. Although some conditioning specialists believe these lifts consist of just a few exercise combinations, like mostly a power clean and another exercise, or a power snatch and another exercise combination, in reality, the list is much larger. (While the barbell combination exercises of the Clean & Jerk are technically Weightlifting exercises, they still are combination lifts because they are being executed without rest.)

The main purpose of combination lifts is to improve and stimulate neuromuscular coordination, increase the workout load and intensity, stimulate the musculoskeletal system, increase the free weight program's cardiovascular quality, and make a program more dynamic and efficient.

The number of combination exercises is unlimited, depending on the coach's knowledge and creativity, the gym's equipment and apparatus, and the goals of the coaches and athletes. In my training programs, I make a distinction between the major lift exercises: snatch, clean, jerk variations, pulls, squats, and auxiliary or assistant exercise combinations, and I categorize them as follows:

Categories of Combination Exercises
A. Simple two major lift exercise combination
B. Complex multiple major lift exercise combinations
C. Auxiliary or assistance lift exercise combinations
Here are some variations of these three categories:
A. Simple Two Major Lift Combination Exercises (Four Major Groups)

Variation 1. Simultaneous repetition of two major lift exercises.
Example: BB from platform snatch grip pull x 4 + BB from platform split snatch x 6

Variation 2. Alternating repetition of two major lift exercises.
Examples:

BB from platform wide, snatch grip pull x 3 + BB from platform split snatch x 2 + BB from platform wide, snatch grip pull x 3 + BB from platform split snatch x 3, etc.
BB from the rack back squat x 4 + BB behind the head squat jump x 4 + BB from the rack back squat x 4 + BB behind the head squat jump x 4
BB from the rack back squat x 10 + BB behind the head wave squat x 25 + BB from the rack back squat x 10
Depending on the goals and a coach's imagination, these combinations-variations are probably unlimited

I. Clean (power, squat or split) and other exercise combination - the clean can be executed from platform, from hang or from box:
BB from platform power clean + BB from the chest overhead press
BB from platform power clean + BB from the chest push press
BB from platform power clean + BB from the chest push jerk
BB from platform power clean + BB from the chest split jerk
BB from platform power clean + BB from the chest front squat
BB from platform power clean + BB from the chest front squat push press

II. Snatch (power, squat or split) and other exercise combination - the snatch can be executed from platform, from the box or from hang:
BB from platform power snatch + BB overhead squat
BB from platform power snatch + BB behind the head press
BB from platform power snatch + BB behind the head push press
BB from platform power snatch + BB behind the head squat push press platform snatch (power, squat or split)

III. Pull and other exercise combination B the pull could be:
Single knee bent pull
Straight knees (dead lift style) pull
Regular so-called double knee bent pull
Clean grip pull or wide, snatch grip pull
From platform, from box or standing on box:
BB from platform single knee bent wide, snatch grip pull + BB from the platform clean (power, squat or split)
BB from platform single knee bent clean grip pull + BB from platform clean (power, squat or split)
BB from platform single knee bent clean grip pull + BB from above the knee up and down shrug

IV. Squat and other Exercises:
BB from rack front squat + BB from rack, from the chest press
BB from rack back squat + BB from rack, behind the head (different grips) press
BB from rack front squat + BB from chest push press (various grip width)
BB from rack back squat + BB from rack, behind the head (different grips) push press
BB from rack back squat + BB from rack, behind the head (different grips) squat push press
BB from rack back squat + BB from rack, behind the head good morning
BB from rack back squat + BB from rack, behind the head squat jump
BB from rack wave squat + BB from the rack back squat jump
BB from rack back squat jump + BB from the rack wave squat
BB from rack back squat + BB from rack wave squat
BB from rack wave squat + BB from rack back squat
BB from rack front squat + BB from platform squat clean
BB from rack front squat + BB from platform power clean
BB from rack, from the chest single leg (or alternate leg) step back, lunges + BB from platform split clean
BB from rack behind the head toe raise + BB back squat
BB from rack, behind the head toe raise + BB wave squat
BB from rack, behind the head toe raise + BB quarter squat
BB from rack, back quarter squat + BB Straight Knees Toe Raise
BB from rack, back quarter squat + BB back squat
BB from rack, back quarter squat + BB wave squat
BB from rack, back quarter squat + BB back squat jump

B. Complex, Multiple Major Lift Exercise Combinations

Variation 1. Pull + clean (squat, power, split) + press variations (military press, push press, squat push press)

Example: BB from platform clean grip pull + BB from platform squat clean + BB from the chest push press

Variation 2. Pull + clean (squat, power, split) + jerk variations (push jerk, split jerk)

Example: BB from platform clean grip single knee bent pull + BB from platform split clean + BB from platform power clean push jerk

Variation 3. Pull, wide, snatch grip + snatch variations (squat, power, split) + press variations (wide grip behind the head press, wide grip behind the head push press, wide grip behind the head squat push press) + overhead squat + behind the head push jerk

Example: BB from hang below the knees wide, snatch grip pull + BB from platform power snatch + BB wide, snatch grip overhead squat + BB wide, snatch grip behind the head push jerk

C. Assistance Exercise Combinations

I have always believed that the order of exercises in a combination should be chosen in a way that avoids interruption, providing a smooth, continuous motion. I also think it is very important to finish this smooth progression of the drill with the combination's most dynamic movement, thus stimulating the athlete's explosive qualities. It is really very simple to combine several assistance exercises to provide this smooth progression.

Depending on the goals of the individual athlete, the numbers of variations are probably unlimited. To satisfy my own coaching goals, I personally developed five BB complex exercises that I use in all sports conditioning. These complexes are included in the following two groups that I consider the major assistance exercise combination groups:

1. Complex Combination Lift Assistance Exercises with Barbells

- Javorek's BB Complex exercise # 1 and #2: BB upright rows + BB high pull snatch + BB squat push press + BB behind the head good morning + BB bent-over row (Complex # 1 is just one cycle performed with 6 repetitions of each exercise. Complex #2 is performed with 3 repetitions of each exercise, repeating the five exercise cycle two or three times from the beginning in a non stop continuous order.)

- Javorek's BB Complex # 3 and 4: BB Supinated curls x 6 + BB upright row x 6 + BB From Hip High Pull Snatch x 6 + BB bent-over row x 8 + BB behind the head press x 6 + BB behind the head good morning x 10 + BB behind the head squat push press x 6 + BB Supinated curls x 6 + BB upright row x 6(Complex # 3 is one cycle performed of each exercise. Complex # 4 is performed with 3 repetitions of each exercise, repeating the five exercise cycle two or three times from the beginning in a non stop continuous order.)

- Javorek's BB Complex # 5 : BB medium grip upright row x 6 + BB medium grip high pull snatch x 4 + BB medium grip bent-over row x 8 + BB back squat push press x 6 + BB upright row x 6 + BB behind the neck alternate leg step-ups on box x (14+14) + BB high pull snatch x 4 + BB good morning x 16 + BB back squat jump x 8

- BB wide, snatch grip upright rows + BB wide, snatch grip high pull snatch + BB wide, snatch grip overhead squat + BB behind the head squat push press + BB back squat jumps

- BB wide, snatch grip upright rows + BB bent-over rows + BB wide, snatch grip high pull snatch + BB behind the head good morning + BB wave squat + BB behind the head push press + BB back squat jumps

2. Complex Combination Lift Exercises with Dumbbells:

(a) With one-hand

- DB one-hand high pull snatch + DB one-hand power clean + DB one-hand squat push press + DB one-hand power snatch

(b) With two hands

- Javorek's DB Complex exercise 1 and 2: DB upright rows + DB high pull snatch + DB squat push press + DB bent-over rows + DB high pull snatch (Complex # 1 is just one cycle performed with 6 repetitions of each exercise. Complex #2 is performed with 3 repetitions of each exercise, repeating the five exercise cycle two or three times from the beginning in a non stop continuous order).

- Javorek's DB Complex # 3 and 4: DB Supinated curls x 6 + DB upright row x 6 + DB bent-over row x 6 + DB high pull snatch x 6 + DB parallel overhead press x 6 + DB rotational curls x 6 + DB upright row x 6 + DB squat or squat jump push press x 6 (Complex 3 is just one cycle performed with 6 repetitions of each exercise. Complex 4 is performed with 3 repetitions of each exercise, repeating the five exercise cycle two or three times from the beginning in a non stop continuous order).

- DB raise to armpit + DB high pull snatch + DB parallel curls + DB bent-over rows + DB parallel press + DB high pull snatch

- DB rotational press + DB rotational push press + DB squat push press + DB push jerk

- DB Supinated curls + DB upright rows + DB parallel press + DB parallel push press + DB high pull snatch

I use combination lift exercises on a year-round basis. The number of repetitions and sets differ, depending on goals and preparation periods that automatically demand different intensities.

In the first part of a workout I use combination exercises as a general warm-up drill. But I also use different variations in the complete workout when I have specific goals for the training. These might include stimulating muscular hypertrophy, strength, specific endurance, muscular tone, muscular coordination or recuperation.

A coach should first teach the proper technique of execution of each exercise, then establish the 1 R.M. for each individual exercise. After these should come the mandatory steps, gradually combining more and more exercises. This is the time when the coach should determine the proper number of repetitions, sets, and intensities that will give the maximum benefit to athletes preparing for a specific sport.

Here are examples of two variations of intensities in preparation for two different sports B cross country and throwing. Both of them incorporate Javorek's DB Complex # 1 and Complex #2 exercises three times a week:

Cross Country

Monday - Javorek's DB Complex #2

For cross-country, I start with the Complex #2's normal three cycles (I consider one cycle three repetitions of each of the five exercises in a continuous, non-stop manner). I gradually increase the number of cycles from three to four and then to five. A sample schedule utilizing the five exercises in a Complex #2 might be:

	Week 1	Week 2
Week 3		
DB upright row x 5 cycles	x 3 cycles	x 4 cycles
DB high pull snatch x 5 cycles	x 3 cycles	x 4 cycles
DB squat push press x 3 cycles	x 4 cycles	x 5 cycles
DB bent-over row x 5 cycles	x 3 cycles	x 4 cycles
DB high pull snatch x 5 cycles	x 3 cycles	x 4 cycles

As the athletes progress, I also increase the repetitions. For example, you can increase to four repetitions of each exercise in four cycles, five reps in four cycles, and then five reps in five cycles. The intensities (intensity is taken from 1 RM of DB upright row) are between 30% and 50% - two sets at 30% ; two at 35% and two at 40% . We perform a total of six sets of Complex #2 a day.

Wednesday - Javorek's DB Complex # 1

For cross country, I start with six repetitions of each of the five exercises per cycle, then gradually increase the reps to seven and then eight per exercise. The intensities are between 30% and 60% (intensity taken from 1 R.M. of DB upright row). We perform a total of six sets of Complex # 1 a day.

Friday - Javorek's DB Complex #2

Six sets of Complex #2, incorporating the same principles of increased repetitions as were done on Monday. I always ask for higher intensities on Friday. For cross country, these would range from 40% to 60% .

Thrower Preparatory Period

Monday - Javorek's DB Complex # 1

Six sets at 50% to 70% intensity - one set at 50% , one set at 55% x , one set at 60% x , two sets at 65% x , and one set at 70% .

Wednesday - Javorek's Complex #2

Six sets with three repetitions of each exercise per cycle at 50% to 65% intensity - two sets at 50% x , two at 55% , one at 60% , and one at 65% .

Friday - Javorek's Complex # 1

Six sets at 60% to 75% intensity - two sets at 60% , two at 65% , one at 70% and one at 75% .

One of the biggest benefits of combination lifts is the ability to use them with novice athletes. Actually, in my opinion, every young athlete should start exercising with assistance exercises and their combinations. The wonderful thing about free weights is the possibility of choosing the intensity, repetition and sets based on any individual athlete's preparation level and goals.

Like any other exercise form, teaching the combination lifts requires professionalism, patience, perseverance, and the gradual involvement of the athlete into a whole combination lifting program.

Javorek's BB and DB Complex Conditioning Exercises

As the head coach of the Clujana Sports Association in Cluj (Kolozsvar, Klausenburg), Romania, I personally experienced two very efficient exercise combinations which I presented for my first class coaching board examination (the highest coaching level in Romania). This experiment took place over a three-year period involving more than three hundred different preparation level athletes.

The main purposes for these exercises were to figure out an easier way to do an exercise complex, which would change the monotony of a workout, and at the same time have a greater influence on the neuro-muscular and osteo-muscular system. The two exercises I am referring to are called Complex # 1 and Complex #2 with BB or DB.

These exercises can be used as a general warm-up in the first part of a workout using lighter weight and only two-three sets, or as a complete part of a workout with a specific purpose.

What is interesting is that both complexes have the same exercises in their circuit, the only difference being the number of repetitions of each and the number of exercise cycles. However is a difference between the BB and DB Complex Exercises, which I will explain later.

My determination for doing this experiment with these two complex exercises it was to try and give more variation to a workout; to try and change the same day-to-day workout routines; to "shock" an athlete's muscles after a hard competitional season and to stimulate the muscular growth or endurance in the preparatory period; to try and build up a specific endurance and cardio-vascular capacity, a specific muscle tone, a good muscular coordination, and a perfectly balanced, well-developed, harmonious musculature. Being an athlete I learned that the coaches do not give too much time and attention for rebuilding an athlete muscular-tendonal system. Also I learned that after each competitional season I had a greater improvement if I introduced in my workout some unusual, non-specific exercises, which were stimulating my whole physiological system. My personal belief and the other sports conditioning coaches, who tried with their athletes my Complex # 1 and 2 exercises, is that they can influence considerably any athlete's improvement.

One of the athletes from this experimental group was Dragomir Cioroslan, former USA Weightlifting Olympic Training Center, Colorado Springs, Co. residence program head coach (bronze medallist in 75 kg (165 lb) weight class, 1984 Summer Olympic Games, Los Angeles), who, from the beginning of his career as a weightlifter regularly practiced these Complexes. He showed an incredible rhythm of improvement from a beginning bodyweight of 37 kg (82 lb) in August 1969 to 63 kg (138 lb) in the spring and 65 kg (143 lb) in the autumn of 1972. His snatch improved from 35 kg (77 lb) in August 1969 to 100 kg (220 lb) in the spring and 107.5 kg (236 lb) in the autumn of 1972. In the Clean & Jerk he went from 50 kg (110 lb) in August 1969 up to 137.5 kg (302.5 lb) in the spring and 142.5 kg (313.5 lb) in the autumn of 1972. Another example could be Aurel Sirbu, who for several years was a member of Romanian National Weightlifting Team, and I started working out with him at age of three, under strict medical supervision, practicing six times a week. His program of course was different from the other older athletes, but still Complex # 1 and Complex #2 was a big part of his program.

I could continue with several examples because I had such a very good overall improvements in all the athletes tested. I do not mean to imply that my athletes improved and continue to improve only because of these exercises, but I can say that I am convinced about of their benefits. What is most important to remember is not to abuse these exercises, but to figure out the best period to utilize them as a special preparatory and conditioning exercise. It is also very important to find the optimal weight for each athlete to have the required benefit of these exercises. Like for any other combined exercises the intensity must be taken from the most difficult exercise. Another thing to remember is that it is essential to have perfect body posture, perfect technique of execution and full range of motion when performing these exercises. It is important not to change the order of the exercises or to do them with too fast a rhythm.

The upright rows should be performed with knees slightly flexed, especially with beginners and children. If it is necessary, bending the knees will allow the legs to assist an athlete when raising the bar or DB to the chin.

The Complex exercises could be a very good test-guideline for a coach. There is some correlation between performance and the best result of Complex # 1 or 2. For example, Istvan Tasnadi from A.S. Clujana (silver medallist in the 110 kg (242 lb) weight class, 1984 Summer Olympic Games, Los Angeles) did his best Complex # 1 with 120 kg (264 lb) snatching 175 kg (385 lb) and Clean and Jerk 225 kg.(495 lb). Wesley Barnett, 1992 US National 100 kg (220 lb) class, Weightlifting champion, my athlete at J.C.C.C between 1988 - 1990, performed Complex # 1 with 85 Kg (187 kb) for a 147.5 kg (324 lb) snatch and 175 kg (385 lb) Clean & Jerk.

During the preparatory phase, these exercises can be performed every day for 2-3 sets or the recommended 5 to 6 sets three times per week. Throughout the competitive period, these exercises should be used as a warm-up, performing 2 sets every day plus 3 times per week with a heavier weight for 3 sets. Four weeks before the main competition, the heavy weight complexes should be omitted from the workout altogether.

For the sport of Weightlifting, all exercises generally are done on flat-feet, but for other sports the athletes should rise onto the toes on last phase of high pull snatch, and of the squat push press.

Complex # 3 and 1 are designed for muscular hypertrophy and basic strength improvement. Complex #2 and # 4 are designed for endurance sports, since they are intended to have a marked effect on remarkable cardiovascular fitness Both Complex exercises improve will power and determination, but Complex #2 and # 4 are aimed at psychologically developing the greatest fighting spirit and tenacity.

BB and DB Complex # 3 and Complex # 4 were developed in 1995 for persons who are working out at home in a basement where the ceiling is low. Also persons with back injuries feel more comfortable with Complexes # 3 and # 4.

Javorek's BB Complex # 1

BB Upright Row	x 6
BB High Pull snatch	x 6
BB Behind the Head Squat Push Press	x 6
BB Behind the Head Good Morning	x 6
BB Bent-Over Row	x 6

Perform in a non-stop, continuous order as listed above :

- 5 exercises x 6 repetitions = 30 repetitions/set. The number of repetitions may be changed to satisfy different goals. Long distance runners, skiers, bikers, wrestlers may gradually increase the number of repetitions and the weight to achieve a higher quality specific endurance and power endurance. In the beginning, one should do only a partial or the full Complex # 1 with fewer repetitions. Is up to the coach to decide when one should practice the full exercise and increase the loading.

Javorek's BB Complex #2

BB Upright Row	x 3
BB High Pull snatch	x 3
BB Behind the Head Squat Push Press	x 3
BB Behind the Head Good Morning	x 3
BB Bent-Over Row	x 3

These five exercises are executed in a non-stop, continuous order, with three repetitions constituting a cycle. Perform in a non-stop, continuous order as listed above. Go through the exercises once for beginners, then gradually increase the number of cycles in one set to two, to three, and even four for different endurance sports, depending on the coach's decision. For strong cardiovascular stimulation, increase the number of repetitions for each exercise gradually, starting for example, with the third

cycle, then the third, next the second, and finally for all three cycles in one set. Never hurry to increase the number of repetitions. Always stress perfect technique of execution and full range of motion.

During my coaching years at Texas A&M (College Station, Texas) and my teaching and coaching years at Johnson County Community College, I tried to devise new complex exercises with dumbbells, since these generally are more specific to most sports conditioning and very suitable for working with a large number of athletes at the same time. After various attempts, I concluded that I just needed to adjust my BB Complex exercises to ones with dumbbells. For example, Upright Rowing, High Pull Snatch, Squat Push Press, Bent-Over Rowing, are also easy to do with DB. I only needed to change the Good Morning Exercise. For that reason I considered it necessary to modify the order of the exercises, so as to exercise the different body segments logically. In the DB Complex exercises, instead of Good Mornings, I introduced the High Pull Snatch. To provide some necessary balance, the Upright Rows, bent-over Rowing and finally, High Pull Snatches follow High Pull Snatch and Squat Push Press, again.

A general recommendation for both barbell and dumbbell Complex exercises is that they should be done without a break in the motion. For example, after the Upright Row, do not stop at hip level but continue with the bent-over phase of the High Pull Snatch; or after the last High Pull Snatch, stop with the BB or DB overhead and move to the next exercise, the Squat Push Press.

Javorek's BB Complex # 3

BB Regular (Supinated) Curls	x 6
BB Upright Row	x 6
BB High Pull Snatch Regular or from Hip	x 6
BB Bent-Over Row	x 8
BB Behind The Head Press	x 6
BB Behind The Head Good Morning	x 10
BB Behind The Head Squat Push Press	x 6
BB Behind The Head Quarter Squat & Up On Toes	x 10
BB In Front Of Thighs Special Good Mornings	x 10

Perform in a non-stop, continuous order as listed above.

Javorek's BB Complex # 4

BB Regular (Supinated) Curls	x 3
BB Upright Row	x 3
BB High Pull Snatch Regular or from Hip	x 3
BB Bent-Over Row	x 3
BB Behind The Head Press	x 3
BB Behind The Head Good Morning	x 5
BB Behind The Head Squat Push Press	x 3
BB Behind The Head Quarter Squat & Up On Toes	x 5
BB In Front Of Thighs Special Good Mornings	x 5

Perform in a non-stop, continuous order as listed above. Go through the exercises twice for beginner, and three times for more advanced athletes. For different sports the number of repetitions for each exercise and the number of cycles (the 9 exercises in a non-stop, continuous order constitute one cycle) could vary, determined by the coach or personal trainer. To make this complex more cardiovascular demanding, increase the number of repetitions for each exercise. For example, first increase only the third cycle from 3 to 4 reps, then the third and second cycles from 3 to 4 reps, and finally all three cycles' repetitions up to four. Every coach should determine by monitoring progress which combination is best for every individual athlete at a given time, although he should never hurry to increase the number of repetitions, and thereby compromise technical proficiency or safety.

Javorek's BB Complex # 5

BB Medium Grip Upright Row	x 6
BB Medium Grip High Pull Snatch	x 4
BB Medium Grip Bent-Over Row	x 8
BB Back Squat Push Press	x 4
BB Alternate Leg Step-up on Box	x 8+8
BB Good Morning	x 16
BB Medium Grip Upright Row	x 6
BB Medium Grip High Pull Snatch	x 4
BB Back Squat Jump	x 8

Perform in a non-stop, continuous order as listed above :

The above Complex comprises 9 exercises for a total of 72 repetitions per set, although the number of repetitions may be changed in order to satisfy different goals. For example, long distance runners, skiers, bikers and wrestlers may gradually increase the number of repetitions and the weight, in order to achieve greater specific endurance and power endurance. In the beginning, one should practice only part of or the full Complex 5 with fewer repetitions, as determined by the coach If the ceiling is low, certain exercises may be performed seated.

Javorek's Barbell Complex # 6.

Barbell Medium Grip Upright Row	x 3
Barbell Medium Grip High Pull Snatch	x 2
Barbell Back Squat Push Press	x 3
Barbell Alternate Leg Step Up On Box or	x 3+3
Barbell Alternate Leg Lunges	x 3+3
Barbell Medium Grip Upright Row	x 3
Barbell Medium Grip Bent Over Row	x 3
Barbell Medium Grip High Pull Snatch	x 2
Barbell Behind The Head Quarter Squat	x 4
Barbell Good Morning	x 4
Barbell Back Squat Jump	x 2

Perform In A Non-Stop, Continuous order As Listed Above. Go Through The Exercises Twice For Beginner, Three Times For More Advanced Athletes. For Different Sport The Number Of Repetitions For Each Exercise And The Number Of Cycles (The 10 Exercises In A Non-Stop, Continuous order Is Equal With One Cycle) Could Vary, Determined By The Coach or Personal Trainer. For A Remarkable Cardio-Vascular Stimulation Of This Exercise, The Number Of Repetition For Each Exercise Could Be Gradually Increased. For Example : First Just The Third Cycle From Three To Four Reps, Then The Third And Second Cycles From Three To Four Reps, And Finally All Three Cycles' Repetitions To Be Increased Up To Four. But Every Coach Could Find Out Which Is The Best Combination For Every Individual Athlete At A Given Time. But Never Hurry In Increasing The Number Of Repetitions, And Always Keep In Mind The Perfect Execution. If Low Ceiling, Certain Exercises Perform Seated

Javorek's Barbell Complex # 7

Barbell Medium Grip Upright Row	x 4
Barbell High Pull Snatch	x 4
Barbell Quarter Squat	x 8
Barbell Squat Push Press	x 4
Barbell Good Morning	x 6
Barbell Back Squat Jump	x 4
Barbell Overhead Triceps Curls	x 4
Barbell Narrow Grip Upright Row	x 4
Barbell From Hip High Pull Snatch	x 3
Barbell Wave Squat +Back Squat + Squat Jump	x 15+6+4

Perform In A Non-Stop, Continuous order As Listed Above :

10 Exercises With A Total Of 66 Repetitions/Set. The Number Of Repetitions Can Be Changed In order To Satisfy Different Goals. Long Distance Runners, Skiers, Bikers, Wrestlers Could Gradually Increase The Number Of Repetitions And The Weight, To Achieve A Higher Quality Specific Endurance And Power In Domain Of Endurance. On The Beginning Should Be Practiced Just Partial or The Integral Complex Vii, But With Less Repetitions. Is Up To The Coaches Decision To Practice The Full Exercise And To Increase The Weight Also. If Low Ceiling, Certain Exercises Perform Seated.

Javorek's Barbell Complex # 8

Barbell Wide Grip Upright Row	x 6
Barbell From Hip High Pull Snatch	x 6
Barbell Behind The Head From Half Squat Press	x 8
Barbell Wide Grip Squat Push Press	x 4
Barbell Wide Grip Shrug	x 6
Barbell Press Under High Pull Snatch	x 6
Barbell Good Morning	x 10
Barbell Wide Grip Bent Over Row	x 6
Barbell From Hip High Pull Snatch	x 6
Barbell Good Morning	x 10
Barbell Back Squat Jump	x 8

Perform In A Non-Stop, Continuous Order As Listed Above :

11 Exercises With A Total Of 76 Repetitions/Set. The Number Of Repetitions Can Be Changed In Order To Satisfy Different Goals. Long Distance Runners, Skiers, Bikers, Wrestlers Could Gradually Increase The Number Of Repetitions And The Weight, To Achieve A Higher Quality Specific Endurance And Power In Domain Of Endurance. On The Beginning Should Be Practiced Just Partial Or The Integral Complex Vii, But With Less Repetitions. Is Up To The Coaches Decision To Practice The Full Exercise And To Increase The Weight Also. If Low Ceiling, Certain Exercises Perform Seated.

Javorek's DB Complex # 1

DB Upright Row	x 6
DB High Pull Snatch	x 6
DB Squat Push Press	x 6
DB Bent-Over Row	x 6
DB High Pull Snatch	x 6

Perform in a non-stop, continuous order as listed above.

Five exercise x 6 reps = 30 reps/set

Javorek's DB Complex #2

DB Upright Row	x 3
DB High Pull Snatch	x 3
DB Squat Push Press	x 3
DB Bent-Over Row	x 3
DB High Pull Snatch	x 3

Note A: Perform in a non-stop, continuous order as listed above. Go through the exercise cycle once for beginners, then gradually increase the number of cycles to two, to three, or as many as the coach or other specialist considers necessary. Increase the number of repetitions for each exercise gradually to enhance its cardiovascular conditioning effects. For example, first increase only the third cycle from 3 to 4 reps, then the third and second cycles from 3 to 4 reps, and finally all three cycles' repetitions up to four. Every coach should determine the best combination for every individual athlete at a given time and never hurry to increase the number of repetitions, while always emphasizing technical perfection.

Javorek's DB Complex # 3

DB Regular (Supinated) Curls	x 6
DB Upright Row	x 6
DB Bent-Over Row	x 6
DB From Hip High Pull Snatch	x 6
DB Parallel Press	x 6
DB Squat Push Press	x 6
DB Upright Row	x 6
DB Rotational Curls	x 6

Perform in a non-stop, continuous order as listed above.

Javorek's DB Complex # 4

DB Regular (supinated) Curls	x 3
DB Upright Row	x 3
DB Bent-Over Row	x 3
DB From Hip High Pull Snatch	x 3
DB Parallel Press	x 3
DB Squat Push Press	x 3
DB Upright Row	x 3
DB Rotational Curls	x 3

Perform in a non-stop, continuous order as listed above.

Perform as detailed in Note A and pay special attention to posture, full range of motion, and technique of execution and stable rhythm of execution. Choose the weight properly so that it is matched to the most difficult exercise in each complex; increase the weight for each set, especially for the last set.

Javorek's DB Complex # 5

DB Upright Row	x 6
DB Alternating Leg Lunges	x 12+12
DB Squat Push Press	x 6
DB Parallel Curls	x 8
DB Alternating Leg Step-up on Box	x 10+10
DB High Pull Snatch	x 6
DB Quarter Squat & Up On Toes Raise To Armpit	x 10
DB Lunge Walk	x 16+16

Javorek's Dumbbell Complex # 6. Exercise

DB. Squat Under Upright Row	x 3
DB. From Hip High Pull Snatch	x 3
DB. Supinated Curls	x 3
DB. Alternate Leg Step Ups On Boxor	x 3+3
DB. Alternate Leg Lunges	x 3+3
DB. Parallel Squat Push Press	x 3
DB. Parallel Bent Over Row.	x 3
DB. In Front Of Thighs Special Good Morning	x 3
DB. Incline Bench Press	x 3
DB. Squat Upright Row	x 3
DB. Squat Jump Raise To Armpit	x 3

Perform In A Non-Stop, Continuous order As Listed Above. Go Through The Exercises Twice For Beginner, Three Times For More Advanced Athletes. For Different Sport The Number Of Repetitions For Each Exercise And The Number Of Cycles (The Nine Exercises In A Non-Stop, Continuous order Is Equal With One Cycle) Could Vary, Determined By The Coach or Personal Trainer. For A Remarkable Cardio-Vascular Stimulation Of This Exercise, The Number Of Repetition For Each Exercise Could Be Gradually Increased. For Example: First Just The Third Cycle From Three To Four Reps, Then The Third And Second Cycles From Three To Four Reps, And Finally All Three Cycles' Repetitions To Be Increased Up To Four. But Every Coach Could Find Out Which Is The Best Combination For Every Individual Athlete At A Given Time. But Never Hurry In Increasing The Number Of Repetitions, And Always Keep In Mind The Perfect Execution. If Low Ceiling, Certain Exercises Perform Seated

Javorek's Dumbbell Complex # 7
Shoulder Reconditioning Program

DB. Hands Bent To Chest Inward-Outward Circle	x 6+6
DB. In Front Of Chest Inward-Outward Rotation	x 6+6
DB. From Hip High Pull Snatch	x 6
DB. Lateral Pronated Arm Raise	x 6
DB. Bent Over Fly	x 6
DB. Bent Over "Kick Back" Triceps Curls	x 6
DB. Breast Stroke Imitation	x 6
DB. Bent Over Parallel Straight Arm Forward-Backward Raise	x 8
DB. Frontal Pronated Arm Raise	x 6
DB. Rotational Bent-Over Row	x 8
DB. Javorek's Shoulder Routine	x 6+6

Perform In A Non-Stop, Continuous order As Listed Above. If Low Ceiling, Certain Exercises Perform Seated.
Six Exercises x 6 Reps = 36 Reps/Set. + 3 Exercises x 12 Reps(6+6)= 36 Reps/Set. Total 72 Reps/Set

Javorek's Dumbbell Complex # 8
Shoulder Reconditioning Program

DB. Hands Bent To Chest Inward-Outward Circle	x 3+3
DB. In Front Of Chest Inward-Outward Rotation	x 3+3
DB. From Hip High Pull Snatch	x 3
DB. Lateral Pronated Arm Raise	x 3
DB. Bent Over Fly	x 3
DB. Bent Over "Kick Back" Triceps Curls	x 3
DB. Breast Stroke Imitation	x 3
DB. Bent Over Parallel Straight Arm Forward-Backward Raise	x 3
DB. Frontal Pronated Arm Raise	x 3
DB. Rotational Bent-Over Row	x 3
DB. Javorek's Shoulder Routine	x 3+3

Perform In A Non-Stop, Continuous order As Listed Above. Go Through The Exercises Twice For Beginner, Three Times For More Advanced Athletes. For Different Sport The Number Of Repetitions For Each Exercise And The Number Of Cycles (The Nine Exercises In A Non-Stop, Continuous order Is Equal With One Cycle) Could Vary, Determined By The Coach or Personal Trainer. For A Remarkable Cardio-Vascular Stimulation Of This Exercise, The Number Of Repetition For Each Exercise Could Be Gradually Increased. For Example: First Just The Third Cycle From Three To Four Reps, Then The Third And Second Cycles From Three To Four Reps, And Finally All Three Cycles' Repetitions To Be Increased Up To Four. But Every Coach Could Find Out Which Is The Best Combination For Every Individual Athlete At A Given Time. But Never Hurry In Increasing The Number Of Repetitions, And Always Keep In Mind The Perfect Execution. If Low Ceiling, Certain Exercises Perform Seated

Javorek's Dumbbell Complex # 9

DB. Lying On Your Back On Bench Fly	x 14
DB. Lying On Your Back On Bench Pull Over	x 12
DB. Lying On Your Back On Bench, Overhead Straight Arm Raise	x 12
DB. Lying On Your Back On Bench Inward & Outward Rotation	x 8+8
DB. Lying On Your Back On Bench In Front Of Chest Scissors	x 10+10
DB. Lying On Your Back On Bench Breast Stroke Imitation	x 12

Perform In A Non-Stop, Continuous order As Listed Above. If Low Ceiling, Certain Exercises Perform Seated.
Three Exercises x 12 Reps = 36 Reps/Set. + 1 Exercise x 14 Reps/Set + 1 Exercise (8+8) 16 reps/Set + 1 Exercise (10+10) 20 reps/Set= Total 86 Reps/Set

Javorek's Dumbbell Complex # 10

DB. Inward Outward Rotation	x 8+8
DB. Lateral Arm Raise	x 12
DB. Frontal Arm Raise	x 12
DB. Breast Stroke Imitation	x 12
DB. From Hip High Pull Snatch	x 12

Perform In A Non-Stop, Continuous order As Listed Above. If Low Ceiling, Certain Exercises Perform Seated.
Four Exercises x 12 Reps = 48 Reps/Set. + 1 Exercise (8+8) 16 Reps/Set = Total 64 Reps/Set

Javorek's Dumbbell Complex # 11

DB. Squat Upright Row	x 8
DB. Supinated Curls	x 8
DB. Alternate Leg Lunges	x 10+10
DB. Squat Push Press	x 10
DB. Squat Under High Pull Snatch	x 10
DB. Squat Jump Push Press	x 8

Perform In A Non-Stop, Continuous order As Listed Above. If Low Ceiling, Certain Exercises Perform Seated. Three Exercises x 8 Reps = 24 Reps/Set. + 2 Exercises x 10 Reps = 20 Reps/Set+ 1 Exercise (10+10) 20 Reps/Set = Total 64 Reps/Set

Javorek's Dumbbell Complex # 12

DB. Supinated Curls	x 8
DB. Parallel Push Press	x 8
DB. Linear Bent Over Row	x 8
DB. Alternate Leg Lunges	x 8+8
DB. Parallel Squat Push Press	x 8
DB. Alternate Leg Step-Ups	x 8+8
DB. Squat Jump	x 8

Perform In A Non-Stop, Continuous order As Listed Above. If Low Ceiling, Certain Exercises Perform Seated.
Five Exercises x 8 Reps = 40 Reps/Set. + 2 Exercises x (8+8) 16 Reps = 32 Reps/Set = Total 72 Reps/Set

Javorek's Dumbbell Complex Just Friday 13th

I am not superstitious, but to have "some fun" in this very demanding and pretty hard conditioning, I developed the "Friday 13-th Complex". So I perform this exercise with my athletes on every Friday 13-th, or I use it just as a form of "punishment" if they don't work hard enough. Also in a situation when I see signs of boring with a program, I like to make "changes" in the routines. So I just announce them, that being a real "sweat heart" I make adjustment in the program, and we just perform 3 sets of Friday 13th.!

DB. Upright Row	x 13
DB. Push Press	x 13
DB. Bent Over "Kick Back" Triceps Curls	x 13
DB. Single Leg Lunges	x 13+13
DB. Squat Push Press	x 13
DB. From Hip High Pull Snatch	x 13
DB. Squat Under Upright Row	x 13
DB. Bent Over Row	x 13
DB. Alternate Leg Lunges	13+13
DB. Squat Upright Row	x 13
DB. Supinated Curls	x 13
DB. High Pull Snatch	x 13
DB. Squat Jump Push Press	x 13

Javorek's Dumbbell Complex Just Friday # 13
For Shoulder Reconditioning
Perform with very light dumbbells - 10% to 20% of 1 RM

DB. Inward-Outward Circle	x 13+13
DB. Bent Over Fly	x 13
DB. Lateral Arm Raise	x 13
DB. Breast Stroke Imitation	x 13
DB. Supinated Parabolic Curls	x 13
DB. Frontal Pronated Arm Raise	x 13
DB. Back Stroke Imitation	x 13
DB. Inward-Outward Rotation	x 13
DB. From Hip High Pull Snatch	x 13
DB. In Front Of Chest Scissors	x 13+13
DB. Free Style Imitation	x 13
DB. Bent Over "Kick Back" Triceps Curls	x 13
DB. Javorek's Shoulder Routine	x 13

Javorek's Dumbbell Complex # 14

DB. Bent Over Kick Back Triceps Curls	x 10
DB. Bent Over Fly	x 12
DB. Overhead Triceps Curls	x 10
DB. From Hip High Pull Snatch	x 10
DB. In Front Of Chest Supinated Parabolic Curls	x 10
DB. Squat Jump Push Press	x 8

Perform In A Non-Stop, Continuous order As Listed Above. If Low Ceiling, Certain Exercises Perform Seated.
Four Exercises x 10 Reps = 40 Reps/Set. + 1 Exercise x 12 Reps = 12 Reps/Set+ 1 Exercise 8 Reps/Set = Total 60 Reps/Set

Javorek's Dumbbell Complex # 15

DB. Squat Upright Row	x 8
DB. Single Leg Lunges	x 8+8
DB. Squat Under High Pull Snatch	x 8
DB. Overhead Parallel Press	x 8
DB. Alternate Leg Lunges	x 8+8
DB. Squat Under Upright Row	x 8
DB. Supinated Curls	x 8
DB. Single +Alternate Leg Lunges	x 4+4+4+4
DB. Squat Jump Raise To Armpit	x 8

Perform In A Non-Stop, Continuous order As Listed Above. If Low Ceiling, Certain Exercises Perform Seated.

Six Exercises x 8 Reps = 48 Reps/Set. + 2 Exercises x (8+8) 16 Reps = 32 Reps/Set+ 1 Exercise (4+4+4+4) 16 Reps/Set = Total 96 Reps/Set

Javorek's Dumbbell Super Complex # 16

DB. Squat Under Upright Row	x 6
Plyo Push Ups (Clapping)	x 6
DB. Alternate Leg Step Ups On Box or	x 8+8
DB. Alternate Leg Lunges	x 8+8
DB. Parallel Squat Push Press	x 6
Pull Ups On High Bar	x 6
DB. In Front Of Thighs Special Good Morning	x 6
Parallel Bar Dips	x 6
DB. High Pull Snatch	x 6
DB. Supinated Curls	x 6
On Box Plyo Push Ups	x 6+6
DB. Squat Jump Raise To Armpit	x 6
DB. Parallel Squat Push Press	x 6
DB. Squat Jump	x 6

Perform In A Non-Stop, Continuous order As Listed Above. Do Not Forget: Perfect Body Posture; Full Range Of Motion; Perfect Technique Of Execution; Stable Rhythm Of Execution; Always Choose The Weight Properly; Accommodate To The Most Difficult Exercise; Increase The Weight For Each Set, But Mandatory For The Last Set.

General Instruction for Javorek's Conditioning and Weightlifting Programs

As general instructions for all of my conditioning and specific Weightlifting programs, I would summarize these as follows: with the

Barbell Upright Row (narrow, medium and wide grip),

Barbell High Pull Snatch (medium and wide grip),

Barbell Bent-Over Row (medium and wide grip),

Barbell Power Snatch,

Barbell Power Clean,

Barbell Behind the Head Push Press,

Barbell Military Press,

Barbell Bench Press, do testing up to 95-100 % of the maximum potential just on Fridays or Saturdays, depending on which day the specific exercise is scheduled for in the entire program. For a realistic 1 RM testing on some of these exercises, we still need to respect the written program. So, after finishing the respective day's sets and repetitions for one of the before mentioned exercise, we could then test the athlete for a 1 Rep Max, which is a indices of the athlete's momentary potential after completing the program

Another variation of testing is, when after the warm-up, we test for 1 RM of the respective day's potential, and after that starts the daily program calculating the intensity from that respective day's 1 RM. The philosophy of this method is that the daily maximum is changing during a week, (and during the day) and is easier to avoid stress or injuries if we know the real daily potential of an athlete.

It is important to respect the order of the exercises in the program schedule, and to be patient in not expecting immediate results or improvement. Generally, the athlete will feel tired after the first days on the program, but gradually the body will adapt to the higher demands. If the program seems too long, divide it in two or three separate sessions (which actually improves an athlete's recovery, and makes the program more efficient). If dividing the program is not possible, shorten it by eliminating as many sets as necessary, but keeping the ratio of sets between the exercises the same. Or could be better, just doing as many exercises as possible from the program and continuing the next time from where it was interrupted. In this way a weekly program may extend to take one and a half or two weeks. Besides suiting individual goals and the available time, this approach still makes it possible to achieve the desired results.

Correct technique is also very important. It gives the athlete a chance to achieve personal goals by preventing injuries and avoiding incorrect body posture. It is a bad idea to change the conditioning program for any minor competitions. Thus, I do not stop my conditioning program before a minor meet, and continue with the scheduled intensity. If possible, I run my conditioning program on the day of the competition, before or after the event.

The rest to exercise ratio depends on the individual's physical and psychological condition. Periodically I check heart pulse rate, bodyweight and blood pressure to gain a clearer idea about the athlete's fitness level. A significantly increased heart rate combined with high blood pressure and decreased bodyweight can be a very strong indicator of overtraining, fatigue or sickness. Never workout with fever! Never workout on injured muscles, or body parts! First treat it and get healthy! Beside the very serious health complications it is proven that it takes much longer to recover working out with sickness or injuries.

When using combination exercises, we must remember that the intensity must be taken from the most difficult exercise in the combination. For example, in the Javorek's DB.Complex # 1., which contains the upright row, high pull snatch, squat push press and bent-over row, the most difficult exercise for the average athlete is the upright row. Therefore, the intensity for the entire DB.Complex # 1 must be taken from the percentage (intensity) of the upright row. In the back squat, push press combination, the push press is more difficult, so the intensity should be taken from it and not from the back squat.

Chapter 14
Dumbbell Programs

This chapter presents several DB programs which can make any programs more enjoyable, by offering more "flavor" in preparation, avoiding monotony and giving the whole musculoskeletal system a different stimulus.

Shorthand Code: It is convenient to abbreviate long descriptions of exercise programs by using a suitable shorthand code. In this case, the well-established shorthand from Weightlifting is especially suitable. For example, the following routine:

DB Parallel Press + High Pull Snatch
60% 8+8   60% 8+8   65% 8+6   70% 8+6

means that one does the DB Press with 60% of 1RM for 8 reps then High Pull Snatch with 60% of 1RM for 8 reps for 2 sets; DB Press with 65% of 1RM for 8 reps then High Pull Snatch with 65% of 1RM for 6 reps for 1 set; the finally the DB Press70% of 1 RM for 8 reps then High Pull Snatch with 70% of 1 RM for 6 reps. In Combination exercises always take the 1 RM from the most difficult exercise (the lowest 1 RM)!.

Javorek's General Fitness DB Conditioning Program

1. DB Upright Row
60% 10   65% 10   70% 8   75% 8   80% 6

2. DB Quarter Squat & Up On Toes Raise to armpit + From Hip High Pull Snatch
60% 8+8   60% 8+8   65% 8+6   70% 8+6
75% 8+6   80% 8+5

3. DB Press + Push Press + High Pull Snatch
60% 6+6+6 65% 5+5+6 70% 4+5+6 75% 4+5+6 80% 4+5+6

4. DB Bent-Over Row + Squat Push Press
65% 8+6 65% 8+6 70% 8+6 80% 6+5 90% 3+3

5. DB High Pull Snatch
65% 10   70% 8   75% 6   80% 5   85% 3   90% 2

6. DB Upright Row + Push Press
60% 10+8   65% 10+8   70% 8+6   75% 6+6

7. DB Parallel Curls + High Pull Snatch
60% 10+8   65% 10+6   70% 8+6   75% 6+4
80% 4+2   85% 3+2

8. DB Push Press + Squat Jump Push Press
60% 8+6   65% 8+6   65% 8+6   70% 8+4
75% 6+4

9. Javorek's DB Complex # 1 or 3
55% 1   60% 1

10.Javorek's DB Complex #2 or 4
45% 1   50% 1

Javorek's Power Athletes DB Program # 1

1. DB Squat Upright Row
60% 10   65% 10   70% 8   75% 8   80% 6

2. DB Squat Raise To Armpit + Parallel Push Press
60% 8+8   60% 8+8   65% 8+6   70% 8+6
75% 8+6   80% 8+5

3. DB Press + Push Press + High Pull Snatch
60% 6+6+6   65% 5+5+6   70% 4+5+6   75% 4+5+6
80% 4+5+6

4. DB Bench Press + Squat Push Press
65% 8+6   65% 8+6   70% 8+6   80% 6+5
90% 3+3

5. DB High Pull Snatch
65% 10   70% 8   75% 6   80% 5   85% 3   90% 2

6. DB One-Hand Power Snatch (Left + Right)
70% 4+4   75% 4+4   80% 3+3   85% 3+3

7. DB One-Hand Squat or Split Snatch (Left + Right)
60% 4+4   65% 4+4   70% 3+3   75% 3+3
80% 2+2   85% 2+2

8. DB One-Hand Power Clean (Left + Right)
70% 3+3   75% 3+3   75% 3+3   80% 2+2
85% 2+2

9. Javorek's DB Complex # 1 or 3
35% 1   40% 1

10. Javorek's DB Complex #2 or 4.
30% 1   35% 1

Javorek's DB Program #2

1. DB Squat Under Upright Row
60% 10   65% 10   70% 8   75% 8   80% 6

2. DB Quarter Squat & Up On Toes Raise To Armpit + From Hip High Pull Snatch
60% 8+8   60% 8+8   65% 8+6   70% 8+6   75% 8+6   80% 8+5

3. DB Parallel Press + Parallel Push Press + High Pull Snatch
60% 6+6+6   65% 5+5+6   70% 4+5+6   75% 4+5+6
80% 4+5+6

4. DB Bent-Over Row + Squat Jump Raise To Armpit
65% 8+6   65% 8+6   70% 8+6   80% 6+5
90% 3+3

5. DB High Pull Snatch
65% 10   70% 8   75% 6   80% 5   85% 3   90% 2

6. DB Squat Upright Rows + High Pull Snatch
60% 10+6   65% 10+6   70% 8+6   75% 6+4

7. DB Parallel Curls + Overhead Parallel Press
60% 14+6   65% 12+6   70% 10+6   75% 8+3
80% 6+2   85% 4+2

8. DB Parallel Push Press + Parallel Squat Push Press
60% 6+6   65% 6+6   65% 6+6   70% 6+4
75% 6+3

9. Javorek's DB Complex # 3. or 5.
50% 1   60% 1

10. Javorek's DB Complex #2 or 4.
40% 1   50% 1

Javorek's DB Program # 3

1. DB Upright Row
60% 10   65% 10   70% 8   75% 8   80% 6

2. DB Quarter Squat & Up On Toes Raise To Armpit
    + Squat Upright Row
60% 8+8   60% 8+8   65% 8+6   70% 8+6
75% 8+6   80% 8+5

3. DB Press + Push Press + Upright Row
60% 6+6+6   65% 5+5+6   70% 4+5+6   75% 4+5+6
80% 4+5+6

4. DB Bent-Over Row + Push Press
65% 8+6   65% 8+6   70% 8+6   80% 6+5
90% 5+3

5. DB Squat Push Press
60% 10   65% 10   70% 8   75% 6   80% 5   85% 3   90% 2

6. DB Bent-Over "Kick-Back" Triceps Curls
40% 14   50% 12   55% 12   60% 10
65% 10   70% 8

7. DB Upright Row + Parallel Bench Press
60% 10+10   65% 10+8   70% 8+8   75% 8+6
80% 5+6

8. DB Regular(Supinated) Curls + Jump Push Press
60% 12+8   65% 12+6   70% 10+6   75% 8+5
80% 6+3   85% 5+2

9. DB Press + Push Press + Squat Jump Push Press
60% 6+6+6   65% 6+6+6   65% 6+6+6   70% 5+6+6
75% 5+5+4   80% 4+4+4

10. Dumbbell Supinated (Regular) Curls x 10 + Upright Row x 8
    + Press x 6 + Bent-Over Row x 8 + Squat Push Press x 6.
50% 1   60% 1

11. DB Upright Row x 8 + Press x 6 + Supinated (Regular) Curls x 6 + Push
Press x 6 + Upright Row x 8 + Squat Push Press x 6 + Squat Jump x 6 +
Split Jump x 10
50% 1   55% 1

Javorek's Endurance DB Program # 1

1. DB Upright Row
50% 18   50% 18   55% 16   60% 14   65% 10   70% 8

2. DB Quarter Squat & Up On Toes Raise To Armpit
    + From Hip High Pull Snatch
40% 10+10   40% 10+10   45% 10+10   50% 10+8
55% 10+6

3. DB Press + Push Press + Upright Row
40% 8+8+8   45% 8+8+8   50% 8+8+8 5   5% 6+6+6
60% 6+6+6

4. DB Bent-Over Row + Push Press
45% 14+10   45% 14+10   50% 12+10   55% 12+10
60% 14+10

5. DB Squat Push Press
40% 16   45% 16   50% 14 14   55% 12   60% 10   65% 10   70% 8

6. DB Bent-Over "Kick-Back" Triceps Curls
30% 18   35% 18   40% 14   45% 12   50% 10   60% 8

7. DB Upright Row + Parallel Curls
40% 15+15   45% 14+14   50% 12+12   55% 10+10
60% 10+10

8. DB Regular (Supinated) Curls + Squat Push Press
40% 16+10   45% 16+10   50% 14+10   55% 12+8
60% 10+8   65% 8+6

9. DB Press + Push Press + Squat Push Press
40% 8+8+8   45% 8+8+8   45% 8+8+8   50% 8+8+8
55% 6+6+6   60% 6+6+6

10. Dumbbell Supinated (Regular) Curls x 16 + Squat Upright Row x 12
    + Parallel Press x 10 + Bent Over Row x 16 + Squat Push Press x 12
50% 1   55% 1

11. DB Upright Row x 14 + Parallel Press x 10 + Supinated (Regular) Curls
    x 12 + Push Press x10 + Squat Upright Row x 12 + Squat Push Press x
    10 + Squat Jump x 10 + Split Jump x 20
50% 1   55% 1

Chapter 15
Dumbbell and Barbell Circuit Conditioning

Circuit training is a variation of exercising which allows a large group of athletes to train at the same time. In a circuit program, instead of continuing several sets with the same exercise, you move to the next exercise downward on the columns instead of completing all sets of one

exercise and then moving to the next. Doing just one set of a given exercise and then followed by one set of a totally different exercise also gives the previous muscle group a chance to recover. In order to be accurate in choosing the right weight of DB or BB, you must first test the whole list of exercises in each circuit program or on the "Introductory" exercise list.

Before you start any circuit program you must master the technique of each exercise. In the Introductory Program you will find a list of the total exercises used with DB, BB, dips bar, high fixed bar, medicine balls and so forth in the following 38 circuits.

The rest interval between the sets depends on several factors such as endurance, cardiovascular, hypertrophy and strength and may vary from 15 seconds to 1-2 minutes.

Javorek's Dumbbell & Barbell Circuit Introductory Program

	Day 1	Day 2	Day 3
1. Dumbbell Inward-Outward Rotation	x 10+10	x 10+10	x 10
2. Dumbbell Bent Over Fly	x 16	x 14	x 10
3. Dumbbell Bent Over Kick Back Triceps Curls	x 14	x 14	x 10
4. Dumbbell Lying On Your Back On Bench Pull Over	x 14	x 14	x 10
5. Dumbbell From Hip High Pull Snatch	x 16	x 12	x 10
6. Dumbbell Supinated (Regular) Curls	x 20	x 12	x 10
7. Dumbbell Parallel Press	x 12	x 12	x 10
8. Dumbbell Parallel Curls	x 20	x 14	x 10
9. Dumbbell Lying On Bench Fly	x 16	x 16	x 10
10. Dumbbell High Pull Snatch	x 12	x 10	x 10
11. Dumbbell Rotational Curls	x 20	x 14	x 10
12. Dumbbell Push Press	x 12	x 10	x 10
13. Dumbbell Jump Push Press	x 10	x 10	x 10
14. Dumbbell Parallel Squat Push Press	x 10	x 10	x 10
15. Dumbbell Squat Jump Push Press	x 10	x 10	x 10
16. Dumbbell Lateral Arm Raise	x 16	x 16	x 10
17. Dumbbell Rotational Bent Over Row	x 20	x 16	x 10
18. Dumbbell Upright Row	x 20	x 16	x 10
19. Dumbbell Squat Upright Row	x 12	x 10	x 10
20. Dumbbell Squat Under Upright Row	x 10	x 10	x 10
21. Dumbbell Pronated Bent Over Row	x 20	x 16	x 10
22. Dumbbell Raises To Armpit	x 20	x 16	x 10
23. Dumbbell Squat Raise To Armpit	x 12	x 10	x 10
24. Dumbbell Jump Raise To Armpit	x 12	x 10	x 10
25. Dumbbell Squat Jump Raise To Armpit	x 12	x 10	x 10
26. Dumbbell Bench Press	x 20	x 14	x 10
27. Bent Knees-Hooked Feet Sit-Ups	x 20	x 20	x 20
28. Crunches	x 15	x 15	x 15
29. Half Jack Knife	x 20	x 20	x 20
30. Dumbbell Single Leg Lunges	x 12+12	x 12+12	x 12+12
31. Dumbbell Alternate Leg Lunges	x 14+14	x 14+14	x 14+14
32. Dumbbell Lunge Walk	x 20+20	x 20+20	x 20+20
33. Javorek's "Special Good Morning"	x 14	x 14	x 14
34. Dumbbell "In Sequences" Upright Row	x 20	x 16	x 16
35. Dumbbell "In Sequences" Supinated Curls	x 20	x 16	x 16
36. Dumbbell Split Jumps	x 12	x 12	x 12
37. Bent Knees-Hooked Feet Sit-Ups	x 20	x 20	x 20
38. Crunches	x 20	x 20	x 2
39. Half Jack Knife	x 20	x 20	x 20
40. Dumbbell Squat Jumps	x 8	x 8	x 8
41. Dumbbell Lunge Walk	x 20+20	x 20+20	x 20+20
42. Dumbbell Javorek's Complex # 1	x 1	x 1	x 1
43. Dumbbell Javorek's Complex #2	x 1	x 1	x 1
44. Bent Knees-Hooked Feet Sit-Ups	x 20	x 20	x 20
45. Crunches	x 20	x 20	x 20
46. Half Jack Knife	x 20	x 20	x 20
47. Dumbbell Squat Under High Pull Snatch	x 14	x 12	x 10
48. Dumbbell Single Leg Step Up On Box	x 12+12	x 12+12	x 12+12
49. Dumbbell Alternate Leg Step Up On Box	x 14+14	x 14+14	x 14+14

50. Javorek's "Special Good Morning"
x 14   x 14   x 14

51. Barbell Back Squat
x 10   x 10   x 10

52. Barbell Wave Squat
x 30   x 30   x 30

53. Barbell Squat Jump
x 6   x 6   x 6

54. Barbell Toes Raise
x 15   x 15   x 15

55. Barbell Quarter Squat & Up On Toes
x 10   x 10   x 10

56. Up-Stair Double Leg Bounding
x 12   x 12   x 12

57. Up-Stair Double Leg Zig-Zag Bounding
x 12   x 12   x.12

58. Up-Stair Run-Jump & Sprint
x 3   x 3   x 3

59. Up-Stair Sprint
x 3   x 3   x 3

Javorek's Introductory BB Circuit Program

    Day 1   Day 2   Day 3

1. BB Narrow Grip Upright Row
x 16   x 12   x 10

2. BB Behind The Head Press
x 16   x 12   x 10

3. BB Medium Grip Upright Row
x 16   x 12   x 10

4. BB Medium Grip From Hip High Pull Snatch
14   x 14   x 10

5. BB Behind The Head Push Press
x 14   x 14   x 10

6. Bent Knees-Hooked Feet Sit-Ups
x 20   x 20   x 20

7. Crunches
x 20   x 20   x 20

8. Half Jack-Knives
x 20   x 20   x 20

9. BB Medium Grip High Pull Snatch
x 12   x 12   x x 10

10. BB Wide Grip Upright Row
x 16   x 14   x 10

11. BB Squat Push Press
x 12   x 10   x 10

12. BB Supinated Curls
x 16   x 14   x 10

13. BB Medium Grip Bent-Over Row
x 16   x 12   x 10

14. BB Overhead Triceps Curls
x 14   x 13   x 10

15. BB In Hand Javorek's Special Good Morning
x 14   x 14   x 14

16. BB Behind The Head Jump Push Press
x 10   x 10   x 10

17. BB Behind The Head Good Morning
x 14   x 14   x 14

18. Bent Knees-Hooked Feet Sit-Ups
x 20   x 20   x 20

19. Crunches
x 20   x 20   x 20

20. Half Jack-Knives
x 20   x 20   x 20

21. BB From Platform Power Clean
x 8   x 8   x 8

22. BB Medium Grip Bench Press
x 14   x 12   x 10

23. BB Behind The Head Squat Jump Push Press
x 10   x 10   x 10

24. High Bar Pull-Ups- Pronated Grip
x ~   x ~   x ~

25. BB Medium "Clean Grip" Up & Down Shrug
x 18   x 18   x 16

26. Bent Knees-Hooked Feet Sit-Ups
x 20   x 20   x 20

27. Crunches
x 20   x 20   x 20

28. Half Jack-Knives
x 20   x 20   x 20

29. BB Wide Grip From Hip High Pull Snatch
x 14   x 12   x 10

30. BB Behind The Head Half Squat Press
x 12   x 12   x 10

31. BB Back Squat
x 12   x 10   x 10

32. BB Wide Grip High Pull Snatch
x 10   x 10   x 10

33. Parallel Bars - Dips
x ~   x ~   x ~

34. BB In Hand Javorek's Special Good Morning
x 14   x 14   x 14

35. BB Behind The Head From Squat Press
x 12   x 12   x 10

36. BB Wave Squat (4+1 Cycle)
x 30   x 30   x 30

37. BB Alternate Leg Lunges
x 12+12   x 12+12   x 12+12

38. Bent Knees-Hooked Feet Sit-Ups
x 20   x 20   x 20

39. Crunches
x 20   x 20   x 20

40. Half Jack-Knives
x 20   x 20   x 20

41. BB Squat Under High Pull Snatch
x 10   x 10   x 10

42. BB Alternate Leg On Box Step-Up
x 10+10   x 10+1   x 10+10

43. BB Front Squat
x 10   x 10   x 10

44. BB Back Squat Jump
x 6   x 6   x 6

45. BB Behind The Head Good Morning
x 14   x 14   x 14

46. BB Javorek's Complex # 1
x 1   x 1   x 1

47. BB Javorek's Complex #2
x 1   x 1   x 1

48. Up-Stair Double Leg Bounding
x 12   x 12   x 12

49. Up-Stair Double Leg Zig-Zag Bounding
x 12   x 12   x 12

50. Up-Stair Run-Jump & Sprint
x 3   x 3   x 3

51. Up-Stair Sprint
x 3   x 3   x 3

52. BB From Platform Power Snatch
x 6   x 6   x 6

53. BB From Hang Below The Knee Power Snatch
x 6   x 6   x 6

54. BB From Platform Alternate Leg Split Snatch
x 4+4   x 4+4   x 4+4

55. BB From Platform Power Clean
x 6   x 6   x 6

56. BB From Hang Split Clean
x 4+4   x 4+4   x 4+4

57. BB Power Clean & Push Jerk
x 2+4   x 2+4   x 2+4

58. BB From Platform Single Knee Bent Snatch Pull
x 6   x 6   x 6

59. BB From Platform Snatch Pull
x 6   x 6   x 6

60. BB From Platform Single Knee Bent Clean Pull
x 6   x 6   x 6

61. BB From Platform Clean Pull
x 6   x 6   x 6

Javorek's DB Circuit Conditioning Program # 1

1 DB Parallel Curls
40% 20   45% 18   50% 14   60% 10

2 DB Rotational Press
40% 18   45% 16   50% 12   60% 10

3 DB Rotational Bent-Over Row
40% 20   45% 18   50% x16   60% 12

4 DB Split Jump
40% 25+25   45% 20+20   50% 18+18   60% 16+16

5 DB Regular (Supinated) Curls
40% 20   45% 18   50% x16   60% 10

6 DB Parallel Push Press
40% 16   45% 14   50% x12   60% 10

7 DB High Pull Snatch
50% 10   55% 10   60% x10   65% 8

8 DB Split Jump
40% 25+25   45% 20+20   50% 18+18   55% 16+16

9 DB Upright Row
40% 20   45% 18   50% x16   60% 10

10 DB Rotational Curls
40% 20   50% 14   60% x10   60% 10

11 Javorek's DB Complex # 1
40% 1   40% 1   40% x1   45% x1

12 Javorek's DB Complex # 2
35% 1   35% 1   35% x1   40% 1

Javorek's DB Circuit Conditioning Program #2

1 DB Quarter Squat & Up On Toes Raise To Armpit
40% 20   45% 18   50% .x16   70% 10

2 DB Parallel Curls
45% 20   50% 16   60% .x.14   70% 10

3 DB Parallel Press
40% 16   45% 14   50% 12   60% 8

4 DB Split Jump
40% 25+25   45% 20+20   50% 18+18
70% 12+12

5 DB Quarter Squat & Up On Toes Raise To Armpit & Bounce
40% 14   45% 12   50% 10   55% 10

6 Dumbbell Supinated (Regular) Curls
45% 20   50% 16   55% 14   70% 10

7 DB Parallel Push Press
45% 14   50% 12   55% 10   70% 8

8 DB Split Jump
40% 25+25   45% 22+22   50% x20+20
55% x16+16

9 DB Upright Row
40% 20   45% 18   50% 16   70% 10

10 DB Parallel Squat Push Press
50% 12   55% 10   65% 10   70% 10

11 DB Rotational Curls
45% 20   50% 16   60% 12   75% 8

12 DB Split Jump
40% 25+25   45% 22+22   50% x20+20
55% x16+16

13 DB Rotational Bent-Over Row
50% 20   55% 16   60% 14   70% 10

14 DB High Pull Snatch
50% 10   55% 10   60% 10   70% 6

15 DB Split Jump
40% 20+25   45% 18+18   50% x16+16
70% 10+10

16 Javorek's DB Complex # 1
40% 1   45% 1   50% 1   50% 1

Javorek's DB Circuit Conditioning Program # 3

1 DB Alternate Raise To Armpit
40% x20+20   45% 18+18   50% 16+16
70% 10+10

2 DB Alternate Supinated (Regular) Curls
40% x20+20   45% 18+18   50% 16+16
70% 10+10

3 DB Alternate Upright Row
40% x20+20   45% 18+18   50% 16+16
70% 10+10

4 DB Alternate Parallel Press
40% x16+16   45% 14+14   50% 12+12
60% 8+8

5 DB Split Jump
40% 25+25   45% 22+22   50% 20+20
55% x16+16

6 DB Alt. From Hip High Pull Snatch
40% 14+14   45% 12+12   50% 10+10

55% 10+10

7 DB Alt. Rotational Curls
40% 20+20   45% 18+18   50% 16+16
70% 10+10

8 DB Pronated Bent-Over Row
40% x20+20   45% x18+18   50% x16+16
70% x10+10

9 DB Split Jump
40% 25+25   45% 22+22   50% x20+20
55% x16+16

10 DB Alt. Parallel Curls
40% x20+20   45% 18+18   50% x16+16
70% 10+10

11 DB Alt.Parallel Push Press
40% x20+20   45% 18+18   50% x16+16
70% 10+10

12 DB High Pull Snatch
50% 10   55% 10   60% 10   70% 6

13 DB Squat Jump
40% 10   45% 10   50% 8   55% 6

14 DB Split Jump
40% 25+25   45% 22+22   50% x20+20
55% x16+16

15 Javorek's DB Complex # 2
40% 1   40% 1   40% 1   45% 1

Javorek's DB Circuit Conditioning Program # 4

1 DB Quarter Squat & Up On Toes Raise To Armpit
50% 16   55% 14   65% 12   75% 8

2 DB Parallel Press
50% 12   55% 12   60% 12   70% 10

3 DB Upright Row
55% 12   65% 12   70% 10   75% 6

4 Dumbbell Supinated (Regular) Curls
55% 14   65% 12   70% 8   75% 6

5 DB Rotational Bent-Over Row
50% 14   60% 14   70% 10   75% 8

6 DB Rotational Push Press
50% 12   55% 12   60% 12   70% 10

7 DB Squat Upright Row
50% 12   55% 12   60% 12   70% 10

8 DB Rotational Curls
55% 14   65% 12   70% 8   75% 6

9 DB Supinated Bent-Over Row
50% 14   60% 14   70% 10   75% 8

10 DB Parallel Squat Push Press
55% 14   65% 12   70% 10   75% 6

11 DB High Pull Snatch
50% 10   55% 10   65% 8   75% 6

12 DB Javorek's Complex # 1
40% 1   45% 1   50% 1   55% 1

Javorek's DB Circuit Conditioning Program # 5

1 DB Alt. From Hip High Pull Snatch
30% x20+20 35% x20+20 40% x16+16 45% 14+14

2 DB Standing Breast Stroke Imitation
30% 20   35% 20   35% 20   40% 14

---

3 DB Bent-Over "Kick-Back" Triceps Curls Triceps Curls
45% 18   50% 16   60% 14   70% 8

4 DB Stnd. Forward Pronated Arm Raise
30% 20   35% 18   40% 16   45% 12

5 DB Bent-Over Breast Stroke Imitation
30% 20   35% 20   35% 20   40% 14

6 DB Stnd. Lateral Pronated Arm Raise
30% 20   35% 18   40% 16   45% 12

7 DB Bent-Over Swimming Free Style Imitation
30% 20   35% 20   35% 20   40% 14

8 DB Stnd. Forward Inside Rotation
30% 20   35% 20   35% 20   40% 14

9 DB Bent-Over Fly
30% 20   35% 18   40% 16   45% 14

10 DB Forward Alternate Press
30% x20+20   35% x20+20   40% x16+16
45% 14+14

11 DB Bent-Over "Kick-Back" Triceps Curls Triceps Curls
45% 18   50% 16   60% 14   70% 8

12 DB Lateral Alternate Press
30% x20+20   35% x20+20   40% x16+16
45% 14+14

13 DB Bent-Over Breast Stroke Imitation
30% 20   35% 20   35% 20   40% 14

14 DB Standing Outside Rotation
30% 20   35% 20   35% 20   40% 14

15 DB Bent-Over "Kick-Back" Triceps Curls Triceps Curls
45% 18   50% 16   60% 14   70% 8

16 DB Alt. From Hip High Pull Snatch
35% x20+20 40% 18+18 45% x16+16 50% 14+14

17 Javorek's DB Complex # 2
40% 1   40% 1   40% 1   45% 1

Javorek's DB Circuit Conditioning Program # 6

1 DB Upright Row
50% 14   60% 12   70% 10   80% 6

2 DB Parallel Press
50% 12   60% 10   70% 8   80% 4

3 DB Parallel Curls
50% 14   60% 12   70% 10   80% 6

4 DB Parallel Bent-Over Row
50% 14   60% 12   70% 10   80% 6

5 DB Linear Press
50% 12   60% 10   70% 8   80% 4

6 Dumbbell Supinated (Regular) Curls
50% 14   60% 12   70% 10   80% 6

7 DB Rotational Press
50% 12   60% 10   70% 8   80% 4

8 DB Pronated Bent-Over Row
50% 14   60% 12   70% 10   80% 6

9 DB Parallel Push Press
50% 12   60% 10   70% 8   80% 4

10 DB Squat Upright Row
50% 14   60% 12   70% 10   80% 6

---

11 DB Parallel Curls
50% 14   60% 12   70% 10   80% 6

12 DB Squat Push Press
50% 12   60% 10   70% 8   80% 4

13 Dumbbell Supinated (Regular) Curls
60% 10   70% 10   80% 6   90% 3

14 DB High Pull Snatch
60% 10   65% 8   70% 6   80% 5

15 Javorek's DB Complex # 1
40% 1   45% 1   50% 1   55% 1

Javorek's DB Circuit Conditioning Program # 7

1 DB Upright Row
60% 12   70% 10   80% 6   90% 3

2 DB Parallel Press
55% 12   65% 10   75% 8   85% 4

3 DB Regular (Supinated) Curls
60% 12   70% 10   80% 6   90% 3

4 DB Parallel Bent-Over Row
60% 12   70% 10   80% 6   90% 3

5 DB Rotational Push Press
60% 12   70% 10   80% 6   90% 3

6 DB Squat Upright Row
60% 12   70% 10   80% 6   90% 3

7 DB Parallel Squat Push Press
60% 12   70% 10   80% 6   90% 3

8 DB High Pull Snatch
50% 10   65% 8   70% 8   80% 5

9 DB Rotational Curls
60% 12   70% 10   80% 6   90% 3

10 DB Javorek's Complex # 1
45% 1   50% 1   55% 1   60% 1

Javorek's DB Circuit Conditioning Program # 8

1 DB Regular (Supinated) Curls
60% 10   65% 8   70% 6   85% 3

2 DB Rotational Press
60% 10   65% 8   70% 6   85% 3

3 DB Parallel Squat Push Press
60% 10   65% 8   70% 6   85% 3

4 DB Upright Row
60% 10   65% 8   70% 6   85% 3

5 DB Rotational Push Press
60% 10   65% 8   70% 6   85% 3

6 DB Parallel Squat Push Press
60% 10   65% 8   70% 6   85% 3

7 DB Rotational Curls
60% 12   65% 10   70% 8   85% 3

8 DB Parallel Jump Push Press
55% 10   60% 8   65% 6   0

9 DB Squat Push Press
60% 10   65% 8   70% 6   85% 3

10 DB Parallel Bent-Over Row
60% 14   65% 12   70% 10   85% 3

11 DB Upright Row
60% 10   65% 8   70% 6   85% 3

12 DB Parallel Squat Jump Push Press
55% 10   60% 8   65% 6   0

13 DB Regular (Supinated) Curls
60% 10   65% 8   70% 6   85% 3

14 DB High Pull Snatch
60% 10   65% 8   70% 6   80% 4

15 DB Squat Jump Push Press
55% 10   60% 8   65% 6   0

16 DB Split Jump
60% x20+20   65% 18+18   70% x16+16
80% 12+12

17 DB Squat Jump
55% 10   60% 8   65% 6   70% 6

18 Javorek's DB Complex # 1
40% 1   40% 1   40% 1   45% 1

Javorek's DB Circuit Conditioning Program # 9

1 DB Upright Row
55% 10   60% 10   65% 8   70% 6

2 DB Parallel Press
55% 10   65% 8   70% 6   75% 4

3 DB Regular (Supinated) Curls
55% 10   65% 8   70% 6   75% 4

4 DB Parallel Squat Push Press
55% 10   65% 8   70% 6   75% 4

5 DB Squat Upright Row
50% 10   55% 10   65% 8   70% 6

6 DB Parallel Press
55% 10   65% 8   70% 6   75% 4

7 DB Rotational Curls
50% 12   55% 10   65% 8   70% 6

8 DB Parallel Squat Jump Push Press
55% 10   65% 8   70% 6   75% 4

9 DB Upright Row
55% 10   65% 8   70% 6   75% 4

10 DB Parallel Push Press
50% 12   55% 10   65% 8   70% 6

11 DB Pronated Bent-Over Row
50% 14   55% 12   60% 10   70% 8

12 DB Parallel Squat Jump Push Press
55% 10   65% 8   70% 6   75% 4

13 DB Rotational Curls
50% 12   55% 10   65% 8   70% 6

14 DB Javorek's Complex # 1
45% 1   50% 1   55% 1   60% 1

15 DB Split Jump
50% x20+20   55% x20+20   60% x20+20
65% x20+20

Javorek's DB Circuit Conditioning Program # 10

1 Dumbbell Supinated (Regular) Curls
50% 14   55% 12   60% 10   65% 8

2 DB Upright Row
50% 14   55% 12   60% 10   70% 8

3 DB Rotational Press
50% 14   55% 12   60% 10   65% 8

4 DB High Pull Snatch
50% 10   55% 10   65% 8   70% 6

5 Dumbbell Supinated (Regular) Curls
50% 14   55% 12   60% 10   65% 8

6 DB Push Press
50% 14   55% 12   60% 10   65% 10

7 DB Split Jump
50% x20+20   55% x20+20   60% x20+20
65% x20+20

8 DB Upright Row
50% 14   55% 12   60% 10   70% 8

9 DB Squat Push Press
50% 12   60% 10   65% 8   70% 6

10 DB Squat Under High Pull Snatch
50% 10   55% 10   60% 8   65% 6

11 DB Squat Jump (Take Intensity From DB Bent-Over Row)
45% 10   50% 8   55% 6   55% 6

12 DB Rotational Curls
50% 14   55% 12   60% 10   65% 8

13 DB Parallel Squat Jump Push Press
50% 10   55% 8   60% 8   65% 6

14 DB Split Jump
50% x20+20   55% x20+20   60% x20+20
65% x20+20

15 Javorek's DB Complex # 1
40% 1   40% 1   40% 1   45% 1

Javorek's DB Circuit Conditioning Program # 11

1 DB Upright Row
50% 12   55% 10   65% 8   70% 6

2 DB Parallel Squat Push Press
55% 10   60% 10   65% 8   70% 6

3 DB Single Leg Step Back Lunges
50% 12+12   55% 10+10   60% 10+10
70% 10+10

4 DB Parallel Squat Jump Push Press
50% 10   60% 8   65% 8   70% 6

5 DB Alt. Leg Step Back Lunges
50% 14+14   55% 14+14   60% 14+14
65% 14+14

6 DB Parallel Squat Push Press
55% 10   60% 10   65% 8   70% 6

7 DB Single + Alt.Leg Step Back Lunges
50% 6+6+6+6   55% 6+6+6+6   60% 6+6+6+6
70% 6+6+6+6

8 DB Squat Push Press
55% 10   65% 8   70% 6   75% 6

9 DB Squat Upright Row
50% 12   50% 10   65% 8   70% 6

10 DB Split Jump
50% x20+20   55% x20+20   60% x20+20
70% x16+16

11 DB Lunge Walk
50% 25+25   55% 25+25   60% 25+25
65% 25+25

12 Javorek's DB Complex # 1
40% 1   50% 1   50% 1   55% 1

Javorek's DB Circuit Conditioning Program # 12

1 DB Upright Row
50% 12   60% 10   70% 8   90% 2

2 DB Rotational Push Press
55% 10   60% 10   65% 8   85% 3

3 DB Split Jump
50% x20+20   50% x20+20   60% x20+20
70% 18+18

4 DB Rotational Squat Push Press
50% 10   60% 10   65% 10   90% 2

5 DB Split Jump
50% x20+20   50% x20+20   60% x20+20
70% 18+18

6 DB Squat Upright Row
50% 12   55% 10   66% 8   85% 3

7 DB High Pull Snatch
50% 10   55% 10   60% 10   80% 4

8 DB Squat Jump(Take From DB. Bent O. Row)
45% 10   45% 10   50% 10   60% 8

9 DB Upright Row
50% 12   65% 8   90% 2

10 DB Parallel Squat Push Press
55% 10   60% 10   65% 8   90% 2

11 DB Split Jump
50% x20+20   50% x20+20   60% x20+20
70% 18+18

12 DB Squat Under Upright Row
50% 12   55% 10   65% 8   70% 3

13 DB High Pull Snatch
50% 10   65% 8   70% 6   80% 4

14 DB Parallel Squat Jump Push Press
50% 10   55% 8   60% 6   65% 6

15 DB Split Jump
50% x20+20   50% x20+20   60% x20+20
70% 18+18

16 DB Squat Jump (Take Intensity From DB Bent-Over Row)
40% 10   45% 10   50% 10   60% 8

17 Javorek's DB Complex # 1
45% 1   55% 1   60% 1   60% 1

Javorek's DB Circuit Conditioning Program # 13

1 DB Supinated Curls
40% 20   45% 16   55% 10   70% 6

2 DB Upright
40% 20   45% 16   55% 10   75% 6

3 DB Bent-Over "Kick-Back" Triceps Curls Triceps Curls
35% 20   45% 16   50% 12   60% 10

4 Parallel Bars Dips
15 or Å   15 or Å   15 or Å   15 or Å

5 High Bar Behind The Head Pull-Ups
6 or Å   6 or Å   6 or Å   6 or Å

6 DB Squat Jump (Take Intensity From DB Bent-Over Row)
40% 10   45% 8   45% 8   50% 6

Note In Case You Cannot Perform The Prescribed Number Of Repetitions, Do As Many As You Can or To Fatigue (Å) On Dip Bar And On Pull-Ups On Each Set.

Javorek's DB Circuit Conditioning Program # 14

1 DB Bent-Over "Kick-Back" Triceps Curls
35% 20   40% 18   45% 16   50% 14

2 DB From Hip High Pull Snatch
40% 18   45% 16   50% 14   55% 12

3 DB Bent-Over Fly
35% 20   40% 18   45% 16   45% 16

4 DB Squat Push Press
45% 14   50% 12   55% 10   65% 8

5 10" Boxes Plyo Push-Ups
10 or Å   10 or Å   10 or Å   10 or Å

6 Parallel Bar Dips
15 or Å   15 or Å   15 or Å   15 or Å

7 High Bar Behind The Head Pull-Ups
8 or Å   8 or Å   8 or Å   8 or Å

8 DB Squat Jump (Take Intensity From DB Bent-Over Row)
40% 10   45% 8   50% 8   55% 8

9. Javorek's DB Complex # 1
50% 1   50% 1   55% 1   60% 1

Note In Case You Cannot Perform The Prescribed Number Of Repetitions, Do As Many As You Can or To Fatigue (Å) On Each Set On Dip Bar, Plyo Push-Ups And On Pull-Ups

Javorek's Circuit Conditioning Program # 15

1 DB Upright Row
40% 20   45% 16   50% 12   70% 6

2 DB Double Step Lunge Walk
60% 25+25   65% 25+25   70% 25+25
75% 25+25

3 Crunches
20   20   20   20

4 DB Squat Push Press
45% 16   50% 14   55% 10   70% 6

5 DB On Box Alternate Leg Step-Up
60% 12+12   65% 12+12   70% 10+10
80% 10+10

6 Parallel Bar Dips
15 or Å   15 or Å   15 or Å   15 or Å

7 BB Back Squat
40% 16   45% 14   50% 12   70% 6

8 Plyo Push-Ups On 10" Boxes
10+10   10+10   10+10   10+10

9 BB Back Squat Jump
30% 10   35% 10   40% 6   45% 6

10 DB Supinated Curls
40% 20   45% 16   55% 12   70% 6

11 Crunches
20 20 20   20

12 DB Double Step Lunge Walk
60% 25+25   65% 25+25   70% 25+25
80% 25+25

13 High Bar Behind The Head Pull-Ups
8 or Å   8 or Å   8 or Å   8 or Å

14 BB Back Squat Jump
30% 10   35% 8   40% 6   45% 6

15 Javorek's DB Complex # 1
50% 1   50% 1   55% 1   60% 1

Note In Case You Cannot Perform The Prescribed Number Of Repetitions, Do As Many As You Can or To Fatigue (Å)

Javorek's Circuit Conditioning Program # 16

1 DB Supinated Curls
45% 20   55% 14   65% 10   80% 5

2 DB Upright Row
45% 20   55% 14   65% 10   80% 6

3 DB Squat Push Press
60% 10   65% 10   70% 10   80% 5

4 DB Bent-Over "Kick-Back" Triceps Curls
50% 14   55% 12   60% 12   70% 8

5 DB Lunge Walk
60% 25+25   65% 22+22   70% x20+20   80% 12+12

6 DB Lying On Bench Pull-Over
50% 18   60% 14   65% 10   75% 8

7 DB Squat Push Press
60% 10   65% 10   75% 8   85% 4

8 Plyo Push-Ups On 6" Boxes
8 or 4   8 or 4   8 or 4   8 or 4

9 DB Alternate Leg Step-Up On Box
60% 14+14   65% 14+14   70% 10+10
75% 10+10

10 Parallel Bar Dips
15 or 4   15 or 4   15 or 4   15 or 4

11 Javorek's DB Complex #2
45% 1   50% 1   50% 1   55% 1

12 DB Squat Jump
60% 10   65% 10   70% 6   75% 6

13 Box Jump 16"-24 "
15   15   15   15

Javorek's Circuit Conditioning Program # 17

1 DB Upright Row
70% 12   80% 8   90% 5   95% 2

2 DB Press
70% 10   80% 8   85% 6   90% 4

3 DB Regular Supinated Curls
70% 10   80% 8   85% 6   85% 6

4 DB Push Press
70% 10   80% 8   90% 4   95% 2

5 Db Single Leg Step Back Lunges
80% 10+10   80% 10+10   90% x (8+8)
90% x (8+8)

6 Db Pronated Bent-Over Row
70% 12   80% 10   85% 6   90% 4

7 Db Squat Push Press
70% 10   80% 8   85% 6   90% 3

8 Db Alternate Leg Lunges
80% 12+12   80% 12+12   85% 12+12
90% x (8+8)

9 Db ""Kick-Back"" Triceps Curls
60% 14   70% 10   75% 8   80% 6

10 Db Squat Push Press
70% 10   80% 8   90% 4   90% 4

11 Javorek's Db Complex # 1
40% 1   45% 1   50% 1   55% 1

12 Db Lunge Walk
80% x20+20   80% x20+20   80% x20+20
90% 10+10

13 Box Jump (16"-32")
15   15   15   15

Javorek's Circuit Conditioning Program # 18

1 DB Upright Row
75% 10   85% 8   90% 4   95% 3

2 Parallel Bars Dips
15 or 4   15 or 4   15 or 4   15 or 4

3 DB Pull-Over
70% 14   75% 10   80% 8   85% 6

4 DB Sit-ups
40% 20   45% 20   50% 20   50% 20

5 DB Parallel Bench Press
75% 10   80% 8   85% 6   90% 3

6 DB Up & Down Shrug
50% 20   60% 16   70% 12   80% 10

7 Medicine Ball (Throw + Push) Sit-Ups
30+10   30+10   30+10   30+10

8 DB Supinated "Regular" Curls
70% 12   80% 8   85% 6   90% 4

9 Javorek's DB Complex # 1
50% 1   50% 1   60% 1   60% 1

10 Box Jumps (16" - 32")
20   18   16   14

Javorek's Circuit Conditioning Program # 19

1 DB Standing Breast Stroke Imitation
30% 20   35% 18   40% 16   45% 16

2 DB Bent-Over "Kick-Back" Triceps Curls
60% 14   70% 12   75% 10   85% 6

3 10" Boxes Plyo Push-Ups
10 or 4   10 or 4   10 or 4   10 or 4

4 DB Quarter Squat & Up On Toes Raise To Armpit
70% 12   80% 10   85% 8   90% 6

5 DB Single Leg Lunges
70% 10+10   75% 10+10   80% 10+10
80% 10+10

6 DB Squat Push Press
70% 10   80% 10   85% 8   90% 5

7 Box Jump (16"-32")
20   20   16   14

8 DB Upright Row
75% 10   80% 8   85% 6   90% 5

9 DB Alternate Leg Lunges
70% 14+14   80% 10+10   85% 10+10
90% 6+6

10 DB Squat Push Press
75% 10   80% 8   85% 6   90% 4

11 10" Boxes Plyo Push-Ups
10 or 4   x 10 or 4   10 or 4   10 or 4

---

12 Box Jump (16"-32")
20   20   16   14

13 DB Pull-Over
70% 14   75% 12   80% 10   85% 8

14 DB Lunge Walk
70% x20+20   75% x20+20   80% x20+20
85% 15+15

15 DB Squat Push Press
70% 12   80% 10   85% 8   90% 4

16 Javorek's DB Complex # 2
45% 1   45% 1   50% 1   55% 1

17 Box Jump (16"-32")
20   20   16   16

Javorek's Circuit Conditioning Program # 20

1 DB Upright Row
60% 12   65% 10   70% 10   75% 10

2 BB Quarter Squat
50% 20   60% 20   70% 15   75% 15

3 DB Bent-Over "Kick-Back" Triceps Curls
50% 16   55% 14   60% 12   70% 10

4 DB Sit-Ups Jump (Take Intensity From DB Bent-Over Row)
50% 25   55% 25   60% 20   65% 20

5. DB From Hip High Pull Snatch
50% 14   55% 14   60% 12   65% 10

6. BB Quarter Squat
50% 20   60% 20   70% 15   75% 15

7. DB Lying On Bench Pull-Over
50% 14   60% 12   70% 10   75% 10

8 DB Alternate Leg Step-Ups
40% 12+12   50% 12+12   60% 10+10
65% 10+10

9 Javorek's DB Complex # 1
50% 1   50% 1   55% 1   65% 1

10 Box Jump (Different Height)
15   15   15   15

11 Upstairs Run
4   4   4   4

Javorek's Circuit Conditioning Program # 21

1 DB Supinated Curls.
55% 16   60% 14   70% 12   75% 10

2 DB Parallel Bench Press
60% 12   65% 12   70% 10   75% 10

3 BB Quarter Squat
50% 20   60% 20   70% 15   75% 15

4 DB Bent-Over "Kick-Back" Triceps Curls
55% 14   65% 12   70% 10   75% 10

5 Parallel Bar Dips
10 or 4   10 or 4   10 or 4   10 or 4

6 DB Lying On Bench Pull-Over
55% 14   65% 12   70% 12   80% 6

7 DB Lying On Back On Bench Fly
40% 20   45% 20   50% 18   65% 12

8 DB Squat Upright Row
50% 12   60% 12   70% 10   80% 6

---

9 DB Sit-Ups
50% 25   55% 25   60% 20   65% 20

10 Double Leg Upstairs Bound-Jumping
5   5   5   5

Javorek's Circuit Conditioning Program # 22

1 DB Upright Row
50% 20   60% 16   70% 12   80% 6

2 DB Squat Push Press
60% 12   70% 10   75% 8   80% 6

3 DB Alternate Leg Lunges
50% x20+20   60% x20+20   70% 18+18
80% 14+14

4 DB From Hip High Pull Snatch
50% 18   55% 16   60% 14   65% 12

5 DB Squat & Raise To Armpit
55% 14   65% 12   75% 8   85% 5

6 DB Lunge Walk
50% x (30+30)   60% 25+25   70% x20+20
80% 14+14

7 DB Bent-Over "Kick-Back" Triceps Curls
55% 14   65% 12   70% 10   75% 10

8 DB Squat Jump & Raise To Armpit
50% 10   60% 10   65% 10   70% 10

9 Javorek's DB Complex # 1
50% 1   55% 1   60% 1   65% 1

10 DB Sit-Ups
50% 30   55% 30   60% 25   65% 20

11 DB Box Jump (Different Height)
20% 10   25% 10   25% 10   30% 10

12 Medicine Ball (Throw + Push) Sit-Ups
20+10   20+10   20+10   20+10

13 Double Leg In Zig-Zag Upstairs Bound-Jumping
6   6   6   6

Javorek's Circuit Conditioning Program # 23

1 BB Narrow Grip Upright Row
50% 16   60% 14   70% 12   80% 6

2 DB Lying On Bench Pull-Over
50% 16   60% 14   65% 12   70% 10

3 BB Medium Grip Upright Row
50% 16   60% 14   70% 10   80% 6

4 DB Lying On Back On Bench Fly
50% 18   55% 18   60% 14   70% 10

5 BB Wide Grip Upright Row
50% 16   55% 14   60% 12   65% 10

6 DB Sit-Ups
50% 30   55% 30   60% 25   65% 20

7 BB Back Squat
50% 12   70% 8   60% 10   80% 6

8 BB Bench Press
60% 12   70% 10   80% 6   85% 5

9 BB Javorek's Complex # 1
50% 2   55% 1   60% 1

10 BB Back Squat Jump
30% 8   35% 8   40% 6   45% 5

11 Medicine Ball (Throw + Push) Sit-Ups
20+10   20+10   20+10   20+10

12 Box Jump (Different Height)
20   20   20   20

13 Upstairs Double Leg Bound-Jumping
4   4   4   4

14 Upstairs Approach-Jump & Sprint
4   4   4   4

15 Upstairs Sprint
4   4   4   4

Javorek's Circuit Conditioning Program # 24

1 DB Supinated Curls
50% 20   60% 14   70% 12   80% 6

2 DB From Hip High Pull Snatch
50% 16   55% 14   60% 12   65% 10

3 DB Lying On Bench Pull-Over
55% 16   65% 12   70% 10   80% 6

4 DB Parallel Press+ Push Press
50% x (8+8)   60% x (8+8)   70% x (8+8)
80% x (4+4)

5 DB Squat & Raise To Armpit
50% 12   60% 12   70% 10   80% 6

6 DB Alternate Leg Lunges
50% x20+20   60% x20+20   70% 18+18
80% 14+14

7 DB Squat Push Press
60% 10   70% 10   75% 8   85% 5

8 DB Lunge Walk
50% x (30+30)   60% 25+25   70% x20+20   80% 14+14

9 Javorek's DB Complex # 1
50% 1   50% 1   60% 1   60% 1

10 DB Sit-Ups
50% 30   55% 30   60% 25   65% 20

11 Plyo (Up & Down On 10"-12" Box) Push-Ups
6+6 6+6   6+6   6+6

12 Medicine Ball (Throw + Push) Sit-Ups
20+10   20+10   20+10   20+10

13 Box Jump (Different Heights)
15 15   15   15

Javorek's Circuit Conditioning Program # 25

1 DB Upright Row
60% 14   65% 12   70% 12   80% 6

2 DB Lunge Walk
50% x (30+30)   60% 25+25   70% x20+20
80% 14+14

3 DB Crunches - Intensity Taken Of From Hip High Pull Snatch
20   20   20   20

4 DB Squat Push Press
60% 10   70% 10   80% 6   85% 6

5 DB Alternate Leg Step-Ups
50% x20+20   60% x20+20   70% 18+18
80% 14+14

6 Parallel Bar Dips
15 or 4   15 or 4   15 or 4   15 or 4

7 BB Back Squat
50% 12   60% 10   70% 10   80% 6

8 Plyo (Up & Down On 10"-12" Box)Push-Ups
6+6   6+6   6+6   6+6

9 BB Back Squat Jump
30% 10   40% 6   35% 8   45% 6

10 DB Supinated Curls
50% 20   70% 10   60% 14   80% 6

11 High Bar Pronated Hand Pull-Ups
10 or 4   10 or 4   10 or 4   10 or 4

12 DB Lunge Walk
50% 30+30   60% 25+25   70% x20+20
80% 14+14

13 DB Squat Under Upright Row
50% 12   55% 12   65% 10   75% 8

14 Javorek's DB Complex # 2
40% 1   45% 1   50% 1   55% 1

15 Box Jump (Different Heights)
15   15   15   15

Javorek's Circuit Conditioning Program # 26

1 DB Parallel Bench Press
60% 12   70% 10   80% 6   85% 4

2 DB Lying On Bench Pull-Over
60% 10   65% 10   75% 10   80% 6

3 DB From Hip High Pull Snatch
50% 18   60% 14   70% 10   75% 8

4 DB Parallel Push Press
60% 10   70% 10   80% 6   85% 4

5 DB Lying On Bench On Your Back Fly
50% 18   55% 18   65% 12   75% 8

6 DB Bent-Over "Kick-Back" Triceps Curls
55% 16   65% 12   70% 10   80% 6

7DB Quarter Squat & Up On Toes Raise To Armpit
60% 20   70% 12   80% 10   85% 6

8 High Bar Pronated Hand Pull-Ups
10 or 4   10 or 4   10 or 4   10 or 4

9 Parallel Bar Dips
15 or 4   15 or 4   15 or 4   15 or 4

10 DB (Throw + Push) Sit-Ups
50% 30+10 55% 30+10 60% 25+10 65% 20+10

11 DB Squat Jump & Raise To Armpit
50% 10   55% 10   60% 10   65% 10

12 Javorek's DB Complex # 1
50% 1   50% 1   60% 1   60% 1

13 Medicine Ball Sit-Ups
20+10   20+10   20+10   20+10

Javorek's Circuit Conditioning Program # 27

1 DB Upright Row
60% 14   70% 12   80% 8   90% 4

2 DB Sit-Ups
50% 30   55% 30   60% 25   65% 20

3 DB Bent-Over "Kick-Back" Triceps Curls
60% 12   65% 12   70% 10   80% 8

4 DB From Hip High Pull Snatch
50% 20   55% 18   60% 16   70% 10

5 High Bar Pronated Hand Pull-Ups
10 or 4   10 or 4   10 or 4   10 or 4

6 DB Bent-Over Fly
50% 16   55% 16   60% 14   70% 10

7 DB Parallel Bench Press
60% 12   70% 10   80% 8   90% 3

8 DB Lying On Bench On Your Back Fly
50% 16   55% 16   65% 12   75% 8

9 DB Lying On Bench Pull-Over
60% 12   65% 10   70% 10   75% 8

10 High Bar Pronated Hand Pull-Ups
10 or 4   10 or 4   10 or 4   10 or 4

11 Parallel Bar Dips
15 or 4   15 or 4   15 or 4   15 or 4

12 Medicine Ball (Throw + Push) Sit-Ups
20+10   20+10   20+10   20+10

13 Plyo (Up & Down On 10"-12" Box) Push-Ups
6+6 6+6   6+6   6+6

14 DB Lunge Walk
50% x (30+30)   60% 25+25   70% x20+20
80% 14+14

15 Javorek's DB Complex # 1
50% 1   50% 1   60% 1   60% 1

16 Upstairs Double Leg Bound-Jumping
4   4   4   4

17 Upstairs Approach-Jump & Sprint
4   4   4   4

18 Upstairs Sprint
4   4   4   4

Javorek's Circuit Conditioning Program # 28

1 DB Upright Row
40% 20   45% 16   50% 12

2 DB From Hip High Pull Snatch
40% 20   45% 16   50% 12

3 DB Bent-Over "Kick-Back" Triceps Curls
40% 16   45% 15   50% 14

4 DB Bent-Over Fly
30% 22   35% 20   40% 18

5 DB Overhead Press
40% 14   45% 14   50% 12

6 DB Bent-Over Row
40% 20   45% 18   50% 16

7 DB Inward-Outward Rotation
30% 10+10   35% 9+9   40% x (8+8)

8 DB Lateral Arm Raise
25% 16   30% 14   35% 14

9 DB Lunge Walk
30% x (30+30)   35% 25+25   40% x20+20

10 DB Squat Jump Push Press
40% 10   45% 10   50% 10

11 DB Breast Stroke Imitation
25% 16   30% 15   40% 14

12 DB Alternate Leg Lunges
40% x20+20 45% x20+20 50% x16+16

13 DB Lying On Your Back On Bench Fly
25% 16   30% 16   35% 16

14 DB Lying On Your Back On Bench Pull-Over
35% 14   40% 14   50% 12

15 DB Bench Press
50% 14   55% 12   60% 12

16 Javorek's DB Complex # 1
50% 1   55% 1   60% 1

Javorek's Circuit Conditioning Program # 29

1 DB From Hip High Pull Snatch
40% 20   45% 18   50% 16

2 DB Lying On Your Back On Bench Fly
30% 20   35% 20   40% 20

3 DB Lying On Your Back On Bench Pull-Over
35% 14   40% 14   50% 12

4 DB Bench Press
50% 14   55% 12   60% 12

5 DB Overhead Press
40% 18   45% 16   50% 14

6 DB Regular (Supinated) Curls
40% 20   45% 18   50% 16

7 DB Bent-Over "Kick-Back" Triceps Curls
40% 16   45% 14   50% 14

8 DB From Hip High Pull Snatch
40% 20   45% 18   50% 16

9 DB Bent-Over Fly
30% 22   35% 20   40% 18

10 DB Lateral Arm Raise
30% 22   35% 20   40% 18

11 DB Quarter Squat & Up On Toes Raise To Armpit or
40% 20   45% 20   50% 18

12 Parallel Bar Dips
x 10 x 10   x 10

13 DB From Hip High Pull Snatch or
40% 20   45% 18   50% 16

14 High Bar Pull-Ups
x 6   x 6   x 6

15 Javorek's DB Complex # 1
50% 1   50% 1   60% 1

16 DB On Chest Sit-Ups
x 30 x 30   x 25

Javorek's Circuit Conditioning Program # 30

1 DB Quarter Squat & Up On Toes Raise To Armpit
40% 20   45% 20   50% 18

2 DB From Hip High Pull Snatch
40% 20   45% 18   50% 16

3 DB Breast Stroke Imitation
20% 20   25% 20   30% 18

4 DB Quarter Squat & Up On Toes Raise To Armpit
40% 16   45% 16   50% 16

5 DB Lateral Arm Raise
40% 20   45% 20   50% 18

6 DB Alternate Leg Lunges
30% x20+20   35% x20+20   40% x20+20

7 DB Squat Push Press
40% 14   45% 14   50% 14

8 DB Lunge Walk
30% x20+20   40% x20+20   50% x20+20

9 DB Squat Upright Row
40% 14   45% 14   50% 14

10 DB Alternate Leg Step-Up
30% x20+20   35% 18+18   40% x16+16

11 DB Javorek's Complex #2
30% 1   35% 1   40% 1

12 DB On Chest Sit-Ups
30   30   25

13 Upstairs Run
6   6   6

Javorek's Circuit Conditioning Program # 31

1 DB Bent-Over "Kick-Back" Triceps Curls
50% 14   55% 12   60% 10

2 DB Upright Row
60% 10   65% 10   70% 10

3 DB From Hip High Pull Snatch
50% 12   55% 12   60% 10

4 Crunches
20   20   20

5 Half Up & Up - Half Down & Down
10   10   10

6 Half Jack-Knives
10   10   10

7 DB Bent-Over Fly
50% 14   50% 14   60% 10

8 DB (Regular) Supinated Curls
60% 12   65% 10   70% 10

9 DB Alternate Leg Lunges
60% x16+16   60% x16+16   70% x16+16

10 Crunches
20   20   20

11 Half Up & Up - Half Down & Down
10   10   10

12 Half Jack-Knives
10   10   10

13 DB Squat Push Press
60% 10   65% 10   70% 10

14 DB Bent-Over "Kick-Back" Triceps Curls
50% 14   55% 12   60% 10

15 DB Lunge Walk
60% x16+16 60% x16+16 70% x16+16

16 DB Inward-Outward Rotation
40% 10+10   45% x (8+8)   50% 6+6

17 Javorek's DB Complex # 1
50% 1   55% 1   60% 1

18 Crunches
20 20   20

19 Half Up & Up - Half Down & Down
10   10   10

20 Half Jack-Knives
10   10   10

Javorek's Circuit Conditioning Program # 32
(For Athletes With Back Injuries)

1 DB Upright Row
40% 12   45% 12   50% 12   60% 10

2 DB Parallel Press
40% 12   45% 12   50% 10   55% 10

3 DB Lying On Bench On Your Back Fly
40% 14   45% 14   50% 12   55% 10

4 DB Parallel Push Press
45% 10   50% 10   55% 10   60% 10

5 DB Pull-Over
40% 14   50% 10   55% 10   60% 10

6 DB Quarter Squat & Up On Toes Raise To Armpit
50% 10   55% 10   60% 10   65% 10

7 DB Supinated Curls
50% 12   55% 12   60% 10   65% 10

8 Parallel Bars Dips
x 10 x 10   x 10   x 10

9 DB From Hip High Pull Snatch
45% 12   50% 10   55% 10   60% 10

10 DB Parallel Bench Press
50% 12   60% 10   65% 10   65% 10

11 DB Inward-Outward Rotation
40% 10+10   45% x (8+8)   50% 6+6
50% 6+6

12 DB Parallel Push Press
50% 10   55% 10   55% 10   60% 10

13 DB Parallel Bench Press
55% 10   60% 10   65% 10   70% 10

14 High Bar Pull-Ups
x 10 x 10   x 10   x 10

15 DB Lateral Arm Raise
40% 12   45% 12   50% 10   55% 10

16 Javorek's DB Complex # 1 (Instead of High Pull Snatch, Perform From Hip High Pull Snatch and Instead of Bent Over Row, Upright Row)
50% 1   50% 1   60% 1   60% 1

Javorek's Circuit Conditioning Program # 33
(For Athletes With Back Injuries)

1 BB Narrow Grip Upright Row
40% 12   45% 12   50% 12   60% 10

2 BB Behind The Head Press
40% 12   45% 12   50% 10   55% 10

3 DB Lying On Bench On Your Back Fly
40% 14   45% 14   50% 12   55% 10

4 BB Behind The Head Push Press
45% 10   50% 10   55% 10   60% 10

5 BB Pull-Over
40% 14   50% 12   55% 10   60% 10

6 BB Up & Down Shrug
50% 10   55% 10   60% 10   65% 10

7 BB Supinated Curls
50% 12   55% 12   60% 10   65% 10

8 Parallel Bars Dips
x 10 x 10   x 10   x 10

9 BB Medium Grip From Hip High Pull Snatch
45% 12   50% 10   55% 10   60% 10

10 BB Wide Grip Bench Press
50% 12   60% 10   65% 10   65% 10

11 DB Inward-Outward Rotation
40% 10+10   45% x (8+8)   50% 6+6
50% 6+6

12 BB Behind The Head Push Press
50% 10   50% 10   55% 10   60% 10

13 BB Behind The Head From Half Squat Press
55% 10   60% 10   65% 10   70% 10

14 High Bar Pull-Ups
x 10 x 10   x 10   x 10

15 BB Behind The Head Toe Raise
20% 14   20% 14   25% 12   25% 12

16 Javorek's Db Complex # 1 (Instead of High Pull Snatch, Perform From Hip High Pull Snatch and instead of Bent Over Row, Upright Row)
50% 1   50% 1   60% 1   60% 1

Javorek's Circuit Conditioning Program # 34
(Before game day)

Every individual athlete should choose the right active rest workout before competition. There are several variations and very specific ones for different sports, but as a general rule the most important is not to stop exercising during the period before a competition or game. What you need to do is just to reduce the amount of time, number of repetitions and intensity. An athlete's physiological system adapts to the high demands of conditioning and develops "Pavlovian" conditioned reflexes. So, when an athlete goes to the workout area, due to the conditioned reflexes, the body starts to build up the necessary neurological and biochemical responses in order to be able to perform at the highest levels. Now when an athlete goes to the weight room before the competition, the same neurological and biochemical orientation will occur in the body. This means that the athlete will not be making use of inefficient processes in training and competition, but will follow a system called peaking and tapering, so that the result in competition will be the desired one. Perform with short breaks between the sets. Usually I perform with my athletes each exercise in the numerical order, but could be performed in Circuit also.

1 DB Upright Row
50% 6   50% 6   60% 6   60% 6   70% 6   80% 4   80% 4

2 DB From Hip High Pull Snatch
50% 6   50% 6   55% 6   55% 6   65% 4   70% 3   70% 3

3 DB Push Press
60% 5   65% 5   70% 4   70% 4   75% 4   75% 4

4 DB Alternate Leg Lunges
60% 10+10   70% 8+8   75% x8+8   75% x8+8   80% 6+6   80% 6+6   80% 6+6

5 DB Squat Push Press
60% 6   70% 4   75% 3   75% 3   80% 2   80% 2   80% 2

6 DB Javorek's Complex # 1
(Perform just with 3 Reps)
50% 1   50% 1   55% 1   55% 1

7 BB Quarter Squat
60% 12   70% 8   75% 6   80% 4   80% 4   80% 4   80% 4

8 Upstairs Double Leg Bound-Jumping
2   2   2   2

9 Upstairs Approach-Jump & Sprint
2   2   2   2

10 Upstairs Sprint
2   2   2   2

Javorek's Cardiovascular Stimulation Program Circuit Conditioning Program # 35

Double Leg Upstairs Bounding x 4	No Break
Double Leg Zigzag x 4	30 Sec. Break
Javorek's Dumbbell Complex # 1 60% 1	30 Sec. Break
Dumbbell Or Barbell Bench Press 65% 15	20 Sec. Break
Dumbbell Alternate Leg Step Up 70% 12+12	20 Sec. Break
Dumbbell Bent Over "Kick Back" Triceps Curls 60% 14	20 Sec. Break
Barbell Back Squat Jump 50% 10	30 Sec. Break
Javorek's Dumbbell Complex # 2 50% 1	30 Sec. Break
Dumbbell Lunge Walk x 20+20	20 Sec. Break
Javorek's Special Abdominal Medicine Ball Sit-Ups Program # 2 x 1	30 Sec. Break
Different Height Box Jump x 15	30 Sec. Break
Alternate Leg Jump-Bounding x 20	20 Sec. Break
Upstairs Sprint (Strides) x 4	30 Sec. Break
Repeat From The Beginning x 3	Without Extra Break Time

Javorek's Step-Ups Cardiovascular Program
Circuit Conditioning Program # 36
INVENTORY:

Set up boxes next to a wall. The boxes may be constructed eight feet long and two feet wide and 16 to 18 inches high (for certain tall or highly prepared athletes could be constructed higher boxes). In case of lack of a longer box, a coach may butt several smaller boxes end to end. organizing a conditioning class or for a big number of athletes line up as many boxes as are available or as long is the wall space. If the team or the group of athletes is too large, a coach could organize athletes in two or three in a group. One group is exercising while the others are waiting for their turn. After each exercise we rotate the groups, without any break.

Each athlete will choose two pairs of adequate weight dumbbells with which she/he will be able to properly perform every exercise of the program. If there are not sufficient quantities of dumbbells, we divide the athletes into group, which match the athletes' physical capacities. This helps avoid injuries and any confusion.

After organizing the class, the coach stands at the middle of the gym behind the athletes, and dictates the rhythm, the intensity and the order of the exercises.

Do not start with the full program from the beginning. First, every athlete must be able of performing six sets of Javorek's Complex # 2. before start this program. Then, start gradually, doing just a certain part of it. The break time between sets is also adjustable. If a coach feels that the group should have longer break he/she could adjust the proper break time.

The proper technique of step-ups:

- head is looking straight ahead

- stable neck, and tight abdominal musculature

- step up on box with a full flat foot and not just with the balls of the feet.

Type of exercises:

1. Single Leg Step Ups: perform the prescribed number of repetitions with same leg continuously, then do same with the other leg

2. Alternate Leg Step Ups: Count the repetitions as steps for both legs, right & left (double count). . Perform the total number of alternate leg step up repetitions. For example: x 10 means x 10 with right leg & x 10 with left leg.

3. Box Jumps: Teach the proper technique of box jumps first without dumbbells, and then once the athletes demonstrate proper technique add light dumbbells first and not high rhythm. Assure enough space between athletes to avoid injuries, potentially caused by bumping into one other. Choose the proper size of boxes, adequate for the athletes' potential.

4. Single or Combination Dumbbell Exercises: Take two pairs of dumbbells -

a) 60% of Dumbbell Upright Row for all dumbbell exercises;

80% of Dumbbell Bent Over Row for all step-ups exercises;

-For certain sports or athletes box jump could be substituted with Tuck Jumps ; Stair Double Leg Bounding or Dumbbell Squat Jump Raise To Armpit;

Javorek's Step-Ups Cardiovascular Program

Standing in front of the box,

1 Dumbbell Upright Row + Dumbbell Squat Jump Push Press x 12 + 5		Twenty seconds break
2 Dumbbells In Hand Single Leg Step-Ups x 14+14		Thirty seconds break
3 Dumbbell High Pull Snatch x 12		Twenty seconds break
4 Dumbbell Parallel Squat Push Press x 10		Twenty seconds break
5 Dumbbell In Hands Alternate Leg Step-Ups x 14+14		Thirty seconds break
6 Javorek's Dumbbell Complex # 1 x 1		Forty-five seconds break
7 Dumbbell In Hands Single Leg Step-Ups x 6+6 +		
Alternate Leg Step-Ups x 8+8 +		
Dumbbell Split Jumps x 6+6		Twenty seconds break
8 Dumbbell Parallel Curls x 14 +		
Dumbbell Bent Over Row x 12		
Dumbbell High Pull Snatch +x 10		Twenty seconds break
9 Dumbbell In Hands Single Leg Step-Ups x 12+12		Thirty seconds break
10 Dumbbell Squat or Squat Jump Push Press x 10		Twenty-five seconds break
11 Dumbbell High Pull Snatch x 12		Twenty seconds break
12 Dumbbell In Hands Single Leg Step-Ups x 6+6 +		
Alternate Leg Step-Ups x 6+6 +		
Single Leg Step-Ups x 6+6 +		
Alternate Leg Step-Ups x 6+6		Thirty seconds break
13 Javorek's Dumbbell Complex # 2 x 1		Sixty seconds break
14 Dumbbell Parallel Curls x 10 +		
Dumbbell Split Jump x 14+14		Twenty seconds break
15 Dumbbell In Hands Alternate Leg Step-Ups x 14+14		Twenty seconds break
16 Dumbbell Bent Over Row x 14		Twenty seconds break
17 Dumbbell Squat or Squat Jump Push Press x 10		Twenty seconds break
18 Box Jump Without Dumbbells x 20		Thirty seconds break
or Tuck Jumps x 20		
or Double Leg Stair Bounding Full length x 5		

Chapter 15

19 **Dumbbell High Pull Snatch**
x 10   Twenty seconds break

20 **Box Jumps With Dumbbell in Hands**
x 15   Forty-five seconds break

   or Dumbbell Squat Jump Raise To Armpit
   x 15

21 **Dumbbell Parallel Curls**
x 12   Fifteen seconds break

22 **Dumbbell High Pull Snatch**
x 10   Twenty seconds break

23 **Dumbbell In Hands Single Leg Step-Ups**
x 8+8   +

   Box Jump
   x 8   + or

   Dumbbell Squat Jump Raise To Armpit
   x 8   Forty-five seconds break

24 **Dumbbell Squat or Squat Jump Push Press**
x 10   Twenty seconds break

25 **Dumbbell Parallel Curls**
x 14   Fifteen seconds break

26 **Dumbbell Split Jumps**
x 14+14   Twenty seconds break

27 **Dumbbell Box Jump or**
x 15

   Dumbbell Squat Jump Raise To Armpit
   x 15   Twenty seconds break

28 **Dumbbell Squat or Squat Jump Push Press**
x 10   Twenty seconds break

29 **Dumbbell High Pull Snatch**
x 10   Twenty seconds break

30 **Dumbbell In Hands Single Leg Step-Ups**
x 6+6   +

   Alternate Leg Step-Ups
   x 6+6   +

   Dumbbell Box Jump
   x 10   or

   Dumbbell Squat Jump Raise To Armpit
   x 10   Sixty seconds break

31 **Javorek's Special Abdominal Program # 1**
   a)Hooked Feet Arms Cross On Chest Sit Ups
   x 10

   b) Hooked Feet Arms Cross On Chest Half Up & Up
      + Half Down & Down Sit Ups
   x 10

   c) Half Jack Knives or Crunches
   x 20

   d) Hooked Feet Arms Cross On Chest Half Up & Down Sit-Ups
   x 10

   e) Half Jack Knives or Crunches
   x 20

   f) Hooked Feet Arms Cross On Chest Half Up & Down Sit-Ups
   x 10

   g) Jack Knives
   x 10

32 **Stair or Shredded Rubber Boxes or Sand Stair Box Double Leg Bounding**
   x 6

   Stair or Shredded Rubber Boxes or Sand Stair Box Sprint
   x 6

Javorek's Calisthenics and Dumbbell Barbell Circuits

Javorek's calisthenics Conditioning Programs

Some of the most challenging tasks for an all sports conditioning coach are to prevent injuries, avoid his/her athletes' lack of interest, burn out or overtraining.

A good conditioning program must be very helpful and should contribute considerably in preventing injuries and improve those necessary qualities for an athlete's success in a given sport. At the same time it could be detrimental, or inefficient if the conditioning program is inadequate and monotonous.

On my own I always preach about program variations and making them as enjoyable as possible and of course as a result of the before mentioned criteria to prevent overtraining and injuries.

In my forty years of active coaching career, I have never experienced overtrained athletes. I think the reason is respecting the principle that I set to myself. As a track and field, weightlifting, as well as an all sports conditioning coach my main concern is my athlete. I always monitor their reaction to the program as well respecting the given sport's characteristics and period of preparation.

I follow very closely their daily feedback and intentionally I intercalate in preparatory phase days of so called calisthenics or other form of physical activities between the regular conditioning programs.

On several surveys I realized that athletes enjoy these days of a very challenging, but very different form of physical activities.

Some of the programs are not a 100% pure calisthenics, but, because the barbell or dumbbell exercises are very simple, "in principle" they fulfill the characteristics of a "free" workout.

I always tell to my athletes, they must enjoy their workout they must be happy. So during the workout, after a very challenging exercise I stop the whole program and I ask them how they feel, and they must smile and answer to me: "Yes, I love it"!!

The followings are my most successful variation of calisthenics conditioning circuit programs:

Organizing the class:

- Set up the stations; be sure every apparatus and equipments are on the right place and in enough number

- Organize the class, dividing equally as numbers of athletes/group. The program should be efficient up to four athletes /group

- Perform a short total body warm up

- Demonstrate the whole program, repeating each exercise (with less intensity) with the whole class

- For Barbell Wave Squat: take from the maximum Barbell Squat Jump

- For Barbell Quarter Squat & Up On Toes: take from the maximum Barbell back Squat

- Allow 1 minute of individual stretching and readiness for the class

Javorek's Calisthenics Circuit Conditioning Program # 1

1 Regular Push-Ups
20 or as many as you can   20 or as many as you can

2 Crunches
20   20

3 Parallel Bar Dips
x 15 or as many as you can   x 15 or as many as you can

4 Fixed Feet, Bent Knees Half Up & Up + Half Down & Down Sit-Ups
10 + 10   10 + 10

5 On High Bar Supinated Half Up& Up + Half Down & Down Pull-Ups
12 or as many as you can   12 or as many as you can

6 Regular "Clapping" Plyo-Push-Ups
15 or as many as you can   15 or as many as you can

7 Crunches
20   20

8 Box Jump (16"-24")
20   20

9 Parallel Bar Half Down & Down+ Half Up & Up Dips
15 or as many as you can   15 or as many as you can

10 Straight Knees Up Half & Half Crunches
20   20

11 On High Bar Pronated Behind The Head Pull-Ups
8 or as many as you can   8 or as many as you can

12 On 6" Boxes Plyo-Push-Ups
6+6 or as many as you can   6+6 or as many as you can

13 Fixed Feet Light Weight On Chest Sit-Ups
20   20

14 Box Jump (16"-32")
20   20

15 Parallel Bar Dips
15 or as many as you can   15 or as many as you can

16 Javorek's DB Complex # 1
40% 1   45% x1

17 Crunches
20   20

18 On High Bar Behind The Head Pronated Pull-Ups
8 or as many as you can   8 or as many as you can

19 Box Jump (16"-32")
20   20

Note In Case You Cannot Perform On Dip Bar, Plyo Push-Ups And On Pull-Ups The Prescribed Number Of Repetitions, Do As Many As You Can Or To Fatigue On Each Set.

Javorek's Calisthenics Circuit Conditioning Program # 2

1 Regular Push-Ups
x 15 or as many as you can   x 15 or as many as you can

2 DB Squat Push Press
70% 12   80% 8

3 Box Jump (16"-32")
15   15

4 On High Bar Supinated In Front Of Chest Pull-Ups
10 or as many as you can   10 or as many as you can

5 Crunches
20   20

6 DB Single Leg Step Back Lunges
70% 12+12   80% 10+10

7 Regular "Clapping" Plyo-Push-Ups
x 15 or as many as you can   x 15 or as many as you can

8 DB Squat Push Press
75% 10   85% 8

9 Box Jump(16"-32")
15   15

10 Jack-Knives
15   15

11 On High Bar Pronated In Front Of Chest Pull-Ups
x 10 or as many as you can   x 10 or as many as you can

12 DB Alternating Leg Lunges
75% 14+14   80% 12+12

13 Parallel Bar Dips
x 20 or as many as you can   x 20 or as many as you can

14 Box Jump (16"-32")
15   15

15 Crunches
20   20

16 Peg Board Walk-Up & Down
1   1

17 DB Squat Push Press
80% 8   85% 6

18 Box Jump (16"-32")
15   15

19 Jack-Knives
15   15

20 On 6" Boxes Plyo Push-Ups
x 6+6 or as many as you can   x 6+6 or as many as you can

21 On High Bar Pronated Behind The Head Pull-Ups
x 10 or as many as you can   x 10 or as many as you can

22 DB Squat Push Press
80% 8   90% 4

23 DB Lunge Walk
80% x20+20   80% x20+20

24 Javorek's DB Complex # 1
50% 1   55% 1

25 Box Jump (16"-32")
15   15

26 Jack-Knives
15   15

Note: In Case Of Not Being Able To Perform The Prescribed Repetitions: The Number Of Repetitions On Dips Bar, Peg Board, Plyo Push-Ups And On Pull-Ups Could Be As Many As You Can Do To Fatigue On Each Set.

Javorek's Calisthenics Circuit Conditioning Program # 3

1 BB Quarter Squat
40% 20   50% 20   60% 20

2 BB Squat Jump
30% 8   35% 8   40% 6

3 Box Jump (16"-32")
10   10   10

4 Regular "Clapping" Plyo- Push-Ups
10   10   10

5 Crunches
20   20   20

6 BB Quarter Squat
40% 20   50% 20   60% 20

7 Regular "Clapping" Plyo Push-Ups
10   10   10

8 Upstairs S Double Leg Bounding (3 Lengths, 28-32 Stairs)
2   2   2

9 Box Jump (16"-32")
10   10   10

10 Jack-Knives
10   10   10

11 Medicine Ball Sit-Ups Chest Pass+Overhead Pass+Chest Pass
10+10+10   10+10+10   10+10+10

12 BB Quarter Squat
50% 20   60% 20   65% 20

13 Javorek's BB Complex # 1
50% 1   50% 1   60% 1   60% 1

14 Upstairs S One Leg (R+L) Bounding
2   2   2

15 Upstairs S Double Leg Bounding (3 Lengths, 28-32 Stairs)
2   2   2

16 Jack-Knives
10   10   10

17 Medicine Ball Sit-Ups Chest Pass+Overhead Pass+Chest Pass
10+10+10   10+10+10   10+10+10

18 Box Jump(16"-32")
10   10   11

19 BB Quarter Squat
55% 20   65% 20   70% 20

20 BB Squat Jump
30% 8   35% 8   40% 6

21 Hooked Feet Weight On Chest Bent Knees Sit-Ups
30   30   30

22 Medicine Ball Sit-Ups Chest Pass+Overhead Pass+Chest Pass
10+10+10   10+10+10   10+10+10

23 Regular "Clapping" Plyo-Push-Ups
10   10   10

24 DB Lunge Walk
80% x20+20   80% x20+20   80% x20+20

25 Jack-Knives
10   10   10

26 Upstairs Double Leg Bounding (3 Lengths, 28-32 Stairs)
2   2   2

27 Upstairs Sprint (3 Lengths, 28-32 Stairs)
2   2   2

28 Javorek's Special Abdominal Program # 1 (Half & Half Sit-Ups Program):

Hooked Feet Sit-Up
x 10

Half Up & Up + Half Down & Down Sit-Up
x 10+10

Half Jack Knives or Crunches
x 20

Half Up & Down Sit-Up
x 10+10

Half Jack Knives or Crunches
x 20

Half Down & Up Sit-Up
x 10+10

Half Jack Knives or Crunches
x 20

Jack-Knives
x 10

Note In Case Of Not Being Able To Perform The Prescribed Number Of Repetitions: The Number Of Repetitions On Box Jumps, Plyo Push-Ups And One Leg Stair Bounding Means You Are Not Ready For This Circuit Program. Conclusion: Don't Do It, Please!

Javorek's Calisthenics Circuit Conditioning Program # 4

1. Dumbbell Single Leg Lunges + Squat Push Press
70% 14+14+10

2. Crunches
x 20

3. Dumbbell Squat Upright Row
70% 16

4. Crunches
x 20

5. Dumbbell Alternate Leg Lunges + Squat Push Press
70% 14+14+10

6. Half Jack Knives
x 20

7. Dumbbell Single Leg Step Ups + Box Jump
70% 12+12+10

8. "Knee Hug" Sit-Ups
x 20

9. Dumbbell Squat Under Upright Row+ Squat Jump
70% 14+10

10. Alternate Knee Bent Twisted Sit-Ups
x 10+10

11. Dumbbell Single Leg Lunges + Squat Jump Push Press
70% 14+14+10

12. Hands Under Butt, Leg Raise
x 20

13. Dumbbell Squat Jump Raise To Armpit
70% 14

14. Dumbbell Alternate Leg Lunges + Squat Jump Push Press
70% 14+14+10

15."Bicycle" Sit-Ups
x 15+15

16.Dumbbell Single Leg Step Ups + Squat Push Press
70% 12+12+10

17.Up & Down Scissors Abdominal exercise
x 30+30

18.Dumbbell Split Jump With Raise To Armpit + Squat Push Press
70% 10+10+10

19.Cross Scissors Abdominal exercise
x 30+30

20.Dumbbell Alternate Leg Step Ups + Squat Push Press
70% 14+14+10

21.Jack Knives
x 20

22.Dumbbell Lunge Walk + Squat Push Press
70% 20+20+10

23.Parallel Bar Dips
x 12 - 15

24.Different Height Box Jump
x 20

Javorek's Calisthenics Circuit Conditioning Program # 5

1. Push Ups	x 15
2. Crunches	x 20
3. Parallel Bar Dips	x 10-15
4. "Knee Hug" Sit-Ups	x 20
5. Regular Plyo (Clapping) Push Ups	x 14
6. Half Jack Knives	x 20
7. High Bar "Chin Ups" Supinated Pull Ups	x 10
8. Alternate Knee Bent Twisted Sit-Ups	x 12+12
9. Parallel Bar Dips	x 10-15
10. Hands Under Butt, Leg Raise	x 20
11. High Bar "Chin Ups" Pronated Pull Ups	x 10
12. Jack Knives	x 20
13. On 3" to 6" Boxes, Plyo Push Ups	x 8+8
14. Jack Knives	x 20
15. Different Heights, Box Jump (12" - 22" Height Box)	x 20
16. Javorek's Special Abdominal Half & Half Sit-Ups Program # 1:	
Hooked Feet Sit-Up	x 10
Half Up & Up + Half Down & Down Sit-Up	x 10+10
Half Jack Knives or Crunches	x 20
Half Up & Down Sit-Up	x 10+10
Half Jack Knives or Crunches	x 20
Half Down & Up Sit-Up	x 10+10
Half Jack Knives or Crunches	x 20
Jack-Knives	x 10

Javorek's Calisthenics Circuit Conditioning Program # 6

Short Variation: # 1

Station # 1
Plyo Push Ups: The Repetitions Varies In Report To The Athletes Conditioning Level — 6 x 6 to 10 x 10

Station # 2
Parallel Bar Dips The Repetitions Varies In Report
To The Athletes Conditioning Level — x 10 - 20

Station # 3

Javorek's Special Medicine Ball Abdominal Program # 2	
Hooked Feet Sit Ups	x 10
Half Up & Up + Half Down & Down	x 10
Hooked Feet Medicine Ball Overhead Pass & Sit-Ups	x 10
Half Jack Knives	x 10
Half Up & Down Sit-Ups	x 10
Hooked Feet Medicine Ball Chest Pass & Sit-Ups	x 10
Half Jack Knives	x 10
Half Down & Up Sit-Ups	x 10
Hooked Feet Medicine Ball Overhead Pass & Sit-Ups	x 10
Hooked Feet Medicine Ball Chest Pass & Sit-Ups	x 10
Jack Knives	x 10

Station # 4
High Bar Behind The Head Or Just Regular Pronated or Supinated Pull Ups. The Repetitions and Hand Positions Varies In Report
To The Athletes' Conditioning Level — x 6 - 12

Station # 5
Different Heights, Box Jump (12" - 22 " Height Box) — x 25

Short Variation: # 2

Station # 1
Plyo Push Ups The Repetitions Varies In Report
To The Athletes Conditioning Level — 6x6 to 10x10

Station # 2
Barbell Wave Squat (3 Quarter Squat & Up On Toes + 1 Jump + 1 Squat Jump) Intensity taken of Barbell Back Squat Jump Maximum
50% 40 (8 series of 3 quarter squat & up on toes + 1 jump + 1 squat jump)

Station 3
Bar Dips. The Repetitions Varies In Report To The Athletes Conditioning Level — x 10 - 20

Station # 4
Barbell Back Squat Jump — 50% 8

Station # 5
High Bar Behind The Head Or Just Regular Pronated or Supinated Pull Ups. The Repetitions and Hand Positions Varies In Report To The Athletes' Conditioning Level — x 6 - 12

Station # 6

Javorek's Special Medicine Ball Abdominal Program #2	
Hooked Feet Sit Ups	x 10
Half Up & Up + Half Down & Down	x 10
Hooked Feet Medicine Ball Overhead Pass & Sit-Ups	x 10
Half Jack Knives	x 10
Half Up & Down Sit-Ups	x 10
Hooked Feet Medicine Ball Chest Pass & Sit-Ups	x 10
Half Jack Knives	x 10
Half Down & Up Sit-Ups	x 10
Hooked Feet Medicine Ball Overhead Pass & Sit-Ups	x 10
Hooked Feet Medicine Ball Chest Pass & Sit-Ups	x 10
Jack Knives	x 10

Station # 7
Different Heights, Box Jump (12" - 22" Height Box) — x 25

The "Challenger" (Variation)

The Stations Are:

Station # 1
Plyo Push Ups The Repetitions Varies In Report
To The Athletes Conditioning Level — 6+6 to 10+10

Station # 2
Barbell Wave Squat (3 Waves + 1 Jump + 1 Squat Jump) — 50% 40

Station # 3

Javorek's Special Abdominal Program # 1	
Hooked Feet Sit-Up	x 10
Half Up & Up + Half Down & Down Sit-Up	x 10+10
Half Jack Knives or Crunches	x 20
Half Up & Down Sit-Up	x 10+10
Half Jack Knives or Crunches	x 20
Half Down & Up Sit-Up	x 10+10
Half Jack Knives or Crunches	x 20
Jack-Knives	x 10

Station # 4
Parallel Bar Dips The Repetitions Varies
In Report To The Athletes Conditioning Level — x 10 - 20

Station # 5
Dumbbell Alternate Leg Lunges
+ Squat Jump Push Press   65% 10+10+10

Station # 6
Barbell Back Squat Jump   50% 8

Station # 7
High Bar Behind The Head Or Just Regular Pronated or Supinated Pull Ups.
The Repetitions and Hand Positions Varies In Report
To The Athletes' Conditioning Level   x 6 - 12

Station # 8

Javorek's Special Medicine Ball Abdominal Program #2
Hooked Feet Sit Ups   · x 10
Half Up & Up + Half Down & Down   x 10
Hooked Feet Medicine Ball Overhead Pass & Sit-Ups   x 10
Half Jack Knives   x 10
Half Up & Down Sit-Ups   x 10
Hooked Feet Medicine Ball Chest Pass & Sit-Ups   x 10
Half Jack Knives   x 10
Half Down & Up Sit-Ups   x 10
Hooked Feet Medicine Ball Overhead Pass & Sit-Ups   x 10
Hooked Feet Medicine Ball Chest Pass & Sit-Ups   x 10
Jack Knives   x 10

Station # 9
Dumbbell Alternate Leg Step Ups
+ Squat Jump Push Press   65% 12+12+8

Station # 10
Box Jump (12" - 22" Height Box)   x 25

Station # 11

Javorek's Special Abdominal Program # 3
Hooked feet arms cross on chest sit-ups   x 10
Hooked feet arms cross on chest half up & up
+ half down & down sit-ups   x 10
Jack-knives or Crunches   x 10
Half jack-knives or Crunches   x 10
Hooked feet arms cross on chest
half up & down sit-ups   x 10
Jack-knives   x 10
Half jack-knives or Crunches   x 10
Hooked feet arms cross on chest
half down & up sit-ups   x 10
Jack-knives   x 10
Hooked feet arms cross on chest half up & up
+ half down & down sit-ups   x 10
Jack-knives   x 10

Station # 12
Upstairs Double Leg Bounding   x 4
Upstairs Strides (Sprint)   x 4

Chapter 16
Javorek's Wrist Shoulder Back Ankle and Leg Injuries
Athletic Reconditioning Programs

Javorek's Wrist Exercises

1. Parallel Dumbbells "Up & Down" Curls	x 10
2. Parallel Dumbbells "Sideways" Curls	x 10
3. Pronated "Up & Down" Curls	x 10
4. Pronated "Sideways" Curls	x 10
5. Supinated "Up & Down" Curls	x 10
6. Supinated "Sideways" Curls	x 10
7. Dumbbell Outside Rotation	x 10
8. Dumbbell Inside Rotation	x 10

Dumbbell parallel sideways wrist curls

Dumbbell pronated sideways wrist curls.

Dumbbell pronated up & down wrist curls.

Dumbbell supinated sideways and up & down wrist curls.

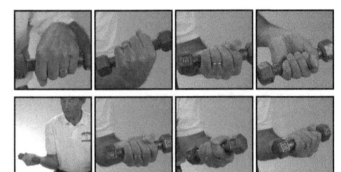

Dumbbell wrist rotation.

Javorek's Shoulder Reconditioning Dumbbell Complex Exercise

1) Hands Bent To Frontal Deltoids, Forward Backward Elbow Rotation	X 10+10
*The elbows should make perfect circular movements	
2) Hands Bent To Frontal Deltoids, Lateral Elbow Raise (Chicken Wings)	X 20
*The elbows should make perfect vertical line movements	
3) Dumbbell Hands Bent To Chest Inward-Outward Circle	X 10+10
*The fists should make perfect circular movements	
4) Dumbbell Rotational (from Pronation to Supination) Curls	X 14
5) Dumbbell Parallel In Front Of Chest Inward-Outward Rotation	X 10+10
6) Dumbbell Lateral Pronated Arm Raise	X 10
7) Dumbbell Frontal Pronated Arm Raise	X 10
8) Dumbbell From Hip High Pull Snatch	X 10
9) Dumbbell Bent Over Fly	X 10
10) Dumbbell Bent Over "Kick Back" Triceps Curls	X 10
11) Dumbbell Lateral Supinated Arm Raise	X 10
12) Dumbbell Frontal Supinated Arm Raise	X 10
13) Dumbbell Breast Stroke Imitation	X 10
14) Dumbbell Frontal Rotational Arm Raise	X 10
15) Dumbbell Lateral Rotational Arm Raise	X 10
16) Dumbbell Rotational Bent Over Row	X 12
17) Dumbbell Javorek's Shoulder Routine	X 10+10

Javorek's shoulder routine.

Javorek's Back Athletic Reconditioning Exercise Routine

I was born with a milder form of "spina bifida" which almost made my athletic career come to a sudden end

After my first back injury not being able to move doctors recommended to stop performance sport. Instead I started to work harder and overcome my very annoying back problem. When I started my studies at University in sport biomechanics classes I was experimenting exercise routines which could help me to survive the hard physical activity load at Physical Education Department and at my preferable sport weightlifting

Following very closely the effect of exercises and different form of back and hamstring stretching I was selecting 8 exercises as the most important in rebuilding a healthy well-balanced back

In my long coaching and athletic career I have concluded that the majority of back problems are generated usually from an unbalanced abdominal and back musculature from an unbalanced quadriceps and hamstring musculature or from a very stiff tight hamstring. Also problems can come from the neglected bad back posture (ciphosis scoliosis and lordosis) which actually are a result of muscular imbalance of incorrect exercise practice or just lack of a well balanced physical activity proper to a young person

With this exercise program which contains seven of my exercises one could prevent certain form of back problems and also if performed the right way could help anyone to reconditioning a damaged back if a doctor releases a person (athlete) to do so

1. Hooked Feet-Bent Knees With Weight On Chest Sit Ups	x 20	3 Sets
2. Javorek's Special Good Mornings With Light Weights	x 10	3 Sets
3. Barbell Behind The Head From Quarter Squat Press	x 10	3 Sets
4. Barbell Regular Good Morning With Light Weights	x 20	3 Sets
5. Barbell Press Under High Pull Snatch	x 10	3 Sets
6. Ballet Hamstring Stretching	x 30 Sec.	3 Sets
7. Yoga Back Stretching	x 30 Sec.	3 Sets

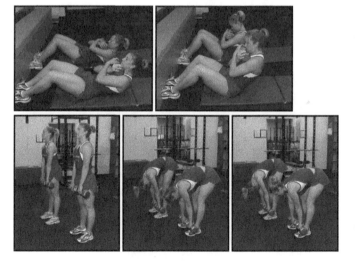

Back reconditioning.

Javorek's General Abdominal Program

* For advanced performance athletes only

Before starting this program, every individual athlete must be capable of performing with perfect body posture each of these exercises with at least 20 repetitions. Depending on individual goals, or the coach's prescription, repeat the program as many times as prescribed. On individual basis, other abdominal exercises could be added to the abdominal program. Do not take longer break than 10-15 seconds between exercises. Do it slowly but with a dynamic and continuous rhythm.

1. Lying Down, arms overhead, simultaneous knee hugs.................................x 15

2. Crunches regular or in four sequences
(*two up & two down*) ....x 20

3. Parallel leg raise, arms under hip ....x 20

4. Lying down, hands bent to head,
alternate knee touch, bicycle ....x 20+20

5. Lying down, straight legs up, half jack knifes.............................x 20

6. Seated, hands behind, pointed toes, legs raised to 30°
up and down scissors ....x 30+30

7. Alternate knee bend, twisted sit ups..................................x 10+10

8. Lying with both shoulders on the floor, arms bent to shoulders, hip twisted to left or right side with the
top foot crossed over, crunches ....x 20+20

9. Jack knifes...x 15

10. Seated, hands behind, pointed toes, legs raised to 30°
side to side cross scissors ....x 30+30

11. Crunches regular or in four sequences
(*two up and two down*) ....x 20

12. Lying down, bent knees, hands bent to head,
alternate leg cross-overs...x 20+20

13. Lying down, arms bent to head, bent knees hooked under heavy dumbbells, or someone stepping on them,
half and half situps ....x 15+15

14. Jack knifes...x 10

15. Lying down, bent knees, feet on the floor,
hold up in crunch up position ....4 x 15 sec.

16. Lying down, straight legs up, half jack knifes ....x 20

17. Seated, hands behind, pointed straight legs, simultaneous knee pull to chest, kick
out 30° from the floor ....x 15

18. Lying on right or left side, bent knees, top hand bent to head, bottom hand cross
on side, *(left — right)*
side crunches in four sequences
(two up and two down) ....x 20+20

19. Jack knifes ....x 15

20. Seated, hands behind, pointed straight legs,
simultaneous 30° leg raise, pull knees to chest,
kick out close to floor ....x 15

21. jack knifes ....x 15

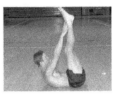

22. Straight legs up, hands on thighs, crunches ....x 20

23. Lying down, arms bent to head, bent knees
and straddled feet, twisted situps ....x 10+10

24. Bent knees feet hooked under heavy dumbbells,
or someone stepping on them,
different size dumbbells on chest sit ups ....x 20

25. Bent knees, feet on the floor,
hold up in crunch up position ....4 x 15 sec.

26. Lying on stomach, arms close to the body, bent at chest level, holding the hip on
the floor, gradually straighten the elbows, looking up on the ceiling, and
hyperextending the back. Hold this position for 15 sec. Then raise onto knees,
curve *(round)* and arch back for 20 sec. Then with straight elbows sit back onto
heels for 20 sec.

Javorek's Ankle-Knee-Hip Exercise Routine:

How I mentioned in several places in my book my main concern is always preventing injuries. With the following ankle &knee & hip exercise program I have the same goal but I am also using for the athletic reconditioning which is the next phase after finishing a physical therapy rehab program

I believe in the importance of developing deep conditioning reflexes in preventing several injuries which could prevent severe damage to an athlete's wrist knee back or ankle caused by brisk unexpected motion. Practicing from the beginning of a pre-competitional period my ankle exercise routine in my long coaching career I received very positive feed back from the athletes and from the trainers. The most important sports which "feel" the benefit of a six to eight weeks daily practice on the ankle routine are basketball volleyball tennis soccer baseball and football.

At the beginning I am explaining the reason why we are performing these pretty boring exercises and after their first practices I receive the very happy feed backs which sounds like this: " Coach I sprained my ankle (I felt in that way) but actually I did not sprained it because I had developed the conditioning reflex and my brained reacted ahead of me!!

Actually that I am telling to my athletes that practicing on a daily basis we are not just strengthening their ankle knee and hip but at the same time we develop a perfect conditioning reflex for those dangerous feet positions which could hurt them and get them out for several days or weeks from their practices or games

1. Running in Place Variations	3 Minutes
2. Stretching	1 Minute
3. Double Leg Toe Raise & Hold	x 10
4. Double Count Split Jump	x 10
5. Ankle Warm Up	1 Minute

Double Leg Toe Raise & Hold & extends onto toes and hold for 10 seconds

- Standing with feet flat with one hand extended to the wall for support quickly roll one foot to the side while raising the other

6. Squat Jump	x 5
7. Double Leg From Side Edge Toe Raise	x 14

Apply body weight to sides of both feet and then return to position with feet flat

Extend to toe raise from side of foot rolling body weight from the heels to little toes. Reverse order and return to start position

8. Double Count Split Jump	x 12+12
9. One Leg Toe Raise(R+L)	x 10+10
10.Squat Jump	x 5
11.Double Leg From Side Edge Toe Raise	x 12

Apply body weight to sides of both feet and then return to position with feet flat

Extend to toe raise from side of foot rolling body weight from the heels to little toes. Reverse order and return to start position

12.Double Count Split Jump	x 14+14
13.Double Leg Bouncing In Place	x 12
14.Double Leg Backward-Forward Bounce	x 10+10
15.Squat Jump	x 5
16.One Leg Toe Raise(R+L)	x 10+10

With one hand extended to the wall for support perform toe raises one leg at a time

17.Double Leg Sideways Bounce	x 10+10
18.Double Leg From Side Edge Toe Raise	x 10
19.Squat Jump	x 5
20.One Leg Bouncing in Place(R+L)	x 10+10
21.Double Count Split Jump	x 14+14

22.One Leg Backward-Forward Bounce(R+L)	x 10+10

Standing on one foot back and fort bouncing

23.Squat Jump	x 5
24.One Leg Toe Raise(R+L)	x 10+10
25.Double Count Split Jump	x 16+16
26.One Leg Sideways Bounce(R+L)	x 10+10
27.Squat Jump	x 5
28.One Leg Twisted Bounce(R+L)	x 10+10
29.Double Count Split Jump	x 14+14
30.Squat Jump	x 5
31.One Leg Toe Raise(R+L)	x 10+10
32.Double Leg From Side Edge Toe Raise	x 12
33.Squat Jump	x 5

Here is a sample of my ankle-knee-hip warm-up routine, performing all of the above exercises. As you will realize between the exercises I intercalated the five repetitions squat jumps, or the ten repetitions split jumps, which makes the program more dynamic, challenging, and itself a good and short conditioning program.

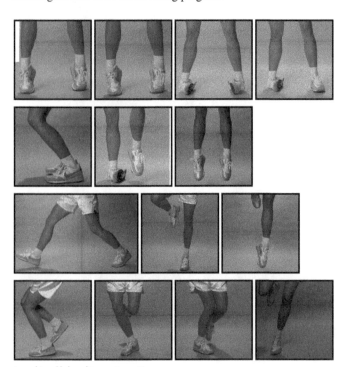

Javorek's ankle-knee-hip exercise routine.

Javorek's Leg Injuries' Athletic Reconditioning After Physical Therapy

One of the most important part in an athlete's leg rehabilitation is after the general physical therapy. After an athlete finishes his physical therapy rehabilitation program and released by his physician to start a complete athletic rehabilitation program I start with a lot of patience and gradually building up all of the lost reflexes and reactions. At the same time I focus on regaining the before injury strength and power level. During in my forty years of coaching I experienced tens and tens of successful stories when athletes were able to participate in their favorite sport on a much higher level than before injury

During my leg rehabilitation program an athlete is working out on other muscle groups gradually getting up with a full total body program parallel with leg rehabilitation

The philosophy of my 56 days rehabilitation program is that starting any kind of jumping and running activities before completing the program would result in a not perfect recovery and shorter post-surgery athletic career

Sports Reconditioning Program
© Istvan "Steve" Javorek

Day # 1 & 3 Slow Barbell Back Squat:
20 Lb. x 10	20 Lb. x 10	20 Lb. x 10	20 Lb. x 10
20 Lb. x 10	20 Lb. x 10	20 Lb. x 10	20 Lb. x 10
20 Lb. x 10	20 Lb. x 10		

Day # 2 & 4 Slow Barbell Back Squat:
20 x 10	25 x 10	30 x 10	20 x 10	25 x 10	30 x 10	20 x 10	25 x 10
30 x 10	30 x 10						

Day # 5 & 7 Slow Barbell Back Squat:
20 x 10	30 x10	20 x10	30 x10	25 x10	30 x10	35 x 10	35 x10
25 x10	35 x10						

Day # 6 & 8 Slow Barbell Back Squat:
20 x 10	30 x 10	30 x 10	40 x 10	30 x 10	30 x 10	35 x 10	40 x 10
40 x 10	40 x 10						

Day # 9 & 11 Slow Barbell Back Squat:
20 x 10	25 x 10	30 x 10	35 x 10	20 x 10	25 x 10	30 x 10	35 x 10
40 x 10	45 x 10						

Day # 10 & 12 Slow Barbell Back Squat:
20 x 10	30 x 10	40 x 10	25 x 10	35 x 10	45 x 10	30 x 10	40 x 10
35 x 10	45 x 10	45 x 10					

Day # 13 & 15 Slow Barbell Back Squat:
20 x 10	30 x 10	40 x 10	45 x 10	30 x 10	35 x 10	40 x 10	45 x 10
45 x 10	45 x 10						

Day # 14 & 16 Slow Barbell Back Squat & Up On Toes:
20 x 10	25 x 10	30 x 10	35 x 10	40 x 10	45 x 10	50 x 10	40 x 10
45 x 10	50 x 10						

Day # 17 & 19 Slow Barbell Back Squat:
30 x 10	40 x 10	35 x 10	45 x 10	30 x 10	40 x 10	50 x 10	35 x 10
45 x 10	55 x 10						

Day # 18 & 20 Slow Barbell Back Squat & Up On Toes:
30 x 10	40 x 10	50 x 10				
30 x 10	40 x 10	50 x 10	35 x 10	45 x 10	55 x 10	55 x 10

Day # 21 & 23 Slow Barbell Back Squat & Up On Toes:
20 x 10	40 x 10	60 x 10	20 x 10	40 x 10	60 x 10	30 x 10	40 x 10
50 x 10	60 x 10						

Day # 22 & 24 Slow Barbell Back Squat & Up On Toes:
30 x 10	50 x 10	60 x 10	65 x 10	65 x 10

Barbell Quarter Squat & Up On Toes:
25 x 40	30 x 40	40 x 40	40 x 35	45 x 35

Day # 25 & 27 Slow Barbell Back Squat & Up On Toes:
30 x 10	60 x 10	70 x 10	40 x 10	70 x 10

Barbell Quarter Squat & Up On Toes:
30 x 40	40 x 40	50 x 35	55 x 35	60 x 30

Day # 26 & 28 Dumbbell Single Leg Continuous Lunges
(L+R) 15+15 x 8 Sets With Light Dumbbells In Hands

Day # 29 & 31 Slow Barbell Back Squat & Up On Toes:
30 x 10	50 x 10	70 x 10	35 x 10	55 x 10	75 x 10

Barbell Wave Squat (4 Quarter Squat & Up On Toes + 1 Jump Combination):
20 x 40	30 x 40	30 x 40	35 x 40	35 x 40	40 x 35	40 x 30

Day # 30 & 32 Dumbbell Single Leg Step Back Lunges
(L+R) 14+14 x 8 Sets With Light Dumbbells In Hands

Day # 33 & 35 Slow Barbell Back Squat & Up On Toes:
40 x 10	60 x 10	80 x 10	40 x 10	60 x 10	80 x 10	80 x 10

Barbell Wave Squat
(4 Quarter Squat & Up On Toes + 1 Jump Combination):
30 x 40	30 x 40	35 x 40	40 x 35	40 x 35	45 x 30	50 x 30

Day # 34 & 36 Dumbbell Alternate Leg Step Back Lunges
(L+R) 14+14 8 Sets With Light Dumbbells In Hands

Day # 37 & 39 Slow Barbell Back Squat & Up On Toes:
40 x 10	60 x 10	80 x 10	90 x 10
50 x 10	70 x 10	90 x 10	70 x 10
90 x 10			

Barbell Wave Squat
(4 Quarter Squat & Up On Toes + 1 Jump Combination):
30 x 40	40 x 40	40 x 40	50 x 35	55 x 30

Day # 38 & 40 Dumbbell Lunge Walk:
25 +25
8 Sets With Light Dumbbells In Hands

Day # 41 & 43 Slow Barbell Back Squat & Up On Toes:
40 x 10	60 x 10	80 x 10	100 x 10

Barbell Wave Squat
(3 Quarter Squat & Up On Toes + 1 Squat Jump + 1 Jump Combination):
30 x 40	40 x 40	40 x 40	45 x 35	45 x 35	50 x 30

Day # 42 & 44 Single Leg Step Ups
The Dumbbells Weight And The Box Height Must Be Individually Determined By The Coach
x 15 Double Steps 6 Sets

Day# 45 & 47 BB.Back Squat+ Wave Squat + Back Squat
30 x 10+30+10	40 x 10+30+10	50 x 10+30+10	50 x 10+30+10
50 x 10+30+10			

Day # 46 & 48 Single Leg Step Ups :
The Dumbbells Weight And The Box Height Must Be Individually Determined By The Coach
x 15 Double Steps 6 Sets

Dumbbell Lunge Walk: 25 + 25
8 Sets With Light Dumbbells In Hands

Day # 49 & 51 BB. Wave Squat +Back Squat+ Wave Squat
30 x 20+10+20	40 x 20+10+20	40 x 20+10+20	40 x 20+10+20
50 x 20+10+20			

Single Leg Step Ups:
The Dumbbells Weight And The Box Height Must Be Individually Determined By The Coach
15 + 15   6 Sets

Day # 50 & 52 Dumbbell Lunge Walk:
25 + 25
8 Sets With Light Dumbbells In Hands

Day # 53 & 55 Barbell Back Squat & Up On Toes:
x 10 Reps Test Start With Light Weight And Gradually Increase To 10 RM.

Barbell Wave Squat
(3 Quarter Squat & Up On Toes + 1 Squat Jump + 1 Jump Combination):
30 x 40	40 x 40	40 x 40	45 x 35	50 x 30	50 x 30	50 x 30

Day # 54 & 56 Barbell Back Squat Jump:
The Barbell's Weight Must Be Individually Determined By The Coach   x 8   6 Sets
For ex: 20 x 8	20 x 8	25 x 8	25 x 8	20 x 8	25 x 8	30 x 8
30 x 8						

Single Leg Step Ups:
The Dumbbells Weight And The Box Height Must Be Individually Determined By The Coach
15 + 15   6 Sets If necessary, Increase The Height Of The Box

With The Personal Physician's Approval. After Day 56 To Start Specific Sport Related Skill Drills Involving Alternating Leg Step Ups Different Height Box Jumps And Lateral Movements Also;

Individuals With Previous (Before Injury) Lesser- Leg Strength The Weight Increment Should Be Slower. (Repeat Several Times The Same Workouts or Just Lower The Weight)

Barbell Back Squat Means As Deep As An Athlete Could Squat Comfortable On Flat Foot With Straight Back, Looking Ahead (Not Down Not Up On The Ceiling!!);

Stop The Program (As Long As Necessary) If An Athlete Complains Pain In The Injured Area Follow Up The Physician And The Physical Therapist Recommendations

Progress Chart

Day. 1 _____

Day. 2 _____

Day. 3 _____

Day. 4 _____

Day. 5 _____

Day. 6 _____

Day. 7 _____

Day. 8 _____

Day. 9 _____

Day. 10 _____

Day. 11 _____

Day. 12 _____

Day. 13 _____

Day. 14 _____

Day. 15 _____

Day. 16 _____

Day. 17 _____

Day. 18 _____

Day. 19 _____

Day. 20 _____

Day. 21 _____

Day. 22 _____

Day. 23 _____

Day. 24 _____

Day. 25 _____

Day. 26 _____

Day. 27 _____

Day. 28 _____

Day. 29 _____

Day. 30 _____

Day. 31 _____

Day. 32 _____

Day. 33 _____

Day. 34 _____

Day. 35 _____

Day. 36 _____

Day. 37 _____

Day. 38 _____

Day. 39 _____

Day. 40 _____

Day. 41 _____

Day. 42 _____

Day. 43 _____

Day. 44 _____

Day. 45 _____

Day. 46 _____

Day. 47 _____

Day. 48 _____

Day. 49 _____

Day. 50 _____

Day. 51 _____

Day. 52 _____

Day. 53 _____

Day. 54 _____

Day. 55 _____

Day. 56 _____

Day. 57 _____

Day. 58 _____

Day. 59 _____

Javorek's Energy Pudding & Drink

Look on You Tube for practical demonstration

http://www.youtube.com/watch?v=4jhFv_3vYpk Energy   Drink
http://www.youtube.com/watch?v=kyoL4_zy7_M Energy Pudding

1. Two Hours before workout: - 200 Gr. boiled rice;
- 1 to 2 Spoon of Honey, or your taste;
- 1 Lemon's juice, or your taste;
- 3 Eggs' yolk mixed them up in a blender.

The left-over egg white, you blend till becomes foamy. After that, mix it up with sugar (two-three spoon) and blend till becomes very hard, then mix it up with a bag of frozen raspberries (of course you defreeze it first), then mix it up with the rice-egg yolk-lemon-honey pudding.

1 spoon of honey - 60 calories - 17 grams of carbohydrate

3 eggs - 210 calories; 12 grams Protein; 2 grams carbohydrate and a lot of antioxidants

3 spoon of Sugar - 135 Calories

200 grams (8Oz) boiled Rice - 200 calories; 25 gram carbohydrate; 2 grams Protein

Raspberry, 12 Oz package 350 calories; 42 gram carbohydrate; 22 gram Dietary Fiber; 15 grams Sugar - 5 grams Protein

1 lemon's juice – 22 calories 12 grams carbohydrates; dietary fibers 5 grams, 1 gram Protein, and a lot of antioxidants, minerals, vitamins

Total: 977 calories; carbohydrates = 124 grams; Protein = 28 grams

Remember if you like sweater, take 2 table spoon of honey, but it increases with 60 calories the grand total of calories!!

Everyone tells me, it is delicious and really gives a lot of energy!

Recommended daily ratio of the three main nutrients for an active athlete are:

(a) 60% Carbohydrate: Muscle glycogen is the most important energy source during a strength workout. Nutritional scientists prove that replacing depleted muscle glycogen stores after workout - by ingesting 1 gram of carbohydrate per kilogram of body mass taken within a maximum of one hour after a workout or practice - will replenish the muscles glycogen stores back to normal level within 24 hours, thereby minimizing the occurrence of overtraining, decreased performance, or fatigue.

(b) 25% Fat (lipids). Medical research shows it is healthier if intake of saturated animal fats is minimized and all hydrogenated oils and transfatty acids (common in most margarines, many cereals, snacks and fast food products) are avoided.

(c) 15% Protein (1-2 grams per kilogram bodyweight per day). Protein is an amino acid compound intended primarily for building and repairing muscle and other tissues of the body. It is not intended to serve as a source of energy, so it is important that you have an adequate intake of carbohydrates and fats.

Vitamins and mineral replacement after workouts I highly recommend, in the form of fruits and vegetables and herbs teas. A few words are necessary about the currently popular Creatine: this is found in the muscles and plays an important part in the energy processes involved with muscle action. Creatine as a nutritional supplement I recommend 1 lb of red meat which contains 3 grams of it. But in the mean time, do not forget that Creatine (and too much protein) may dehydrate the body if you do not have an adequate intake of fluid.

Chapter 17
Cycling Conditioning

Motto: in this time of drug scandals in every sport and specifically in cycling, I can state that cyclist does not need any "special help" just a scientific and year-round athletic preparation This program will pass the most sophisticated drug test, and any cyclist could sleep quietly after every random or mandatory drug test during any level of competition, including Tour de France!!

Cycling, Boxing, Cross Country Running and Skiing, Swimming and Wrestling, has one thing in common: all of them require muscular endurance, stamina and high quality cardio-vascular endurance.

For endurance sports I consider that a perfect combination of general physical conditioning, cardio-vascular free weights conditioning, and interval running, swimming or biking conditioning could develop the highest quality of an overall physical and psychological shape (state). During heavy practice, I ponder general conditioning -in a form of an active rest- as the best and very efficient tool of recovery during heavy practice time.

The endurance sports, being a very complex notion with their several events and races, the conditioning also must be a harmonious combination of aerobic and free weights cardio-vascular endurance, general muscular strength, power and endurance, exercises and programs.

The endurance exercises must follow a ratio of high repetitions with short breaks, achieving a very elevated muscular & cardio-vascular endurance, parallel with a very increased (augmented) degree of will power, which is indispensable in performance cycling.

In the sport of cycling -if any- I consider as one of the most important factors of being able to fight the "big two F" of all endurance performance sports: Fear and Fatigue. Fatigue is a result of an unsatisfactory conditioning: is a combination of physical and mental tiredness-. Fear is an obvious result of the fatigue. In several sports (which includes cycling), will power has an immeasurable significance, especially in fighting the "Fatigue and Fear "and could help athletes to overcome every negative psychological manifestation and help them to become a successful athlete. Will power is a psychological quality, which could be developed on the same principles as muscle fibers: gradually and continuously.

I could say, that every athlete should have as a psychological motivator an old and very wise motto:" Everybody has unlimited potential to be the person that they want to be ", which (at least personally) sounds more human and helps develop a positive mental attitude toward the modern time's increased load in practice and in sports conditioning versus the so popular "No pain, no gain ".

In a yearly plan of preparation - as the best method of preventing injuries and emphasizing on overall body strengthening-, I consider for every sport to sacrifice a certain amount of time for an off-season "clean " general conditioning. During this general conditioning, gradually more, specific cycling conditioning could be introduced in the programs. In my personal opinion of a yearly cycling conditioning I would include:

- To balance the undeveloped musculature

- To develop a harmonious abdominal and lower back musculature

- To improve the upper and lower body strength with a special attention to shoulders-middle back-lower back-hip-knee-ankle lever

- To develop the highest quality of possible fast twitch leg musculature

- To correct any sign of a bad body posture

- Improving the hamstrings' flexibility

- Combining aerobic and muscular cardio-vascular conditioning with general strength, power and speed conditioning exercises

- Special conditioning for high mileage, developing an outstanding cardio-vascular and muscular endurance

- Accommodate the whole body functions in developing a high standard fighting spirit

- Combining of biking practice, general and gradually more specific biking conditioning in order to achieve the highest standard of physical and mental state

- Developing special "on bike "interval circuit combinations of conditioning in order to stress the circulatory and respiratory systems (cardio-vascular and pulmonary)

The two weeks of introductory conditioning, as outlined in the following training schedules, are more time consuming than a free weight conditioning program. However, the athletes must be prepared to complete the introductory program without struggling.

The importance of technical proficiency must be emphasized from the start of the program. Poor technique is difficult to correct and may lead to tendon or muscle injuries.

A primary question facing all coaches is, "How can I determine the maximum weight for each athlete in a particular exercise." This question can be answered during the two-week preparatory program. During the first part of the preparatory program approximate intensities are used. Then, in the final days of the two-week period, athletes are tested for a five-repetition maximum. For the dumbbell exercises ten pounds or five kilograms are added for each hand to those five repetitions maximum weights to determine a one-repetition maximum. For exercises with barbell (barbell upright row, barbell back squat, etc.) twenty-two pounds or ten kilograms are added to the five repetitions maximum weight to determine a one-repetition maximum.

Because significant portions of the exercises in cycling conditioning programs are performed with dumbbells, the selection of appropriate weights is necessary before the start of the daily program. Before conditioning, athletes set up their dumbbells in order of use. Usually I use three to four intensities. For the sport of cycling (working with a smaller number of athletes at the same time) I think it is not difficult to find dumbbells with the right intensities. To simplify this problem I chose for each athlete the closest intensities possible. For example an athlete does Dumbbell Upright Row five repetitions with a 35 pounds dumbbell in each hand, meaning that his 1 RM is (35 + 10 pounds)'45 pounds. In case that this athlete has in his program

Dumbbell Upright Row:
60%10   65%10   70%10   70%10

the exact weight for 60% would be 27 pounds, 65% 29 pounds and 70% 32 pounds. In my weight room I have dumbbells of 5, 8, 10, 12, 15, 20, 25, 30, 35, 40 pounds, etc. he will perform the 60%10 set with 25 pound instead of 27 pound, then the 65%10 still with 25 pound instead of 29 pound and the 70% 10 70%10 with a pair of 30 pounds dumbbells instead of 32 pounds dumbbells. If an athlete is very well prepared, - very individually-, I chose for the 65%10 the 30 pounds dumbbells and then I will prefer for the 70%10 70%10, the same weight of 30 pounds, instead of the next available set of dumbbells of 35 pounds.

When performing the dumbbell program, a rhythm is established for the total program and for each exercise within the program. A ten, fifteen, twenty etc. second of rest is permitted between exercises, depending on the difficulty of the exercise. For example, the dumbbell raise to the armpit at ten repetitions is followed by a ten second break prior to performing the second set of the same exercise. A fifteen second break is permitted between sets of the dumbbell standing Simultaneous Parallel Squat & Up on Toes Push Press, and twenty seconds is permitted between sets of the Barbell Back Up on Toes Squat & Up on Toes Push Press, etc. The athletes are lined up, and everyone has his/her own sets of dumbbells. In case that the group is greater than the available dumbbell sets I make groups of two athletes for the same sets of dumbbells and they share them. one of them is lifting the other one is resting. In my school's weight room I can accommodate twenty-five athletes at the same time with four sets of dumbbells. For the barbell exercises, teams of two or three athletes work through the program.

Athletes must understand that conditioning for cycling requires very high pulmonary ventilation, as well as a relaxed musculature. The program has high rhythm and utilizes lightweights to develop physical abilities consistent with the demands of the sports. These demands include muscular power, explosiveness, coordination, flexibility and endurance. Every effort is made to strengthen the muscles, tendons and ligaments to reduce the incidence of injury.

The following programs are samples, which may be modified to meet particular conditioning needs. Each coach determines the specific training cycle based upon considerations of individual philosophy, the capacity of the conditioning area, available equipment and goals of the conditioning program. While it is permissible to repeat the four-week cycles Pre-Season Preparatory Period Conditioning, variations are recommended.

During the course of the weekly cycle, day one features the lowest intensity. In the four-week cycle, week one is of the lowest intensity, week two features increased intensity and the third and fourth week consists of greatest intensity. This follows the golden rule of periodization: the first week accumulation; the second week gain and stimulation, the third week is more stimulation and fourth is the highest intensity coupled with testing and evaluation. Following this system, the next four week cycle -of course- can begin at a higher intensity and a heavier first week load.

I believe in a high intensity, good quality conditioning for any sports. This is why my whole programs' philosophy is built upon a muscular strength-power-explosiveness-general and special endurance-flexibility-neuromuscular coordination and orientation in space combination.

In my personal opinion the best specific physical conditioning for cycling (for several other sports also) I can achieve executing short but frequent sets of running, jumping, bounding and sprinting variations, especially when we have a chance doing it uphill, and combined with a well designed free weight, jump boxes, sand stair boxes (see NSCA Journal, Volume 13, Number 5, 1991, Pages 84-87 "Sand Stair Boxes and their use in developing explosive response "), shredded rubber boxes and uphill ramp (see T&C Training & Conditioning, May/June 2003, pages 85-90 "King of The Hill") and in this book at Chapter 11 pages 48-50 stairs conditioning program. I do not say that I am completely against distance cross country style running, and in the sport of cycling it depends very much on the event which an athlete performs for what type of endurance we choose. I always emphasize that every coach should develop his/her own conditioning program and adopt it to a specific weight room's given condition and situation. I just try to give some samples of exercises and exercise combinations, because there are so many variations possible, which should fill up several pages. In my conditioning programs I often change the exercise combinations, because when doing a program I get new ideas and I try to improve the quality of it. Because I live in Kansas in a four-season climate zone a part of the program must be practiced indoors. This is why I am using indoor stairs, and more times the jump box combinations. See my chapter 11 pages 48 – 54. In an outdoor uphill cardiovascular conditioning program for cycling in general I would use the following exercises and programs:

Sample 1

1. Uphill running 80 yards
x 8 to 10 sets - jogging back in 35 seconds

2. Uphill alternate bounding 60 yards
x 6 sets- jogging back in 20 seconds

3. Uphill frog jumps, 40 yards
x 4 sets- walk back 30-40 seconds

4. Uphill backward running 100 yards
x 4 sets- jogging back in 30 seconds

5. Uphill sprint combination:
100 yards x 1 - 80 % intensity - jogging back in 30 seconds
80 yards   x 1 - 80 % intensity - jogging back in 25 seconds
70 yards   x 1 - 85 % intensity - jogging back in 25 seconds
60 yards   x 1 - 90 % intensity- jogging back in 25 seconds
50 yards   x 3 - 95 % intensity - jogging back in 25 seconds
40 yards   x 4 - 100% intensity - jogging back in 20 seconds
30 yards   x 1 - 100% intensity

Sample #2

1. Uphill running 100 yards
x 6 80 % intensity - jogging back in 30 - 35 seconds

2. Uphill double leg zigzag jump-bounding 40 yards
x 4 - jogging back in 20 seconds

3. Uphill one leg bounding, 50 yards
x 3 for right leg x 3 for left leg- jogging back in 25 seconds;

4. Uphill sideways in zigzag (back & forth) double leg jump-bounding 50 yards
x 2 with right shoulder forward x 2 with left shoulder forward- jogging back in 25 seconds

5. Sample 1. Uphill sprint combination

The Javorek's Uphill Super-Set for cycling. I would start gradually in a program and just after considering that the whole group is capable to do it, I would do the complete set and never in the same day with a Sand Stair Box Javorek's Super Set:

Uphill Sprint 100 yards
x 1 - 100 % intensity jogging back in 30 seconds

Uphill Frog or Squat jumps 40 yards
x 1 100 % intensity jogging back in 20 seconds

Uphill Double leg bounding 60 yards
x 1 100 % intensity- jogging back in 20 seconds

Uphill Frog or Squat jumps 30 yards
x 1 100 % intensity- jogging back in 25 seconds

Uphill one leg bounding 80 yards
x 1 for each leg 100 % intensity jogging back in 25 seconds

Uphill Sprint 100 yards
x 1 - 100 % intensity - jogging back in 35 seconds

Uphill Frog or Squat jumps 30 yards
x 1 - 100 % intensity - jogging back in 25 seconds

Uphill Sprint 100 yards
x 1 - 100 % intensity jogging back in 35 seconds

Uphill Frog or Squat jumps 30 yards
x 1 - 100 % intensity - jogging back in 25 seconds

Uphill Sprint 40 yards
x 3 100 % intensity- jogging back in 20 seconds

on every uphill exercise I mark the distances with signed cones and I try to get the whole group of athletes in a very close time up. It is better to wait a few seconds to get everyone up and then order the whole group to get down hill in a counted time. It is very important to ask the athletes to respect the intensity.

The Stair-Sand Stair Boxes or shredded rubber boxes and uphill ramp Combination Javorek's Super Set is the basic indicator about an individual athlete or of a team's cardio-vascular conditioning level.

How I mention in Sand Stair Box chapter, I am combining different exercise variations for different sports, or the same exercises but with smaller or greater number of repetitions. During the years of experiments with this Super Set I came on a conclusion about the number of repetitions, which should indicate an individual athlete or a team's readiness to be able of handling the most difficult practices.

1. Sand stair box double leg jump bounding
x 10

2. Stairs double leg takeoff,
double leg jump up then sprint two-three steps and again double leg takeoff continued with a double leg jump up and sprint all the way up on stair way. Indoor I am asking the team to return on the right side of the stairway, to avoid traffic jam x 10

3. Consecutive one leg jump bounding:
- for right leg x 10

- for left leg in an alternating way
x 10

1-mile cross-country style running in
7-8 minutes (which varies on individual goals)

4. Sand stair boxes or shredded rubber boxes double leg zigzag jump bounding
x 10

5. Double leg squat jump or jump bounding
x 10

6. Sand stair boxes or shredded rubber boxes
100 % intensity sprint up x 10

In case of missing the possibility of having sand stair boxes and outdoor stairs I choose a hill, which could accommodate 12-16 athletes in a line. I perform the same program.

Jump Bounding is a series of continuous "bound together" single leg hops or double leg jump combination

Running is considered a 60%-70% of an athlete's maximum speed

Sprint is considered when an athlete runs with over 80% of his maximum speed

Regardless the athletes' conditioning level, the Super Set I start gradually. First I perform each exercise separately. Then, more exercises are combined in a non-stop execution. After a few practice I try to do a Super Set but just with four repetitions of each exercises, then I gradually increase to the designated number for that respective sport or team. The general conditioning level of each individual athlete or team determines the number of exercises and sets in each workout. As a general safety rule: I never require for any injured or physically not able athlete to perform certain exercises, which could be harmful for their physical integrity and could produce greater injuries. Usually I am asking them to perform instead of one leg hop bounding or two legs jump bounding just sprints up, if they have a release from the trainers.

The Stair-Sand Stair or Shredded Rubber Boxes and Uphill Ramp Combination Javorek's Super Set is the basic indicator about a cyclist cardio-vascular conditioning level.

How I mention in Sand Stair Box chapter, I am combining different exercise variations for different sports, or the same exercises but with smaller or greater number of repetitions. During the years of experiments with this Super Set I have gotten a conclusion about the number of repetitions which should indicate a team's or an athlete's readiness to be able to handle the most difficult practices.

For cycling I recommend the following combination:

1. Stairs or Sand Stair or Shredded Rubber Boxes Double leg jump bounding
x 14

2. Stairs or Sand Stair or Shredded Rubber Boxes Sprint
x 10

3. Cross Country running
1 mile

4. Stairs or Sand Stair or Shredded Rubber Boxes Consecutive one leg bounding:
for right leg x 8
for left leg in an alternating way x 8

5. Stairs or Sand Stair or Shredded Rubber Boxes Double leg zigzag jump bounding
x 10

6. Cross Country running -
  1 mile

7. Stair or Sand Stair or Shredded Rubber Boxes 100 % intensity Sprint up
  x 14

I recommend a specific biking "combination" conditioning exercise also:

- 100 m uphill 100% intensity sprint +
- 1000 m 80% intensity biking +
- 100 m 100% intensity sprint +
- 1000 m 85% intensity biking +
- 100 m uphill 100% intensity sprint

From my coaching experience I would recommend including a certain amount of general conditioning during the competitional season also. During the season the conditioning program must have a more active rest and recuperative character.

Javorek Endurance Dumbbell Program # 1

1. Dumbbell Up on Toes Upright Row
50% 18   50% 18   55% 16   60% 14   65%10 70%8

2. Dumbbell Quarter Squat & Up on Toes Raise To Armpit
  + From Hip Up on Toes High Pull Snatch
40%10+10   40%10+10   45%10+10   50%10+8
55%10+6

3. Dumbbell Straight Knees & Up on Toes Press + Quarter Squat & Up on
  Toes Push Press + Up on Toes Upright Row
40%8+8+8   45%8+8+8   50%8+8+8   55%6+6+6
60%6+6+6

4. Dumbbell Bent-Over Row + Quarter Squat & Up on Toes Push Press
45%14+10   45%14+10   50%12+10   55%12+10
60%14+10

5. Dumbbell Squat & Up on Toes Push Press
40%16   45%16   50%14   50%14
55%12   60%10   65%10   70%8

6. Dumbbell Bent-Over "Kick-Back" Triceps Curls
30%18   35%18   40%14   45%12   50%10   60%8

7. Dumbbell Up on Toes Upright Row + Parallel Curls
40%15+15   45%14+14   50%12+12   55%10+10
60% 10+10

8. Dumbbell (Regular) Supinated Curls + Squat & Up on Toes Push Press
40%16+10   45%16+10   50%14+10   55%12+
60%10+   65%8+6

9. Dumbbell Press + Quarter Squat & Up on Toes Push Press
  + Up on Toes Squat & Up on Toes Push Press
40%8+8+8   45%8+8+8   45%8+8+8   50%8+8+8
55%6+6+6   60%6+6+6

10. Dumbbell Regular Curls x 16 + Squat & Up on Toes Upright Row x 12 +
  Dumbbell Straight Knees & Up on Toes Parallel Press x 10 + Bent Over
  Row x 16 + Up on Toes Squat & Up on Toes Push Press x 12
Take intensity of 100% Dumbbell Straight Knees & Up on Toes Parallel Press Intensity
50%1 Set   55%1 Set

11. Dumbbell Up on Toes Upright Row x 14 + Straight Knees & Up on Toes
  Parallel Press x 10 + Regular Curls x 12 + Quarter Squat & Up on Toes
  Push Press x 10 + Squat & Up on Toes Upright Row x 12 + p on Toes
  Squat & Up on Toes Push Press x 10 + Squat Jump x 10 + Split Jump
  x 20
Take intensity of 100% Dumbbell Straight Knees & Up on Toes Parallel Press Intensity
50%1 Set   55%1 Set

Cycling General Conditioning Preparatory Period

Two Week Introductory Program
Week 1 Workout # 1
Dumbbell Quarter Squat & Up on Toes Raise To Armpit
50%16   50%16   60%14   60%14   70%12   70%12   80%8

Dumbbell Upright Row & Up on Toes
50%14   50%14   55%14   55%14
60%12   60%12   65%12   65%12

Dumbbell Rotational, From Supinated To Pronated Curls
50%14   55%14   60%12   65%12 7   0%10

Dumbbell Linear Pronated Bent Over Row
50%14   60%14   65%12   65%12   75%10

Dumbbell Standing Continuous Single Leg Lunge
50%16+16   55%16+16   60%14+14   65%14+14
70%14+14   75%14+14

Dumbbell Single Leg Step Up on Box
50%16+16   60%14+14   55%16+16   65%14+14   5%14+14

Barbell Back Squat & Up on Toes
40%12   45%12   50%12   55%10   60%10   65%10

Double Leg Stair or Sand Stair Box Bounding
4 Sets x 3

Stair or Sand Stair Box Sprint
4 Sets x 6

Workout # 2
Dumbbell Split Jump With Raise To Armpit
50%20   50%20   55%20   60%20   60%20   70%15

Dumbbell Simultaneous Parallel Curls
50%14   60%14   55%14   65%14   70%12   75%10

Dumbbell Parallel Bent Over Row
50%14   60%14   70%12   70%12   80%8   80%8

Dumbbell Standing Simultaneous Parallel Press
50%14   55%14   60%12   65%12   70%10   75%8

Dumbbell Standing Simultaneous Parallel Squat Push Press
50%14   60%12   55%14   65%12   60%12   70%12

Dumbbell Standing Alternate Leg Lunge
50%20   55%20   60%20   65%20   70%18   75%18

Dumbbell Alternate Leg Step Up on Box
50%18   55%18   60%16   65%14   70%12   75%10

Barbell Wave Squat
(9 Quarter Squat & Up on Toes +2 Quarter Squat Jumps)
30%44   35%44   40%44   45%44   50%44

Workout # 3

Dumbbell Standing Simultaneous Parallel Push Press
50%14   60%14   70%12   80%8   65%12   80%8

Dumbbell Bent Over "Kick Back" Triceps Curls
50%14   55%12   60%10   65%10   70%8   75%8

Barbell Upright Row Narrow Grip
50%14   55%12   60%14   65%12   70%10

Barbell Bent Over Row Wide Grip
50%15   55%14   60%12   65%10   70%10

Javorek's Dumbbell Special Good Mornings
50%16   55%16   60%14   65%12   70%12

Dumbbell Alternate Leg Lunge Walk
50%30,30   55%30   60%30   65%25   70%20

Barbell Back Squat & Up on Toes Jump
30%10   35%10   40%8   45%6

Double Leg Stair or Sand Stair Box Bounding
4 Sets x 3

Stair or Sand Stair Box Sprint
4 Sets x 6

Week 2 Workout # 4

Dumbbell Quarter Squat & Up on Toes Raise To Armpit
50%16   55%16   60%14   65%14   70%12   75%10

Dumbbell Simultaneous Parallel Curls
50%14   55%14   60%12   65%12   70%12   70%12

Dumbbell Simultaneous Linear Pronated Bent Over Row
50%16   60%14   55%16   65%14
60%14   70%12   75%10   80%8

Dumbbell Standing Simultaneous Parallel Squat Push Press
50%14   55%12   60%12   65%10   70%10   60%12   70%10

Dumbbell Standing Alternate Leg "Step Back" Lunge.
50%16+16   60%14+14   55%16+16   65%14+14
60%14+14   70%12+12

Dumbbell Alternate Leg Step Up on Box
40%18   45%18   50%16   55%16   60%14   65%14

Barbell Wave Squat
(9 Quarter Squat & Up on Toes +2 Quarter Squat Jumps)
25%44   30%44   30%44   35%44   35%44

Stair or Sand Stair Box Sprint
6 Sets x 6

Workout # 5

Dumbbell Simultaneous Raise To Armpit and Split Jump
40%18   45%18   50%18   55%16   60%16   65%16

Dumbbell Simultaneous Rotational From Supinated To Pronated Curls
40%16   45%16   50%14   55%14   60%12   65%12

Dumbbell Standing or Seated Simultaneous Parallel Press
45%14   50%12   55%12   60%10   65%10   70%8

Dumbbell Bent Over Simultaneous Kick Back Triceps Curls
40%14   40%14   45%14   45%14
50%12   50%12   55%12   60%10

Dumbbell Alternate Leg Lunge Walk
30%30   35%30   40%30   45%30
Double Steps Count (30 + 30)

Barbell Upright Row Medium Grip
40%12   45%12   50%12   55%10   60%10   65%8

Barbell Back Squat & Up on Toes Jump
25%10   30%10   30%10   35%10   35%10

Workout # 6

Dumbbell Standing Simultaneous Parallel Push Press
50%14 5   5%14   65%12   60%12   70%10   65%12   75%8

Dumbbell Bent Over Simultaneous Kick Back Triceps Curls
40%14   50%12   45%14   55%10   50%12   60%10

Barbell Upright Row Wide Grip
40%12   45%12   50%10   55%10   60%10   60%10

Barbell Back Squat & Up on Toes + Barbell Wave Squat + Barbell Back Squat & Up on Toes
30%10+40+10   35%10+40+10   40%10+30+10   45%10+30+10

Barbell Single Leg Continuous Lunges
20%18+18   25%16+16   25%16+16   30%14+14

Double Leg Stair or Sand Stair Box Bounding
4 Sets x 3

one Leg Stair or Sand Stair Box Bounding (R+L)
3 Sets x 3+3

Stair or Sand Stair Box Sprint
6 Sets x 10

Cycling Preparatory Period Week 1
Workout # 1

Dumbbell Simultaneous Up on Toes Upright Row.
Ten seconds break between the sets
50%14   50%14   55%14   55%14   60%14   60%14

Dumbbell Simultaneous Parallel Bent Over Row.
Ten seconds break between the sets
50%14   50%14   60%14   60%14   65%12   65%12

Dumbbell Lunge Walk With 3 Parallel Curls or From Hip High Pull Snatch on Each Step.
Thirty seconds break between the sets
30%30+ 30   35%30+ 30   40%30+30   45%30+30
50%30+30

Dumbbell Straight Knees Simultaneous Parallel Up on Toes Overhead Press.
Ten seconds break between the sets
50%14   50%14   60%14   60%14   55%14   55%14   60%14
60%14

Dumbbell Standing Continuous Single Leg Lunge.
Twenty seconds break between the sets
50%16+16   50%16+16   55%16+16   60%14+14
60%14+14

Barbell Back Squat & Up on Toes.
Thirty seconds break between the sets
40%12   40%12   45%12   45%12
50%12   50%12   55%10   55%10

Double Leg Stair or Sand Stair Box Bounding.
Thirty seconds break between the sets
6 sets x 4

Stair or Sand Stair Box Sprint.
Thirty seconds break between the sets
6 sets x 4

Workout # 2

Dumbbell Split Jump & Raise To Armpit.
Twenty seconds break between the sets

50%20	50%20	55%18	55%18	60%16	60%16

Dumbbell Simultaneous Parallel Curls.
5Ten seconds break between the sets

50%16	50%16	55%16	55%16
60%12	60%12	65%10	65%10

Dumbbell Quarter Squat & Up on Toes Simultaneous Parallel Push Press.
Fifteen seconds break between the sets

50%14	50%14	60%12	60%12
55%14	55%14	65%10	65%10

Dumbbell Standing Alternate Leg Lunge.
Thirty seconds break between the sets

50%30	50%30	60%30	60%30

Barbell Back Squat & Up on Toes Push Press.
Twenty seconds break between the sets

50%10	55%10	55%10	60%10
65%8	65%8	70%6	70%6

Barbell Back Squat Jump.
Twenty seconds break between the sets

30%10	30%10	35%10	35%10	40%10

Stair or Sand Stair Box Sprint.
Thirty seconds break between the sets

6 Sets x 4

Workout # 3

Dumbbell Standing Simultaneous Rotational Curls.
Ten seconds break between the sets

50%14	50%14	55%14	55%14
60%12	60%12	70%8	70%8

Dumbbell Quarter Squat & Up on Toes Simultaneous Parallel Push Press
Twenty seconds break between the sets

50%14	50%14	60%12	60%12
65%10	65%10	60%12	70%10

Dumbbell Lunge Walk With 3 Parallel Curls
or From Hip High Pull Snatch on Each Step.
Thirty seconds break between the sets

30%30+ 30	35%30+ 30	40%30+30	45%30+30
50%30+30			

Barbell Back Squat Jump.
Twenty seconds break between the sets

30%10	30%10	40%10	40%10
35%10	35%10	45%6	45%6

Stair or Sand Stair Box Sprint.
Thirty seconds break between the sets

6 Sets x 4

Preparatory Week 2
Workout # 1

Barbell Standing Up on Toes Upright Row Narrow Grip.
Fifteen seconds break between the sets

50%14	50%14	55%12	55%12
60%12	60%12	70%8	70%8

Barbell Medium Grip Up on Toes High Pull Snatch.
Twenty five seconds break between the sets

50%12	50%12	60%10	60%10
55%12	55%12	65%10	65%10

Barbell Back Squat & Up on Toes Push Press.
Twenty seconds break between the sets

50%10	50%10	60%10	60%10	55%10	65%10	70%8
70%8					

Barbell Wave Squat +Barbell Back Squat & Up on Toes +Barbell Wave Squat.
Thirty to Fifty seconds break between the sets
(The wave Squat in this program is 4 x 9 reps of Quarter Squat & Up on Toes + 1 Quarter Squat Jump)

40%44+10+44	40%44+10+44	45%44+10+44
50%44+10+44	50%44+10+44	

Stair or Sand Stair Box Sprint.
Thirty seconds break between the sets

6 Sets x 5

Workout # 2

Javorek's Dumbbell Complex # 1
Thirty to Fifty seconds break between the sets.

45%1	50%1	55%1	50%1	55%	60%1

Barbell Back Squat & Up on Toes +Barbell Wave Squat +
Barbell Back Squat & Up on Toes
Thirty to Fifty seconds break between the sets

40%10+40+10	45%10+40+10	50%10+40+10	40%10+40+10
45%10+40+10	50%10+40+10		

Barbell Standing Good Morning.
Twenty five seconds break between the sets

30%15	30%15	35%15	35%15
40%15	40%15	45%15	45%15

Stair or Sand Stair Box Sprint.
Thirty seconds break between the sets

6 Sets x 4

Workout # 3

Javorek's Barbell Complex # 5
one minute break between the sets

35%1	40%1	45%1	50%1
55%1	45%1	50%1	55%1

Dumbbell Lunge Walk With 3 Parallel Curls
or From Hip High Pull Snatch on Each Step.
Thirty seconds break between the sets

30%30+ 30	35%30+ 30	40%30+30	45%30+30
50%30+30			

Stair or Sand Stair Box Sprint.
Thirty seconds break between the sets

6 Sets x 6

Preparatory Week 3
Workout # 1

Javorek's Dumbbell Complex # 2
Forty to Fifty seconds break between the sets

40%1	45%1	45%1	45%1
50%1	55%1	60%1	60%1

Barbell Standing Toe Raise.
Twenty seconds break between the sets

40%25	40%25	45%25	45%25	50%20	50%20

Barbell Standing Alternate Leg Step Up on Box.
Thirty seconds break between the sets

25%16+16	30%16+16	35%16+16	40%14+14

Stair or Sand Stair Box Sprint. Thirty seconds break between the sets
6 Sets x 6

Workout # 2

Javorek's Dumbbell Complex # 3
Forty to Fifty seconds break between the sets

40%1	45%1	45%1	45%1	50%1	50%1	55%1
60%1	65%1					

Barbell Standing Quarter Squat and Raise Up on Toes.
Thirty seconds break between the sets

30%30	35%25	40%20	45%20	50%16

Dumbbell Lunge Walk With 3 Parallel Curls or From Hip High Pull Snatch on Each Step.
Thirty seconds break between the sets

30%30+ 30	35%30+ 30	40%30+30	45%30+30
50%30+30			

Barbell Back Squat Jump.
Thirty seconds break between the sets

30%10	30%10	35%10	40%10	45%8

Stair or Sand Stair Box Sprint.
Thirty seconds break between the sets

6 Sets x 4

Workout # 3

Javorek's Barbell Complex # 5
One minute break between the sets

35%1	35%1	40%1	40%1	45%1	45%1	50%1
55%1	50%1	55%1	60%1			

Barbell Standing Good Morning.
Twenty seconds break between the sets

30%20	30%20	35%20	35%20	40%20	40%20

Stair or Sand Stair Box Sprint.
Thirty seconds break between the sets

After this introductory program, everyone should practice the exercises from the 12 Weeks Cycling General Fitness # 1 program's exercise list in order to get familiar with them.

Then, test for your five repetition maximums in each exercise so you can find the correct amount of weight for each set's intensity.

Cycling General Fitness # 1
12 Weeks program

Dumbbell Quarter Squat & Up On Toes Raise To Armpit
Dumbbell Alternate Leg Split Snatch
Dumbbell From Hang Bellow The Knee Power Snatch
Dumbbell Alternate Leg Split Clean
Dumbbell Up On Toes Upright Row
Dumbbell Up On Toes Squat Upright Row
Dumbbell Up On Toes From Hip High Pull Snatch
Dumbbell Up On Toes High Pull Snatch
Dumbbell Up On Toes Parallel Press
Dumbbell Quarter Squat & Up On Toes Parallel Push Press
Dumbbell Parallel Jump Push Press
Dumbbell Up On Toes Parallel Squat Push Press
Barbell Behind The Head From Squat Overhead Press
Dumbbell Rotational Bent Over Row
Dumbbell Bent Over "Kick Back" Triceps Curls
Dumbbell Bent Over Fly
Dumbbell Alternate Raise To Armpit & Running In Place
Dumbbell Horizontal Parallel Inward-Outward Rotation
Dumbbell Alternate Overhead Press & High Knees Running In Place
Dumbbell Split Jump & Alternate Raise To Armpit
Dumbbell Alternate Leg Lunges
Dumbbell Lunge Walk & From Lunge, Hip High Pull Snatch
Dumbbell Alternate Leg Step Ups
Dumbbell Single Leg Lunges + Up On Toes Squat Push Press
Dumbbell Upstairs Run (Minimum 20 Steps Stairway)
Javorek's Dumbbell Complex # 1
Javorek's Dumbbell Complex # 2
Barbell Back Squat & Up On Toes
Barbell Wave Squat (9 Quarter Squat & Up On Toes + 2 Quarter Squat Jumps)
Barbell Back Squat Jump
Barbell Wave Squat + Back Squat & Up On Toes + Wave Squat
General Plyometrics Exercises On Stairs Or Sand Stair Boxes
Dumbbell Frontal + Lateral Straight Arm Raise
Javorek's Special Abdominal # 3

Javorek's 12 Weeks
1 Cycling and 6 Weeks
Tapering Conditioning Program
The Whole Program In Circuit !!!

Week 1 Day 1

Dumbbell Quarter Squat & Up on Toes Raise To Armpit

						40s Break
50%14	55%14	55%14	60%12	60%12	65%10	65%10

5 Dumbbell Up on Toes Upright Row

						40s Break
50%14	55%14	55%12	65%10	60%10	60%10	70%10

8 Dumbbell Up on Toes High Pull Snatch

						40s Break
50%10	55%10	55%10	60%10	60%10	65%10	70%10

10 Dumbbell Quarter Squat & Up on Toes Parallel Push Press

						35s Break
50%10	55%10	55%10	60%10	60%10	65%10	70%10

28 Barbell Back Squat & Up on Toes

						60s Break
40%12	40%12	50%12	45%12	45%12	55%10 60%10	

30 Barbell Back Squat Jump

						60s Break
25%6	40%6	35%6	25%6	40%6	35%6	40%6

33 Dumbbell Frontal + Lateral Straight Arm Raise

				15s Break
40%12 +12	40%12 +12	40%12 +12	45%10+10	
45%10+10	45%10+10	50%8+8		

32 General Plyometrics Exercises on Stairs or Sand Stair Boxes

			40s Break
4xstair D.L.B.	4xjump & Sprint	4x D.L Zig-Zag	4xstair Sprint 4xstair
D.L.B.	4xstair Sprint	4xstair Sprint	

D.L.B.= Double Leg Bounding   D.L.Zig-Zag B.= Double Leg Zig-Zag Bounding

34 Javorek's Special Abdominal # 3

						No Break
1	1	1	1	1	1	1

Week 1 Day 2

2 Dumbbell Alternate Leg Split Snatch

			30s Break
60%8+8	65%8+8	65%8+8	65%8+8
70%6+6	70%6+6	70%6+6	

7 Dumbbell Up on Toes From Hip High Pull Snatch

			30s Break
50%12	50%12	55%10	55%10
60%12	65%10	70%10	

9 Dumbbell Up on Toes Parallel Press

			40s Break
50%12	50%12	55%10	55%10
60%12	65%10	70%10	

21 Dumbbell Alternate Leg Lunges

			35s Break
40%16+16	40%16+16	45%16+16	45%16+16
50%14+14	50%14+14	50%14+14	

11 Dumbbell Parallel Jump Push Press

						35s Break
35%10	40%10	50%10	45%10	55%8	45%10	55%10

22 Dumbbell Lunge Walk & From Lunge, Hip High Pull Snatch

			40s Break
40%22+22+22+22	40%22+22+22+22	45%22+22+22+22	
45%22+22+22+22	45%22+22+22+22	45%22+22+22+22	
45%22+22+22+22			

32 General Plyometrics Exercises on Stairs or Sand Stair Boxes

			40s Break
4xstair D.L.B.	4xjump & Sprint	4x D.L Zig-Zag	4xstair Sprint
4xstair D.L.B.	4xstair Sprint	4xstair Sprint	

34 Javorek's Special Abdominal # 3

						No Break
1	1	1	1	1	1	1

Week 1 Day 3

3 Dumbbell From Hang Bellow The Knee Power Snatch

						30s Break
50%8	50%8	60%6	65%6	65%6	65%6	70%6

12 Dumbbell Up on Toes Parallel Squat Push Press

						40s Break
50%12	50%12	55%10	55%10	60%12	65%10	70%10

14 Dumbbell Rotational Bent Over Row

						30s Break
40%16	45%16	50%14	55%12	60%10	55%12	60%10

18 Dumbbell Horizontal Parallel Inward-Outward Rotation

						30s Break
40%8+8	40%8+8	35%8+8	40%7+7	40%7+7	45%6+6	45%6+6

19 Dumbbell Alternate Overhead Press & High Knees Running In Place

			30s Break
35%20+20	35%20+20	40%20+20	40%20+20
40%20+20	40%20+20	40%20+20	

29 Barbell Wave Squat
(9 Quarter Squat & Up on Toes + 2 Quarter Squat Jumps)

						60s Break
40%44	35%44	35%44	40%44	45%36	40%44	45%33

30 Barbell Back Squat Jump

						60s Break
40%8	35%8	45%6	40%8	35%8	45%6	45%6

33 Dumbbell Frontal + Lateral Straight Arm Raise

			15s Break
40%12 +12	40%12 +12	40%12 +12	45%10+10
45%10+10	45%10+10	50%8+8	

32 General Plyometrics Exercises on Stairs or Sand Stair Boxes

40s Break

4xstair D.L.B.	4xjump & Sprint	4x D.L Zig-Zag	4xstair Sprint
4xstair D.L.B.	4xstair Sprint	4xstair Sprint	

34 Javorek's Special Abdominal # 3

No Break

1	1	1	1	1	1	1

Week 2 Day 1
2   Dumbbell Alternate Leg Split Snatch

30s Break

60%8+8	65%8+8	65%8+8	65%8+8	70%6+6	70%6+6	70%6+6

10 Dumbbell Quarter Squat & Up on Toes Parallel Push Press

30s Break

45%10	50%10	55%10	60%10	65%8	70%8	70%8

13 Barbell Behind The Head From Squat Overhead Press

40s Break

55%12	60%10	65%10	70%10	65%10	70%10	75%8

15 Dumbbell Bent Over "Kick Back" Triceps Curls

30s Break

40%14	40%14	45%12	50%10	55%10	60%10	60%10

22 Dumbbell Lunge Walk & From Lunge, Hip High Pull Snatch

40s Break

40%22+22+22+22	40%22+22+22+22	45%22+22+22+22	45%22+22+22+22
45%22+22+22+22	45%22+22+22+22	22+22+22+50%22	

33 Dumbbell Frontal + Lateral Straight Arm Raise

15s Break

40%12 +12	40%12 +12	40%12 +12	45%10+10
45%10+10	45%10+10	50%8+8	

32 General Plyometrics Exercises on Stairs or Sand Stair Boxes

40s Break

4xstair D.L.B.	4xjump & Sprint	4x D.L Zig-Zag	4xstair Sprint
4xstair D.L.B.	4xstair Sprint	4xstair Sprint	

34 Javorek's Special Abdominal # 3

No Break

1	1	1	1	1	1	1

Week 2 Day 2
4   Dumbbell Alternate Leg Split Clean

30s Break

50%8+8	50%8+8	60%8+8	65%6+6	65%6+6	70%6+6	75%4+4

7   Dumbbell Up on Toes From Hip High Pull Snatch

30s Break

40%14	45%12	55%10	60%8	65%6	65%6

23 Dumbbell Alternate Leg Step Ups

50s Break

50%12+12	50%12+12	55%12+12	55%12+12
60%10+10	65%10+10	65%10+10	

11 Dumbbell Parallel Jump Push Press

40s Break

50%10	55%10	60%10	65%8	65%8	70%6	70%6

16 Dumbbell Bent Over Fly

25s Break

50%16	55%12	60%10	55%12	70%8	60%10	70%8

20 Dumbbell Split Jump & Alternate Raise To Armpit

30s Break

50%15+15	60%14+14	65%12+12	65%12+12
70%10+10	65%12+12	70%10+1	

32 General Plyometrics Exercises on Stairs or Sand Stair Boxes

40s Break

4xstair D.L.B.	4xjump & Sprint	4x D.L Zig-Zag	4xstair Sprint
4xstair D.L.B.	4xstair Sprint	4xstair Sprint	

34 Javorek's Special Abdominal # 3

No Break

1	1	1	1	1	1	1

Week 2 Day 3
6   Dumbbell Up on Toes Squat Upright Row

35s Break

50%12	60%12	70%12	55%12
65%10	75%8	75%8	

13 Barbell Behind The Head From Squat Overhead Press

40s Break

40%10	45%10	50%10	55%10	60%8	65%6	65%6

8   Dumbbell Up on Toes High Pull Snatch

40s Break

50%12	60%12	65%10	60%12	70%10	75%8	75%8

15 Dumbbell Bent Over "Kick Back" Triceps Curls

25s Break

50%12	55%12	60%10	55%12	60%12	65%10	65%10

24 Dumbbell Single Leg Lunges + Up on Toes Squat Push Press

40s Break

50%12+12+8	55%12+12+8	12 + 12 + 60%8	65%12+12+8
65%12+12+8	65%12+12+8	65%12+12+8	

25 Dumbbell Upstairs Run (Minimum 20 Steps Stairway)

35s Break

25%3	40%3	35%3	25%3
40%3	35%3	35%3	

33 Dumbbell Frontal + Lateral Straight Arm Raise

15s Break

40%12 +12	40%12 +12	40%12 +12	45%10+10
45%10+10	45%10+10	45%10+10	

32 General Plyometrics Exercises on Stairs or Sand Stair Boxes

40s Break

4xstair D.L.B.	4xjump & Sprint	4x D.L Zig-Zag	4xstair Sprint
4xstair D.L.B.	4xstair Sprint	4xstair Sprint	

34 Javorek's Special Abdominal # 3

No Break

1	1	1	1	1	1	1

Week 3 Day 1
26 Javorek's Dumbbell Complex # 1

60s Break

45%1	45%1	45%1	50%1	50%1	50%1	50%1

17 Dumbbell Alternate Raise To Armpit & Running In Place

25s Break

40%20+20	40%20+20	40%20+20	45%20+20
45%20+20	50%16+16	50%16+16	

19 Dumbbell Alternate Overhead Press & High Knees Running In Place

30s Break

50%20+20	50%20+20	55%20+20	60%16+16
65%12+12	70%12+12	70%12+12	

30 Barbell Back Squat Jump

60s Break

40%10	35%10	40%10	45%8	50%6	55%4	55%4

32 General Plyometrics Exercises on Stairs or Sand Stair Boxes

40s Break

4xstair D.L.B.	4xjump & Sprint	4x D.L Zig-Zag	4xstair Sprint
4xstair D.L.B.	4xstair Sprint	4xstair Sprint	

34 Javorek's Special Abdominal # 3

No Break

1	1	1	1	1	1	1

Week 3 Day 2

9 Dumbbell Up on Toes Parallel Press

						30s Break
50%12	50%12	60%12	65%10	65%10	75%8	75%8

10 Dumbbell Quarter Squat & Up on Toes Parallel Push Press

						30s Break
50%14	50%12	55%12	60%12	65%10	70%10	70%10

4 Dumbbell Alternate Leg Split Clean

						30s Break
50%8+8	50%8+8	60%8+8	65%6+6	65%6+6	70%6+6	75%4+4

12 Dumbbell Up on Toes Parallel Squat Push Press

						40s Break
40%14	45%12	50%12	55%10	65%8	80%6	80%6

18 Dumbbell Horizontal Parallel Inward-Outward Rotation

			30s Break
50%10+10	60%8+8	55%10+10	65%6+6
55%10+10	65%6+6	65%6+6	

31 Barbell Wave Squat + Back Squat & Up on Toes + Wave Squat

			60s Break
40%33+10+33	40%33+10+33	45%33+6+33	45%33+6+33
50%22+6+22	50%22+6+22	50%22+6+22	

33 Dumbbell Frontal + Lateral Straight Arm Raise

			15s Break
40%12 +12	40%12 +12	40%12 +12	45%10+10
45%10+10	45%10+10	50%8+8	

32 General Plyometrics Exercises on Stairs or Sand Stair Boxes

			40s Break
4xstair D.L.B.	4xjump & Sprint	4x D.L Zig-Zag	4xstair Sprint
4xstair D.L.B.	4xstair Sprint	4xstair Sprint	

34 Javorek's Special Abdominal # 3

						No Break
1	1	1	1	1	1	1

Week 3 Day 3

27 Javorek's Dumbbell Complex # 2

						60s Break
40%1	40%1	40%1	40%1	45%1	45%1	45%1

22 Dumbbell Lunge Walk & From Lunge, Hip High Pull Snatch

		40s Break
40%22+22+22+22	40%22+22+22+22	45%22+22+22+22
45%22+22+22+22	45%22+22+22+22	45%22+22+22+22
22+22+22+50%22		

28 Barbell Back Squat & Up on Toes

						60s Break
50%12	60%10	70%6	65%10	75%6	70%6	75%6

25 Dumbbell Upstairs Run (Minimum 20 Steps Stairway)

						40s Break
25%3	40%3	35%3	25%3	40%3	35%3	35%3

33 Dumbbell Frontal + Lateral Straight Arm Raise

			15s Break
40%12 +12	40%12 +12	40%12 +12	45%10+10
45%10+10	45%10+10	50%8+8	

32 General Plyometrics Exercises on Stairs or Sand Stair Boxes

			40s Break
4xstair D.L.B.	4xjump & Sprint	4x D.L Zig-Zag	4xstair Sprint
4xstair D.L.B.	4xstair Sprint	4xstair Sprint	

34 Javorek's Special Abdominal # 3

						No Break
1	1	1	1	1	1	1

Week 4 Day 1

1 Dumbbell Quarter Squat & Up on Toes Raise To Armpit

						35s Break
50%16	60%14	70%10	75%8	80%6	80%6	80%6

15 Dumbbell Bent Over "Kick Back" Triceps Curls

						30s Break
50%14	60%10	55%12	65%10	70%8	75%6	75%6

21 Dumbbell Alternate Leg Lunges

			35s Break
50%16+16	55%16+16	60%12+12	65%12+12
70%12+12	70%12+12	70%12+12	

14 Dumbbell Rotational Bent Over Row

						30s Break
50%14	60%12	65%10	70%10	75%8	80%6	80%6

29 Barbell Wave Squat
(9 Quarter Squat & Up on Toes + 2 Quarter Squat Jumps)

						60s Break
40%44	40%44	45%44	50%33	55%33	60%33	60%33

20 Dumbbell Split Jump & Alternate Raise To Armpit

			40s Break
50%15+15	60%14 + 14	65%12+12	65%12+12
70%10 +10	70%10 +10	70%10 +10	

33 Dumbbell Frontal + Lateral Straight Arm Raise

			15s Break
40%12 +12	40%12 +12	40%12 +12	45%10+10
45%10+10	45%10+10	50%8+8	

32 General Plyometrics Exercises on Stairs or Sand Stair Boxes

			40s Break
4xstair D.L.B.	4xjump & Sprint	4x D.L Zig-Zag	4xstair Sprint
4xstair D.L.B.	4xstair Sprint	4xstair Sprint	

34 Javorek's Special Abdominal # 3

						No Break
1	1	1	1	1	1	1

Week 4 Day 2

7 Dumbbell Up on Toes From Hip High Pull Snatch

						30s Break
50%10	60%10	70%8	75%8	60%10	70%8	75%8

12 Dumbbell Up on Toes Parallel Squat Push Press

						30s Break
50%10	55%10	60%10	65%10	70%8	75%6	80%6

18 Dumbbell Horizontal Parallel Inward-Outward Rotation

			25s Break
50%10+10	60%8+8	55%10+10	65%6+6
55%10+10	65%6+6	65%6+6	

23 Dumbbell Alternate Leg Step Ups

			40s Break
50%12+12	50%12+12	55%12+12	55%12+12
60%10+10	65%10+10	65%10+10	

26 Javorek's Dumbbell Complex # 1

						60s Break
40%1	45%1	45%1	50%1	50%1	55%1	60%1

4 Dumbbell Alternate Leg Split Clean

						30s Break
50%8+8	50%8+8	60%8+8	65%6+6	65%6+6	70%6+6	75%4+4

30 Barbell Back Squat Jump

						60s Break
40%10	35%10	40%8	6@45%	50%6	60%6	60%6

33 Dumbbell Frontal + Lateral Straight Arm Raise

			15s Break
40%12 +12	40%12 +12	40%12 +12	45%10+10
45%10+10	45%10+10	50%8+8	

32 General Plyometrics Exercises on Stairs or Sand Stair Boxes

40s Break

| 4xstair D.L.B. | 4xjump & Sprint | 4x D.L Zig-Zag | 4xstair Sprint |
| 4xstair D.L.B. | 4xstair Sprint | 4xstair Sprint | |

34 Javorek's Special Abdominal # 3

No Break

| 1 | 1 | 1 | 1 | 1 | 1 | 1 |

Week 4 Day 3

27 Javorek's Dumbbell Complex # 2

60s Break

| 35%1 | 40%1 | 35%1 | 40%1 | 45%1 | 45%1 | 45%1 |

15 Dumbbell Bent Over "Kick Back" Triceps Curls

30s Break

| 50%14 | 55%12 | 60%10 | 65%8 | 70%6 | 70%6 | 70%6 |

29 Barbell Wave Squat
(9 Quarter Squat & Up on Toes + 2 Quarter Squat Jumps)

60s Break

| 40%44 | 45%44 | 50%33 | 55%33 | 60%33 | 60%33 | 60%33 |

33 Dumbbell Frontal + Lateral Straight Arm Raise

15s Break

| 40%12 +12 | 40%12 +12 | 40%12 +12 | 45%10+10 |
| 45%10+10 | 45%10+10 | 50%8+8 | |

32 General Plyometrics Exercises on Stairs or Sand Stair Boxes

40s Break

| 4xstair D.L.B. | 4xjump & Sprint | 4x D.L Zig-Zag | 4xstair Sprint |
| 4xstair D.L.B. | 4xstair Sprint | 4xstair Sprint | |

34 Javorek's Special Abdominal # 3

No Break

| 1 | 1 | 1 | 1 | 1 | 1 | 1 |

Week 5 Day 1

2   Dumbbell Alternate Leg Split Snatch

30s Break

| 60%8+8 | 65%8+8 | 65%8+8 | 65%8+8 | 70%6+6 | 70%6+6 | 70%6+6 |

9   Dumbbell Up on Toes Parallel Press

30s Break

| 50%10 | 55%10 | 60%10 | 65%10 | 70%8 | 75%6 | 75%6 |

13 Barbell Behind The Head From Squat Overhead Press

30s Break

| 55%12 | 60%10 | 65%10 | 70%10 | 65%10 | 70%10 | 75%8 |

16 Dumbbell Bent Over Fly

30s Break

| 40%16 | 45%16 | 50%14 | 55%12 | 60%10 | 55%12 | 60%10 |

31 Barbell Wave Squat + Back Squat & Up on Toes + Wave Squat

60s Break

| 40%44+10+44 | 40%44+10+44 | 50%33+10+33 | 50%33+10+33 |
| 55%33+10+33 | 55%33+10+33 | 55%33+10+33 | |

33 Dumbbell Frontal + Lateral Straight Arm Raise

15s Break

| 40%12 +12 | 40%12 +12 | 40%12 +12 | 45%10+10 |
| 45%10+10 | 45%10+10 | 50%8+8 | |

32 General Plyometrics Exercises on Stairs or Sand Stair Boxes

40s Break

| 4xstair D.L.B. | 4xjump & Sprint | 4x D.L Zig-Zag | 4xstair Sprint |
| 4xstair D.L.B. | 4xstair Sprint | 4xstair Sprint | |

34 Javorek's Special Abdominal # 3

No Break

| 1 | 1 | 1 | 1 | 1 | 1 | 1 |

Week 5 Day 2

5   Dumbbell Up on Toes Upright Row

30s Break

| 50%12 | 60%12 70%10 | 65%10 | 70%10 | 75%6 80%6 |

8   Dumbbell Up on Toes High Pull Snatch

30s Break

| 50%10 | 60%10 | 70%10 | 75%8 | 80%6 | 75%8 | 80%6 |

11 Dumbbell Parallel Jump Push Press

30s Break

| 50%10 | 60%10 | 65%8 | 70%8 | 60%10 | 65%8 | 70%8 |

19 Dumbbell Alternate Overhead Press & High Knees Running In Place

30s Break

| 50%20+20 | 50%20+20 | 55%20+20 | 60%16+16 |
| 65%12+12 | 70%12+12 | 70%12+12 | |

22 Dumbbell Lunge Walk & From Lunge, Hip High Pull Snatch

40s Break

40%22+22+22+22	40%22+22+22+22	45%22+22+22+22
45%22+22+22+22	45%22+22+22+22	45%22+22+22+22
22+22+22+50%22		

30 Barbell Back Squat Jump

60s Break

| 40%10 | 35%10 | 40%8 | 45%8 | 40%8 | 45%8 | 45%8 |

32 General Plyometrics Exercises on Stairs or Sand Stair Boxes

40s Break

| 4xstair D.L.B. | 4xjump & Sprint | 4x D.L Zig-Zag | 4xstair Sprint |
| 4xstair D.L.B. | 4xstair Sprint | 4xstair Sprint | |

34 Javorek's Special Abdominal # 3

No Break

| 1 | 1 | 1 | 1 | 1 | 1 | 1 |

Week 5 Day 3

27 Javorek's Dumbbell Complex # 2

60s Break

| 35%1 | 40%1 | 35%1 | 40%1 | 45%1 | 45%1 | 45%1 |

28 Barbell Back Squat & Up on Toes

60s Break

| 50%10 | 60%10 | 70%8 | 80%6 | 85%4 | 80%6 | 85%4 |

17 Dumbbell Alternate Raise To Armpit & Running In Place

30s Break

| 40%20+20 | 45%20+20 | 50%20+20 | 55%20+20 |
| 50%20+20 | 55%20+20 | 60%20+20 | |

29 Barbell Wave Squat
(9 Quarter Squat & Up on Toes + 2 Quarter Squat Jumps)

60s Break

| 40%44 50%44 | 55%44 | 60%33 | 60%33 | 60%33 | 60%33 |

30 Barbell Back Squat Jump

60s Break

| 40%12 | 35%12 | 40%10 | 45%8 | 40%10 | 45%8 | 50%6 |

33 Dumbbell Frontal + Lateral Straight Arm Raise

15s Break

| 40%12 +12 | 40%12 +12 | 40%12 +12 | 45%10+10 |
| 45%10+10 | 45%10+10 | 50%8+8 | |

32 General Plyometrics Exercises on Stairs or Sand Stair Boxes

40s Break

| 4xstair D.L.B. | 4xjump & Sprint | 4x D.L Zig-Zag | 4xstair Sprint |
| 4xstair D.L.B. | 4xstair Sprint | 4xstair Sprint | |

34 Javorek's Special Abdominal # 3

No Break

| 1 | 1 | 1 | 1 | 1 | 1 | 1 |

Week 6 Day 1

3 Dumbbell From Hang Bellow The Knee Power Snatch
40s Break
50%12	55%12	60%12	65%10	70%10	75%6	80%4

9 Dumbbell Up on Toes Parallel Press
35s Break
50%10	55%10	60%10	65%8	70%8	75%6	80%6

6 Dumbbell Up on Toes Squat Upright Row
40s Break
50%12	50%12	55%10	55%10	60%10	65%10	65%10

12 Dumbbell Up on Toes Parallel Squat Push Press
35s Break
50%10	55%10	60%8	65%8	70%6	75%6	80%4

30 Barbell Back Squat Jump
60s Break
40%12	40%12	35%10	40%8	40%12	35%10	40%8

33 Dumbbell Frontal + Lateral Straight Arm Raise
15s Break
40%12 +12	40%12 +12	40%12 +12	45%10+10
45%10+10	45%10+10	50%8+8	

32 General Plyometrics Exercises on Stairs or Sand Stair Boxes
40s Break
4xstair D.L.B.	4xjump & Sprint	4x D.L Zig-Zag	4xstair Sprint
4xstair D.L.B.	4xstair Sprint	4xstair Sprint	

34 Javorek's Special Abdominal # 3
No Break
1	1	1	1	1	1	1

Week 6 Day 2

12 Dumbbell Up on Toes Parallel Squat Push Press
40s Break
50%10	55%10	60%8	65%8	70%6	75%6	80%6

21 Dumbbell Alternate Leg Lunges
40s Break
40%16+16	45%16+16	50%14+14	55%14+14
60%14+14	55%14+14	60%14+14	

15 Dumbbell Bent Over "Kick Back" Triceps Curls
30s Break
45%14	50%12	55%10	60%10	65%10	70%10	75%8

23 Dumbbell Alternate Leg Step Ups
40s Break
40%14+14	45%14+14	50%14+14	55%12+12
60%10+10	65%10+10	65%10+10	

19 Dumbbell Alternate Overhead Press & High Knees Running In Place
30s Break
35%20+20	35%20+20	40%20+20
40%20+20	40%20+20	40%20+20

28 Barbell Back Squat & Up on Toes
60s Break
50%10	60%10	70%10	65%10
75%6 85%4	85%4		

25 Dumbbell Upstairs Run (Minimum 20 Steps Stairway)
40s Break
25%3	40%3	35%3	45%3	40%3	35%3	45%3

33 Dumbbell Frontal + Lateral Straight Arm Raise
15s Break
40%12 +12	40%12 +12	40%12 +12	45%10+10
45%10+10	45%10+10	50%8+8	

32 General Plyometrics Exercises on Stairs or Sand Stair Boxes
40s Break
4xstair D.L.B.	4xjump & Sprint	4x D.L Zig-Zag	4xstair Sprint
4xstair D.L.B.	4xstair Sprint	4xstair Sprint	

34 Javorek's Special Abdominal # 3
No Break
1	1	1	1	1	1	1

Week 6 Day 3

4 Dumbbell Alternate Leg Split Clean
35s Break
50%8+8	50%8+8	60%8+8	65%6+6	65%6+6	70%6+6	75%4+4

23 Dumbbell Alternate Leg Step Ups
40s Break
50%12+12	50%12+12	55%12+12	55%12+12
60%10+10	65%10+10	65%10+10	

5 Dumbbell Up on Toes Upright Row
40s Break
50%12	55%12	60%12	65%10	70%10	70%10	70%10

7 Dumbbell Up on Toes From Hip High Pull Snatch
35s Break
40%14	45%12	50%12	55%10	60%8	55%10	60%8

25 Dumbbell Upstairs Run (Minimum 20 Steps Stairway)
40s Break
25%3	40%3	35%3	45%3	40%3	35%3	45%3

11 Dumbbell Parallel Jump Push Press
40s Break
50%10	50%10	55%10	55%8	60%8	65%6	65%6

20 Dumbbell Split Jump & Alternate Raise To Armpit
60s Break
40%12+12	50%10+10	55%10+10	60%10+10
65%10+10	60%10+10	65%10+10	

33 Dumbbell Frontal + Lateral Straight Arm Raise
15s Break
40%12 +12	40%12 +12	40%12 +12	45%10+10
45%10+10	45%10+10	50%8+8	

32 General Plyometrics Exercises on Stairs or Sand Stair Boxes
40s Break
4xstair D.L.B.	4xjump & Sprint	4x D.L Zig-Zag	4xstair Sprint
4xstair D.L.B.	4xstair Sprint	4xstair Sprint	

34 Javorek's Special Abdominal # 3
No Break
1	1	1	1	1	1	1

Week 7 Day 1

13 Barbell Behind The Head From Squat Overhead Press
35s Break
55%12	60%10	65%10	70%10	65%10	70%10	75%8

22 Dumbbell Lunge Walk & From Lunge, Hip High Pull Snatch
40s Break
40%22+22+22+22	40%22+22+22+22	45%22+22+22+22
45%22+22+22+22	45%22+22+22+22	45%22+22+22+22
22+22+22+50%22		

14 Dumbbell Rotational Bent Over Row
35s Break
50%12	60%12	65%12	80%8	80%8

20 Dumbbell Split Jump & Alternate Raise To Armpit
40s Break
40%12+12	50%10+10	55%10+10	60%10+10
65%10+10	60%10+10	65%10+10	

8 Dumbbell Up on Toes High Pull Snatch
40s Break

40%10	45%10	50%10	55%10	60%10	55%10	60%10

28 Barbell Back Squat & Up on Toes
60s Break

40%10	45%10	50%10	60%8	70%5	70%5	70%5

29 Barbell Wave Squat
(9 Quarter Squat & Up on Toes + 2 Quarter Squat Jumps)
60s Break

25%44	40%44	35%44	40%44	45%44	40%44	45%44

32 General Plyometrics Exercises on Stairs or Sand Stair Boxes
40s Break

4xstair D.L.B.   4xjump & Sprint   4x D.L Zig-Zag   4xstair Sprint
4xstair D.L.B.   4xstair Sprint   4xstair Sprint

34 Javorek's Special Abdominal # 3
No Break

1   1   1   1   1   1   1

Week 7 Day 2
1 Dumbbell Quarter Squat & Up on Toes Raise To Armpit
35s Break

50%12	60%10	70%10	80%6	80%6	90%3	90%3

16 Dumbbell Bent Over Fly
30s Break

40%14	45%14	50%12	55%12	60%10	65%10	65%10

18 Dumbbell Horizontal Parallel Inward-Outward Rotation
35s Break

40%8+8 35%7+7		40%6+6	45%6+6	50%5+5	50%5+5	50%5+5

26 Javorek's Dumbbell Complex # 1
60s Break

50%1	50%1	55%1	55%1	60%1	55%1	60%1

22 Dumbbell Lunge Walk & From Lunge, Hip High Pull Snatch
40s Break

40%22+22+22+22   40%22+22+22+22   45%22+22+22+22
45%22+22+22+22   45%22+22+22+22   45%22+22+22+22
22+22+22+50%22

33 Dumbbell Frontal + Lateral Straight Arm Raise
15s Break

40%12 +12   40%12 +12   40%12 +12   45%10+10
45%10+10   45%10+10   50%8+8

32 General Plyometrics Exercises on Stairs or Sand Stair Boxes
40s Break

4xstair D.L.B.   4xjump & Sprint   4x D.L Zig-Zag   4xstair Sprint
4xstair D.L.B.   4xstair Sprint   4xstair Sprint

34 Javorek's Special Abdominal # 3
No Break

1   1   1   1   1   1   1

Week 7 Day 3
27 Javorek's Dumbbell Complex # 2
60s Break

45%1	45%1	50%1	50%1	55%1	45%1	55%1

24 Dumbbell Single Leg Lunges + Up on Toes Squat Push Press
40s Break

50%12+12+8   55%12+12+8   60%12+12+8   65%12+12+8
70%12+12+8   75%12+12+8   75%12+12+8

25 Dumbbell Upstairs Run (Minimum 20 Steps Stairway)
40s Break

25%3	25%3	40%3	40%3	40%3	35%3	40%3

31 Barbell Wave Squat + Back Squat & Up on Toes + Wave Squat
60s Break

35%27+10+27   35%27+10+27   45%27+6+27   45%27+6+27
55%18+6+18   55%18+6+18   55%18+6+18

30 Barbell Back Squat Jump
60s Break

35%10	40%8	50%6	60%6	60%6	60%6	60%6

33 Dumbbell Frontal + Lateral Straight Arm Raise
15s Break

40%12 +12   40%12 +12   40%12 +12   45%10+10
45%10+10   45%10+10   50%8+8

32 General Plyometrics Exercises on Stairs or Sand Stair Boxes
40s Break

4xstair D.L.B.   4xjump & Sprint   4x D.L Zig-Zag   4xstair Sprint
4xstair D.L.B.   4xstair Sprint   4xstair Sprint

34 Javorek's Special Abdominal # 3
No Break

1   1   1   1   1   1   1

Week 8 Day 1
2 Dumbbell Alternate Leg Split Snatch
35s Break

60%8+8	65%8+8	65%8+8	65%8+8	70%6+6	70%6+6	70%6+6

6 Dumbbell Up on Toes Squat Upright Row
35s Break

50%10	50%10	60%10	70%10	80%8	80%6	80%6

4 Dumbbell Alternate Leg Split Clean
30s Break

50%8+8	50%8+8	60%8+8	65%6+6	65%6+6	70%6+6	75%4+4

23 Dumbbell Alternate Leg Step Ups
60s Break

50%16+16   50%16+16   55%16 + 16   55%16 + 16
60%16+16   65%16+16   65%16+16

8 Dumbbell Up on Toes High Pull Snatch
35s Break

60%10	65%10	70%10	75%8	80%8	70%10	80%6

12 Dumbbell Up on Toes Parallel Squat Push Press
40s Break

50%10	60%10	70%8	75%8	80%6	80%6	80%6

28 Barbell Back Squat & Up on Toes
60s Break

40%12	50%10	55%10	65%8	60%10	70%10	80%5

33 Dumbbell Frontal + Lateral Straight Arm Raise
15s Break

40%12 +12   40%12 +12   40%12 +12   45%10+10
45%10+10   45%10+10   50%8+8

32 General Plyometrics Exercises on Stairs or Sand Stair Boxes
40s Break

4xstair D.L.B.   4xjump & Sprint   4x D.L Zig-Zag   4xstair Sprint
4xstair D.L.B.   4xstair Sprint   4xstair Sprint

34 Javorek's Special Abdominal # 3
No Break

1   1   1   1   1   1   1

Week 8 Day 2
3 Dumbbell From Hang Bellow The Knee Power Snatch
30s Break

50%12	55%12	60%12	65%10	70%10	75%6	80%4

7 Dumbbell Up on Toes From Hip High Pull Snatch
30s Break

40%12	50%10	55%10	60%10	65%8	70%6	70%6

22 Dumbbell Lunge Walk & From Lunge, Hip High Pull Snatch

60s Break

40%22+22+22+22   40%22+22+22+22   45%22+22+22+22   45%22+22+22+22
45%22+22+22+22   45%22+22+22+22   22+22+22+2250%   22+22+22+2250%

18 Dumbbell Horizontal Parallel Inward-Outward Rotation

30s Break

40%10 + 10   40%10 + 10   45%8+8   50%8+8
55%7+7   60%6+6   60%6+6

29 Barbell Wave Squat
(9 Quarter Squat & Up on Toes + 2 Quarter Squat Jumps)

60s Break

35%44   45%44   55%44   55%44   60%33   65%33   65%33

20 Dumbbell Split Jump & Alternate Raise To Armpit

40s Break

40%12+12   50%10+10   55%10+10   60%10+10
65%10+10   65%10+10   65%10+10

32 General Plyometrics Exercises on Stairs or Sand Stair Boxes

40s Break

4xstair D.L.B.   4xjump & Sprint   4x D.L Zig-Zag   4xstair Sprint
4xstair D.L.B.   4xstair Sprint   4xstair Sprint

34 Javorek's Special Abdominal # 3

No Break

1   1   1   1   1   1   1

Week 8 Day 3

4   Dumbbell Alternate Leg Split Clean

35s Break

50%8+8   50%8+8   60%8+8   65%6+6   65%6+6   70%6+6   75%4+4

5   Dumbbell Up on Toes Upright Row

35s Break

50%14   50%14   55%12   60%12   65%10   70%10   70%10

7   Dumbbell Up on Toes From Hip High Pull Snatch

35s Break

40%14   45%12   50%12   55%10   65%8   70%6   70%6

14 Dumbbell Rotational Bent Over Row

35s Break

60%14   70%12   65%12   75%10   80%8   90%6
90%6

29 Barbell Wave Squat
(9 Quarter Squat & Up on Toes + 2 Quarter Squat Jumps)

60s Break

50%44   55%44   60%44   65%33   70%22   75%22   75%22

33 Dumbbell Frontal + Lateral Straight Arm Raise

15s Break

40%12 +12   40%12 +12   40%12 +12   45%10+10
45%10+10   45%10+10   50%8+8

32 General Plyometrics Exercises on Stairs or Sand Stair Boxes

40s Break

4xstair D.L.B.   4xjump & Sprint   4x D.L Zig-Zag   4xstair Sprint
4xstair D.L.B.   4xstair Sprint   4xstair Sprint

34 Javorek's Special Abdominal # 3

No Break

1   1   1   1   1   1   1

Week 9 Day 1

8   Dumbbell Up on Toes High Pull Snatch

35s Break

60%10   65%10   70%10   75%8   80%8   75%8   80%8

21 Dumbbell Alternate Leg Lunges

30s Break

50%16+16   55%16+16   60%16+16   65%16+16
70%16+16   75%16+16   75%16+16

10 Dumbbell Quarter Squat & Up on Toes Parallel Push Press

30s Break

60%10   65%10   70%8   75%6   80%6   85%5   85%5

22 Dumbbell Lunge Walk & From Lunge, Hip High Pull Snatch

40s Break

40%22+22+22+22   40%22+22+22+22   45%22+22+22+22   45%22+22+22+22
45%22+22+22+22   45%22+22+22+22   22+22+22+50%22

19 Dumbbell Alternate Overhead Press & High Knees Running In Place

30s Break

35%20+20   35%20+20   40%20+20   40%20+20
40%20+20   40%20+20   40%20+20

13 Barbell Behind The Head From Squat Overhead Press

30s Break

55%12   60%10   65%10   70%10   65%10   70%10   75%8

25 Dumbbell Upstairs Run (Minimum 20 Steps Stairway)

40s Break

25%3   25%3   25%3   25%3   25%3   25%3   25%3

31 Barbell Wave Squat + Back Squat & Up on Toes + Wave Squat

60s Break

35%44+10+44   35%44+10+44   45%33+8+33   50%33+8+33
50%33+8+33   60%22+6+22   60%22+6+22

32 General Plyometrics Exercises on Stairs or Sand Stair Boxes

40s Break

4xstair D.L.B.   4xjump & Sprint   4x D.L Zig-Zag   4xstair Sprint
4xstair D.L.B.   4xstair Sprint   4xstair Sprint

34 Javorek's Special Abdominal # 3

No Break

1   1   1   1   1   1   1

Week 9 Day 2

1   Dumbbell Quarter Squat & Up on Toes Raise To Armpit

35s Break

50%12   60%12   70%12   65%10   75%10   85%8   85%8

17 Dumbbell Alternate Raise To Armpit & Running In Place

35s Break

40%14   45%14   50%12   55%12   60%10   60%10   60%10

15 Dumbbell Bent Over "Kick Back" Triceps Curls

35s Break

50%12   60%12   65%10   70%10   75%10   80%8   80%8

26 Javorek's Dumbbell Complex # 1

60s Break

50%1   50%1   55%1   55%1   60%1   60%1   65%1

28 Barbell Back Squat & Up on Toes

60s Break

25 Dumbbell Upstairs Run (Minimum 20 Steps Stairway)

40s Break

25%5   40%5   40%5   35%5   35%5   35%5   35%5

30 Barbell Back Squat Jump

60s Break

40%10   35%10   40%8   40%8   35%10   40%8   45%8

33 Dumbbell Frontal + Lateral Straight Arm Raise
15s Break

40%12 +12   40%12 +12   40%12 +12   45%10+10
45%10+10   45%10+10   50%8+8

32 General Plyometrics Exercises on Stairs or Sand Stair Boxes
40s Break

4xstair D.L.B.   4xjump & Sprint   4x D.L Zig-Zag   4xstair Sprint
4xstair D.L.B.   4xstair Sprint   4xstair Sprint

34 Javorek's Special Abdominal # 3
No Break

1   1   1   1   1   1   1

Week 9 Day 3

3 Dumbbell From Hang Bellow The Knee Power Snatch
35s Break

50%12   55%12   60%12   65%10   70%10   75%6 80%4

4 Dumbbell Alternate Leg Split Clean
35s Break

50%8+8   50%8+8   60%8+8   65%6+6   65%6+6   70%6+6   75%4+4

5 Dumbbell Up on Toes Upright Row
35s Break

60%12   70%10   80%8   80%8   80%8   80%8   80%8

23 Dumbbell Alternate Leg Step Ups
40s Break

60%14+14   65%12+12   70%12+12   70%12+12
70%12+12   70%12+12   70%12+12

8 Dumbbell Up on Toes High Pull Snatch
35s Break

60%10   65%10   70%10   70%10   70%10   70%10   70%10

12 Dumbbell Up on Toes Parallel Squat Push Press
40s Break

55%10   65%10   80%8   80%8   80%8   80%8   80%8

22 Dumbbell Lunge Walk & From Lunge, Hip High Pull Snatch
40s Break

40%22+22+22+22   40%22+22+22+22   45%22+22+22+22
45%22+22+22+22   45%22+22+22+22   45%22+22+22+22
45%22+22+22+22

18 Dumbbell Horizontal Parallel Inward-Outward Rotation
35s Break

50%8+8   55%7+7   60%6+6   60%6+6   60%6+6   60%6+6   60%6+6

29 Barbell Wave Squat
(9 Quarter Squat & Up on Toes + 2 Quarter Squat Jumps)
60s Break

50%44   55%44   50%44   50%44   50%44   50%44   50%44

20 Dumbbell Split Jump & Alternate Raise To Armpit
40s Break

55%10+10   60%10+10   65%10+10   65%10+10
65%10+10   65%10+10   65%10+10

33 Dumbbell Frontal + Lateral Straight Arm Raise
15s Break

40%12 +12   40%12 +12   40%12 +12   45%10+10
45%10+10   45%10+10   45%10+10

32 General Plyometrics Exercises on Stairs or Sand Stair Boxes
40s Break

4xstair D.L.B.   4xjump & Sprint   4x D.L Zig-Zag   4xstair Sprint
4xstair D.L.B.   4xstair Sprint   4xstair Sprint

34 Javorek's Special Abdominal # 3
No Break

1   1   1   1   1   1   1

Week 10 Day 1

1 Dumbbell Quarter Squat & Up on Toes Raise To Armpit
30s Break

60%12   70%12   80%8   80%8   80%8   80%8   80%8

2 Dumbbell Alternate Leg Split Snatch
30s Break

60%8+8   65%8+8   65%8+8   70%8+8   70%6+6   75%4+4   75%4+4

21 Dumbbell Alternate Leg Lunges
40s Break

50%16+16   60%16+16   70%16+16   70%16+16
70%16+16   70%16+16   70%16+16

7 Dumbbell Up on Toes From Hip High Pull Snatch
30s Break

40%14   45%12   50%12   50%12   50%12   50%12   50%12

14 Dumbbell Rotational Bent Over Row
30s Break

60%14   70%12   80%8   80%8   80%8   80%8   80%8

22 Dumbbell Lunge Walk & From Lunge, Hip High Pull Snatch
40s Break

40%22+22+22+22   40%22+22+22+22   45%22+22+22+22
45%22+22+22+22   45%22+22+22+22   45%22+22+22+22
45%22+22+22+22

8 Dumbbell Up on Toes High Pull Snatch
30s Break

60%10   70%10   80%6   80%6   80%6   80%6   80%6

10 Dumbbell Quarter Squat & Up on Toes Parallel Push Press
30s Break

60%10   70%10   85%6   85%6   85%6   85%6   85%6

13 Barbell Behind The Head From Squat Overhead Press
40s Break

55%10   65%10   75%6   75%6   75%6   75%6   75%6

19 Dumbbell Alternate Overhead Press & High Knees Running In Place
40s Break

50%20+20   50%20+20   55%20+20   60%16+16
65%12+12   70%12+12   70%12+12

24 Dumbbell Single Leg Lunges + Up on Toes Squat Push Press
40s Break

65%12+12+8   70%12+12+8   75%12+12+8   75%12+12+8
75%12+12+8   75%12+12+8   75%12+12+8

31 Barbell Wave Squat + Back Squat & Up on Toes + Wave Squat
60s Break

40%44+10+44   40%44+10+44   50%33+8+33   50%33+8+33
50%33+8+33   50%33+8+33   50%33+8+33

33 Dumbbell Frontal + Lateral Straight Arm Raise
15s Break

40%12 +12   40%12 +12   40%12 +12   45%10+10
45%10+10   45%10+10   45%10+10

32 General Plyometrics Exercises on Stairs or Sand Stair Boxes
40s Break

4xstair D.L.B.   4xjump & Sprint   4x D.L Zig-Zag   4xstair Sprint
4xstair D.L.B.   4xstair Sprint   4xstair Sprint

34 Javorek's Special Abdominal # 3
No Break

1   1   1   1   1   1   1

Week 10 Day 2

3 Dumbbell From Hang Bellow The Knee Power Snatch — 30s Break

| 50%12 | 55%12 | 60%12 | 65%10 | 70%10 | 75%6 | 80%4 |

6 Dumbbell Up on Toes Squat Upright Row — 30s Break

| 70%10 | 80%8 | 90%4 | 90%4 | 90%4 | 90%4 | 90%4 |

23 Dumbbell Alternate Leg Step Ups — 40s Break

| 60%16+16 | 60%16+16 | 60%16+16 | 60%16+16 |
| 60%16+16 | 60%16+16 | 60%16+16 | |

8 Dumbbell Up on Toes High Pull Snatch — 30s Break

| 75%8 | 80%6 | 85%6 | 85%6 | 85%6 | 85%6 | 85%6 |

12 Dumbbell Up on Toes Parallel Squat Push Press — 40s Break

| 75%8 | 80%6 | 90%4 | 90%4 | 90%4 | 90%4 | 90%4 |

22 Dumbbell Lunge Walk & From Lunge, Hip High Pull Snatch — 40s Break

40%22+22+22+22	40%22+22+22+22	45%22+22+22+22
45%22+22+22+22	45%22+22+22+22	45%22+22+22+22
45%22+22+22+22		

17 Dumbbell Alternate Raise To Armpit & Running In Place — 30s Break

| 50%12 | 60%10 | 70%10 | 70%10 | 70%10 | 70%10 | 70%10 |

15 Dumbbell Bent Over "Kick Back" Triceps Curls — 30s Break

| 50%12 | 55%10 | 60%10 | 60%10 | 60%10 | 60%10 | 60%10 |

29 Barbell Wave Squat
(9 Quarter Squat & Up on Toes + 2 Quarter Squat Jumps) — 60s Break

| 45%44 | 55%33 | 65%33 | 65%33 | 65%33 | 65%33 | 65%33 |

20 Dumbbell Split Jump & Alternate Raise To Armpit — 40s Break

| 55%10+10 | 60%10+10 | 65%10+10 | 65%10+10 |
| 65%10+10 | 65%10+10 | 65%10+10 | |

32 General Plyometrics Exercises on Stairs or Sand Stair Boxes — 40s Break

| 4xstair D.L.B. | 4xjump & Sprint | 4x D.L Zig-Zag | 4xstair Sprint |
| 4xstair D.L.B. | 4xstair Sprint | 4xstair Sprint | |

34 Javorek's Special Abdominal # 3 — No Break

| 1 | 1 | 1 | 1 | 1 | 1 | 1 |

Week 10 Day 3

1 Dumbbell Quarter Squat & Up on Toes Raise To Armpit — 30s Break

| 65%10 | 75%10 | 85%8 | 85%8 | 85%8 | 85%8 | 85%8 |

3 Dumbbell From Hang Bellow The Knee Power Snatch — 30s Break

| 50%12 | 55%12 | 60%12 | 65%10 | 70%10 | 75%6 | 80%4 |

21 Dumbbell Alternate Leg Lunges — 30s Break

| 55%16+16 | 65%16+16 | 75%16+16 | 75%16+16 |
| 75%16+16 | 75%16+16 | 75%16+16 | |

7 Dumbbell Up on Toes From Hip High Pull Snatch — 30s Break

| 55%10 | 65%8 | 80%6 | 80%6 | 80%6 | 80%6 | 80%6 |

---

14 Dumbbell Rotational Bent Over Row — 30s Break

| 75%10 | 80%8 | 90%6 | 90%6 | 90%6 | 90%6 | 90%6 |

22 Dumbbell Lunge Walk & From Lunge, Hip High Pull Snatch — 40s Break

40%22+22+22+22	40%22+22+22+22	45%22+22+22+22
45%22+22+22+22	45%22+22+22+22	45%22+22+22+22
45%22+22+22+22		

8 Dumbbell Up on Toes High Pull Snatch — 30s Break

| 50%12 | 60%10 | 70%10 | 70%10 | 70%10 | 70%10 | 70%10 |

19 Dumbbell Alternate Overhead Press & High Knees Running In Place — 30s Break

| 35%20+20 | 35%20+20 | 40%20+20 | 40%20+20 |
| 40%20+20 | 40%20+20 | 40%20+20 | |

10 Dumbbell Quarter Squat & Up on Toes Parallel Push Press — 30s Break

| 75%6 | 80%6 | 85%5 | 85%5 | 85%5 | 85%5 | 85%5 |

11 Dumbbell Parallel Jump Push Press — 30s Break

| 60%8 | 65%6 | 70%6 | 60%8 | 70%6 | 60%8 | 70%6 |

24 Dumbbell Single Leg Lunges + Up on Toes Squat Push Press — 40s Break

| 65%12+12+8 | 70%12+12+8 | 75%12+12+8 | 75%12+12+8 |
| 75%12+12+8 | 75%12+12+8 | 75%12+12+8 | |

17 Dumbbell Alternate Raise To Armpit & Running In Place — 30s Break

| 50%14 | 60%12 | 70%10 | 70%10 | 70%10 | 70%10 | 70%10 |

13 Barbell Behind The Head From Squat Overhead Press — 40s Break

| 55%12 | 60%10 | 65%10 | 70%10 | 65%10 | 70%10 | 75%8 |

31 Barbell Wave Squat + Back Squat & Up on Toes + Wave Squat — 60s Break

| 40%33+8+33 | 50%33+6+33 | 60%33+6+33 | 60%33+6+33 |
| 60%33+6+33 | 60%33+6+33 | 60%33+6+33 | |

33 Dumbbell Frontal + Lateral Straight Arm Raise — 15s Break

| 40%12 +12 | 40%12 +12 | 40%12 +12 | 45%10+10 |
| 45%10+10 | 45%10+10 | 45%10+10 | |

32 General Plyometrics Exercises on Stairs or Sand Stair Boxes — 40s Break

| 4xstair D.L.B. | 4xjump & Sprint | 4x D.L Zig-Zag | 4xstair Sprint |
| 4xstair D.L.B. | 4xstair Sprint | 4xstair Sprint | |

34 Javorek's Special Abdominal # 3 — No Break

| 1 | 1 | 1 | 1 | 1 | 1 | 1 |

Week 11 Day 1

1 Dumbbell Quarter Squat & Up on Toes Raise To Armpit — 30s Break

| 70%12 | 80%8 | 85%6 | 85%6 | 85%6 | 85%6 | 85%6 |

4 Dumbbell Alternate Leg Split Clean — 30s Break

| 50%8+8 | 50%8+8 | 60%8+8 | 65%6+6 | 65%6+6 | 70%6+6 | 75%4+4 |

23 Dumbbell Alternate Leg Step Ups — 40s Break

| 55%16+16 | 55%16+16 | 55%16+16 | 55%16+16 |
| 55%16+16 | 55%16+16 | 55%16+16 | |

6 Dumbbell Up on Toes Squat Upright Row — 30s Break

| 65%10 | 75%10 | 85%6 | 85%6 | 85%6 | 85%6 | 85%6 |

8 Dumbbell Up on Toes High Pull Snatc
h
30s Break

| 75%8 | 80%8 | 85%6 | 85%6 | 85%6 | 85%6 | 85%6 |

22 Dumbbell Lunge Walk & From Lunge, Hip High Pull Snatch
40s Break

| 40%22+22+22+22 | 40%22+22+22+22 | 45%22+22+22+22 | 45%22+22+22+22 |
| 45%22+22+22+22 | 45%22+22+22+22 | 45%22+22+22+22 | |

12 Dumbbell Up on Toes Parallel Squat Push Press
30s Break

| 70%10 | 80%8 | 90%4 | 90%4 | 90%4 | 90%4 | 90%4 |

16 Dumbbell Bent Over Fly
30s Break

| 60%12 | 70%10 | 80%6 | 80%6 | 80%6 | 80%6 | 80%6 |

20 Dumbbell Split Jump & Alternate Raise To Armpit
40s Break

| 55%10+10 | 60%10+10 | 65%10+10 | 65%10+10 |
| 65%10+10 | 65%10+10 | 65%10+10 | |

18 Dumbbell Horizontal Parallel Inward-Outward Rotation
30s Break

| 50%8+8 | 55%7+7 | 60%6+6 | 60%6+6 | 60%6+6 | 60%6+6 | 60%6+6 |

29 Barbell Wave Squat
(9 Quarter Squat & Up on Toes + 2 Quarter Squat Jumps)
60s Break

| 40%44 | 55%44 | 65%33 | 65%33 | 65%33 | 65%33 | 65%33 |

33 Dumbbell Frontal + Lateral Straight Arm Raise
15s Break

| 40%12 +12 | 40%12 +12 | 40%12 +12 | 45%10+10 |
| 45%10+10 | 45%10+10 | 45%10+10 | |

32 General Plyometrics Exercises on Stairs or Sand Stair Boxes
40s Break

| 4xstair D.L.B. | 4xjump & Sprint | 4x D.L Zig-Zag | 4xstair Sprint |
| 4xstair D.L.B. | 4xstair Sprint | 4xstair Sprint | |

34 Javorek's Special Abdominal # 3
No Break

| 1 | 1 | 1 | 1 | 1 | 1 | 1 |

Week 11 Day 2

3   Dumbbell From Hang Bellow The Knee Power Snatch
30s Break

| 50%12 | 55%12 | 60%12 | 65%10 | 70%10 | 75%6 | 80%4 |

16 Dumbbell Bent Over Fly
30s Break

| 40%14 | 45%14 | 50%12 | 50%12 | 50%12 | 50%12 | 50%12 |

18 Dumbbell Horizontal Parallel Inward-Outward Rotation
30s Break

| 50%8+8 | 55%7+7 | 60%6+6 | 60%6+6 | 60%6+6 | 60%6+6 | 60%6+6 |

26 Javorek's Dumbbell Complex # 1
60s Break

| 50%1 | 50%1 | 55%1 | 55%1 | 60%1 | 60%1 | 65%1 |

25 Dumbbell Upstairs Run (Minimum 20 Steps Stairway)
40s Break

| 40%5 | 40%5 | 35%5 | 35%5 | 40%5 | 40%5 | 40%5 |

29 Barbell Wave Squat
(9 Quarter Squat & Up on Toes + 2 Quarter Squat Jumps)
60s Break

| 40%44 | 45%44 | 50%33 | 50%33 | 55%33 | 60%33 | 65%33 |

33 Dumbbell Frontal + Lateral Straight Arm Raise
15s Break

| 40%12 +12 | 40%12 +12 | 40%12 +12 | 45%10+10 |
| 45%10+10 | 45%10+10 | 45%10+10 | |

32 General Plyometrics Exercises on Stairs or Sand Stair Boxes
40s Break

| 4xstair D.L.B. | 4xjump & Sprint | 4x D.L Zig-Zag | 4xstair Sprint |
| 4xstair D.L.B. | 4xstair Sprint | 4xstair Sprint | |

34 Javorek's Special Abdominal # 3
No Break

| 1 | 1 | 1 | 1 | 1 | 1 | 1 |

Week 11 Day 3

1   Dumbbell Quarter Squat & Up on Toes Raise To Armpit
30s Break

| 70%12 | 80%8 | 90%5 | 90%5 | 90%5 | 90%5 | 90%5 |

5   Dumbbell Up on Toes Upright Row
30s Break

| 70%10 | 80%6 | 90%5 | 90%5 | 90%5 | 90%5 | 90%5 |

23 Dumbbell Alternate Leg Step Ups
40s Break

| 65%16+16 | 65%16+16 | 65%16+16 | 65%16+16 |
| 65%16+16 | 65%16+16 | 65%16+16 | |

8   Dumbbell Up on Toes High Pull Snatch
30s Break

| 75%8 | 80%6 | 85%4 | 85%4 | 85%4 | 85%4 | 85%4 |

12 Dumbbell Up on Toes Parallel Squat Push Press
30s Break

| 70%8 | 80%6 | 90%4 | 90%4 | 90%4 | 90%4 | 90%4 |

22 Dumbbell Lunge Walk & From Lunge, Hip High Pull Snatch
40s Break

40%22+22+22+22	40%22+22+22+22	45%22+22+22+22
45%22+22+22+22	45%22+22+22+22	45%22+22+22+22
45%22+22+22+22		

18 Dumbbell Horizontal Parallel Inward-Outward Rotation
30s Break

| 50%8+8 | 55%6+6 | 60%5+5 | 60%5+5 | 60%5+5 | 60%5+5 | 60%5+5 |

29 Barbell Wave Squat
(9 Quarter Squat & Up on Toes + 2 Quarter Squat Jumps)
60s Break

| 50%44 | 55%44 | 65%33 | 65%33 | 65%33 | 65%33 | 65%33 |

20 Dumbbell Split Jump & Alternate Raise To Armpit
40s Break

| 55%10+10 | 60%10+10 | 65%10+10 | 65%10+10 |
| 65%10+10 | 65%10+10 | 65%10+10 | |

33 Dumbbell Frontal + Lateral Straight Arm Raise
15s Break

| 40%12 +12 | 40%12 +12 | 40%12 +12 | 45%10+10 |
| 45%10+10 | 45%10+10 | 45%10+10 | |

32 General Plyometrics Exercises on Stairs or Sand Stair Boxes
40s Break

| 4xstair D.L.B. | 4xjump & Sprint | 4x D.L Zig-Zag | 4xstair Sprint |
| 4xstair D.L.B. | 4xstair Sprint | 4xstair Sprint | |

34 Javorek's Special Abdominal # 3
No Break

| 1 | 1 | 1 | 1 | 1 | 1 | 1 |

Week 12 Day 1

1   Dumbbell Quarter Squat & Up on Toes Raise To Armpit
30s Break

| 65%12 | 80%8 | 90%5 | 90%5 | 90%5 | 90%5 | 90%5 |

13 Barbell Behind The Head From Squat Overhead Press
30s Break

| 55%12 | 60%10 | 65%10 | 70%10 | 65%10 | 70%10 | 75%8 |

14 Dumbbell Rotational Bent Over Row

30s Break

| 70%10 | 80%8 | 90%5 | 90%5 | 90%5 | 90%5 | 90%5 |

21 Dumbbell Alternate Leg Lunges

40s Break

| 60%16+16 | | 70%16+16 | | 80%14+14 | | 80%14+14 |
| 80%14+14 | | 80%14+14 | | 80%14+14 | | |

20 Dumbbell Split Jump & Alternate Raise To Armpit

40s Break

| 55%10+10 | | 10+60%10 | | 65%10+10 | | 65%10+10 |
| 65%10+10 | | 65%10+10 | | 65%10+10 | | |

24 Dumbbell Single Leg Lunges + Up on Toes Squat Push Press

40s Break

| 65%12+12+8 | | 70%12+12+8 | | 75%12+12+8 | | 75%12+12+8 |
| 75%12+12+8 | | 75%12+12+8 | | 75%12+12+8 | | |

27 Javorek's Dumbbell Complex # 2

60s Break

| 40%1 | 45%1 | 50%1 | 50%1 | 55%1 | 55%1 | 55%1 |

32 General Plyometrics Exercises on Stairs or Sand Stair Boxes

40s Break

| 4xstair D.L.B. | 4xjump & Sprint | 4x D.L Zig-Zag | 4xstair Sprint |
| 4xstair D.L.B. | 4xstair Sprint | 4xstair Sprint | |

34 Javorek's Special Abdominal # 3

No Break

| 1 | 1 | 1 | 1 | 1 | 1 |

Week 12 Day 2

1 Dumbbell Quarter Squat & Up on Toes Raise To Armpit

40s Break

| 70%8 | 80%6 | 85%5 | 85%5 | 90%3 | 90%3 | 90%3 |

12 Dumbbell Up on Toes Parallel Squat Push Press

40s Break

| 60%10 | 70%10 | 80%6 | 85%5 | 90%3 | 90%3 | 90%3 |

23 Dumbbell Alternate Leg Step Ups

40s Break

| 70%8+8 | 75%6+6 | 80%6+6 | 85%4+4 | 90%3+3 | 90%3+3 | 90%3+3 |

3 Dumbbell From Hang Bellow The Knee Power Snatch

40s Break

| 70%10 | 75%10 | 80%8 | 85%6 | 90%4 | 95%2 | 95%2 |

21 Dumbbell Alternate Leg Lunges

40s Break

| 60%16+16 | | 70%16+16 | | 80%14+14 | | 85%12+12 |
| 85%12+12 | | 85%12+12 | | 85%12+12 | | |

20 Dumbbell Split Jump & Alternate Raise To Armpit

40s Break

| 55%10+10 | | 60%10+10 | | 65%10+10 | | 55%10+10 |
| 60%10+10 | | 65%10+10 | | 65%10+10 | | |

26 Javorek's Dumbbell Complex # 1

60s Break

| 50%1 | 55%1 | 60%1 | 60%1 | 65%1 | 70%1 | 70%1 |

4 Dumbbell Alternate Leg Split Clean

35s Break

| 50%8+8 | 50%8+8 | 60%8+8 | 65%6+6 | 65%6+6 | 70%6+6 | 75%4+4 |

33 Dumbbell Frontal + Lateral Straight Arm Raise

15s Break

| 40%12 +12 | | 40%12 +12 | | 40%12 +12 | | 45%10+10 |
| 45%10+10 | | 45%10+10 | | 45%10+10 | | |

32 General Plyometrics Exercises on Stairs or Sand Stair Boxes

40s Break

| 4xstair D.L.B. | 4xjump & Sprint | 4x D.L Zig-Zag | 4xstair Sprint |
| 4xstair D.L.B. | 4xstair Sprint | 4xstair Sprintxstair | |

34 Javorek's Special Abdominal # 3

No Break

| 1 | 1 | 1 | 1 | 1 | 1 | 1 |

Week 12 Day 3

3 Dumbbell From Hang Bellow The Knee Power Snatch

40s Break

| 50%12 | 55%12 | 60%12 | 65%10 | 70%10 | 75%6 80%4 |

12 Dumbbell Up on Toes Parallel Squat Push Press

40s Break

| 60%10 | 70%10 | 80%6 | 85%5 | 90%3 | 90%3 | 90%3 |

4 Dumbbell Alternate Leg Split Clean

35s Break

| 50%8+8 | 50%8+8 | 60%8+8 | 65%6+6 | 65%6+6 | 70%6+6 | 75%4+4 |

14 Dumbbell Rotational Bent Over Row

40s Break

| 70%10 | 75%10 | 80%8 | 85%6 | 90%4 | 90%4 | 90%4 |

18 Dumbbell Horizontal Parallel Inward-Outward Rotation

40s Break

| 50%8+8 | 55%8+8 | 60%6+6 | 55%5+5 | 55%5+5 | 55%5+5 | 55%5+5 |

19 Dumbbell Alternate Overhead Press & High Knees Running In Place

40s Break

| 50%20+20 | | 50%20+20 | | 55%20+20 | | 55%20+20 |
| 60%16+16 | | 60%16+16 | | 60%16+16 | | |

29 Barbell Wave Squat
(9 Quarter Squat & Up on Toes + 2 Quarter Squat Jumps)

60s Break

| 40%44 | 45%44 | 45%44 | 50%33 | 55%33 | 55%33 | 60%33 |

28 Barbell Back Squat & Up on Toes

60s Break

| 70%8 | 75%6 | 80%6 | 85%4 | 75%6 80%6 85%4 |

33 Dumbbell Frontal + Lateral Straight Arm Raise

15s Break

| 40%12 +12 | | 40%12 +12 | | 40%12 +12 | | 45%10+10 |
| 45%10+10 | | 45%10+10 | | 50%8+8 | | |

32 General Plyometrics Exercises on Stairs or Sand Stair Boxes

40s Break

| 4xstair D.L.B. | 4xjump & Sprint | 4x D.L Zig-Zag | 4xstair Sprint |
| 4xstair D.L.B. | 4xstair Sprint | 4xstair Sprintxstair | |

34 Javorek's Special Abdominal # 3

No Break

| 1 | 1 | 1 | 1 | 1 | 1 | 1 |

6 Weeks Tapering

Week 1 Day 1

3 Dumbbell From Hang Bellow The Knee Power Snatch

40s Break

| 60%4 | 65%4 | 70%2 | 80%2 |

9 Dumbbell Up on Toes Parallel Press

35s Break

| 60%4 | 5%4 | 70%2 | 80%2 |

6 Dumbbell Up on Toes Squat Upright Row

40s Break

| 60%4 | 65%4 | 70%2 | 80%2 |

12 Dumbbell Up on Toes Parallel Squat Push Press

35s Break

| 60%4 | 65%4 | 70%2 | 80%2 |

30 Barbell Back Squat Jump

				60s Break
40%4	35%4	40%4	45%2	

33 Dumbbell Frontal + Lateral Straight Arm Raise

				15s Break
40%4+4	40%4+4	40%4+4	50%4+4	

32 General Plyometrics Exercises on Stairs or Sand Stair Boxes

				40s Break
4xstair D.L.B.	4xstair D.L.B.	4xjump & Sprint	4xstair D.L.B.	

34 Javorek's Special Abdominal # 3

				No Break
1	1	1	1	

Week 1 Day 2

12 Dumbbell Up on Toes Parallel Squat Push Press

				40s Break
60%4	65%4	65%3	70%3	

21 Dumbbell Alternate Leg Lunges

				40s Break
50%6+6	55%5+5	60%5+5	65%4+4	

15 Dumbbell Bent Over "Kick Back" Triceps Curls

				30s Break
60%4	65%4	65%3	70%3	

23 Dumbbell Alternate Leg Step Ups

				40s Break
50%6+6	55%5+5	60%5+5	65%4+4	

19 Dumbbell Alternate Overhead Press & High Knees Running In Place

				30s Break
35%6+6	35%6+6	40%6+6	40%6+6	

28 Barbell Back Squat & Up on Toes

				60s Break
50%2	60%2	70%2	70%2	

25 Dumbbell Upstairs Run (Minimum 20 Steps Stairway)

				40s Break
25%3	40%3	35%3	45%3	

33 Dumbbell Frontal + Lateral Straight Arm Raise

				15s Break
40%4+4	40%4+4	40%4+4	50%4+4	

32 General Plyometrics Exercises on Stairs or Sand Stair Boxes

				40s Break
4xstair D.L.B.	4xstair D.L.B.	4xjump & Sprint	4xstair D.L.B.	

34 Javorek's Special Abdominal # 3

				No Break
1	1	1	1	

Week 1 Day 3

4 Dumbbell Alternate Leg Split Clean

				35s Break
60%3+3	65%3+3	70%+3	75%2+2	

23 Dumbbell Alternate Leg Step Ups

				40s Break
50%6+6	55%6+6	60%6+6	65%4+4	

5 Dumbbell Up on Toes Upright Row

				40s Break
55%6	65%6	70%4	75%4	

7 Dumbbell Up on Toes From Hip High Pull Snatch

				35s Break
55%6	65%6	70%4	75%4	

25 Dumbbell Upstairs Run (Minimum 20 Steps Stairway)

				40s Break
25%3	40%3	35%3	45%3	

11 Dumbbell Parallel Jump Push Press

40s Break

55%6	65%6	70%4	70%4

20 Dumbbell Split Jump & Alternate Raise To Armpit

60s Break

50%6+6	55%6+6	60%6+ 6	65%4+4

33 Dumbbell Frontal + Lateral Straight Arm Raise

15s Break

40%6+6	40%6+6	40%6+6	45%4+4

32 General Plyometrics Exercises on Stairs or Sand Stair Boxes

4xstair D.L.B.	4xstair D.L.B.	4xjump & Sprint	4xstair D.L.B.

34 Javorek's Special Abdominal # 3

				No Break
1	1	1	1	

Week 2 Day 1

13 Barbell Behind The Head From Squat Overhead Press

				35s Break
55%6	60%4	65%4	70%4	

22 Dumbbell Lunge Walk & From Lunge, Hip High Pull Snatch

				40s Break
40%10+10+10+10	40%10+10+10+10	45%10+10+10+10	45%10+10+10+10	

14 Dumbbell Rotational Bent Over Row

				35s Break
60%6	60%6	65%6	70%4	

20 Dumbbell Split Jump & Alternate Raise To Armpit

				40s Break
50%6+6	55%6+6	60%6+ 6	65%4+4	

8 Dumbbell Up on Toes High Pull Snatch

				40s Break
60%6	60%6	65%6	70%4	

28 Barbell Back Squat & Up on Toes

				60s Break
60%4	65%4	65%4	70%3	

29 Barbell Wave Squat
(9 Quarter Squat & Up on Toes + 2 Quarter Squat Jumps)

				60s Break
35%22	40%22	40%22	45%11	

32 General Plyometrics Exercises on Stairs or Sand Stair Boxes

				40s Break
4xstair D.L.B.	4xstair D.L.B.	4xjump & Sprint	4xstair D.L.B.	

34 Javorek's Special Abdominal # 3

				No Break
1	1	1	1	

Week 2 Day 2

1 Dumbbell Quarter Squat & Up on Toes Raise To Armpit

				35s Break
60%6	60%4	70%4	80%3	

16 Dumbbell Bent Over Fly

				30s Break
40%6	45%6	50%6	55%6	

18 Dumbbell Horizontal Parallel Inward-Outward Rotation

				35s Break
40%4+4	35%3+3	40%2+2	45%2+2	

26 Javorek's Dumbbell Complex # 1

60s Break

50%1	50%1	55%1	55%1

22 Dumbbell Lunge Walk & From Lunge, Hip High Pull Snatch

30sBreak

40%10+10+10+10	40%10+10+10+10	45%10+10+10+10	
45%10+10+10+10			

33 Dumbbell Frontal + Lateral Straight Arm Raise

15s Break

40%6+6	40%6+6	40%6+6	45%4+4

32 General Plyometrics Exercises on Stairs or Sand Stair Boxes

40s Break

4xstair D.L.B.	4xstair D.L.B.	4xjump & Sprint	4xstair D.L.B.

34 Javorek's Special Abdominal # 3

No Break

1	1	1	1

Week 2 Day 3

27 Javorek's Dumbbell Complex # 2

60s Break

45%1	45%1	50%1	50%1

24 Dumbbell Single Leg Lunges + Up on Toes Squat Push Press

40s Break

60%6+6+4	60%6+6+4	65%6+6+4	65%6+6+4

25 Dumbbell Upstairs Run (Minimum 20 Steps Stairway)

40s Break

25%3	30%3	40%3	40%3

31 Barbell Wave Squat + Back Squat & Up on Toes + Wave Squat

60s Break

35%11+4+11	35%11+4+11	45%11+3+11	45%11+3+11

30 Barbell Back Squat Jump

60s Break

35%8	40%8	45%6	50%6

33 Dumbbell Frontal + Lateral Straight Arm Raise

15s Break

40%6+6	40%6+6	40%6+6	45%4+4

32 General Plyometrics Exercises on Stairs or Sand Stair Boxes

40s Break

4xstair D.L.B.	4xstair D.L.B.	4xjump & Sprint	4xstair D.L.B.

34 Javorek's Special Abdominal # 3

No Break

1	1	1	1

Week 3 Day 1

2 Dumbbell Alternate Leg Split Snatch

35s Break

60%4+4	65%3+3	65%3+3	70%2+2

6 Dumbbell Up on Toes Squat Upright Row

35s Break

50%4	60%4	65%4	70%4

4 Dumbbell Alternate Leg Split Clean

30s Break

65%3+3	65%3+3	70%2+2	75%2+2

23 Dumbbell Alternate Leg Step Ups

60s Break

55%6+6	60%6+ 6	65%6+6	70%6+6

8 Dumbbell Up on Toes High Pull Snatch

35s Break

60%4	65%4	70%4	75%2

12 Dumbbell Up on Toes Parallel Squat Push Press

40s Break

50%4	60%4	70%2	75%2

28 Barbell Back Squat & Up on Toes

60s Break

50%6	60%4	70%3	75%2

33 Dumbbell Frontal + Lateral Straight Arm Raise

15s Break

40%6+6	40%6+6	40%6+6	45%4+4

32 General Plyometrics Exercises on Stairs or Sand Stair Boxes

40s Break

4xstair D.L.B.	4xstair D.L.B.	4xjump & Sprint	4xstair D.L.B.

34 Javorek's Special Abdominal # 3

No Break

1	1	1	1

Week 3 Day 2

3 Dumbbell From Hang Bellow The Knee Power Snatch

30s Break

55%3	60%3	65%3	70%2

7 Dumbbell Up on Toes From Hip High Pull Snatch

30s Break

55%3	60%3	65%3	70%2

22 Dumbbell Lunge Walk & From Lunge, Hip High Pull Snatch

60s Break

18 Dumbbell Horizontal Parallel Inward-Outward Rotation

30s Break

40%4+4	40%4+4	45%4+4	50%4+4

**29 Barbell Wave Squat
(9 Quarter Squat & Up on Toes + 2 Quarter Squat Jumps)**

60s Break

35%22	45%22	55%22	55%22

20 Dumbbell Split Jump & Alternate Raise To Armpit

40s Break

40%6+6	50%4+4	55%6+6	60%4+4

32 General Plyometrics Exercises on Stairs or Sand Stair Boxes

40s Break

4xstair D.L.B.	4xstair D.L.B.	4xjump & Sprint	4xstair D.L.B.

34 Javorek's Special Abdominal # 3

No Break

1	1	1	1

Week 3 Day 3

4 Dumbbell Alternate Leg Split Clean

35s Break

60%3+3	65%3+3	70%3+3	70%2+2

5 Dumbbell Up on Toes Upright Row

35s Break

50%6	50%6	55%6	60%6

7 Dumbbell Up on Toes From Hip High Pull Snatch

35s Break

40%6	45%6	50%6	55%4

14 Dumbbell Rotational Bent Over Row

35s Break

60%6	70%6	65%6	75%4

**29 Barbell Wave Squat
(9 Quarter Squat & Up on Toes + 2 Quarter Squat Jumps)**

60s Break

50%22	55%22	60%22	65%11

33 Dumbbell Frontal + Lateral Straight Arm Raise

				15s Break
40%6+6	40%6+6	40%6+6	45%4+4	

32 General Plyometrics Exercises on Stairs or Sand Stair Boxes

				40s Break
4xstair D.L.B.	4xstair D.L.B.	4xjump & Sprint	4xstair D.L.B.	

34 Javorek's Special Abdominal # 3

				No Break
1	1	1	1	

Week 4 Day 1

8   Dumbbell Up on Toes High Pull Snatch

				35s Break
60%4	65%4	70%4	75%2	

21 Dumbbell Alternate Leg Lunges

				30s Break
50%6+6	55%6+6	60%6+ 6	65%6+6	

10 Dumbbell Quarter Squat & Up on Toes Parallel Push Press

				30s Break
60%4	65%4	70%3	75%2	

22 Dumbbell Lunge Walk & From Lunge, Hip High Pull Snatch

				40s Break
40%10+10+10+10	40%10+10+10+10	45%10+10+10+10	45%10+10+10+10	

19 Dumbbell Alternate Overhead Press & High Knees Running In Place

				30s Break
35%10+10	35%10+10	40%10+10	40%10+10	

13 Barbell Behind The Head From Squat Overhead Press
30s Break

55%6	60%4	65%4	70%4

25 Dumbbell Upstairs Run (Minimum 20 Steps Stairway)

				40s Break
25%3	25%3	25%3	25%3	

31 Barbell Wave Squat + Back Squat & Up on Toes + Wave Squat

				60s Break
35%11+5+11	35%11+5+11	45%11+4+11	50%11+4+11	

32 General Plyometrics Exercises on Stairs or Sand Stair Boxes

				40s Break
4xstair D.L.B.	4xstair D.L.B.	4xjump & Sprint	4xstair D.L.B.	

34 Javorek's Special Abdominal # 3

				No Break
1	1	1	1	

Week 4 Day 2

1   Dumbbell Quarter Squat & Up on Toes Raise To Armpit

				35s Break
60%6	60%6	70%4	75%3	

17 Dumbbell Alternate Raise To Armpit & Running In Place

				35s Break
40%8+8	45%8+8	50%8+8	55%8+8	

15 Dumbbell Bent Over "Kick Back" Triceps Curls

				35s Break
50%6	60%6	65%4	70%4	

26 Javorek's Dumbbell Complex # 1

				60s Break
50%1	50%1	55%1 55%1		

28 Barbell Back Squat & Up on Toes

				60s Break
60%6	60%6	70%4	75%3	

25 Dumbbell Upstairs Run (Minimum 20 Steps Stairway)

				40s Break
25%5	40%5	40%5	35%5	

30 Barbell Back Squat Jump

				60s Break
35%4	35%4	40%4	40%4	

33 Dumbbell Frontal + Lateral Straight Arm Raise

				15s Break
40%6+6	40%6+6	40%6+6	45%4+4	

32 General Plyometrics Exercises on Stairs or Sand Stair Boxes

				40s Break
4xstair D.L.B.	4xstair D.L.B.	4xjump & Sprint	4xstair D.L.B.	

34 Javorek's Special Abdominal # 3

				No Break
1	1	1	1	

Week 4 Day 3

3   Dumbbell From Hang Bellow The Knee Power Snatch

				35s Break
60%3	65%3	70%3	70%	

4   Dumbbell Alternate Leg Split Clean

				35s Break
60%3+3	65%3+3	70%+3	75%2+2	

5   Dumbbell Up on Toes Upright Row

				35s Break
60%6	70%4	80%2	80%2	

23 Dumbbell Alternate Leg Step Ups

				40s Break
60%6+ 6	65%6+6	70%6+6	70%6+6	

8   Dumbbell Up on Toes High Pull Snatch

				35s Break
60%3	65%3	70%3	70%	

12 Dumbbell Up on Toes Parallel Squat Push Press

				40s Break
60%3	65%3	70%3	70%3	

22 Dumbbell Lunge Walk & From Lunge, Hip High Pull Snatch

			40s Break
40%10+10+10+10	40%10+10+10+10	45%10+10+10+10	
45%10+10+10+10			

18 Dumbbell Horizontal Parallel Inward-Outward Rotation

				35s Break
50%4+4	55%3+3	60%2+2	60%2+2	

29 Barbell Wave Squat
(9 Quarter Squat & Up on Toes + 2 Quarter Squat Jumps)

				60s Break
50%22	55%22	60%22	65%11	

20 Dumbbell Split Jump & Alternate Raise To Armpit

				40s Break
55%6+6	60%4+4	65%6+6	65%6+6	

33 Dumbbell Frontal + Lateral Straight Arm Raise

				15s Break
40%6+6	40%6+6	40%6+6	45%4+4	

32 General Plyometrics Exercises on Stairs or Sand Stair Boxes

				40s Break
4xstair D.L.B.	4xstair D.L.B.	4xjump & Sprint	4xstair D.L.B.	

34 Javorek's Special Abdominal # 3

				No Break
1	1	1	1	

Week 5 Day 1

1 Dumbbell Quarter Squat & Up on Toes Raise To Armpit

30s Break

| 60%6 | 70%6 | 80%2 | 80%2 |

2 Dumbbell Alternate Leg Split Snatch

30s Break

| 60%4+4 | 65%4+4 | 65%4+4 | 70%4+4 |

21 Dumbbell Alternate Leg Lunges

40s Break

| 50%6+6 | 60%6+ 6 | 70%6+6 | 70%6+6 |

7 Dumbbell Up on Toes From Hip High Pull Snatch

30s Break

| 40%6 | 45%6 | 50%6 | 50%6 |

14 Dumbbell Rotational Bent Over Row

30s Break

| 60%6 | 70%4 | 80%2 | 80%2 |

22 Dumbbell Lunge Walk & From Lunge, Hip High Pull Snatch

40s Break

| 40%10+10+10+10 | 40%10+10+10+10 | 45%10+10+10+10 |
| 45%10+10+10+10 | | |

8 Dumbbell Up on Toes High Pull Snatch

30s Break

| 60%4 | 70%4 | 80%2 | 80%2 |

10 Dumbbell Quarter Squat & Up on Toes Parallel Push Press

30s Break

| 70%3 | 75%3 | 80%2 | 85%1 |

13 Barbell Behind The Head From Squat Overhead Press

40s Break

| 70%3 | 70%3 | 75%3 | 75%3 |

19 Dumbbell Alternate Overhead Press & High Knees Running In Place

40s Break

| 50%10+10 | 50%10+10 | 55%10+10 | 60%16+16 |

24 Dumbbell Single Leg Lunges + Up on Toes Squat Push Press

40s Break

| 65%6+6+4 | 70%6+6+4 | 75%6+6+4 | 75%6+6+4 |

31 Barbell Wave Squat + Back Squat & Up on Toes + Wave Squat

60s Break

| 40%11+5+11 | 45%11+5+11 | 55%11+4+11 | 55%11+4+11 |

33 Dumbbell Frontal + Lateral Straight Arm Raise

15s Break

| 40%6+6 | 40%6+6 | 40%6+6 | 45%4+4 |

32 General Plyometrics Exercises on Stairs or Sand Stair Boxes

40s Break

| 4xstair D.L.B. | 4xstair D.L.B. | 4xjump & Sprint | 4xstair D.L.B. |

34 Javorek's Special Abdominal # 3

No Break

| 1 | 1 | 1 | 1 |

Week 5 Day 2

3 Dumbbell From Hang Bellow The Knee Power Snatch

30s Break

| 60%4 | 65%4 | 70%3 | 75%2 |

6 Dumbbell Up on Toes Squat Upright Row

30s Break

| 70%4 | 80%2 | 90%1 | 90%1 |

23 Dumbbell Alternate Leg Step Ups

40s Break

| 60%6+ 6 | 60%6+ 6 | 65%6+6 | 65%6+6 |

8 Dumbbell Up on Toes High Pull Snatch

30s Break

| 75%3 | 80%2 | 85%2 | 85%2 |

12 Dumbbell Up on Toes Parallel Squat Push Press

40s Break

| 75%3 | 80%2 | 85%2 | 85%2 |

22 Dumbbell Lunge Walk & From Lunge, Hip High Pull Snatch

40s Break

| 40%10+10+10+10 | 40%10+10+10+10 | 45%10+10+10+10 |
| 45%10+10+10+10 | | |

17 Dumbbell Alternate Raise To Armpit & Running In Place

30s Break

| 50%6+6 | 60%6+ 6 | 70%4+4 | 70%4+4 |

15 Dumbbell Bent Over "Kick Back" Triceps Curls

30s Break

| 50%4 | 55%4 | 60%4 | 60%4 |

29 Barbell Wave Squat
(9 Quarter Squat & Up on Toes + 2 Quarter Squat Jumps)

60s Break

| 45%22 | 55%22 | 65%11 | 65%11 |

20 Dumbbell Split Jump & Alternate Raise To Armpit

40s Break

| 55%4+4 | 60%4+4 | 65%6+6 | 65%6+6 |

32 General Plyometrics Exercises on Stairs or Sand Stair Boxes

40s Break

| 4xstair D.L.B. | 4xstair D.L.B. | 4xjump & Sprint | 4xstair D.L.B. |

34 Javorek's Special Abdominal # 3

No Break

| 1 | 1 | 1 | 1 |

Week 5 Day 3

3 Dumbbell From Hang Bellow The Knee Power Snatch

30s Break

| 50%6 | 55%5 | 60%4 | 65%4 |

21 Dumbbell Alternate Leg Lunges

30s Break

| 55%6+6 | 65%6+6 | 75%6+6 | 75%6+6 |

7 Dumbbell Up on Toes From Hip High Pull Snatch

30s Break

| 65%4 | 75%3 | 80%2 | 80%2 |

22 Dumbbell Lunge Walk & From Lunge, Hip High Pull Snatch

40s Break

| 40%10+10+10+10 | 40%10+10+10+10 | 45%10+10+10+10 |
| 45%10+10+10+10 | | |

8 Dumbbell Up on Toes High Pull Snatch

30s Break

| 50%6 | 60%6 | 70%4 | 75%3 |

19 Dumbbell Alternate Overhead Press & High Knees Running In Place

30s Break

| 35%6+6 | 35%6+6 | 40%6+6 | 40%6+6 |

10 Dumbbell Quarter Squat & Up on Toes Parallel Push Press

30s Break

| 50%6 | 60%6 | 70%4 | 75%3 |

17 Dumbbell Alternate Raise To Armpit & Running In Place

30s Break

| 50%6+6 | 60%6+ 6 | 70%4+4 | 70%4+4 |

31 Barbell Wave Squat + Back Squat & Up on Toes + Wave Squat

60s Break

| 40%11+4+11 | 50%11+4+11 | 60%11+4+11 | 60%11+4+11 |

32 General Plyometrics Exercises on Stairs or Sand Stair Boxes

				40s Break
4xstair D.L.B.	4xstair D.L.B.	4xjump & Sprint	4xstair D.L.B.	

34 Javorek's Special Abdominal # 3

				No Break
1	1	1	1	

Week 6 Day 1

1 Dumbbell Quarter Squat & Up on Toes Raise To Armpit

			30s Break
70%3	70%3	75%3	

4 Dumbbell Alternate Leg Split Clean

			30s Break
50%2+2	55%2+2	60%2+2	

23 Dumbbell Alternate Leg Step Ups

			40s Break
55%6+6	60%4+4	65%4+4	

6 Dumbbell Up on Toes Squat Upright Row

			30s Break
65%4	75%2	85%1	

22 Dumbbell Lunge Walk & From Lunge, Hip High Pull Snatch

			40s Break
40%6+6+6	40%6+6+6	45%6+6+6	

16 Dumbbell Bent Over Fly

			30s Break
60%6	70%4	80%6	

20 Dumbbell Split Jump & Alternate Raise To Armpit

			40s Break
55%3+3	60%3+3	65%3+3	

18 Dumbbell Horizontal Parallel Inward-Outward Rotation

			30s Break
50%2+2	50%2+2	60%2+2	

29 Barbell Wave Squat
(9 Quarter Squat & Up on Toes + 2 Quarter Squat Jumps)

			60s Break
40%11	55%11	65%11	

33 Dumbbell Frontal + Lateral Straight Arm Raise

			15s Break
40%6+6	40%6+6	40%6+6	

32 General Plyometrics Exercises on Stairs or Sand Stair Boxes

			40s Break
4xstair D.L.B.	4xstair D.L.B.	4xjump & Sprint	

34 Javorek's Special Abdominal # 3

			No Break
1	1	1	

Week 6 Day 2

3 Dumbbell From Hang Bellow The Knee Power Snatch

			30s Break
50%2	55%2	60%2	

16 Dumbbell Bent Over Fly

			30s Break
40%2	45%2	50%2	

18 Dumbbell Horizontal Parallel Inward-Outward Rotation

			30s Break
50%2+2	55%2+2	60%2+2	

26 Javorek's Dumbbell Complex # 1

			60s Break
50%1	50%1	55%1	

25 Dumbbell Upstairs Run (Minimum 20 Steps Stairway)

			40s Break
40%2	40%2	35%2	

29 Barbell Wave Squat
(9 Quarter Squat & Up on Toes + 2 Quarter Squat Jumps)

			60s Break
40%11	45%11	50%11	

32 General Plyometrics Exercises on Stairs or Sand Stair Boxes

			40s Break
4xstair D.L.B.	4xstair D.L.B.	4xjump & Sprint	

34 Javorek's Special Abdominal # 3

			No Break
1	1	1	

Week 6 Day 3

1 Dumbbell Quarter Squat & Up on Toes Raise To Armpit

			30s Break
70%3	80%2	85%1	

5 Dumbbell Up on Toes Upright Row

			30s Break
70%3	80%2	85%1	

8 Dumbbell Up on Toes High Pull Snatch

			30s Break
75%2	80%1	85%1	

22 Dumbbell Lunge Walk & From Lunge, Hip High Pull Snatch

			40s Break
40%4+4+4+4	40%4+4+4+4	45%4+4+4+4	

18 Dumbbell Horizontal Parallel Inward-Outward Rotation

			30s Break
50%2+2	55%2+2	55%2+2	

29 Barbell Wave Squat
(9 Quarter Squat & Up on Toes + 2 Quarter Squat Jumps)

			60s Break
50%11	55%11	55%11	

34 Javorek's Special Abdominal # 3

			No Break
1	1	1	

"Super Challenger" Circuit Conditioning Program

In my long, over forty years of coaching career I learned that athletes and coaches have a great tendency to skip a "step by step" preparatory program that would be appropriate for their level of ability and instead jump to an Olympic champion's or world record holder's "miraculous" workouts. I guess those coaches are thinking the reason their athletes are not Olympic champions is because they have been doing the wrong program. The coaches believe is that as soon as they switch, their athlete's performance will reach world-class levels.

Assuming they have in their hands a world-class elite athlete's conditioning program, the big question is: are they ready for it? Does it actually make any athletic improvements? or will doing it just will ruin their dreams?

My answer categorically is that usually the third statement happens and their dreams are ruined.

once in my coaching career a new young coach came to work at my college and introduced himself, having in his hand two big folders. He was telling me, that these programs are the US Olympic team's conditioning programs for his sport and he wishes to perform that program with his athletes. Very polite I explained to him the following:

First, is my responsibility to decide on a conditioning program and I will choose what program we will perform. of course I will discuss it with him in detail, and let him express his concerns and offer suggestions. Also I explained to him, if after a season the program does not work, and then we can make the necessary changes;

Secondly, I tried to explain to him, the Olympic program was actually developed for the "cream" of US athletes and his team in this moment is at the last place in the conference. None of his athletes are close to being placed even in the Conference's third team. I tried to explain that performing a program developed for the most talented athletes in this country probably would do more harm than good;

Finally I assured him that we would work together, I would explain to him the whole year preparatory plan, and I would try to satisfy his concerns about certain issues of conditioning. That it is the best for a new program to build up gradually from the base all the way to the top and I am sure that in a short time several of his athletes will be selected in the Conference team.

As a general statement of my philosophy of athletic preparation (and not just in conditioning) is:

Never consider yourself already an Olympic champion, just because you have talent in that respective sport. Rather work hard, following the golden rules of gradualism: from simple to complex and from easy to more difficult.

Try to develop a well-balanced musculature, learning the perfect technique of conditioning exercises (as well as your sport's skills), in order to prevent and minimize injuries.

Here is my success "secret": In a yearly or in a four-year cycle of preparation plan, during a period of transition, or in a certain phase of preparatory period, I will introduce some very different conditioning programs, with the main goal of "shocking" the athlete's' neuro-muscular system, avoiding the monotonous core of preparation, giving some "color" into the hard conditioning and achieving a very high quality of what I call "active rest."

With a very carefully planned approach, a coach should decide when his/her team is ready for an extra stimulatory challenge. In my long experience these programs don't just revitalize an athlete's total morpho-functional system, but the coach and athletes will enjoy the changes in the daily routine.

I always compare dieting with exercising. With either, to achieve the goal you must be consistent and perseverant. In other words, you must hold steady for a long period of time. Otherwise you just waste you time and energy.

Someone could ask, "then why not to pick the Olympic champion's program?" You could, if your athletic skills and performances are up to that level. But remember, most of you are not at that level.

I never forget when as a young athlete I was studying different world and Olympic champion's training methods. But I was selecting only certain exercises from them, what could be beneficial for my specific athletic improvement. I would experiment with them for months and only then was I implementing them in my program (and later in my coaching career in my athlete's programs).

This program, which I developed, is a three weeks Circuit Type program, which could be repeated several times in a yearly or in a four-year plan of preparation. Please remember what I said before! This program is just for athletes with a high preparation level and even if they are in great athletic shape, when they perform this program first time in their preparation they still need to:

a) learn the perfect technique of exercises from this program

b) be able to perform six sets of 12 reps of the first 25 exercises for a period of two to four weeks before the start of this program

c) practice exercises # 26 and# 27 at least a minimum of six sets with 50% of the weight used in "From Hip High Pull Snatch," then continue with exercise # 28 for another week or two!!

d) When they will perform the program a second time, they would perform just a minimum six sets of each exercises and get into the program, without those weeks of learning and practicing the exercises (b and c above).

Javorek's Super Challenger Conditioning Circuit Program Exercise List:

1. Dumbbell Straight Knees Overhead Parallel Up on Toes Press: standing, feet shoulder with, dumbbells in hand, over the shoulders.

The dumbbells position can be parallel, or linear, depending on the goals. Tight abdominal muscles, locked knees head looking forward.

Press the dumbbells overhead and getting up on toes, without bending the knees, (locked knees) or changing the body position. The body balance in the shoulder-hip-ankle, perfect vertical line, between the balls of feet and heels. There are several variations of dumbbell position during press: start with parallel dumbbells and finish up with parallel dumbbells; start with parallel dumbbell and finish up with linear dumbbell, doing a rotational movement; start with linear and finish up with linear dumbbells; start with linear dumbbells and finish up with parallel dumbbells, doing a rotational movement with the palms facing each other; start with linear dumbbells and finish up with parallel dumbbells, doing a rotational movement with the forehands facing each other (swimming, diving, volleyball, basketball); simultaneous or alternating pressing.

2. Dumbbell From Hip Up on Toes High Pull Snatch: Same exercise like # 3, the difference is, those instead of doing the full bend over and then overhead high pull snatch movement, the start from the hip will be continued in high pull snatch, and never get bend over. The perfect technique

of execution is very important. The first phase, of the From Hip High Pull Snatch technically it is similar to upright row, than continued in the snatching the bar overhead. Remember, keeping the elbow up as long is possible; accelerate the motion; turn the elbows in the upward position. Is technically wrong when at the shoulder's level the elbows suddenly are rotated downward, executing a pressing movement overhead. The correct return motion should be required, similar to the regular high pull snatch exercise.

3. Dumbbell Standing Two Hands Simultaneous High Pull Snatch. Stand with dumbbells in hand in linear Pronated position at the hip level.

Bend over with head down; back curved straight arms, slightly bent knees, and flat footed, with the center of gravity shifted back from the balls of the feet toward the heels. Raise the dumbbells up to an upright row "up" position, and without a stop, - with a continued acceleration- raise the dumbbells over your head, and at the same time coming up on toes. For sport of weightlifting we should not come up on toes, just flat footed. It is very important that after the 'up' position phase do not let the elbows turned down, and executing an overhead press, but to keep the elbows up with the help of acceleration and turn the wrist over head locking the elbows overhead. During the lift, the dumbbells should be kept as close as possible to the body. After the overhead phase, leading the dumbbells down should be executed with the same technique and in an opposite return order of execution. First the wrist will be curled and pushed down lower than the elbows, and very close to the trunk, followed by the bend over phase with relatively straight knees.

38. Dumbbell Supinated (Regular) Curls: the hand is supinated, the elbows 1-2 inch apart from the Hip.

Curl the arms upward, bend the arms from the elbows without changing the elbow position relative to the trunk, and finish the curl up position in front of the chest. The exercise has several variations: (a) inward rotational movement, finishing in a pronated hands position, or (B) holding the elbows higher and doing an oblique curl, or (c) parabolic curls: curl up your arms and in the highest fist position extend with a greater speed the arms upward-in front of your eyes, than with

straight elbows slowly return to the start position. Pay attention to a tight abdominal musculature and holding the shoulders-hip-ankle aligned on a perfect vertical line.

39. Dumbbell Parallel Curls: similar to supinated curls, just now hold the dumbbells in a parallel position.

Keep your elbows in a stable (fixed) position.

36. Dumbbell Standing Two Hands Simultaneous Quarter Squat & Up on Toes, Raise To Armpit: standing with dumbbells in hands at the hip level.

Bend your knees and simultaneously with the knees extension, raise the dumbbells up to your armpit, and at the same time coming up on your toes. Hold your body in a vertical position, and do not lean your trunk or your head forward. Keep your arms on both side of your body. Hang the dumbbells and do not reverse curl your wrist.

37. Dumbbell Standing Two Hands Simultaneous Upright Row: Standing, with dumbbells in hand in front of your thighs in a linear position.

Arms straight, elbows turned slightly outward, shoulders turned in. The head looking straight ahead, with a very firm chin position. The chest is in an "up" (tight) position, with a straight back and a tight abdominal musculature. Raise the dumbbells up to your neck level, holding the dumbbells in its linear position and pointing the elbows upward as much as possible, and raising up on toes.

4. Dumbbell Single Leg Lunges – Intensity taken of Dumbbell Squat Push Press

5. Dumbbell Alternate Leg Lunges – Intensity taken of Dumbbell Squat Push Press

6. Dumbbell Parallel or Rotational Quarter Squat & Up on Toes Push Press : stand with dumbbell in each hand at shoulder level.

Hold a tight neck and abdominal muscles. The head is looking straight ahead. Bend the knees less than a quarter squat, balancing the body weight toward the heels, between balls of the feet and the heels. Keep the shoulder-hip-ankle alignment in a perfect vertical line.

A continuous accelerating pressing overhead movement follows the knee bend and up on toes and always hold it for a second, then continue the exercise. Never stop with straight knees after you performed a repetition.

7. Dumbbell Overhead Parallel or Rotational Up on Toes Squat Push Press : Standing with dumbbells in each hand at shoulder level.

It is same body position like in Dumbbell Push press. Do the squat with the dumbbells at your shoulder, without changing the body's verticality. The flat foot position should be kept. The knees must be pointed outward in the squat position, allowing to the hip's joint to be pushed between the heels. The back should be concave (arched and not curved), head looking forward. Rise up from the squat, maintaining the trunk's relatively vertical position and pushing the dumbbells overhead with a dynamic, explosive motion, flat footed or coming up on toes (depending on coach's indication) and then recover again with bending the knees and getting in the squat position..

8. Dumbbell Overhead Parallel or Rotational Squat Jump Push Press- it is a similar exercise to Squat push press.

The only difference is that after a full squat you are arising upward with a brisk jump movement. It is very important that after the jump do not stop with straight knees, but continue slowly back again in a full squat position.

9. **Dumbbell Single Leg, on Different Height Box Step Ups**– Intensity taken of Dumbbell Squat Push Press: Standing, with dumbbells in hand, at hip level.

There are several variations possible: a) the height of the step up box could be different, depending on goals; different arms movements: 1) arms raise overhead on each step up (simultaneous, or alternating) depending on goals; 2) overhead press (alternating or simultaneous) on each step up; 3) alternating arm swing forward or in front of the chest. 4) Alternating or simultaneous arms rotation, forward or backward, on each step up.

10. **Dumbbell Alternate Leg, on Different Height Box Step Ups** – Intensity taken of Dumbbell Squat Push Press As general safety rules: step up with full foot on the box, not just the toes; hold the trunk straight, do not lean forward, and tight the abdominal musculature; increase the weight gradually, do not try too heavy dumbbells on the different arms variations;

11. **Dumbbell Javorek's "The Challenger" Complex # 1:**
Up on Toes Upright Row x 6 + Up on Toes High Pull Snatch x 6 + Parallel Curls x 6 + Overhead Quarter Squat & Up on Toes Parallel Push Press x 6 + Up on Toes Squat Upright Row x 6 + Bent Over Row x 6 + Up on Toes High Pull Snatch x 6 + Up on Toes Squat Push Press x 6 + Squat Jump Raise To Armpit x6 Intensity taken of The weakest exercise maximum

12. **Dumbbell Lunge Walk**– Intensity taken of Dumbbell Squat Push Press

13. **Dumbbell From Lunge Supinated Curls** – Intensity taken of Supinated Curls - Perform equal number of reps, by changing the lunge position, on both legs.

14. **Dumbbell From Lunge Overhead Press** – Intensity taken of Overhead press - Perform equal number of reps, by changing the lunge position, on both legs.

15. **Dumbbell from Lunge, From Hip High Pull Snatch** – Intensity taken of From Hip High Pull Snatch - Perform equal number of reps, by changing the lunge position, on both legs.

16. **Dumbbell Single Leg, on Different Height Box Step up & Overhead up on Toes Press** – Intensity taken of Overhead Press

17. **Dumbbell Single Leg, on Different Height Box Step up & from Hip High Pull Snatch** – Intensity taken of From Hip High Pull Snatch

18. **Dumbbell Single Leg, on Different Height Box Step up & up on Toes Raise to Armpit** – Intensity taken of Raise To Armpit

19. **Dumbbell Alternate Leg, on Different Height Box & Overhead up on Toes Press** – Intensity taken of Overhead Press

20. **Dumbbell Alternate Leg, on Different Height Box Step up & from Hip High Pull Snatch** – Intensity taken of From Hip High Pull Snatch

21. **Dumbbell Alternate Leg, on Different Height Box Step up & up on Toes Raise to Armpit** – Intensity taken of Raise To Armpit

22. **Dumbbell Lunge Walk + Up on Toes Squat Push Press** – Intensity taken of Squat Push Press

23. **Dumbbell Lunge Walk & From Lunge Overhead Press** – Intensity taken of Overhead Press

24. **Dumbbell Lunge Walk & from Lunge, From Hip High Pull Snatch** – Intensity taken of From Hip High Pull Snatch

25. **Dumbbell Lunge Walk & From Lunge Supinated Curls** – Intensity taken of Supinated Curls

26. **Dumbbell Javorek's "Novice" Athletes Killer Lunge Walk Variation** – Intensity taken of weakest performance among Supinated Curls, From Hip High Pull Snatch and Overhead Press

27. **Dumbbell Javorek's "Advanced" Athletes Killer Lunge Walk Variation** – Intensity taken of weakest performance among Supinated Curls, From Hip High Pull Snatch and Overhead Press

28. **Dumbbell Javorek's "The Marines" Elite Athletes Killer Lunge Walk Variation**– Intensity taken of weakest performance among Supinated Curls, From Hip High Pull Snatch and Overhead Press

29. **Dumbbell Squat Jump**– Intensity taken of Dumbbell Squat Push Press

30. **Barbell Wave Squat + Back Squat & Up on Toes + Wave Squat**

31. **on High Bar Behind The Head Pull Ups**

32. **Parallel Bar Dips**

33. **on 12 inch High Boxes Plyo Push Ups**

34. **Javorek's Special Abdominal Program # 1**

35. **Javorek's Special Abdominal Program # 3**

Javorek's "Killer" Lunge Walk Exercises

These 3 variations to Lunge Walk are for highly conditioned athletes, who wants to challenge his/her muscular and cardio-vascular endurance and to stimulate to the extreme their lactic acid built up. Also I use this exercise to "shock or shake-up" an athlete's neuro-muscular system from lethargy, to burn more calories or just for simple reason of eliminating the monotonous core of regular lunge walk.

To perform these variations of Lunge Walk an athlete "MUST" be in perfect physical health, and "MUST" master the perfect technique of lunge walk and of Overhead Press from Lunge, Supinated Curls from Lunge, From Hip High Pull Snatch from Lunge, Split jump, Squat Push Press and Squat Jump

Novice Athletes Variation
(1 Right Leg Lunge Walk & 1 From Lunge Overhead Press + 1 Left Leg Lunge Walk & 1 From Lunge Supinated Curls + 1 Right Leg Lunge Walk & 1 From Lunge From Hip High Pull Snatch) x 4 Then Continue + 1 Right Leg Lunge Walk & 3 From Lunge Overhead Press + 1 Left Leg Lunge Walk & 3 From Lunge Supinated Curl + 1 Right Leg Lunge Walk & 3 From Lunge From Hip High Pull Snatch + Lunge Walk x 4 + 4 + Squat Push Press x 4

Advanced Athletes Variation
(1 Right Leg Lunge Walk & 3 From Lunge Overhead Press + 1 Left Leg Lunge Walk & 3 From Lunge Supinated Curl + 1 Right Leg Lunge Walk & 3 From Lunge From Hip High Pull Snatch) x 3 Then Continue + 1 Left Leg Lunge Walk & 4 From Lunge Overhead Press + 1 Right Leg Lunge Walk & 4 From Lunge Supinated Curl + 1 Left Leg Lunge Walk & 4 From Lunge From Hip High Pull Snatch +Lunge Walk x 6 + 6 + Squat Push Press x 8

"The Marines", Elite Athletes Variation
(1 Right Leg Lunge & 3 From Lunge Overhead Press + 1 Left Leg Lunge & 3 From Lunge Supinated Curl s + 1 Right Leg Lunge & 3 From Lunge From Hip High Pull Snatch) x 6 (repeat 6 times) + 1 Right Leg Lunge Walk & 6 From Lunge Overhead Press + 1 Left Leg Lunge Walk & 6 From Lunge Supinated Curls + 1 Right Leg Lunge Walk & 6 From Lunge From Hip High Pull Snatch + Lunge Walk 8 + 8 +Up on Toes Squat Push Press x 8+ Split Jump x 6+6+ Squat Jump & Raise To Armpit x 6

Killer Lunge Walk You Tube
http://www.youtube.com/watch?v=bH_jB0foCMg

Killer Lunge Walk Exercise Descriptions:

Dumbbell Straight Knees Overhead Parallel Up on Toes Press

Dumbbell From Hip Up on Toes High Pull Snatch

Dumbbell Supinated (Regular) Curls

Dumbbell Single Leg Lunges – Intensity taken of Dumbbell Squat Push Press

Dumbbell Alternate Leg Lunges – Intensity taken of Dumbbell Squat Push Press

Dumbbell Parallel or Rotational Quarter Squat & Up on Toes Push Press

Dumbbell Overhead Parallel or Rotational Up on Toes Squat Push Press

Dumbbell Overhead Parallel or Rotational Squat Jump Push Press

Dumbbell Single Leg, on Different Height Box Step Ups– Intensity taken of Dumbbell Squat Push Press

Dumbbell Alternate Leg, on Different Height Box Step Ups – Intensity taken of Dumbbell Squat Push Press

Dumbbell From Lunge Simultaneous From Hip High Pull Snatch: Standing in lunge with dumbbells in hand in linear Pronated position at the hip level. Raise the dumbbells up to an up-right row "up" position, and without a stop, - with a continued acceleration- raise the dumbbells over your head (elbows finish first the upward motion followed by the wrists, holding firmly a static lunge position. During the lift, the dumbbells should be kept as close as possible to the body.

After the overhead phase, leading the dumbbells down should be executed with the same technique and in an opposite return order of execution. First the wrist will be curled and pushed down lower than the elbows, and very close to the trunk.

If there is more repetition, perform equal number of reps, by changing the lunge position, on both legs.

Dumbbell From Lunge Supinated Curls: Standing in lunge with dumbbells in hand.

The hand is supinated and dumbbells are in a linear position. The elbows must be set 1-2 inch apart from the hip. Curl the arms upward, bending the arms from the elbows, without changing the elbows position related to the trunk, finishing the curl up position in front of chest, holding firmly a static lunge position. If there is more repetition, perform equal number of reps, by changing the lunge position, on both legs.

Dumbbell From Lunge Overhead Parallel Press: Standing in lunge with dumbbells in hand, dumbbells in hand, over the shoulders.

The dumbbells position can be parallel, or linear, depending on the goals. Tight abdominal muscles, head looking forward. Press overhead without changing the static lunge position, or changing the body position. If there is more repetition, perform equal number of reps, by changing the lunge position, on both legs.

Dumbbell Lunge Walk: Standing, dumbbells in hand at hip level. Step forward with high knees, pushing the fore leg forward, landing on heels and gradually rolling on flat foot.

The trunk should be holding on perfect vertical line, the back knee as straight as possible, the lower leg almost parallel with the floor, heel pointed perfectly upward with all toes on the floor. Each giant step is a separate unit. The athlete must stop for 1-2 second after each step. Without to slow down the stepping motion, push the back foot forward, bending the back foot's knee, rising as high as possible, continuing the lunge walk with the next giant step or stop in a perfectly balanced lunge and perform one of the prescribed from lunge exercise.

Dumbbell Lunge Walk + Up on Toes Squat Push Press

Perform the prescribed number of repetitions for the lunge walk then continue with the Up on Toes Squat Push Press

Dumbbell Lunge Walk & From Lunge Overhead Press

on each step of lunge walk stop and perform the respective exercise with the described repetitions (from lunge overhead press)

Dumbbell Lunge Walk & From Lunge, From Hip High Pull Snatch

on each step of lunge walk stop and perform respective exercise with the described repetitions (from lunge from hip high pull snatch)

Dumbbell Lunge Walk & From Lunge Supinated Curls

on each step of lunge walk stop and perform the respective exercise with the described repetitions (from lunge supinated curls)

Dumbbell Standing Overhead Parallel or Rotational Up on Toes Squat Push Press: Standing with dumbbells in each hand at shoulder level.

Squat with the dumbbells at your shoulder, without changing the body's verticality. The flat foot position should be kept. The knees must be pointed outward in the squat position, following the pointed out feet, allowing to the hip's joint to be pushed between the heels. The best way to learn is imagining sitting down on a stair. The back should be concave (arched and not curved), head looking forward. Raise up from the squat, maintaining the trunk's relatively vertical position and pushing the dumbbells overhead with a dynamic, explosive motion, coming up on toes and then recover again with bending the knees and getting in the squat position..

Dumbbell Split Jump: Star from a shorter lunge.

Shift the feet as close as possible to the floor, always landing with a bent back knee, lower leg almost parallel with the floor and front feet landing always slightly toward the heel or just flat foot. Never land with your front leg on toes. In landing phase the front leg's foot must be in front of the knee. Never extend your knee during the exercise. The back foot heel must be pointed perfectly upward with all toes on the floor; the front feet must be with heel slightly pointed out for a better balance.

Dumbbell Standing Squat Jump: Standing, dumbbells in hand, at hip level, feet shoulder width. Holding the arms sideways, regular squatting (flat foot, straight back, looking forward) and jump up.

on the recovery phase, land on balls of the feet, rolling back on flat foot.

Dumbbell Single Leg, on Different Height Box Step Up & Overhead Up on Toes Press – Intensity taken of Overhead Press –during the step up with the knee extension gradually perform the described exercise of raise to armpit, or from hip high pull snatch or overhead press. Same principal on alternate leg step-ups also

Week # 1 – Learning The Perfect Technique

Attention:

This Program is for advanced athletes only! The Novice or Unprepared athletes should follow the Cycling Preparatory and Cycling General Fitness # 1 programs and just in case they are physically and mentally ready could try it.

Practice Week # 1 Day # 1 Circuit # 1

Dumbbell Straight Knees Overhead Parallel Up on Toes Press

50%12	55%12	60%12	60%12
65%10	65%10	70%10	70%10

Dumbbell Single Leg Lunges

50%12+12	50%12+12	55%12+12	55%12+12
60%12+12	65%10+10	65%10+10	70%10+10

Dumbbell Lunge Walk

50%20+20	50%20+20	55%20+20	55%20+20
60%20+20	60%20+20	60%20+20	65%20+20

on High Bar Behind The Head Pull Ups

8	8	8	8
8	8	8	8

Dumbbell Alternate Leg, on Different Height Box Step Up & Overhead Up on Toes Press

50%12+12	50%12+12	50%12+12	55%10+10
55%10+10	55%10+10	60%8+8	60%8+8

Javorek's Special Abdominal Program # 1

1 1   1   1   1   1   1   1

Practice Week # 1 Day # 2 Circuit # 2

Dumbbell From Hip Up on Toes High Pull Snatch

55%14	60%12	65%12	70%10
75%8	75%8	70%10	80%6

Dumbbell Alternate Leg Lunges

60%14+14	65%12+12	70%10+10	75%10+10
60%14+14	65%12+12	70%10+10	75%10+10

Dumbbell Parallel or Rotational Quarter Squat & Up on Toes Push Press

70%10	70%10	75%8	75%8
80%6	80%6	85%5	85%5

Dumbbell Alternate Leg, on Different Height Box Step Up & Up on Toes Raise To Armpit

60%8+8	60%8+8	65%6+6	70%5+5
60%8+8	60%8+8	65%6+6	70%5+5

Dumbbell Javorek's "The Challenger" Complex # 1

Upright Row x 6 + High Pull Snatch x 6 + Parallel Curls x 6 + Overhead Quarter Squat & Up on Toes Parallel Push Press x 6 + Squat Upright Row x 6 + Bent Over Row x 6 + High Pull Snatch x 6 + Squat Push Press x 6

50%	50%	50%	50%
55%	55%	55%	55%

Barbell Wave Squat + Back Squat & Up on Toes + Wave Squat (3 Quarter Squat & Up on Toes +2 Quarter Squat Jumps)

50%30+10+30	55%30+10+30	55%30+10+30	60%25+10+25
50%30+10+30	55%30+10+30	55%30+10+30	60%25+10+25

Javorek's Special Abdominal Program # 1

1 1   1   1   1   1   1   1

Practice Week # 1 Day # 3 Circuit # 3

Dumbbell Supinated (Regular) Curls

50%14	55%14	60%12	65%12
70%10	75%8	70%10	75%8

Dumbbell Lunge Walk + Up on Toes Squat Push Press

50%25+25+10	55%25+25+10	60%22+22+10	65%20+20+10
65%20+20+10	70%20+20+10	75%16+16+8	75%16+16+8

Dumbbell From Lunge Supinated Curls

50%14	55%12	60%12	65%12
70%10	75%8	70%10	75%8

on 12 inch High Boxes Plyo Push Ups

8+8	8+8	8+8	8+8
8+8	8+8	8+8	8+8

Dumbbell Straight Knees Overhead Parallel Up on Toes Press

60%12	60%12	65%12	65%12
70%10	70%10	75%8	80%6

Dumbbell Single Leg, on Different Height Box Step Up & From Hip High Pull Snatch

50%10+10	50%10+10	55%8+8	55%8+8
60%6+6	60%6+6	65%6+6	65%6+6

Javorek's Special Abdominal Program # 1

1 1   1   1   1   1   1   1

Practice Week # 2 Day # 1 Circuit # 4

Dumbbell Overhead Parallel or Rotational Up on Toes Squat Push Press

60%12	65%10	70%10	65%10
70%10	75%8	80%6	80%6

Dumbbell From Hip Up on Toes High Pull Snatch

60%10	60%10	60%10	65%10
65%10	70%10	75%8	75%8

Dumbbell Single Leg, on Different Height Box Step Ups

60%12+12	70%12+12	65%12+12	75%10+10
70%12+12	80%10+10	75%10+10	80%10+10

Dumbbell Lunge Walk & From Lunge Overhead Press

50%10+10+10+10	50%10+10+10+10	55%10+10+10+10
55%10+10+10+10	60%10+10+10+10	65%10+10+10+10
70%8+8+8+8	70%8+8+8+8	

Dumbbell Supinated (Regular) Curls

60%12	60%12	65%12	65%12
70%10	70%10	75%8	75%8

Dumbbell Alternate Leg, on Different Height Box Step Up & From Hip High Pull Snatch

60%8+8	60%8+8	70%5+5	70%5+5
65%6+6	75%4+4	70%5+5	75%4+4

Parallel Bar Dips

15	15	15	15
15	15	15	15

Javorek's Special Abdominal Program # 1

1 1   1   1   1   1   1   1

Practice Week # 2 Day # 2 Circuit # 5

Dumbbell Overhead Parallel or Rotational Squat Jump Push Press

60%10	65%10	70%10	65%10	70%10	75%8	80%6
80%6						

Dumbbell From Hip Up on Toes High Pull Snatch

60%10	70%10	65%10	75%8
70%10	80%6	75%8	85%4

Dumbbell Alternate Leg, on Different Height Box Step Ups

60%14+14	65%14+14	70%12+12	75%12+12
80%10+10		70%12+12	75%12+12
80%10+10			

Dumbbell From Lunge Overhead Press
60%10	60%10	65%10	65%10	70%10	75%8	75%8
80%6						

Dumbbell Lunge Walk & From Lunge Supinated Curls
50%10+10+10+10	50%10+10+10+10	55%10+10+10+10
55%10+10+10+10	60%10+10+10+10	65%10+10+10+10
70%8+8+8+8	70%8+8+8+8	

Parallel Bar Dips
15	15	15	15
15	15	15	15

Javorek's Special Abdominal Program # 3
1	1	1	1	1	1	1	1

Practice Week # 2 Day # 3 Circuit # 6

Dumbbell Javorek's "The Challenger" Complex # 1

Up on Toes Upright Row x 6 + Up on Toes High Pull Snatch x 6 + Parallel Curls x 6 + Overhead Quarter Squat & Up on Toes Parallel Push Press x 6 + Up on Toes Squat Upright Row x 6 + Bent Over Row x 6 + Up on Toes High Pull Snatch x 6 + Up on Toes Squat Push Press x 6
50%1	50%1	50%1	55%1
55%1	55%1	60%1	65%1

Dumbbell From Lunge, From Hip Up on Toes High Pull Snatch
50%10	55%10	55%10	60%10
65%10	70%10	75%6	75%6

Dumbbell Squat Jump
50%10	55%10	60%8	65%6
70%5	70%5	75%5	80%4

Dumbbell Straight Knees Overhead Parallel Up on Toes Press
60%10	65%10	70%10	75%8
80%6	85%4	80%6	85%4

Barbell Wave Squat + Back Squat & Up on Toes + Wave Squat
50%30+10+30	55%30+10+30	60%25+10+25	65%20+10+20
50%30+10+30	55%30+10+30	60%25+10+25	65%20+10+20

on 12 inch High Boxes Plyo Push Ups
8+8	8+8	8+8	8+8
8+8	8+8	8+8	8+8

Javorek's Special Abdominal Program # 1
1	1	1	1	1	1	1	1

Practice Week # 3 Day # 1 Circuit # 7

Dumbbell Parallel or Rotational Quarter Squat & Up on Toes Push Press
60%10	75%8	65%10	80%6
70%10	90%4	75%8	90%4

Dumbbell Single Leg, on Different Height Box Step Up & Overhead Up on Toes Press
50%10+10	55%9+9	60%8+8	65%7+7
70%6+6	75%5+5	80%3+3	80%3+3

Dumbbell Lunge Walk & From Lunge, From Hip High Pull Snatch
50%10+10+10+10	50%10+10+10+10	55%10+10+10+10
55%10+10+10+10	60%10+10+10+10	65%10+10+10+10
70%8+8+8+8	70%8+8+8+8	

Dumbbell From Lunge Supinated Curls
55%12	60%10	55%12	65%10
70%10	75%8	65%10	75%8

Dumbbell Single Leg, on Different Height Box Step Up & Up on Toes Raise To Armpit
50%12+12	55%10+10	60%8+8	65%7+7
70%6+6	75%5+5	80%3+3	85%2+2

Javorek's Special Abdominal Program # 1
1	1	1	1	1	1	1	1

Practice Week # 3 Day # 2 Circuit # 8

Dumbbell From Hip Up on Toes High Pull Snatch
60%10	65%10	70%10	75%8
70%10	75%8	80%6	80%6

Dumbbell Javorek's "Novice" Athletes Killer Lunge Walk Variation
50%	55%	60%	55%
60%	65%	65%	70%

Barbell Wave Squat + Back Squat & Up on Toes + Wave Squat
50%30+10+30	60%25+10+25	55%30+10+30	65%20+10+20
60%25+10+25	70%15+6+15	65%20+10+20	75%10+5+10

Dumbbell Javorek's "The Challenger" Complex # 1

Up on Toes Upright Row x 6 + Up on Toes High Pull Snatch x 6 + Parallel Curls x 6 + Overhead Quarter Squat & Up on Toes Parallel Push Press x 6 + Up on Toes Squat Upright Row x 6 + Bent Over Row x 6 + Up on Toes High Pull Snatch x 6 + Up on Toes Squat Push Press x 6
50%	55%	50%	55%	60%	55%	60%
65%						

on High Bar Behind The Head Pull Ups
8	8	8	8	8	8
8					

Javorek's Special Abdominal Program # 3
1	1	1	1	1	1	1	1

Practice Week # 3 Day # 3 Circuit # 9

Dumbbell Supinated (Regular) Curls
60%10	80%6	65%10	85%4	70%10	90%3	75%8
90%3						

Dumbbell Single Leg Lunges
60%12+12	65%12+12	70%12+12	75%10+10
80%10+10	85%8+8	85%8+8	90%6+6

Dumbbell From Lunge Overhead Press
50%12	55%12	60%10	65%10
70%10	75%8	75%8	80%6

Dumbbell Alternate Leg, on Different Height Box Step Up & Overhead Up on Toes Press
50%12+12	55%10+10	60%8+8	65%6+6
70%5+5	75%4+4	80%3+3	85%2+2

Parallel Bar Dips
15	15	15	15
15	15	15	15

Javorek's Special Abdominal Program # 1
1	1	1	1	1	1	1	1	1

Practice Week # 4 Day # 1 Circuit # 10

Dumbbell Javorek's "The Challenger" Complex # 1

Up on Toes Upright Row x 6 + Up on Toes High Pull Snatch x 6 + Parallel Curls x 6 + Overhead Quarter Squat & Up on Toes Parallel Push Press x 6 + Up on Toes Squat Upright Row x 6 + Bent Over Row x 6 + Up on Toes High Pull Snatch x 6 + Up on Toes Squat Push Press x 6
50%	50%	50%	55%
55%	55%	60%	60%

Dumbbell Straight Knees Overhead Parallel Up on Toes Press
60%10	65%10	70%10	75%8
80%6	70%10	75%8	80%6

Dumbbell Javorek's "Advanced" Athletes Killer Lunge Walk Variation
50%	55%	60%	50%
55%	60%	60%	60%

Dumbbell Squat Jump

60%6	60%6	65%6	65%6
70%5	70%5	75%4	75%4

on 12 inch High Boxes Plyo Push Ups

8+8	8+8	8+8	8+8
8+8	8+8	8+8	8+8

Javorek's Special Abdominal Program # 3

1 1 1 1 1 1 1 1

Practice Week # 4 Day # 2 Circuit # 11

Dumbbell From Hip Up on Toes High Pull Snatch

60%10	70%10	60%10	70%10
65%10	75%8	80%6	85%4

Dumbbell Overhead Parallel or Rotational Up on Toes Squat Push Press

60%10	65%10	70%10	75%8
80%6	85%4	90%2	90%2

Dumbbell Single Leg, on Different Height Box Step Ups

50%10+10	60%10+10	70%10+10	80%8+8
75%10+10	80%8+8	85%5+5	85%5+5

Dumbbell Javorek's "Advanced" Athletes Killer Lunge Walk Variation

50%	60%	50%	60%
50%	60%	50%	60%

Dumbbell Lunge Walk + Up on Toes Squat Push Press

60%20+20+10	65%20+20+10	70%20+20+10	75%15+15+6
80%12+12+5	80%12+12+5	85%8+8+4	85%8+8+4

on High Bar Behind The Head Pull Ups

8	8	8	8
8	8	8	8

Javorek's Special Abdominal Program # 1

1 1 1 1 1 1 1 1

Practice Week # 4 Day # 3 Circuit # 12

Dumbbell Alternate Leg, on Different Height Box Step Ups

60%14+14	65%12+12	70%12+12	75%10+10
80%10+10	85%8+8	80%10+10	85%8+8

Dumbbell Javorek's "The Marines" Elite Athletes Killer Lunge Walk Variation

50%	50%	55%	55%
60%	60%	50%	60%

Dumbbell Javorek's "The Challenger" Complex # 1

Up on Toes Upright Row x 6 + Up on Toes High Pull Snatch x 6 + Parallel Curls x 6 + Overhead Quarter Squat & Up on Toes Parallel Push Press x 6 + Up on Toes Squat Upright Row x 6 + Bent Over Row x 6 + Up on Toes High Pull Snatch x 6 + Up on Toes Squat Push Press x 6

55%	60%	65%	70%
55%	60%	65%	70%

Barbell Wave Squat + Back Squat & Up on Toes + Wave Squat

50%30+10+30	60%25+10+25	55%30+10+30	65%20+10+20
60%25+10+25	70%15+6+15	65%20+10+20	75%10+5+10

Parallel Bar Dips

15	15	15	15
15	15	15	15

Javorek's Special Abdominal Program # 3

1 1 1 1 1 1 1 1

Javorek's Super Challenger Circuit Conditioning Program

Week 1 Day 1 Circuit # 1

Dumbbell Straight Knees Overhead Parallel Up on Toes Press

70%10	70%10	80%6	80%6

Dumbbell Supinated (Regular) Curls

65%12	70%10	75%8	80%6

Dumbbell Parallel or Rotational Quarter Squat & Up on Toes Push Press

70%10	75%10	80%6	85%5

Dumbbell Single Leg, on Different Height Box Step Ups

60%12+12	65%12+12	70%10+10	80%8+8

Dumbbell Lunge Walk

60%25+25	65%25+25	70%20+20	80%20+20

Dumbbell From Lunge, From Hip Up on Toes High Pull Snatch

55%14	60%12	65%12	70%10

Dumbbell Single Leg, on Different Height Box Step Up & Up on Toes Raise To Armpit

60%8+8	65%6+6	70%5+5	75%4+4

Dumbbell Alternate Leg, on Different Height Box & Up on Toes Raise To Armpit

60%8+8	65%6+6	70%4+4	80%3+3

Dumbbell Lunge Walk & From Lunge, From Hip High Pull Snatch

50%15+15+15+15	55%12+12+12+12	60%10+10+10+10	65%0+10+10+10

Dumbbell Javorek's "Advanced" Athletes Killer Lunge Walk Variation

50%	55%	60%	65%

BB. Wave Squat + Back Squat & Up on Toes + Wave Squat

50%30+10+30	55%30+10+30	60%25+10+25	65%20+10+20

on 12 inch High Boxes Plyo Push Ups

8+8	8+8	8+8	8+8

Javorek's Special Abdominal Program # 1

1 1 1 1

Week 1 Day 2 Circuit # 2

Dumbbell From Hip Up on Toes High Pull Snatch

55%14	60%12	65%12	70%10

Dumbbell Alternate Leg Lunges

65%12+12	70%12+12	75%12+12	80%10+10

Dumbbell Overhead Parallel or Rotational Squat Jump Push Press

70%10	75%8	80%6	85%5

Dumbbell Javorek's "The Challenger" Complex # 1

Up on Toes Upright Row x 6 + Up on Toes High Pull Snatch x 6 + Parallel Curls x 6 + Overhead Quarter Squat & Up on Toes Parallel Push Press x 6 + Up on Toes Squat Upright Row x 6 + Bent Over Row x 6 + Up on Toes High Pull Snatch x 6 + Up on Toes Squat Push Press x 6

50%	55%	60%	65%

Dumbbell Single Leg, on Different Height Box Step Up & From Hip High Pull Snatch

50%10+10	55%10+10	60%8+8	65%6+6

Dumbbell From Lunge Overhead Press

60%10	65%10	70%10	75%8

Dumbbell Alternate Leg, on Different Height Box Step Up & From Hip High Pull Snatch

60%6+6	65%6+6	70%5+5	75%4+4

Dumbbell Javorek's "Novice" Athletes Killer Lunge Walk Variation

50%	60%	65%	70%

Dumbbell Lunge Walk & From Lunge Overhead Press

60%10+10+10+10	65%10+10+10+10	70%10+10+10+10	80%8+8+8+8

Dumbbell Squat Jump

60%10	70%6	75%6	80%5

Parallel Bar Dips

15	15	15	15

Javorek's Special Abdominal Program # 3

1	1	1	1

Week 1 Day 3 Circuit # 3

Dumbbell Single Leg Lunges

60%12+12	70%12+12	80%10+10	85%8+8

Dumbbell Overhead Parallel or Rotational Up on Toes Squat Push Press

70%10	75%8	80%6	85%5

Dumbbell Alternate Leg, on Different Height Box Step Ups

70%10+10	70%10+10	75%10+10	80%8+8

Dumbbell From Lunge Supinated Curls

60%12	65%12	70%10	75%8

Dumbbell Single Leg, on Different Height Box Step Up & Overhead Up on Toes Press

55%8+8	60%7+7	65%6+6	70%5+5

Dumbbell Alternate Leg, on Different Height Box Step Up & Overhead Up on Toes Press

60%10+10	65%10+10	70%10+10	75%8+8

Dumbbell Lunge Walk + Up on Toes Squat Push Press

60%20+20+10	65%20+20+10	70%20+20+8	80%14+14+6

Dumbbell Lunge Walk +& From Lunge Supinated Curls

60%10+10+10+10	65%10+10+10+10	70%8+8+8+8	80%6+6+6+6

Dumbbell Javorek's "The Marines" Elite Athletes Killer Lunge Walk Variation

55%	60%	65%	70%

on High Bar Behind The Head Pull Ups

8	8	8	8

Dumbbell From Hip Up on Toes High Pull Snatch

65%12	70%10	75%8	80%6

Javorek's Special Abdominal Program # 1

1	1	1	1

Week 2 Day 1 Circuit # 4

Dumbbell Straight Knees Overhead Parallel Up on Toes Press

60%10	70%10	80%6	90%3

Dumbbell Alternate Leg Lunges

70%12+12	75%12+12	80%10+10	85%10+10

Dumbbell Single Leg, on Different Height Box Step Ups

70%12+12	80%10+10	75%10+10	90%5+5

Dumbbell From Lunge Overhead Press

60%12	65%12	70%10	75%8

Dumbbell Alternate Leg, on Different Height Box Step Up & From Hip High Pull Snatch

55%8+8	60%6+6	65%6+6	70%5+5

Dumbbell Lunge Walk & From Lunge, From Hip High Pull Snatch

50%12+12+12+12	55%12+12+12+12	60%10+10+10+10	65%10+10+10+10

Dumbbell Supinated (Regular) Curls

70%12	80%6	75%8	90%3

Dumbbell Javorek's "Novice" Athletes Killer Lunge Walk Variation

60%	65%	70%	70%

Dumbbell Squat Jump

60%8	70%6	80%4	85%4

on 12 inch High Boxes Plyo Push Ups

8+8	8+8	8+8	8+8

on High Bar Behind The Head Pull Ups

10	10	10	10

Javorek's Special Abdominal Program # 3

1	1	1	1

Week 2 Day 2 Circuit # 5

Dumbbell Supinated (Regular) Curls

70%10	75%8	80%6	90%3

Dumbbell Parallel or Rotational Quarter Squat & Up on Toes Push Press

70%10	80%6	75%8	90%3

Dumbbell Single Leg, on Different Height Box Step Ups

60%12+12	70%12+12	80%8+8	90%4+4

Dumbbell Single Leg Lunges

70%10+10	75%10+10	80%10+10	85%8+8

Dumbbell Alternate Leg, on Different Height Box Step Ups

70%12+12	75%10+10	80%8+8	85%6+6

Dumbbell Javorek's "The Challenger" Complex # 1

Up on Toes Upright Row x 6 + Up on Toes High Pull Snatch x 6 + Parallel Curls x 6 + Overhead Quarter Squat & Up on Toes Parallel Push Press x 6 + Up on Toes Squat Upright Row x 6 + Bent Over Row x 6 + Up on Toes High Pull Snatch x 6 + Up on Toes Squat Push Press x 6

60%	65%	60%	70%

Dumbbell From Hip Up on Toes High Pull Snatch

60%12	65%12	60%12	70%10

Dumbbell Alternate Leg, on Different Height Box & Overhead Up on Toes Press

50%8+8	55%6+6	60%6+6	70%5+5

Dumbbell Squat Jump

70%5	75%5	80%5	85%4

on 12 inch High Boxes Plyo Push Ups

8+8	8+8	8+8	8+8

Dumbbell Javorek's "Advanced" Athletes Killer Lunge Walk Variation

55%	60%	65%	70%

Parallel Bar Dips

20	20	20	20

Barbell Wave Squat + Back Squat & Up on Toes + Wave Squat

60%20+10+20	70%15+10+15	80%10+6+10	80%10+6+10

Javorek's Special Abdominal Program # 1

1	1	1	1

Week 2 Day 3 Circuit # 6

Dumbbell Straight Knees Overhead Parallel Up on Toes Press

70%10	80%6	75%8	90%3

Dumbbell Alternate Leg Lunges

80%10+10	80%10+10	8/5%10+10	85%10+10

Dumbbell Overhead Parallel or Rotational Up on Toes Squat Push Press

70%10	80%5	85%5	90%3

Dumbbell Javorek's "The Marines" Elite Athletes Killer Lunge Walk Variation

60%	65%	70%	70%

on High Bar Behind The Head Pull Ups

10	10	10	10

Dumbbell From Lunge Supinated Curls

70%10	75%8	80%6	85%6

Dumbbell Single Leg, on Different Height Box Step Up & Overhead Up on Toes Press

60%6+6	65%5+5	70%5+5	80%3+3

Parallel Bar Dips

20	20	20	20

Dumbbell Alternate Leg, on Different Height Box Step Up & From Hip High Pull Snatch

60%8+8	70%5+5	80%3+3	80%3+3

Javorek's Special Abdominal Program # 3

1	1	1	1

Week 3 Day 1 Circuit # 7

Dumbbell From Hip Up on Toes High Pull Snatch

70%10	80%6	85%5	90%3

Dumbbell Single Leg Lunges

70%10+10	80%10+10	85%8+8	90%5+5

Dumbbell Parallel or Rotational Quarter Squat & Up on Toes Push Press

70%10	80%6	75%8	90%4

Dumbbell Overhead Parallel or Rotational Squat Jump Push Press

60%10	65%8	70%	75%5

Dumbbell Javorek's "The Challenger" Complex # 1
Up on Toes Upright Row x 6 + Up on Toes High Pull Snatch x 6 + Parallel Curls x 6 + Overhead Quarter Squat & Up on Toes Parallel Push Press x 6 + Up on Toes Squat Upright Row x 6 + Bent Over Row x 6 + Up on Toes High Pull Snatch x 6 + Up on Toes Squat Push Press x 6

60%	65%	60%	70%

Dumbbell Supinated (Regular) Curls

70%10	80%6	85%5	90%3

Dumbbell Single Leg, on Different Height Box Step Ups

70%10+10	75%10+10	80%10+10	85%8+8

Dumbbell Javorek's "Novice" Athletes Killer Lunge Walk Variation

60%	65%	70%	70%

on 12 inch High Boxes Plyo Push Ups

8+8	8+8	8+8	8+8

on High Bar Behind The Head Pull Ups

10	10	10	10

Barbell Wave Squat + Back Squat & Up on Toes + Wave Squat

70%15+10+15	75%10+8+10	80%10+5+10	80%10+5+10

Javorek's Special Abdominal Program # 1

1	1	1	1

Week 3 Day 2 Circuit # 8

Dumbbell Supinated (Regular) Curls

70%10	75%8	70%10	75%8

Dumbbell Javorek's "Advanced" Athletes Killer Lunge Walk Variation

50%	55%	60%	60%

Dumbbell Overhead Parallel or Rotational Up on Toes Squat Push Press

65%10	70%10	75%8	80%6

Dumbbell Single Leg, on Different Height Box Step Ups

65%12+12	70%10+10	75%10+10	80%10+10

Dumbbell From Lunge Supinated Curls

70%10	75%8	70%10	75%8

Dumbbell Lunge Walk

60%25+25	65%22+22	70%20+20	75%20+20

Dumbbell From Lunge Overhead Press

60%10	65%10	70%10	75%8

Dumbbell Javorek's "The Challenger" Complex # 1
Up on Toes Upright Row x 6 + Up on Toes High Pull Snatch x 6 + Parallel Curls x 6 + Overhead Quarter Squat & Up on Toes Parallel Push Press x 6 + Up on Toes Squat Upright Row x 6 + Bent Over Row x 6 + Up on Toes High Pull Snatch x 6 + Up on Toes Squat Push Press x 6

50%	50%	50%	60%

Dumbbell Squat Jump

50%8	55%8	60%8	65%8

Parallel Bar Dips

20	20	20	20

Javorek's Special Abdominal Program # 3

1	1	1	1

Week 3 Day 3 Circuit # 9

Dumbbell Straight Knees Overhead Parallel Up on Toes Press

70%10	80%6	85%5	90%3

Dumbbell Lunge Walk + From Lunge, From Hip High Pull Snatch

60%20+20+8	65%18+18+6	70%18+18+6	80%12+12+4

Dumbbell From Hip Up on Toes High Pull Snatch

70%10	80%6	85%5	90%3

Dumbbell Supinated (Regular) Curls

70%10	80%6	85%5	90%3

Dumbbell From Lunge, From Hip Up on Toes High Pull Snatch

70%10	75%8	80%6	85%4

Dumbbell Single Leg, on Different Height Box Step Up & Up on Toes Raise To Armpit

70%5+5	75%4+4	80%3+3	85%2+2

Dumbbell Javorek's "The Marines" Elite Athletes Killer Lunge Walk Variation

60%	65%	70%	70%

Dumbbell Javorek's "The Challenger" Complex # 1
Up on Toes Upright Row x 6 + Up on Toes High Pull Snatch x 6 + Parallel Curls x 6 + Overhead Quarter Squat & Up on Toes Parallel Push Press x 6 + Up on Toes Squat Upright Row x 6 + Bent Over Row x 6 + Up on Toes High Pull Snatch x 6 + Up on Toes Squat Push Press x 6

60%	70%	60%	70%

Dumbbell Alternate Leg, on Different Height Box & Overhead Up on Toes Press

70%5+5	75%4+4	80%3+3	85%2+2

Dumbbell Javorek's "The Marines" Elite Athletes Killer Lunge Walk Variation

60%	65%	70%	70%

Barbell Wave Squat + Back Squat & Up on Toes + Wave Squat

70%15+10+15	75%10+8+10	80%10+5+10
80%10+5+10		

Javorek's Special Abdominal Program # 1

1	1	1

Dumbbell Javorek's "The Challenger" Complex # 1
Up on Toes Upright Row x 6 + Up on Toes High Pull Snatch x 6 + Parallel Curls x 6 + Overhead Quarter Squat & Up on Toes Parallel Push Press x 6 + Up on Toes Squat Upright Row x 6 + Bent Over Row x 6 + Up on Toes High Pull Snatch x 6 + Up on Toes Squat Push Press x 6

60%	70%	65%	70%

Javorek's "Whoop Ass" General Fitness Program

After receiving hundreds of letters from readers requesting a more specific program for elite athletes, I decided to develop a 12 weeks demanding program.

This program includes the majority of dumbbell and barbell exercises "beloved" by athletes, of course in a set, which follows my philosophy of general and specific conditioning.

I am a believer of total body involvement in a daily routine and not of isolating certain muscle groups/workout. When you change the body part or muscle group involved in an exercise it will give a chance to the body neuro-muscular system to "refresh" the previously exercised muscles and build up the necessary quantity of minerals and energy sources. I would also call this approach as exercising with the benefit of a so-called "active rest." This active rest time will contribute to the body physiological system to rebuild the necessary "fuels" in a previously exercised muscle group so that while we do exercise another body part, those muscles are resting and recuperating. In this way the body feels fresher and the result in gaining strength, hypertrophy or you name it, would be greater.

In this 12 weeks general fitness program I chose six to ten exercises/sessions with a total of maximum eight sets/exercises. I am sure a lot of you will ask the reason of eight sets/exercise circuit. My answer is that in order to achieve a great improvement you should stimulate for several sets your muscle fibers, but always starting with lighter intensities (warming up the tendonal-muscular system for that respective exercise) and finishing with the heaviest sets. As you will find out in this program also, I am using different variations on intensities during an exercise and also during a four weeks cycle of preparation.

So week # 1 is the lowest intensity, followed by the second, third and fourth week higher and higher, then dropped again to a lower intensity and gradually getting up to the highest intensities in week eight. Also you will realize an oscillation of intensities during the week. Monday would be medium- Wednesday the low and Friday the highest intensity. I did not follow exactly this principle on power clean, power snatch and dead lift because I consider that someone who starts this program should be in a higher grade of athletic preparation.

The program will be performed in Circuit

The intensity for an exercise will be also very various.

one exercise will go with a continuous increase of intensity, like 50% 55% 60% 65% etc.

Other exercise with a double stepping intensities, like 50% 50% 55% 55% 60% 60% etc,

Other day the exercise with skip intensity like 50% 60% 70% 80%

Other day or exercise performed with "in wave" intensities like: 50% 60% 55% 65% 60% 70% and the list could be endless! So don't be surprised if you don't find the same intensity cycle or routine on each exercise while I was developing the program with this concept.

My main reason is that I like to avoid the monotonous core of exercising. The monotonous "all of them look alike" programs are tiring an athlete neuro-muscular system, the dreamed performance is delayed and the whole body will suffer from the lack of success and satisfaction. I consider that my programs are like some sentimental and nice, but in the mean time very enthusiastic poems. Poems which should invigorate an athlete's soul and body and not just ruining it if would be performing the same variation of intensities, without any "color" into the daily workout routines. All of those varieties of inten-

sities and exercises in each day routines are the rhythms and rhymes of my "poems", which makes your whole neuro-emotional-muscular system to enjoy the workout and to refresh the body and mind.

I would like to make a short (few pages) association of ideas about athletic conditioning, and mind, which is so important for the sport of Cycling.

Can you imagine a fifteen years old 77 lb. kid with a rheumatic heart disease and visible signs of rickets, who spent more years in hospitals than out, to be transformed in a 170 lb harmoniously built Olympic bronze medalist athlete? It is not advertising for a wonder drug. It is a real story of Dragomir Cioroslan's, the former head coach of US Olympic Training Center Weightlifting Residence Program from Colorado Springs, Co. He was the lucky kid, who I just recruited on his friends' insistence in my experimental group. From the beginning Dragomir had special sparkle in his eyes, to be the best. on my warning that the road "up there" is very long and difficult he did not hesitate telling me, that he is ready for it. So I wasn't surprised when in a short time of three years Dragomir overcame every physical and mental obstacle and was already a member of Romanian Olympic team and a European Junior record holder. With hard work and fanaticism, he improved from 110 lb clean and jerk to a 445 lb life's best with a 164 lb body weight, winning several times the national body building championship also. Dragomir had a desire for excellence and his body was able to transform from a sick kid into a healthy athlete, just because of his power of eliminating the big two

F-words of athletic preparation: Fatigue and Fear. He had high goals and enjoyed his activities. His cells were "fulfilled" with happiness and joy, and those cells are capable for more physical and mental challenge.

There are millions of youths with exceptional physical qualities, but for someone to excel in sport, or in any other form of life, they must possess properties of desire, crave, perseverance, ambition, tenacity, interest to train, passion," never give up"- fighting spirit and motivation with one word Fanaticism.

I consider motivation as the most powerful tool, the greatest psychological drug in developing those so-called "supernatural" athletes. I am sure that Lance Armstrong possesses these qualities. After an almost fatal testicular cancer, and winning six consecutive Tour de France proves his fantastic motivational abilities and will power.

Actually I consider motivation as a spiritual manifestation of will power, which everybody could build up the same way like the muscles and strength: gradually and with patience. Set up small goals and never rush the result. I was the lucky person to learn from a famous Romanian psychiatrist, Dr. Bilcea, the Schultz Autogenic Training Method, which I suggest to my athletes to practice. It is very simple and easy to learn.

I consider that Soul and Spirit constitutes a reflection of the reality, of the material earth in the human brain and practicing special mental relaxation, such as the Schultz Autogenic Training Method, combined with general conditioning we can eliminate (reduce) the sign of fatigue and compel our mind and body for more mental and physical work. We can control and eliminate the stress and accelerate the recovery time after an exhausting effort (minimizing the symptom of fear). With a well-planned mental preparation an athlete should be capable to control his actions in workout and prepare himself for more detailed, highly demanding workouts or competition. The human organism has invisible strength reservation (latent forces), which can be mobilized in a definite situation with significant energy development in a short period of time.

The ancient Greeks and Romans were recognizing the values of sport psychology, selecting the best athletes for the Olympic Games or soldiers for special units. The principle of selection was very simple:

those who turned paled (vascular-constriction, or so called negative emotion), showing clear sign of fear before a contest were dropped.

In my coaching career I did not and I do not consider respecting these methods. With a good and continuous preparation it is possible transforming a timid athlete in a fearful fighter. I was witnessing athletes with high quality mental preparation being able to improve their in practice performance up to 15 percent during a competition and to endure without any negative effect the most demanding workouts and practices.

I consider this could be an ideal philosophy for any athlete's approach of preparation in sport of Cycling!

In my opinion the mental strength is a very important component in an athlete preparation. I consider sport and competition more than 70 percent mental and just 20-30 percent physical challenge, and I feel necessary to quote an unknown author:" Everybody has unlimited potential to be the person they want to be".

Every individual athlete is a totally different micro cosmos, but one thing is very sure: it is very important to enjoy the life, the sport, physical activities, everything around you, the sky, the bird, the flowers, teammates, etc. because the cells filled with joy and happiness are capable for more activities, are living longer and there is a permanent desire for all kind of physical and psychological activities. Set high goals in small doses and you will be able to control your body and mind, avoiding any stress related symptoms and achieving your goals, aim and dream.

For an athlete the most important words should be: I will, I can, I must, I shall and the most important slogan should be "The ones who succeed in sports are those who know the art of relaxation". I consider that as far as someone is able to relax will be able to focus to concentrate on the same degree.

I would like to finish with a few quotas from one of the Rudyard Kipling's poem, "If", which as a very young kid became my life's philosophy:"

**"If you can keep your head when all about you
are losing theirs and blaming it on you,
If you can trust yourself when all men doubt you,**

....

If you can dream—and not make dream your master;

....

**If you can meet with Triumph and Disaster
And treat those two imposters just the same;**

....

If you can make one heap of all your winnings:

....

**And lose, and start again at your beginnings
And never breathe a word about your loss;
If you can force your heart and nerve and sinew
To serve your turn long after they are gone
And so hold when there is nothing in you
Except the will, this says to them: "Hold on"
Yours is the Earth and everything that's in it
And which is more you'll be a man, my son!"**

After this long philosophical introduction I am sure that everyone is waiting to read my sentimental "poem," which does not sound like Rudyard Kipling, but I am sure that reading and performing it, all of you will cry, if not for other reason, but because of sore muscles and tremendously improved performance. .

Week # 1 Day # 1

DB. Up on Toes Upright Row

55%14	55%14	60%12	60%12
60%12	60%12	70%10	70%10

DB. Parallel (Hammer) Curls

50%14	60%12	70%10	70%10
50%14	60%12	70%10	70%10

BB. Comfortable Grip Bench Press

55%14	60%12	65%10	70%10
60%12	65%10	70%10	75%6

BB. Quarter Squat & Up on Toes

60%10	60%10	60%10	70%10
70%10	70%10	60%10	70%10

DB. Bent Over "Kick Back" Triceps Curls

50%14	55%12	60%12	65%10
70%10	75%8	70%10	75%8

DB. Javorek's Whoop Ass Complex # 1: intensity taken from the exercise of lowest maximum.

Up on Toes Upright Row x 6 + Supinated Curl x 6 + Overhead Rotational Up on Toes Press x 6 + Right Leg Forward, From Lunge Parallel Curl x 6 + Up on Toes Rotational Squat Push Press x 6 + Bent Over Row x 6 + Left Leg Forward, From Lunge Parallel Curl x 6 Up on Toes High Pull Snatch x 6:

50%1	60%1	50%1	60%1
50%1	60%1	60%1	60%1

BB. From The Floor Power Snatch

60%6	65%6	70%5	75%5
75%5	75%5	75%5	75%5

Javorek's Special Abdominal Program # 1

1 Set	1 Set	1 Set	1 Set
1 Set	1 Set	1 Set	1 Set

40 Yards Sprint

x 1	x 1	x 1	x 1
x 1	x 1	x 1	x 1

Week # 1 Day # 2

DB. Up on Toes Squat Upright Row

50%14	50%14	50%14	55%12
55%12	55%12	60%10	60%10

DB. Parallel or Rotational Up on Toes Overhead Press

45%14	60%10	50%12	65%10
45%14	60%10	50%12	65%10

BB. Pronated (Reverse) Curls

40%14	45%14	50%14	55%12
60%12	65%10	65%10	65%10

BB. Back Squat & Up on Toes

40%10	60%10	45%10	65%10
50%10	70%10	50%10	70%10

DB. Lying on Bench Fly

35%16	40%16	45%14	50%14
55%14	60%12	65%10	65%10

BB. Romanian Dead Lift

60%10	70%10	70%10	75%8
75%8	80%6	85%5	90%5

BB. From Hang Bellow the Knee Power Clean
60%6   65%6   70%5   70%5   75%5   75%5   80%4
80%4

Javorek's Special Abdominal Program # 1

1 Set	1 Set	1 Set	1 Set
1 Set	1 Set	1 Set	1 Set

40 Yards Sprint

x 1	x 1	x 1	x 1
x 1	x 1	x 1	x 1

Week # 1 Day # 3

DB. Supinated (Regular) Curls

60%12	65%12	65%12	70%10
65%10	75%8	75%8	75%8

DB. Quarter Squat & Up on Toes Parallel or Rotational Overhead Push Press

60%12	60%12	65%12	65%12
70%10	70%10	75%8	80%6

DB. Incline Bench Press

60%12	80%6	60%12	80%6
60%12	80%6	60%12	80%6

BB. Wave Squat (3 Quarter Squat + 1 Jump + 1 Squat Jump Combination/cycle)

50%30	50%30	60%30	60%30
55%30	65%20	55%30	65%20

BB. Narrow Grip Up on Toes Upright Row

65%12	70%10	65%12	75%8
70%10	80%6	70%10	85%4

DB. In Front of Chest Parallel Inward-Outward Rotation

50%10+10	55%8+8	60%6+6	65%6+6
65%6+6	70%5+5	70%5+5	70%5+5

BB. From The Floor Power Snatch

60%6	65%6	70%5	70%5
75%5	75%5	80%4	80%4

Javorek's Special Abdominal Program # 1

1 Set	1 Set	1 Set	1 Set
1 Set	1 Set	1 Set	1 Set

40 Yards Sprint

x 1	x 1	x 1	x 1
x 1	x 1	x 1	x 1

Week # 2 Day # 1

DB. Pronated (Reverse) Curls

50%14	55%12	60%12	65%10
70%10	75%8	75%8	75%8

BB. Back Squat Jump

50%8	55%8	60%8	65%6
70%4	70%4	75%4	75%4

DB. Rotational Up on Toes Overhead Squat Push Press

60%10	65%10	70%10	75%8
70%10	75%8	80%6	80%6

BB. Javorek's Whoop Ass Complex # 1: intensity taken from the weakest link of this Complex Exercise.

: Barbell Up on Toes Upright Row x 6 + Up on Toes High Pull Snatch x 6 + Overhead Up on Toes Squat Push Press x 6 + Behind The Head Good Morning x 6 + Behind The Head Alternate Leg Lunges + Bent-Over Row x 6 + Supinated Curl x 6 + Up on Toes Upright Row x 6 + Up on Toes High Pull Snatch x 6

50%1	55%1	50%1	55%1
60%1	60%1	65%1	65%1

DB. Lateral Arm Raise

40%16	45%14	50%14	55%12
60%10	65%10	70%10	75%8

BB. Romanian Dead Lift

70%10	70%10	80%6	80%6
85%5	85%5	90%5	95%5

BB. From Hang Bellow the Knee Power Clean
60%6   65%6   70%5   70%5   75%5   75%5   80%4
80%4

Javorek's Special Abdominal Program # 1

1 Set	1 Set	1 Set	1 Set
1 Set	1 Set	1 Set	1 Set

40 Yards Sprint

x 1	x 1	x 1	x 1
x 1	x 1	x 1	x 1

Week # 2 Day # 2

DB. Parallel Bent Over Row

50%14	60%12	55%14	65%12	60%12	70%10	60%12
70%10						

DB. Seated Overhead Press

50%14	50%14	55%14	55%14
60%12	60%12	65%10	70%10

DB. Frontal Arm Raise

40%16	50%14	50%14	55%12
60%12	65%10	60%12	65%10

BB. Back Squat & Up on Toes + Wave Squat + Back Squat & Up on Toes

50%10+30+10	55%10+30+10	60%10+20+10	50%10+30+10
55%10+30+10	60%10+20+10	65%8+15+8	70%6+10+6

DB. Alternate Leg on Different Height Box Step Ups + Squat Push Press

50%14+14+6	55%14+14+6	55%14+14+6	60%12+12+6
60%12+12+6	65%12+12+6	65%12+12+6	70%10+10+6

BB. From The Floor Power Snatch

60%6	65%6	70%5	70%5
75%5	75%5	80%4	80%4

Javorek's Special Abdominal Program # 2

1 Set	1 Set	1 Set	1 Set
1 Set	1 Set	1 Set	1 Set

40 Yards Sprint

x 1	x 1	x 1	x 1
x 1	x 1	x 1	x 1

Week # 2 Day # 3

DB. Bent Over Fly

60%12	60%12	80%6	80%6
65%12	85%4	70%10	85%4

BB. Narrow Grip Up on Toes Upright Row

60%12	70%10	70%10	75%8
80%6	75%8	75%8	85%5

BB. From Half Squat Behind The Head Overhead Press

50%14	70%10	60%12	80%6
70%10	80%6	75%8	85%4

BB. Back Squat & Up on Toes

60%10	60%10	85%4	70%10
85%4	60%10	70%10	85%4

DB. Javorek's Whoop Ass Complex # 1: intensity taken from the exercise of lowest maximum.

Up on Toes Upright Row x 6 + Supinated Curl x 6 + Overhead Rotational Up on Toes Press x 6 + Right Leg Forward, From Lunge Parallel Curl x 6 + Up on Toes Rotational Squat Push Press x 6 + Bent Over Row x 6 + Left Leg Forward, From Lunge Parallel Curl x 6 Up on Toes High Pull Snatch x 6:

50%1	70%1	50%1	50%1
70%1	60%1	60%1	70%1

BB. Romanian Dead Lift

70%10	75%8	80%6	85%5
85%5	90%5	95%5	100%4

BB. From Hang Bellow the Knee Power Clean

60%6	65%6	70%5	70%5
75%5	75%5	80%4	85%4

Javorek's Special Abdominal Program # 1

1 Set	1 Set	1 Set	1 Set
1 Set	1 Set	1 Set	1 Set

40 Yards Sprint

x 1	x 1	x 1	x 1
x 1	x 1	x 1	x 1

Week # 3 Day # 1

DB. Overhead Triceps Curls

55%14	65%12	75%8	65%12
70%10	75%8	70%10	80%5

BB. Medium Grip Up on Toes Upright Row

65%12	70%10	75%8	80%6
70%10	70%10	75%8	80%6

BB. Overhead Triceps Curls

60%10	60%10	70%10	70%10
80%6	75%8	75%8	80%6

BB. Back Squat & Up on Toes + Wave Squat + Back Squat & Up on Toes

50%10+20+10	55%10+20+10	60%10+20+10	65%8+15+8
70%6+10+6	75%6+10+6	70%6+10+6	75%6+10+6

BB. Back Squat Jump

50%8	55%8	60%8	65%8
70%6	75%4	70%6	75%4

BB. Incline Bench Press

70%10	70%10	80%6	75%8
75%8	80%6	85%4	90%2

BB. From The Floor Power Snatch

65%6	70%5	75%5	75%5
80%4	85%5	85%4	88%4

Javorek's Special Abdominal Program # 2

1 Set	1 Set	1 Set	1 Set
1 Set	1 Set	1 Set	1 Set

40 Yards Sprint

x 1	x 1	x 1	x 1
x 1	x 1	x 1	x 1

Week # 3 Day # 2

BB. Wave Squat

50%30	55%30	60%30	65%25
60%30	65%25	70%20	70%20

DB. Javorek's Whoop Ass Complex # 1: intensity taken from the exercise of lowest maximum.

Up on Toes Upright Row x 6 + Supinated Curl x 6 + Overhead Rotational Up on Toes Press x 6 + Right Leg Forward, From Lunge Parallel Curl x 6 + Up on Toes Rotational Squat Push Press x 6 + Bent Over Row x 6 + Left Leg Forward, From Lunge Parallel Curl x 6 Up on Toes High Pull Snatch x 6:

50%1	50%1	50%1	55%1
55%1	60%1	60%1	65%1

BB. Wide Grip Up on Toes Upright Row

50%14	55%12	60%12	65%12
70%10	60%12	65%12	70%10

BB. Supinated (Regular) Curls

50%14	60%12	55%12	65%12
60%12	70%10	65%12	75%8

BB. Javorek's Whoop Ass Complex # 1: intensity taken from the weakest link of this Complex Exercise.

: Barbell Up on Toes Upright Row x 6 + Up on Toes High Pull Snatch x 6 + Overhead Up on Toes Squat Push Press x 6 + Behind The Head Good Morning x 6 + Behind The Head Alternate Leg Lunges + Bent-Over Row x 6 + Supinated Curl x 6 + Up on Toes Upright Row x 6 + Up on Toes High Pull Snatch x 6

50%1	65%1	50%1	65%1
55%1	65%1	60%1	65%1

BB. From Hang Bellow the Knee Power Clean

60%6	65%6	70%5	70%5
75%5	75%5	80%4	85%4

BB. Romanian Dead Lift

70%10	75%8	80%6	85%5
85%5	90%5	95%5	100%4

Javorek's Special Abdominal Program # 3

1 Set	1 Set	1 Set	1 Set
1 Set	1 Set	1 Set	1 Set

40 Yards Sprint

x 1	x 1	x 1	x 1
x 1	x 1	x 1	x 1

Week # 3 Day # 3

BB. Behind The Head Up on Toes Squat Push Press

60%10	70%10	80%6	65%10
75%10	70%10	80%6	85%4

BB. Quarter Squat & Up on Toes

60%12	75%10	70%10	80%10
85%10	80%10	85%10	85%10

DB. Linear Flat Bench Press

70%10	80%6	90%3	75%8
80%6	90%3	80%6	90%3

BB. Javorek's Whoop Ass Complex # 3: intensity taken from the weakest link of this Complex Exercise

Barbell Supinated Curls X 6 + Barbell Comfortable Grip Up on Toes Upright Row X 6 + Barbell Flat Footed Squat Under High Pull Snatch X 6 + Barbell Behind The Head From Half Squat Press X 6 + Barbell Comfortable Grip Bent Over Row X 6 + Barbell Flat Footed Squat Under Upright Row X 6 + Barbell Behind The Head Good Morning X 6 + Barbell Behind The Head Squat Push Press x 6 + Barbell Comfortable Grip Overhead Squat X 6 + Barbell Behind The Head Squat Jump X 6 + Barbell In Front of Thighs Special Good Morning X 6

55%1	60%1	65%1	70%1
55%1	60%1	65%1	70%1

on High Bar Supinated Grip Chin Ups

8	8	8	8
8	8	8	8

BB. From The Floor Power Snatch

65%6	70%5	75%5	75%5
80%4	85%5	85%4	85%4

Javorek's Special Abdominal Program # 1

1 Set	1 Set	1 Set	1 Set
1 Set	1 Set	1 Set	1 Set

40 Yards Sprint

x 1	x 1	x 1	x 1
x 1	x 1	x 1	x 1

Week # 4 Day # 1

DB. Up on Toes Squat Upright Row

70%10	80%8	70%10	85%6
75%8	80%6	85%4	85%6

DB. Quarter Squat & Up on Toes Parallel or Rotational Overhead Push Press

70%10	80%8	75%8	85%5
75%8	85%5	80%6	85%5

BB. Back Squat & Up on Toes

60%10	70%10	80%6	65%10
85%3	80%6	85%3	85%3

DB. Incline Bench Press

70%10	75%8	80%6	85%5
80%6	85%4	80%6	85%4

BB. From Hang Bellow the Knee Power Clean

65%6	70%5	75%5	75%5
80%4	85%4	85%4	85%4

BB. Romanian Dead Lift

70%10	75%8	80%6	85%5
85%5	90%5	95%5	100%4

BB. From The Floor Power Snatch

65%6	70%5	75%5	75%5
80%4	85%4	85%4	90%2

on High Bar Behind The Head Pull Ups

8	8	8	8
8	8	8	8

Javorek's Special Abdominal Program # 2

1 Set	1 Set	1 Set	1 Set
1 Set	1 Set	1 Set	1 Set

40 Yards Sprint

x 1	x 1	x 1	x 1
x 1	x 1	x 1	x 1

Week # 4 Day # 2

DB. Supinated (Regular) Curls

60%12	65%12	70%10	75%8
80%6	70%10	75%8	80%6

BB. Back Squat & Up on Toes+ Wave Squat + Back Squat & Up on Toes

50%10+20+10	60%10+20+10	70%8+15+8	60%10+20+10
70%8+15+8	65%20+10+20	75%6+15+6	80%5+10+5

DB. Rotational Up on Toes Overhead Squat Push Press

65%10	75%8	70%10	80%6
65%10	75%8	70%10	80%6

DB. Javorek's Whoop Ass Complex # 1: intensity taken from the exercise of lowest maximum.

Up on Toes Upright Row x 6 + Supinated Curl x 6 + Overhead Rotational Up on Toes Press x 6 + Right Leg Forward, From Lunge Parallel Curl x 6 + Up on Toes Rotational Squat Push Press x 6 + Bent Over Row x 6 + Left Leg Forward, From Lunge Parallel Curl x 6 Up on Toes High Pull Snatch x 6:

50%1	60%1	55%1	65%1
60%1	65%1	55%1	70%1

With or Without Weight Parallel Bar Dips

15	15	15	15
15	15	15	15

BB. From The Floor Power Snatch

65%6	70%5	75%5	80%5
80%5	85%4	85%4	90%2

Javorek's Special Abdominal Program # 3

1 Set	1 Set	1 Set	1 Set
1 Set	1 Set	1 Set	1 Set

40 Yards Sprint

x 1	x 1	x 1	x 1
x 1	x 1	x 1	x 1

Week # 4 Day # 3

BB. Back Squat & Up on Toes

70%10	80%4	75%5	85%3
90%2	75%5	85%4	90%2

DB. Pronated (Reverse) Curls

60%12	75%8	70%10	80%6
85%5	85%5	85%5	85%5

DB. Parallel Bent Over Row

80%6	85%5	90%3	80%6
90%3	85%5	80%6	90%3

DB. Decline Bench Press

70%10	80%6	90%2	85%5
90%2	75%8	90%2	90%2

on Push Up Bars Push Ups

20	20	20	20
20	20	20	20

BB. From Hang Bellow the Knee Power Clean

65%6	70%5	75%5	75%5
80%4	85%4	85%4	85%4

BB. Romanian Dead Lift

70%10	75%8	80%6	85%5
85%5	90%5	95%5	100%4

Javorek's Special Abdominal Program # 1

1 Set	1 Set	1 Set	1 Set
1 Set	1 Set	1 Set	1 Set

40 Yards Sprint

x 1	x 1	x 1	x 1
x 1	x 1	x 1	x 1

Week # 5 Day # 1

DB. Parallel (Hammer) Curls

65%12	70%10	75%8	65%12
75%8	70%10	80%6	80%6

DB. Parallel or Rotational Flat Bench Press

70%10	80%6	75%8	80%6
70%10	80%6	75%8	80%6

DB. Bent Over "Kick Back" Triceps Curls

65%12	70%10	75%8	80%6
65%12	70%10	75%8	80%6

BB. Back Squat Jump

60%6	65%6	70%4	75%4
60%6	65%6	70%4	75%4

on Different Height Push Ups Boxes, Plyo Push Ups

6+6	6+6	6+6	6+6
6+6	6+6	6+6	6+6

BB. From The Floor Power Snatch

65%6	70%5	75%5	75%5
80%5	85%4	85%4	85%4

Javorek's Special Abdominal Program # 2

1 Set	1 Set	1 Set	1 Set
1 Set	1 Set	1 Set	1 Set

40 Yards Sprint

x 1	x 1	x 1	x 1
x 1	x 1	x 1	x 1

Week # 5 Day # 2

DB. Parallel or Rotational Up on Toes Overhead Press

55%14	60%12	65%12	70%10
75%8	65%12	70%10	75%8

BB. Wave Squat

55%30	60%30	65%25	70%20
55%30	60%30	65%25	70%20

BB. Javorek's Whoop Ass Complex # 1: intensity taken from the weakest link of this Complex Exercise.

: Barbell Up on Toes Upright Row x 6 + Up on Toes High Pull Snatch x 6 + Overhead Up on Toes Squat Push Press x 6 + Behind The Head Good Morning x 6 + Behind The Head Alternate Leg Lunges + Bent-Over Row x 6 + Supinated Curl x 6 + Up on Toes Upright Row x 6 + Up on Toes High Pull Snatch x 6

50%1	55%1	60%1	55%1
60%1	65%1	60%1	70%1

DB. Lying on Your Back on Bench Fly

50%14	55%12	60%12	65%12
70%10	60%12	65%12	70%10

DB. Overhead Triceps Curls

55%14	60%12	55%14	65%12
65%12	70%10	65%12	70%10

BB. Romanian Dead Lift

75%8	80%6	85%5	90%5
95%5	100%5	105%4	105%4

BB. From Hang Bellow the Knee Power Clean

65%6	70%5	75%5	80%4
80%4	85%4	90%2	90%2

Javorek's General Abdominal Program: Perform in chronological order

3 exercise	3 exercise	3 exercise	3 exercise
3 exercise	3 exercise	3 exercise	3 exercise

Javorek's Special Abdominal Program # 3

1 Set	1 Set	1 Set	1 Set
1 Set	1 Set	1 Set	1 Set

40 Yards Sprint

x 1	x 1	x 1	x 1
x 1	x 1	x 1	x 1

Week # 5 Day # 3

BB. Incline Bench Press

70%10	80%6	75%8	85%4
70%10	80%6	75%8	85%4

DB. on Different Height Box Alternate Leg Step Ups+ Squat Push Press

60%12+12+8	65%12+12+8	70%10+10+6	80%6+6+4
80%6+6+4	70%10+10+6	80%6+6+4	85%6+6+4

BB. Quarter Squat & Up on Toes

70%10	75%8	80%6	75%8
80%6	85%5	75%8	85%5

DB. Lateral Arm Raise

50%14	55%14	60%12	65%12
70%10	75%8	80%6	85%5

on High Bar Behind The Head Pull Ups

8	8	8	8
8	8	8	8

BB. From The Floor Power Snatch

65%6	70%5	75%5	80%4
80%4	85%4	90%2	90%2

Javorek's Special Abdominal Program # 1

1 Set	1 Set	1 Set	1 Set
1 Set	1 Set	1 Set	1 Set

40 Yards Sprint

x 1	x 1	x 1	x 1
x 1	x 1	x 1	x 1

Week # 6 Day # 1

BB. Javorek's Whoop Ass Complex # 1: intensity taken from the weakest link of this Complex Exercise.

: Barbell Up on Toes Upright Row x 6 + Up on Toes High Pull Snatch x 6 + Overhead Up on Toes Squat Push Press x 6 + Behind The Head Good Morning x 6 + Behind The Head Alternate Leg Lunges + Bent-Over Row x 6 + Supinated Curl x 6 + Up on Toes Upright Row x 6 + Up on Toes High Pull Snatch x 6

60%1	70%1	60%1	70%1
60%1	70%1	60%1	70%1

BB. Back Squat & Up on Toes

60%10	70%10	80%5	75%5
85%4	85%4	65%10	85%4

DB. Bent Over "Kick Back" Triceps Curls

65%10	70%10	75%8	80%6
75%8	80%6	85%4	85%4

With or Without Weight Parallel Bar Dips

15	15	15	15
15	15	15	15

BB. Back Squat Jump

60%6	65%6	70%5	75%5
80%4	70%5	75%5	80%4

BB. From Hang Bellow the Knee Power Clean

65%6	70%5	75%5	75%5
80%4	85%4	85%4	85%4

BB. Romanian Dead Lift

75%8	80%6	85%5	90%5
95%5	100%5	105%4	105%4

Javorek's Special Abdominal Program # 2

1 Set	1 Set	1 Set	1 Set
1 Set	1 Set	1 Set	1 Set

40 Yards Sprint

x 1	x 1	x 1	x 1
x 1	x 1	x 1	x 1

Week # 6 Day # 2

BB. Javorek's Whoop Ass Complex # 3: intensity taken from the weakest link of this Complex Exercise

Barbell Supinated Curls X 6 + Barbell Comfortable Grip Up on Toes Upright Row X 6 + Barbell Flat Footed Squat Under High Pull Snatch X 6 + Barbell Behind The Head From Half Squat Press X 6 + Barbell Comfortable Grip Bent Over Row X 6 + Barbell Flat Footed Squat Under Upright Row X 6 + Barbell Behind The Head Good Morning X 6 + Barbell Behind The Head Squat Push Press x 6 + Barbell Comfortable Grip Overhead Squat X 6 + Barbell Behind The Head Squat Jump X 6 + Barbell In Front of Thighs Special Good Morning X 6

50%1	55%1	60%1	65%1
50%1	55%1	60%1	65%1

DB. Linear Flat Bench Press

50%14	60%12	55%14	65%12
70%10	75%8	80%6	80%6

BB. Back Squat & Up on Toes+ Wave Squat + Back Squat & Up on Toes

60%10+20+10	65%10+20+10	70%8+15+8	65%10+20+10
60%10+20+10	70%8+15+8	65%10+20+10	75%4+10+4

DB. Frontal Arm Raise

50%16	55%14	60%12	55%14
60%12	65%12	70%10	70%10

on Push Up Bars Push Ups

20	20	20	20
20	20	20	20

BB. From The Floor Power Snatch

65%6	70%5	75%5	75%5
80%4	85%4	85%4	85%4

Javorek's Special Abdominal Program # 3

1 Set	1 Set	1 Set	1 Set
1 Set	1 Set	1 Set	1 Set

40 Yards Sprint

x 1	x 1	x 1	x 1
x 1	x 1	x 1	x 1

Week # 6 Day # 3

BB. Narrow Grip Upright Row

70%10	80%6	75%8	85%5
80%6	85%5	80%6	85%6

BB. Overhead Triceps Curls

65%12	75%8	70%10	80%6
85%5	80%6	85%5	85%5

BB. Wave Squat

60%30	65%30	70%25	75%20
80%15	70%25	75%20	80%15

DB. Up on Toes Upright Row

80%6	85%4	80%6	85%4
90%3	80%6	85%4	90%3

on Different Height Push Ups Boxes, Plyo Push Ups

10+10	10+10	10+10	
10+10	10+10	10+10	10+10
			10+10

BB. Romanian Dead Lift

75%8	80%6	85%5	90%5
95%5	100%5	105%4	105%4

BB. From Hang Bellow the Knee Power Clean

65%6	70%5	75%5	80%4
85%4	75%5	80%4	85%4

Javorek's Special Abdominal Program # 1

1 Set	1 Set	1 Set	1 Set
1 Set	1 Set	1 Set	1 Set

40 Yards Sprint

x 1	x 1	x 1	x 1
x 1	x 1	x 1	x 1

Week # 7 Day # 1

DB. In Front of Chest Parallel Inward-Outward Rotation

60%6+6	65%6+6	70%5+5	75%4+4
80%3+3	70%5+5	80%3+3	85%2+2

BB. From Half Squat Behind The Head Overhead Press

70%10	70%10	80%6	80%6
85%4	90%2	85%4	90%2

DB. Javorek's Whoop Ass Complex # 1: intensity taken from the exercise of lowest maximum.

Up on Toes Upright Row x 6 + Supinated Curl x 6 + Overhead Rotational Up on Toes Press x 6 + Right Leg Forward, From Lunge Parallel Curl x 6 + Up on Toes Rotational Squat Push Press x 6 + Bent Over Row x 6 + Left Leg Forward, From Lunge Parallel Curl x 6 Up on Toes High Pull Snatch x 6:

60%1	65%1	70%1	60%1
65%1	70%1	70%1	70%1

BB. Back Squat & Up on Toes

70%8	80%6	90%2	70%10
90%2	80%4	75%5	90%3

BB. Medium Grip Up on Toes Upright Row

80%6	85%4	80%6	90%3
80%6	85%4	80%6	90%3

BB. From The Floor Power Snatch

65%6	70%5	75%5	80%4
85%4	75%5	80%4	85%4

Javorek's General Abdominal Program: Perform in chronological order

3 exercise	3 exercise	3 exercise	3 exercise
3 exercise	3 exercise	3 exercise	3 exercise

40 Yards Sprint

x 1	x 1	x 1	x 1
x 1	x 1	x 1	x 1

Week # 7 Day # 2

DB. Bent Over Fly

65%12	65%12	70%10	70%10
75%8	75%8	65%12	75%8

BB. Supinated (Regular) Curls

65%10	70%10	75%8	80%6
65%10	70%10	75%8	80%6

DB. Parallel or Rotational Flat Bench Press

60%14	80%6	65%12	85%5
70%10	80%6	80%6	85%4

BB. From Hang Bellow the Knee Power Clean

70%5	75%5	80%4	85%4
80%4	85%4	85%4	90%2

on High Bar Behind The Head Pull Ups

8	8	8	8
8	8	8	8

BB. Back Squat & Up on Toes+ Wave Squat + Back Squat & Up on Toes

60%10+25+10	65%10+25+10	70%8+20+8	75%6+15+6
65%10+25+10	70%8+20+8	75%6+15+6	80%6+10+6

BB. Romanian Dead Lift

80%6	85%5	90%5	95%5
100%5	105%4	110%4	110%4

Javorek's Special Abdominal Program # 1

1 Set	1 Set	1 Set	1 Set
1 Set	1 Set	1 Set	1 Set

40 Yards Sprint

x 1	x 1	x 1	x 1
x 1	x 1	x 1	x 1

Week # 7 Day # 3

BB. Back Squat & Up on Toes

70%10	90%2	70%10	80%5
75%6	90%2	80%3	90%2

DB. Overhead Triceps Curls

70%10	75%8	80%6	85%4
90%3	80%6	85%4	90%3

BB. Javorek's Whoop Ass Complex # 3: intensity taken from the weakest link of this Complex Exercise

Barbell Supinated Curls X 6 + Barbell Comfortable Grip Up on Toes Upright Row X 6 + Barbell Flat Footed Squat Under High Pull Snatch X 6 + Barbell Behind The Head From Half Squat Press X 6 + Barbell Comfortable Grip Bent Over Row X 6 + Barbell Flat Footed Squat Under Upright Row X 6 + Barbell Behind The Head Good Morning X 6 + Barbell Behind The Head Squat Push Press x 6 + Barbell Comfortable Grip Overhead Squat X 6 + Barbell Behind The Head Squat Jump X 6 + Barbell In Front of Thighs Special Good Morning X 6

60%1	60%1	70%1	70%1
65%1	65%1	70%1	70%1

DB. Pronated (Reverse) Curls

60%12	70%10	80%6	90%2
80%6	85%4	90%2	90%2

on High Bar Supinated Grip Chin Ups

14	14	14	14
14	14	14	14

BB. From Hang Bellow the Knee Power Clean

80%5	85%4	80%5	85%4
80%5	85%4	85%4	90%2

Javorek's Special Abdominal Program # 2

1 Set	1 Set	1 Set	1 Set
1 Set	1 Set	1 Set	1 Set

40 Yards Sprint

x 1	x 1	x 1	x 1
x 1	x 1	x 1	x 1

Week # 8 Day # 1

DB. Javorek's Whoop Ass Complex # 1: intensity taken from the exercise of lowest maximum.

Up on Toes Upright Row x 6 + Supinated Curl x 6 + Overhead Rotational Up on Toes Press x 6 + Right Leg Forward, From Lunge Parallel Curl x 6 + Up on Toes Rotational Squat Push Press x 6 + Bent Over Row x 6 + Left Leg Forward, From Lunge Parallel Curl x 6 Up on Toes High Pull Snatch x 6:

55%1	60%1	65%1	70%1
60%1	60%1	60%1	75%1

BB. Wide Grip Up on Toes Upright Row

80%6	80%6	90%3	90%3
85%4	90%3	80%6	90%4

BB. From Hang Bellow the Knee Power Clean

70%6	75%6	80%5	85%4
80%5	85%4	85%4	90%2

BB. Quarter Squat & Up on Toes

80%6	85%5	90%4	95%2
80%6	95%3	85%5	95%3

DB. Quarter Squat & Up on Toes Parallel or Rotational Overhead Push Press

80%6	806	85%4	85%4
90%3	90%3	85%4	95%2

With or Without Weight Parallel Bar Dips

16	16	16	16
16	16	16	16

BB. Romanian Dead Lift

75%8	80%6	85%5	90%5
95%5	100%4	105%4	105%4

Javorek's General Abdominal Program: Perform in chronological order

3 exercise	3 exercise	3 exercise	3 exercise
3 exercise	3 exercise	3 exercise	3 exercise

40 Yards Sprint

x 1	x 1	x 1	x 1
x 1	x 1	x 1	x 1

Week # 8 Day # 2

BB. Behind The Head Up on Toes Squat Push Press

70%10	75%8	80%6	85%5
75%8	70%10	85%5	85%5

on Different Height Push Ups Boxes Plyo Push Ups

8+8	8+8	8+8	8+8
8+8	8+8	8+8	8+8

BB. Javorek's Whoop Ass Complex # 1: intensity taken from the weakest link of this Complex Exercise.

: Barbell Up on Toes Upright Row x 6 + Up on Toes High Pull Snatch x 6 + Overhead Up on Toes Squat Push Press x 6 + Behind The Head Good Morning x 6 + Behind The Head Alternate Leg Lunges + Bent-Over Row x 6 + Supinated Curl x 6 + Up on Toes Upright Row x 6 + Up on Toes High Pull Snatch x 6

50%1	55%1	60%1	65%1
70%1	65%1	60%1	75%1

DB. on Different Height Box Alternate Leg Step Ups + Squat Push Press

60%14+14+8	70%12+12+8	80%10+10+5	85%8+8+5

65%12+12+875%10+10+8   80%10+10+585%8+8+5

DB. Linear Flat Bench Press

70%10	80%6	75%8	85%5
75%8	80%6	80%6	85%4

BB. From The Floor Power Snatch

70%5	75%5	80%5	90%2
80%5	90%2	85%4	90%2

Javorek's Special Abdominal Program # 3

1 Set	1 Set	1 Set	1 Set
1 Set	1 Set	1 Set	1 Set

40 Yards Sprint

x 1	x 1	x 1	x 1
x 1	x 1	x 1	x 1

Week # 8 Day # 3

BB. Pronated (Reverse) Curls

70%10	80%6	75%8	85%5
90%3	80%6	95%2	95%2

BB. Comfortable Grip Bench Press

80%6	90%3	80%6	90%2
85%3	95%2	85%4	95%2

BB. Javorek's Whoop Ass Complex # 3: intensity taken from the weakest link of this Complex Exercise

Barbell Supinated Curls X 6 + Barbell Comfortable Grip Up on Toes Upright Row X 6 + Barbell Flat Footed Squat Under High Pull Snatch X 6 + Barbell Behind The Head From Half Squat Press X 6 + Barbell Comfortable Grip Bent Over Row X 6 + Barbell Flat Footed Squat Under Upright Row X 6 + Barbell Behind The Head Good Morning X 6 + Barbell Behind The Head Squat Push Press x 6 + Barbell Comfortable Grip Overhead Squat X 6 + Barbell Behind The Head Squat Jump X 6 + Barbell In Front of Thighs Special Good Morning X 6

60%1	70%1	60%1	70%1
60%1	70%1	60%1	75%1

DB. Supinated (Regular) Curls

70%10	80%6	90%3	75%8
85%4	95%2	70%10	95%3

DB. Bent Over "Kick Back" Triceps Curls

70%10	80%6	75%8	85%4
80%6	90%3	95%2	95%2

BB. Romanian Dead Lift

80%6	85%5	90%5	95%5
100%5	105%4	110%4	110%4

BB. From Hang Bellow the Knee Power Clean

70%6	75%6	80%5	90%2
80%5	90%2	85%4	90%2

Javorek's Special Abdominal Program # 3

1 Set	1 Set	1 Set	1 Set
1 Set	1 Set	1 Set	1 Set

40 Yards Sprint

x 1	x 1	x 1	x 1
x 1	x 1	x 1	x 1

Week # 9 Day # 1

DB. Up on Toes Squat Upright Row

60%12	65%12	70%10	60%12
65%12	70%10	75%8	75%8

DB. Rotational Up on Toes Overhead Squat Push Press

60%10	70%10	65%10	75%8
60%10	70%10	65%10	75%8

DB. Incline Bench Press

50%14	75%8	55%12	75%8
60%12	80%6	65%10	80%6

DB. Pronated (Reverse) Curls

50%14	55%14	60%12	65%12
70%10	75%8	75%8	80%6

BB. Back Squat & Up on Toes

50%10	80%6	60%10	80%6
55%10	85%4	70%10	85%4

BB. From The Floor Power Snatch

70%6	75%6	80%5	90%2
80%5	90%2	85%4	90%2

Javorek's Special Abdominal Program # 1

1 Set	1 Set	1 Set	1 Set
1 Set	1 Set	1 Set	1 Set

40 Yards Sprint

x 1	x 1	x 1	x 1
x 1	x 1	x 1	x 1

Week # 9 Day # 2

DB. Decline Bench Press

50%14	50%14	60%12	60%12
55%14	55%14	70%10	70%10

DB. Parallel Bent Over Row

50%16	55%14	60%12	65%12
70%10	75%8	65%12	75%8

DB. Up on Toes Upright Row

50%12	70%10	55%12	75%8
50%12	70%10	55%12	75%8

DB. Parallel or Rotational Flat Bench Press

60%12	60%12	60%12	65%12
65%12	65%12	75%8	80%6

BB. Quarter Squat & Up on Toes

50%14	55%14	60%14	65%14
70%12	75%10	65%14	75%10

BB. From Hang Bellow the Knee Power Clean

70%6	80%5	85%4	90%2
80%5	90%2	85%4	90%2

BB. Romanian Dead Lift

80%6	85%5	90%5	95%5
100%5	105%4	110%4	110%4

Javorek's Special Abdominal Program # 2

1 Set	1 Set	1 Set	1 Set
1 Set	1 Set	1 Set	1 Set

40 Yards Sprint

x 1	x 1	x 1	x 1
x 1	x 1	x 1	x 1

Week # 9 Day # 3

DB. Seated Overhead Press

60%12	60%12	70%10	70%10
65%12	65%12	75%8	80%6

DB. In Front of Chest Parallel Inward-Outward Rotation

40%10+10	45%10+10	50%8+8	55%7+7
60%6+6	60%6+6	65%5+5	70%4+4

BB. Pronated (Reverse) Curls

50%12	60%12	55%12	65%12
60%12	70%10	80%6	80%6

BB. Overhead Triceps Curls

50%14	75%8	55%14	75%8
60%12	75%8	65%12	80%6

BB. Back Squat & Up on Toes

50%10	80%6	60%10	80%6
55%10	85%4	70%10	85%4

BB. From The Floor Power Snatch

70%6	75%6	80%5	85%4
80%5	90%2	85%4	90%2

BB. Back Squat Jump

40%10	45%8	50%6	55%6
60%6	55%6	65%5	70%4

Javorek's Special Abdominal Program # 3

1 Set	1 Set	1 Set	1 Set
1 Set	1 Set	1 Set	1 Set

40 Yards Sprint

x 1	x 1	x 1	x 1
x 1	x 1	x 1	x 1

Week # 10 Day # 1

DB. Supinated (Regular) Curls

65%10	70%10	80%6	75%8
85%4	80%6	85%4	85%4

DB. Linear Bench Press

70%10	80%6	75%8	85%4
80%6	90%2	85%6	90%2

BB. Javorek's Whoop Ass Complex # 1: intensity taken from the weakest link of this Complex Exercise.

: Barbell Up on Toes Upright Row x 6 + Up on Toes High Pull Snatch x 6 + Overhead Up on Toes Squat Push Press x 6 + Behind The Head Good Morning x 6 + Behind The Head Alternate Leg Lunges + Bent-Over Row x 6 + Supinated Curl x 6 + Up on Toes Upright Row x 6 + Up on Toes High Pull Snatch x 6

50%1	55%1	60%1	65%1
70%1	65%1	60%1	75%1

BB. From Hang Bellow the Knee Power Clean

70%6	75%6	80%5	85%4
80%5	85%4	90%2	90%2

BB. Medium Grip Up on Toes Upright Row

70%10	70%10	80%6	80%6
75%8	85%4	90%3	90%3

BB. Romanian Dead Lift

80%6	85%5	90%5	95%5
100%5	105%4	110%4	110%4

BB. Wave Squat

40%40	45%40	50%35	55%30
60%25	65%25	70%20	70%20

Javorek's General Abdominal Program: Perform in chronological order

3 exercise	3 exercise	3 exercise	3 exercise
3 exercise	3 exercise	3 exercise	3 exercise

40 Yards Sprint

x 1	x 1	x 1	x 1
x 1	x 1	x 1	x 1

Week # 10 Day # 2

DB. Parallel (Hammer) Curls

60%12	70%10	80%6	75%8
85%5	75%8	80%6	85%5

DB. Quarter Squat & Up on Toes Parallel or Rotational Overhead Push Press

70%10	80%6	70%10	80%6
75%8	85%4	75%8	85%4

on High Bar Behind The Head Pull Ups

10	10	10	10
10	10	10	10

BB. Wide Grip Up on Toes Upright Row

60%12	80%6	65%12	85%4
70%10	85%4	75%8	85%4

BB. Back Squat & Up on Toes

60%10	80%4	70%6	85%4
75%6	85%3	70%10	85%4

BB. From The Floor Power Snatch

65%6	70%5	75%5	75%5
80%4	85%4	85%4	85%4

BB. Comfortable Grip Bench Press

70%10	80%6	75%8	85%4
80%6	90%2	85%6	90%2

Javorek's Special Abdominal Program # 1

1 Set	1 Set	1 Set	1 Set
1 Set	1 Set	1 Set	1 Set

40 Yards Sprint

x 1	x 1	x 1	x 1
x 1	x 1	x 1	x 1

Week # 10 Day # 3

DB. Parallel or Rotational Up on Toes Overhead Press

70%10	80%6	90%3	75%8
85%4	85%4	90%3	90%3

DB. Lying on Your Back on Bench Fly

60%12	70%10	75%8	80%6
90%2	85%4	90%2	90%2

DB. Frontal Arm Raise

50%14	55%12	60%12	65%12
70%10	75%8	80%6	85%4

BB. Romanian Dead Lift

80%6	85%5	90%5	95%5
100%5	105%4	110%4	110%4

DB. Parallel or Rotational Flat Bench Press

80%6	90%3	80%6	90%3
85%4	95%2	85%4	95%2

BB. From Hang Bellow the Knee Power Clean

65%6	70%5	75%5	75%5
80%4	85%4	85%4	85%4

BB. Back Squat & Up on Toes + Wave Squat + Back Squat & Up on Toes

60%10+20+10	65%10+20+10	70%6+15+6	75%4+10+4
65%10+20+10	70%6+15+6	75%4+10+4	80%3+10+3

Javorek's Special Abdominal Program # 2

1 Set	1 Set	1 Set	1 Set
1 Set	1 Set	1 Set	1 Set

40 Yards Sprint

x 1	x 1	x 1	x 1
x 1	x 1	x 1	x 1

Week # 11 Day # 1

DB. Javorek's Whoop Ass Complex # 1: intensity taken from the exercise of lowest maximum.

Up on Toes Upright Row x 6 + Supinated Curl x 6 + Overhead Rotational Up on Toes Press x 6 + Right Leg Forward, From Lunge Parallel Curl x 6 + Up on Toes Rotational Squat Push Press x 6 + Bent Over Row x 6 + Left Leg Forward, From Lunge Parallel Curl x 6 Up on Toes High Pull Snatch x 6:

55%1	60%1	65%1	70%1
60%1	60%1	70%1	75%1

BB. Incline Bench Press

60%10	65%10	70%10	75%8
80%6	85%4	70%10	85%4

With or Without Weight Parallel Bar Dips

12	12	12	12
12	12	12	12

BB. Back Squat & Up on Toes

60%10	80%4	70%10	80%3
65%10	75%6	70%8	80%4

BB. From Half Squat, Behind The Head Overhead Press

60%12	70%10	65%10	80%6
75%8	85%4	80%6	85%4

BB. From The Floor Power Snatch

70%5	75%5	75%5	80%4
85%4	85%4	90%2	90%2

Javorek's Special Abdominal Program # 3

1 Set	1 Set	1 Set	1 Set
1 Set	1 Set	1 Set	1 Set

40 Yards Sprint

x 1	x 1	x 1	x 1
x 1	x 1	x 1	x 1

Week # 11 Day # 2

BB. From Hang Bellow the Knee Power Clean

70%6	75%5	80%4	85%4
75%5	80%4	85%4	85%4

DB. Supinated (Regular) Curls

60%14	65%12	70%10	75%8
80%6	70%10	75%8	80%6

DB. Parallel or Rotational Flat Bench Press

70%10	80%6	70%10	80%6
70%10	80%6	70%10	80%6

BB. Narrow Grip Up on Toes Upright Row

65%12	70%10	75%8	70%10
75%8	80%6	75%8	85%4

on Push Ups Bar Push Up

12	12	12	12
12	12	12	12

BB. Romanian Dead Lift

80%6	85%5	90%5	95%5
100%5	105%4	110%4	110%4

BB. Back Squat Jump

40%10	45%8	50%6	55%6
60%5	65%5	65%5	70%3

Javorek's Special Abdominal Program # 1

1 Set	1 Set	1 Set	1 Set
1 Set	1 Set	1 Set	1 Set

40 Yards Sprint

x 1	x 1	x 1	x 1
x 1	x 1	x 1	x 1

Week # 11 Day # 3

DB. Incline Bench Press

70%10	70%10	70%10	75%8
80%6	85%4	85%4	90%3

DB. Bent Over "Kick Back" Triceps Curls

60%12	65%12	70%10	75%8
80%6	85%4	90%3	90%2

BB. Supinated (Regular) Curls

60%12	75%8	65%12	80%6
70%10	85%4	80%6	90%3

on High Bar Behind The Head Pull Ups

10	10	10	10
10	10	10	10

BB. Quarter Squat & Up on Toes

60%14	70%12	80%8	75%10
85%6	85%6	90%4	90%4

BB. From The Floor Power Snatch

65%6	70%5	75%5	75%5
80%4	85%4	85%4	85%4

Javorek's Special Abdominal Program # 2

1 Set	1 Set	1 Set	1 Set
1 Set	1 Set	1 Set	1 Set

40 Yards Sprint

x 1	x 1	x 1	x 1
x 1	x 1	x 1	x 1

Week # 12 Day # 1

BB. From Hang Bellow the Knee Power Clean

70%6	75%5	80%4	85%4
90%2	84%4	90%2	90%2

DB. Up on Toes Upright Row

70%10	**80%6**	**75%8**	**85%4**	**80%6**
90%3	**90%3**	**90%3**		

DB. Decline Bench Press

80%6	80%6	90%2	90%2
85%6	85%6	90%2	90%2

DB. In Front of Chest Parallel Inward-Outward Rotation

50%8+8	50%8+8	55%7+7	60%6+6
60%6+6	65%4+4	65%4+4	70%3+3

on Different Height Push Ups Boxes Plyo Push Ups

8+8	8+8	8+8	8+8
8+8	8+8	8+8	8+8

BB. Romanian Dead Lift

80%6	85%5	90%5	95%5
100%5	105%4	110%4	110%4

BB. Back Squat & Up on Toes+ Wave Squat + Back Squat & Up on Toes

60%10+20+10	65%8+20+8	70%6+15+6	75%4+10+4
70%6+15+6	75%4+10+4	80%3+10+3	80%3+10+3

Javorek's Special Abdominal Program # 3

1 Set	1 Set	1 Set	1 Set
1 Set	1 Set	1 Set	1 Set

40 Yards Sprint

x 1	x 1	x 1	x 1
x 1	x 1	x 1	x 1

Week # 12 Day # 2

DB. Up on Toes Squat Upright Row

75%8	80%6	75%8	80%6
80%6	90%3	85%4	90%3

DB. Lying on Your Back on Bench Fly

60%10	65%10	70%10	75%8
80%6	85%5	90%3	90%3

DB. Supinated (Regular) Curls

70%10	85%5	75%8	90%3
75%8	85%5	90%3	90%3

BB. Incline Bench Press

75%8	85%5	75%8	85%5
75%8	85%5	75%8	85%5

BB. From The Floor Power Snatch

70%6	75%5	80%4	85%4
90%2	85%4	90%2	90%2

BB. Back Squat Jump

50%8	55%8	60%6	65%4
70%3	60%6	65%4	70%3

Javorek's Special Abdominal Program # 2

1 Set	1 Set	1 Set	1 Set
1 Set	1 Set	1 Set	1 Set

40 Yards Sprint

x 1	x 1	x 1	x 1
x 1	x 1	x 1	x 1

Week # 12 Day # 3

BB. Comfortable Grip Bench Press

70%10	90%2	75%8	95%2
80%6	95%2	100%1	100%1

DB. Javorek's Whoop Ass Complex # 1: intensity taken from the exercise of lowest maximum.

Up on Toes Upright Row x 6 + Supinated Curl x 6 + Overhead Rotational Up on Toes Press x 6 + Right Leg Forward, From Lunge Parallel Curl x 6 + Up on Toes Rotational Squat Push Press x 6 + Bent Over Row x 6 + Left Leg Forward, From Lunge Parallel Curl x 6 Up on Toes High Pull Snatch x 6:

55%1	60%1	65%1	70%1
60%1	60%1	60%1	75%1

BB. Overhead Triceps Curls

65%12	75%8	70%10	80%6
75%8	85%5	90%3	95%2

BB. Javorek's Whoop Ass Complex # 3: intensity taken from the weakest link of this Complex Exercise

Barbell Supinated Curls X 6 + Barbell Comfortable Grip Up on Toes Upright Row X 6 + Barbell Flat Footed Squat Under High Pull Snatch X 6 + Barbell Behind The Head From Half Squat Press X 6 + Barbell Comfortable Grip Bent Over Row X 6 + Barbell Flat Footed Squat Under Upright Row X 6 + Barbell Behind The Head Good Morning X 6 + Barbell Behind The Head Squat Push Press X 6 + Barbell Comfortable Grip Overhead Squat X 6 + Barbell Behind The Head Squat Jump X 6 + Barbell In Front of Thighs Special Good Morning X 6

60%1	70%1	60%1	70%1
60%1	70%1	60%1	75%1

BB. Back Squat & Up on Toes

70%6	90%2	75%5	90%2
80%3	95%1	85%3	95%1

BB. Romanian Dead Lift

80%6	85%5	90%5	95%5
100%5	105%4	110%4	110%4

BB. From Hang Bellow the Knee Power Clean

80%4	80%4	80%4	80%4
90%2	90%2	90%2	90%2

Javorek's General Abdominal Program: Perform in chronological order

3 exercise	3 exercise	3 exercise	3 exercise
3 exercise	3 exercise	3 exercise	3 exercise

40 Yards Sprint

x 1	x 1	x 1	x 1
x 1	x 1	x 1	x 1

Test Exercise List

1. DB. Up on Toes Upright Row
2. DB. Up on Toes Squat Upright Row
3. DB. Supinated (Regular) Curls
4. DB. Pronated (Reverse) Curls
5. DB. Parallel (Hammer) Curls
6. DB. Parallel or Rotational Up on Toes Overhead Press
7. DB. Quarter Squat & Up on Toes Parallel or Rotational Overhead Push Press
8. DB. Rotational Up on Toes Overhead Squat Push Press
9. DB. Parallel Bent Over Row
10. DB. Parallel or Rotational Flat Bench Press
11. DB. Linear Flat Bench Press
12. DB. Incline Bench Press
13. DB. Decline Bench Press
14. DB. Seated Overhead Press
15. DB. Bent Over "Kick Back" Triceps Curls
16. DB. Lying on Your Back on Bench Fly
17. DB. In Front of Chest Parallel Inward-Outward Rotation
18. DB. Lateral Arm Raise
19. DB. Frontal Arm Raise
20. DB. Bent Over Fly
21. DB. Overhead Triceps Curls
22. DB. Javorek's Whoop Ass Complex # 1:
23. DB. on Different Height Box Alternate Leg Step Ups + Up on Toes Squat Push Press
24. BB. Narrow Grip Up on Toes Upright Row
25. BB. Medium Grip Up on Toes Upright Row
26. BB. Wide Grip Up on Toes Upright Row
27. BB. Behind The Head Up on Toes Squat Push Press
28. BB. From Half Squat, Behind The Head Overhead Press
29. BB. Overhead Triceps Curls
30. BB. Supinated (Regular) Curls
31. BB. Pronated (Reverse) Curls
32. BB. Comfortable Grip Bench Press
33. BB. Incline Bench Press
34. BB. Javorek's Whoop Ass Complex # 1:
35. BB. Javorek's Whoop Ass Complex # 3:
36. BB. Back Squat & Up on Toes
37. BB. Back Squat & Up on Toes+ Wave Squat + Back Squat & Up on Toes
38. BB. Quarter Squat & Up on Toes
39. BB. Back Squat Jump
40. BB. Wave Squat.
41. on High Bar Behind The Head Pull Ups
42. on High Bar Pronated Grip Behind The Head Chin Ups
43. With or Without Weight Parallel Bar Dips
44. on Push Ups Bar Push Up
45. on Different Height Push Ups Boxes Plyo Push Ups
46. Javorek's Special Abdominal Program # 1
47. Javorek's Special Abdominal Program # 2
48. Javorek's Special Abdominal Program # 3
49. Javorek's General Abdominal Program

Exercise description of Less Known Exercises:

Barbell Quarter Squat + Calf Raise: Perform a quarter squat, then, at the top of the rep, go up on your toes with your knees extended – that's one rep. Perform these two movements as one fluid motion.

Dumbbell Quarter Squat & Up on Toes Rotational Push Press: Standing with a dumbbell in each hand at shoulder level, facing straight ahead with your abdominal muscles tight. Bend your knees less than with a quarter squat, keeping your weight centered between the balls of your feet and heels. Keep your shoulders, hips, and ankles in a perfect vertical line. Follow the knee bend with an explosive pressing overhead movement, all in one fluid motion. Depending on your goals, this move can be done flat-footed or up on your toes, but preferably up on the toes.

Barbell Wave Squat: In one continuous motion, do a barbell quarter squat and raise up onto your toes at the top (calf raise). Do this for three reps. on the fourth rep, jump up slightly after going up onto your toes. on the fifth rep, do a full squat plus a jump at the top. Repeat this 5-rep cycle six times when the program calls for 30 reps, and four times when it calls for 20.

Dumbbell Inward/Outward Rotation: Stand holding light dumbbells directly in front of your chest with your elbows bent and arms parallel to the floor. Start the rotation by extending your elbows until your arms are straight out at your sides, (palms facing forward) in an "iron cross" position. From here, bring the dumbbells together in front of you, keeping your elbows straight, until they meet. Perform the movement in the opposite position to return to the start position.

Barbell Squat Jump: Go into a deep regular squat and jump up at the top of the motion. Always go slowly down into the squat and land on balls of feet when landing from the jump.

Dumbbell Overhead Up on Toes Rotational Squat Push Press: Stand with a dumbbell in each hand at shoulder level. Squat with the dumbbells at your shoulders with your feet flat on the floor and your knees pointed outward. Keep you back slightly arched, head facing forward. Raise up from the squat, maintaining the trunk's relatively vertical position, and push the dumbbells overhead in a dynamic, explosive motion, either remaining flat footed or coming up on toes. Recover by coming down with soft (bent) knees and going directly into a squat for the next rep.

Dumbbell Step-Up + Up on Toes Rotational Squat Push Press: As noted in the program, perform all prescribed reps for step-ups (onto a plyometrics box), then do all reps for squat push presses on the floor.

Barbell Behind The Head From Half Squat + Behind The Head Overhead Up on Toes Press: Upon reaching the down position of a half squat, press the bar overhead without extending your legs. It's very important for balance to stay flatfooted and to keep your shoulders, hips, and ankles aligned.

Javorek's Whoop Ass Dumbbell Complex # 1: Up on Toes Upright Row x 6 + Supinated Curl x 6 + Overhead Rotational Up on Toes Press x 6 + Right Leg Forward, From Lunge Parallel Curl x 6 + Up on Toes Rotational Squat Push Press x 6 + Bent Over Row x 6 + Left Leg Forward, From Lunge Parallel Curl x 6 Up on Toes High Pull Snatch x 6: Perform these movements in succession (non-stop) as a combination exercise. Do six reps of dumbbell upright rows, then six reps for standing curls and so on. on Parallel Curl from lunge, it is very important to balance the body weight equally on both legs (front leg the feet must be in front of the knee, and the back lower leg parallel with the floor holding the balance on balls of the feet .Hold the trunk stiff, tight core muscles and do not extend or bend your legs during the exercise.

Javorek's Whoop Ass Barbell Complex # 1: Barbell Up on Toes Upright Row x 6 + Up on Toes High Pull Snatch x 6 + Overhead Up on Toes Squat Push Press x 6 + Behind The Head Good Morning x 6 + Behind The Head Alternate Leg Lunges + Bent-Over Row x 6 + Supinated Curl x 6 + Up on Toes Upright Row x 6 + Up on Toes High Pull Snatch x 6

Perform these movements in succession (non-stop) as a combination exercise. Do six reps of barbell upright rows, then six reps for high pull snatches and so on.

Javorek's Whoop Ass Barbell Complex # 3: Perform these movements in succession (non-stop) as a combination exercise.

Barbell Supinated Curls X 6 + Barbell Comfortable Grip Up on Toes Upright Row X 6 + Barbell Flat Footed Squat Under High Pull Snatch X 6 + Barbell Behind The Head From Half Squat Press X 6 + Barbell Comfortable Grip Bent Over Row X 6 + Barbell Flat Footed Squat Under Upright Row X 6 + Barbell Behind The Head Good Morning X 6 + Barbell Behind The Head Squat Push Press x 6 + Barbell Comfortable Grip Overhead Squat X 6 + Barbell Behind The Head Squat Jump X 6 + Barbell In Front of Thighs Special Good Morning X 6

Push-Ups (on push-up bars): Perform push-ups using specially designed raised bars instead of on the floor. If this equipment is not available to you, do regular push-ups.

Half Sit-Up (bottom half) + Half Sit-Up (top half): Hook your feet on something stable at floor level, cross your arms over your chest and perform a sit-up only halfway up. Pause, and then continue all the way up. Lower back to the halfway position, the pause again and lower down all the way. That's one rep.

on half sit-ups (bottom half), go only to halfway up, pause, and then back down. on top half sit-ups, start all the way and go halfway down, pause, then back up.

Jack Knifes: Lay flat on your back, on the floor with your legs together and straight and your arms straight overhead. Raise your legs and arms up at the same time until your hands and feet touch over your body.

Complete exercise techniques information you can find on my 3.5 hrs long great quality "Javorek's Exercise techniques DVD" and in my book "Javorek Complex Conditioning". order form available on my website: www.istvanjavorek.com

Javorek's Dumbbell Whoop Ass Complex # 1 Exercise:

Up on Toes Upright Row	X 6
Supinated Curls	X 6
Overhead Rotational Up on Toes Press	X 6
Right Leg Forward, From Lunge Parallel Curls	X 6
Rotational Up on Toes Squat Push Press	X 6
Bent Over Row	X 6
Left Leg Forward, From Lunge Parallel Curls	X 6
Up on Toes High Pull Snatch	X 6

Perform In A Non-Stop, Continuous order As Listed Above: 8 Exercise X 6 reps = 48 reps. on The Beginning Should Be Practiced Just Partial or The Integral Complex #1 , But With Less Repetitions. It Is Up To The Individual or Coach's Decision To Practice The Full Exercise And To Increase The Weight Also.

Take the intensity from the lowest weight maximum of these 8 exercises.

Javorek's Whoop Ass Barbell Complex # 1 Exercise

Up on Toes Upright Row	X 6
Up on Toes High Pull Snatch	X 6
Behind The Head Up on Toes Squat Push Press	X 6
Behind The Head Good Morning	X 6
Behind The Head Alternate Leg Lunges	X 6 + 6
Bent-Over Row	X 6
Supinated Curls	X 6
Up on Toes Upright Row	X 6
Up on Toes High Pull Snatch	X 6

Perform In A Non-Stop, Continuous order As Listed Above: 9 Exercise X 6 reps = 60 reps.(Lunges counted 12 reps!!) on The Beginning Should Be Practiced Just Partial or The Integral Complex #1 , But With Less Repetitions. It Is Up To The Individual or Coach's Decision To Practice The Full Exercise And To Increase The Weight also.

Javorek's Whoop Ass Barbell Complex # 3:

Barbell Supinated Curls	X 6
Barbell Comfortable Grip Up on Toes Upright Row	X 6
Barbell Flat Footed Squat Under High Pull Snatch	X 6
Barbell Behind The Head From Half Squat Press	X 6
Barbell Comfortable Grip Bent Over Row	X 6
Barbell Flat Footed Squat Under Upright Row	X 6
Barbell Behind The Head Good Morning	X 6
Barbell behind The Head Squat Push Press	X 6
Barbell Comfortable Grip Overhead Squat	X 6
Barbell Behind The Head Squat Jump	X 6
Barbell In Front of Thighs Special Good Morning	X 6

Perform In A Non-Stop, Continuous order As Listed Above: 11Exercise X 6 Reps = 66 Reps. on The Beginning Should Be Practiced Just Partial or The Integral Complex #1, But With Less Repetition. It Is Up To The Individual or Coach's Decision To Practice The Full Exercise And To Increase The Weight also

Javorek's "Tremendous Pleasure" Conditioning Program

Copyright @ 2000 Istvan "Steve" Javorek

This new program unlike the six weeks six times a week " Javorek's Big Fun # 1" program is a 12 weeks, three times a week program. I call it "Javorek's Big Fun #2" or "Javorek's Millennium Elite Athletes Tremendous Pleasure Program". Because of the high load, it may be performed in two different sessions daily, and performed three times a week for 12 weeks, or dividing into two separate workouts and performed for 24 weeks. of course the neuro-muscular and hormonal stimulation will be very different, achieving the best result with the original version.

As everyone can see in my programs, I finish each day with abdominal and general explosive drills. The reason is that in my forty years of coaching experience I have come to the conclusion that it is much more beneficial to do explosive drills at the end of a daily program for a shorter period of time instead of performing a full hour separate workout. For sport of Cycling I increased the repetition in each set, for a greater cardiovascular stimulation.

As I mentioned previously, I was born with the East-European plyo-metrics movement (which we just called "explosive drills"). I have helped athletes achieve great performance applying my philosophy to my hundreds of programs, which develop quick, fast and explosive musculature.

A major feature of my programs is the very different approach to using shorter breaks between the sets of exercises. This must be modified for anyone who does not fit into an elite athlete's physical shape by increasing and adjusting the break times to a trainee's individual adaptation level! In the mean time respecting the repetition, the short breaks I can guarantee any cyclist will achieve their best physical shape of their life. Just combine the right way this program with a special cycling training.

Decreasing the break times between the sets has been a long experiment. During my own, and later my athletes' athletic preparation, I realized that by shortening the breaks and increasing the intensity I can achieve higher quality muscular fitness and strength improvement. I have had very positive feed back from other coaches and athletes around the world. From the many positive comments, I have come to the conclusion that a greater variation of exercises will stimulate the cardio-vascular and hormonal and lactic acid system. The human body (after a period of "fighting") will adapt to the increased demand, and new doors will open in a clean, drug free athletic preparation.

one of the most important points what I realized in program design is that of exercise technique. Everyone must feel comfortable with all of the exercises within a program and must posses the correct technique for all of them. During my years of publishing articles in different journals and magazines, I realized that several exercises from my programs are not familiar to the general public. My dumbbell and barbell exercise videotapes show "in detail" information and descriptions of the exercises I utilize.

I feel it necessary to share with the readers several pieces of general information about the exercises from this program.

In the "Tremendous Pleasure" program there are dumbbell, barbell and general fitness exercises, including box jumps, step ups, lunges, walk lunges, pull ups on high bar, dips on parallel bar, abdominal programs and up-stairs activities.

Exercises with dumbbells always involve more active minor, major and balance muscles at the same time, using a wide range of motion. Dumbbell exercises are very dynamic and stimulatory.

Exercises with barbells are another group from the free weights family. In most of the cases with barbells, an athlete can isolate more effectively a muscle or muscle group, because the barbell itself eliminates some of the balance muscles' involvement, or changes the order, the biomechanics and number of balance muscles participation.

Alternating and mixing up dumbbell and barbell exercises makes the program more enjoyable and it produces great stimulation on the whole vital body function.

Both the dumbbell and the barbell exercise groups produce a continuous stimulation on the muscular-skeletal (bones, ligaments, tendons, muscles) the cardio-vascular and the morpho-functional system. My personal experiences confirm the quasi-general knowledge that weight-bearing exercises can help to prevent injury, and osteoporosis. Research proves that weight training is not just preventive, but also very beneficial in recovering damaged joints due to arthritis, or after serious injuries.

Cycling editors and athletes are questioning why a cyclist should perform a program like this. As a general conclusion in favor of doing this kind of preparation, I would like to present my philosophy of a new concept of athletics, athletic bodybuilding and general fitness:

Avoid monotony in your workouts - doing year round almost the same routines make the neuro-muscular system tired, which drives the body to burn out or "over-train". Give your body a chance to enjoy your hard work. This program has a great number of exercise variations, which makes it more enjoyable and stimulatory. Everyone who performs this program, (of course this includes only those who are physically and mentally ready to do it) will become, strong, vigorous, healthy and with perfectly balanced musculature.

At least after every six months take time off from your general exercise routines. Changing from a general routine will "shock" your body. At first, the change will act as active rest and later as a new form of stimulation to your body.

If you are a beginner, then start with basic exercises - one or two exercises per muscle group. Build up your program and exercise groups gradually. Each exercise must be performed with perfect technique!

High performance athletes , novice athletes and general fitness enthusiasts should benefit from this program

So, give your body an opportunity to take off from your year-round routine. Enjoy the hard work, and refresh your body's improvement, and show to the world how you did improve your performance without "juices".

Special Instruction to the program: Javorek's Barbell and Dumbbell Complex Exercises. Take the intensity always from the most difficult exercise of a respective complex, avoiding the chance of choosing too heavy weights and not being able of performing correctly.

Week 1 Day 1

Dumbbell Up on Toes Upright Row 30s Break between the sets

60% 12	60% 12	65% 10	70% 10	75%8	80% 8

Dumbbell Pronated Curls 25s Break between the sets

55%14	60%12	65%12	70%10	75%8	80%6

Barbell Wide Grip Bent Over Row 30s Break between the sets

55%10	60%10	65%10	70%10	75%8	80%6

Dumbbell Overhead, From Parallel To Linear, Rotational Press 30s Break between the sets

55%14	60% 12	65%10	70%10	75%8	80%6

Dumbbell Parallel Squat Push Press 35s Break between the sets

60%10	70%10	65%10	75%8	80%6	80%6

Dumbbell Alternate Leg Lunges - Double Steps Count 40s Break between the sets

50%16+16	60%16+16	65%16+16	70%14+14
75%14+14	75%14+14		

Javorek's Dumbbell Complex 3 60s Break between the sets

40%1	45%1	50%1	55%1	50%1	55%1

Barbell Back Squat & Up on Toes | | **60s Break between the sets**

60%10	70%10	80%6	65%10	80%6	80%6

Double Leg Up-Stairs Bounding - Minimum 22-24 Stairs (2 Flights) 30s Break between the sets
3 Length on Each Circuit

one Leg(Right) Up-Stairs Bounding - Minimum 22-24 Stairs (2 Flights)
30s Break between the sets
3 Length on Each Circuit

one Leg(Left) Up-Stairs Bounding - Minimum 22-24 Stairs (2 Flights)
30s Break between the sets
3 Length on Each Circuit

Up-Stairs Sprint - Minimum 22-24 Stairs (2 Flights)
30s Break between the sets
3 Length on Each Circuit

Javorek's General Abdominal Program (Four exercises on each circuit)

Ex.1-4	Ex 5-8	Ex 9-12	Ex.13-16	Ex. 17-20	Ex. 21-24

Week 1 Day 2

Barbell Narrow Grip Upright Row

40s Break between the sets

50%12	55%12	60%10	65%10	70%10	75%8

Barbell Supinated (Regular) Curls

35s Break between the sets

40%14	45%12	50%12	60%10	55%12	70%10

Barbell Overhead Triceps Curls

35s Break between the sets

50%12	60%10	65%10	70%10	65%10	70%10

Barbell Incline Bench Press

40s Break between the sets

50%10	55%10	65%10	60%10	70%10	75%8

Barbell (Comfortable Width Grip) Behind The Head From Half Squat Press

35s Break between the sets

40%14	45%14	50%12	50%12	55%10	55%10

High Bar Pronated Grip Behind The Head Pull Ups or Regular Chin-Ups Pull (With Weight or Without Weight)

60s Break between the sets

10%10	15%10	15%10	15%10	20%8	25%6

Or 6 Set As Many You Can Perform With Correct Form

Dumbbell Walk Lunges With 6 From Hip High Pull Snatch on Each Step - Double Steps Count.

45s Break between the sets

40%20+20	45%20+20	45%20+20	50%20+20
55%18+18	55%18+18		

Barbell Wave Squat (4 Wave + 1 Jump)

45s Break between the sets

40%40	45%40	50%35	60%30	65%30	65%30

Javorek's Barbell Complex 4

60s Break between the sets

40%1	45%1	50%1	50%1
55%1	55%1		

Barbell Back Squat & Up on Toes

30s Break between the sets

40%14	50%12	60%10	50%12	70%10	80%6, 6

Box Jump (The Height Must Be Individually Chosen)

60s Break between the sets

6 Sets of 10 Box Jumps or Sets of 10 Tuck Jumps

Double Leg Up-Stairs Zig-Zag Bounding - Minimum 22-24 Stairs (2 Flights)

30s Break between the sets

3 Length on Each Circuit

Run-Jump & Sprint - Minimum 22-24 Stairs (2 Flights)

30s Break between the sets

3 Length on Each Circuit

Up-Stairs Sprint - Minimum 22-24 Stairs (2 Flights)

30s Break between the sets

3 Length on Each Circuit

Javorek's Special Abdominal Program # 1

1 Set on each circuit

Week 1 Day 3

Dumbbell Lying on Back on Bench Fly

45s Break between the sets

50%14	60%12	65%10	70%10	75%8	80%6

Dumbbell Parallel Bench Press 45s Break between the sets

60%10	65%10	70%8	75%8	80%6	85%5

Dumbbell Bent Over Row + "Kick Back " Triceps Curls

40s Break between the sets

40%16+12	50%16+12	60%12+10	70%10+8
80%6+6	85%5+5		

Dumbbell Lying on Bench Pull Over

35s Break between the sets

60%10	65%10	70%10	75%8	80%6	85%5

Dumbbell Incline Bench Press

45s Break between the sets

60%10	70%10	75%8	65%10	85%4	85%4

Dumbbell Regular Curls X 10 + Upright Row X 8 + Press X 6 + Bent Over Row X 8 + Squat Push Press X 6

60s Break between the sets

40%1	45%1	50%1	55%1	60%1	60%1

Dumbbell Up on Toes Upright Row X 8 + Press X 6 + Regular Curls X 6 + Push Press X 6 + Upright Row X 8 + Squat Push Press X 6 + Squat Jump X 6 + Split Jump X 10

60s Break between the sets

45%1	50%1	55%1	60%1	55%1	60%1

Barbell Front Squat

45s Break between the sets

50%10	60%10	60% 10	65%10	70%10	75%6

Double Leg Up-Stairs Bounding - Minimum 22-24 Stairs (2 Flights)

30s Break between the sets

3 Length on Each Circuit

one Leg(Right) Up-Stairs Bounding - Minimum 22-24 Stairs (2 Flights)

30s Break between the sets

3 Length on Each Circuit

one Leg(Left) Up-Stairs Bounding - Minimum 22-24 Stairs (2 Flights)

30s Break between the sets

3 Length on Each Circuit

Up-Stairs Sprint - Minimum 22-24 Stairs (2 Flights)

30s Break between the sets

3 Length on Each Circuit

Javorek's Medicine Ball Abdominal Program # 2

30s Break between the sets

1 Set on each Circuit

Week 2 Day 1

Barbell Wide Grip Upright Row 40s Break between the sets

55%14	60%12	65%10	70%10	75%8	80%6

Barbell Medium Grip From Hip High Pull Snatch

35s Break between the sets

50%10	55%10	65%10	70%8	75%8	80%6

Barbell Medium Grip Behind The Head Press

35s Break between the sets

50%10	55%10	60%10	65%10	75%8	75%8

Dumbbell Bent Over Row + "Kick Back " Triceps Curls

30s Break between the sets

40%14+10	50%10+8	45%12+8	65%10+8
60%10+8	75%8+6		

Barbell Lying on Bench on Your Back Pull Over

40s Break between the sets

50%10	60%10	65%1	70%10	75%8	80%8	85%6

Barbell Medium Grip Bench Press 45s Break between the sets

50%12	60%12	70%10	65%10	75%8	80%6

Parallel Bar Dips (With Waist Weight or Without)

60s Break between the sets

30%14	35%12	40%12	45%10	50%10	55%8 or

6 Sets X 14 Without Weight

Javorek's Barbell Complex 3

60s Break between the sets

50%1	55%1	60%1	50%1 55%1 60%1	

Barbell Back Squat Jump

50s Break between the sets

| 50%10 | 60%10 | 70%10 | 60%10 | 80%8 | 70%8 | 85%6 |

one Leg(Right) Up-Stairs Zig-Zag Bounding - Minimum 22-24 Stairs (2 Flights)

30s Break between the sets

3 Length on Each Circuit

one Leg(Left) Up-Stairs Zig-Zag Bounding - Minimum 22-24 Stairs (2 Flights)

30s Break between the sets

3 Length on Each Circuit

Up-Stairs Sprint - Minimum 22-24 Stairs (2 Flights)

30s Break between the sets

3 Length on Each Circuit

Javorek's Abdominal Program # 3

30s Break between the sets

1 Set on Each Circuit

Week 2 Day 2

Dumbbell Incline Bench Press   40s Break between the sets

| 60%10 | 65%10 | 70%10 | 75%8 | 80%8 | 85%6 |

Dumbbell Alternate Leg Step Ups - Double Steps Count

45s Break between the sets

| 50%12+12 | 55%12+12 | 60%10+10 | 65%10+10 |
| 60%10+10 | 65%10+10 | | |

Dumbbell Lateral Arm Raise

25s Break between the sets

| 40%14 | 45%12 | 50%12 | 55%10 | 60%8 | 65%6 |

High Bar Pronated Grip Behind The Head Pull Ups or Regular Chin-Ups Pull (With Weight or Without Weight)

60s Break between the sets

| 10%14 | 15%12 | 20%8 | 20%8 | 10%14 | 20%8 |
| or 6 Sets X 10 Without Weight | | | | | |

Barbell Medium Grip Behind The Head Press

40s Break between the sets

| 60%10 | 65%10 | 70%10 | 75%10 | 80%8 | 85%6 |

Dumbbell Lying on Bench Pull Over

35s Break between the sets

| 50%14 | 60%12 | 70%10 | 65%12 | 75%10 | 80%6 |

Dumbbell Push Press + Squat Jump Push Press

50s Break between the sets

| 50%6+6 | 60%6+6 | 70%5+5 | 75%4+4 | 80%3+3 | 80%3+3 |

Javorek's Dumbbell Complex 4

60s Break between the sets

| 50%1 | 55%1 | 60%1 | 55%1 | 60%1 | 65%1 |

Barbell Back Squat & Up on Toes

60s Break between the sets

| 50%10 | 70%6 | 60%10 | 80%4 | 60%12 | 85%4 |

Double Leg Up-Stairs Bounding - Minimum 22-24 Stairs (2 Flights)

30s Break between the sets

3 Length on Each Circuit

Double Leg Up-Stairs Zig-Zag Bounding - Minimum 22-24 Stairs (2 Flights)

3 Length on Each Circuit

Run-Jump & Sprint - Minimum 22-24 Stairs (2 Flights)

50s Break between the sets

3 Length on Each Circuit

Up-Stairs Sprint - Minimum 22-24 Stairs (2 Flights)

30s Break between the sets

3 Length on Each Circuit

Javorek's General Abdominal Program

| Ex.1-4 | Ex 5-8 | Ex 9-12 | Ex.13-16 | Ex. 17-20 | Ex. 21-24 |

Week 2 Day 3

Javorek's General Fitness Dumbbell Conditioning Program:

Dumbbell Up on Toes Upright Row

30s Break between the sets

| 60%10 | 65%10 | 70%8 | 75%8 | 80%6 | 80%6 |

Dumbbell Raise To Armpit + From Hip High Pull Snatch

35s Break between the sets

| 60%8+8 | 65%8+6 | 70%8+6 | 75%8+6 | 80%8+5 | 80%8+5 |

Dumbbell Press + Push Press + High Pull Snatch

40s Break between the sets

| 60%6+6+6 | 65%5+5+6 | 70%4+5+6 | 75%4+5+6 |
| 80%4+5+6 | | | |

Dumbbell Bent Over Row + Squat Push Press

40s Break between the sets

| 65%8+6 | 70%8+6 | 80%6+5 | 90%3+3 | 80%6+5 | 90%3+3 |

Dumbbell High Pull Snatch

40s Break between the sets

| 65%10 | 70%8 | 75%6 | 80%5 |
| 85%3 | 90%2 | | |

Dumbbell Up on Toes Upright Row + Push Press

40s Break between the sets

| 60%10+8 | 65%10+8 | 70%8+6 | 75%6+6 | 70%8+6 | 75%6+6 |

Dumbbell Parallel Curls + High Pull Snatch

40s Break between the sets

| 60%10+8 | 65%10+6 | 70%8+6 | 75%6+4 | 80%4+4 | 85%3+2 |

Dumbbell Push Press + Squat Jump Push Press

45s Break between the sets

| 60%8+6 | 65%8+6 | 70%8+4 | 75%6+4 | 70%8+4 | 75%6+4 |

Javorek's Dumbbell Complex 1.

60s Break between the sets

| 55%1 | 60%1 | 60%1 | — | — | — |

Javorek's Dumbbell Complex 2

60s Break between the sets

| — | — | — | 45%1 | 50%1 | 50%1 |

Barbell Front Squat

60s Break between the sets

| 50%10 | 60%10 | 70%10 | 65%10 | 75%6 | 80%4 |

Box Jump (The Height Must Be Individually Chosen)

30s Break between the sets

6 Sets X 10   Jumps or
6 Sets X 10 Tuck Jump

Javorek's Half & Half Abdominal Program # 1
1 Set

Week 3 Day 1

Dumbbell Up on Toes Upright Row

30s Break between the sets

| 50%12 | 60%10 | 65%10 | 70%10 | 80%6 | 85%4 |

Barbell Supinated (Regular) Curls

25s Break between the sets

| 50%14 | 60%12 | 70%10 | 65%12 | 80%6 | 85%4 |

Dumbbell Lying on Bench Pull Over

25s Break between the sets

| 50%14 | 55%12 | 60%12 | 65%12 | 70%10 | 80%6 |

Barbell Medium Grip Behind The Head Press

30s Break between the sets

| 60%12 | 65%12 | 70%10 | 75%8 | 80%6 | 85%3 |

Dumbbell Parallel Squat Push Press

30s Break between the sets

| 60%10 | 70%10 | 65%10 | 75%8 | 80%6 | 85%4 |

Barbell Overhead Triceps Curls

30s Break between the sets

| 60%12 | 65%12 | 70%10 | 75%8 | 80%6 | 85%4 |

High Bar Pronated Grip Behind The Head Pull Ups or Regular Chin-Ups Pull (With Weight or Without Weight)

50s Break between the sets

| 10%14 | 15%12 | 20%8 | 20%8 | 10%14 | 20%8 |

or 6 Sets X 10 Without Weight

Dumbbell Lateral Arm Raise

25s Break between the sets

| 50%14 | 50%14 | 60%12 | 55%12 | 60%12 | 65%10 |

on 6-8" Boxes Up & Down Plyo-Push Ups

45s Break between the sets

6 Sets X 8+8

Double Leg Up-Stairs Bounding - Minimum 22-24 Stairs (2 Flights)

30s Break between the sets

3 Length on Each Circuit

Run-Jump & Sprint - Minimum 22-24 Stairs (2 Flights)

45s Break between the sets

3 Length on Each Circuit

Up-Stairs Sprint - Minimum 22-24 Stairs (2 Flights)

60s Break between the sets

3 Length on Each Circuit

Javorek's Medicine Ball Abdominal Program # 2

30s Break between the sets

1 Set on Each Circuit

Week 3 Day 2

Barbell Narrow Grip Upright Row

35s Break between the sets

| 50%12 | 60%12 | 70%12 | 75%10 | 75%10 | 80%8 |

Barbell Medium Grip From Hip High Pull Snatch

35s Break between the sets

| 50%14 | 55%12 | 60%12 | 65%12 | 70%10 | 75%8 |

Barbell (Comfortable Width Grip) Behind The Head From Half Squat Press

35s Break between the sets

| 40%14 | 45%12 | 50%12 | 55%10 | 60%10 | 70%10 |

Barbell Wide Grip Upright Row

30s Break between the sets

| 55%12 | 60%10 | 55%12 | 65%10 | 70%10 | 75%8 |

Barbell Medium Grip Behind The Head Squat Push Press

40s Break between the sets

| 50%12 | 60%12 | 70%12 | 75%10 | 65%12 | 80%8 |

Barbell Supinated (Regular) Curls

25s Break between the sets

| 50%14 | 55%12 | 60%12 | 65%10 | 70%10 | 75%8 |

Parallel Bar Dips (With Waist Weight or Without)

50s Break between the sets

| 30%14 | 35%12 | 40%12 | 45%10 | 50%10 | 55%8 |

or 6 Sets X 14 Without Weight

on 6-8" Boxes Up & Down Plyo-Push Ups

40s Break between the sets

6 Sets X 8+8

Barbell Back Squat & Up on Toes

60s Break between the sets

| 50%12 | 60%8 | 55%12 | 75%6 | 65%12 | 80%6 |

Barbell Back Squat Jump

45s Break between the sets

| 40%8 | 50%6 | 45%8 | 50%6 | 55%4 | 60%4 |

Up-Stairs Sprint - Minimum 22-24 Stairs (2 Flights)

30s Break between the sets

3 Length on Each Circuit

Javorek's Abdominal Program # 3

30s Break between the sets

1 Set on Each Circuit

Week 3 Day 3

Dumbbell Lying on Back on Bench Fly

30s Break between the sets

| 45%14 | 50%12 | 55%12 | 60%10 | 65%10 | 70%10 |

Dumbbell Pronated Curls

30s Break between the sets

| 60%12 | 55%12 | 65%10 | 60%12 | 70%10 | 80%6 |

Dumbbell Up on Toes Upright Row

30s Break between the sets

| 60%12 | 65%10 | 70%10 | 75%8 | 65%10 | 80%6 |

Dumbbell Overhead, From Parallel To Linear, Rotational Press

30s Break between the sets

| 60%10 | 70%10 | 65%10 | 75%8 | 70%10 | 80%6 |

Dumbbell Lying on Bench Pull Over

30s Break between the sets

| 50%12 | 60%10 | 55%12 | 65%10 | 70%10 | 65%10 |

Dumbbell Bent Over Row + "Kick Back " Triceps Curls

30s Break between the sets

| 55%14+8 | 60%12+8 | 65%10+8 | 70%10+8 | 65%10+8 | 80%6+4 |

Dumbbell Alternate Leg Lunges - Double Steps Count

30s Break between the sets

| 60%20+20 | 65%18+18 | 70%16+16 | 75%16+16 |
| 80%14+14 | 80%14+14 | | |

Dumbbell Parallel Squat Push Press

30s Break between the sets

| 65%10 | 75%8 | 80%6 | 65%10 | 75%8 | 80%6 |

Dumbbell Alternate Leg Step Ups - Double Steps Count

30s Break between the sets

| 50%10+10 | 55%10+10 | 60%10+10 | 65%10+10 |
| 70%10+10 | 75%10+10 | | |

Barbell Back Squat Jump

45s Break between the sets

| 50%8 | 60%6 | 55%8 | 65%5 | 60%6 | 70%3 |

Double Leg Up-Stairs Bounding - Minimum 22-24 Stairs (2 Flights)

30s Break between the sets

6 Sets of 3 Length

one Leg(Right) Up-Stairs Bounding - Minimum 22-24 Stairs (2 Flights)

30s Break between the sets

6 Sets of 3 Length

one Leg(Left) Up-Stairs Bounding - Minimum 22-24 Stairs (2 Flights)

30s Break between the sets

6 Sets of 3 Length

Up-Stairs Sprint - Minimum 22-24 Stairs (2 Flights)

30s Break between the sets

6 Sets of 3 Length

Javorek's General Abdominal Program

| Ex.1-4 | Ex 5-8 | Ex 9-12 | Ex.13-16 | Ex. 17-20 | Ex. 21-24 |

Week 4 Day 1

Javorek's Dumbbell Program # 2:

Dumbbell Up on Toes Upright Row

30s Break between the sets

60%10	65%10	70%8	75%8	80%6

Dumbbell Raise To Armpit + From Hip High Pull Snatch

30s Break between the sets

60%8+8	60%8+8	65%8+6	70%8+6	75%8+6	80%8+5

Dumbbell Up on Toes Parallel Press + Parallel Push Press + High Pull Snatch

35s Break between the sets

60%6+6+6	65%5+5+6	70%4+5+6	75%4+5+6
80%4+5+6	80%4+5+6		

Dumbbell Bent Over Row + From Hip High Pull Snatch

35s Break between the sets

65%8+6	65%8+6	70%8+6	70%8+6	80%6+5	90%3+3

Dumbbell High Pull Snatch

30s Break between the sets

65%10	70%8	75%6	80%5	85%3	90%2

Dumbbell Up on Toes Upright Rows + From Hip High Pull Snatch

30s Break between the sets

60%10+6	65%10+6	70%8+6	75%6+4
70%8+6	75%6+4		

Dumbbell Parallel Curls + High Pull Snatch

30s Break between the sets

60%14+6	65%12+6	70%10+6	75%8+3
80%6+2	85%4+2		

Dumbbell Parallel Push Press + Parallel Squat Jump Push Press

30s Break between the sets

60%6+6	65%6+6	65%6+6	70%6+4	75%6+3	75%6+3

Javorek's Dumbbell Complex 3

60s Break between the sets

55%1	60%1	60%1	—	—	—

Javorek's Dumbbell Complex 4

60s Break between the sets

—	—	—	45%1	50%1	50%1

Barbell Front Squat

60s Break between the sets

50%10	55%10	60%10	65%10	70%10	75%8

Box Jump (The Height Must Be Individually Chosen)

60s Break between the sets

6 Sets X 10 Jumps or
6 Sets X 10 Tuck Jump

Double Leg Up-Stairs Zig-Zag Bounding - Minimum 22-24 Stairs (2 Flights)

60s Break between the sets

3 Length on Each Circuit

Run-Jump & Sprint - Minimum 22-24 Stairs (2 Flights)

60s Break between the sets

3 Length on Each Circuit

Up-Stairs Sprint - Minimum 22-24 Stairs (2 Flights)

30s Break between the sets

3 Length on Each Circuit

Javorek's Half & Half Abdominal Program # 1

30s Break between the sets

1 Set on Each Circuit

Week 4 Day 2

Barbell Supinated (Regular) Curls

40s Break between the sets

50%10	60%10	70%10	75%8	70%10	75%8

Barbell Medium Grip From Hip High Pull Snatch

40s Break between the sets

55%10	60%10	65%10	70%8	75%6	80%6

Barbell (Comfortable Width Grip) Behind The Head From Half Squat Press

40s Break between the sets

50%10	55%10	60%10	65%10	70%8	75%6

Barbell Overhead Triceps Curls

40s Break between the sets

50%12	60%10	55%10	65%10	70%10	75%8

Barbell Medium Grip Behind The Head Squat Push Press

40s Break between the sets

65%10	60%10	75%8	70%10	75%8	80%6

Barbell Lying on Bench on Your Back Pull Over

40s Break between the sets

55%12	60%10	65%10	70%10	75%8	80%6

Barbell Incline Bench Press

40s Break between the sets

60%10	65%10	75%8	80%6	70%10	80%6

Dumbbell Walk Lunges With 6 From Hip High Pull Snatch on Each Step - Double Steps Count

40s Break between the sets

50%20+20	60%20+20	55%20+20	65%20+20
60%20+20	70%20+20		

High Bar Pronated Grip Behind The Head Pull Ups or Regular Chin-Ups Pull (With Weight or Without Weight)

60s Break between the sets

10%14	15%12	20%8	20%8	10%14	20%8

or 6 Sets X 10 Without Weight

Barbell Back Squat Jump

60s Break between the sets

50%8	55%8	60%6	65%4	70%3	70%3

Double Leg Up-Stairs Bounding - Minimum 22-24 Stairs (2 Flights)

30s Break between the sets

3 Length on Each Circuit

Double Leg Up-Stairs Zig-Zag Bounding - Minimum 22-24 Stairs (2 Flights)

30s Break between the sets

3 Length on Each Circuit

Up-Stairs Sprint - Minimum 22-24 Stairs (2 Flights)

30s Break between the sets

3 Length on Each Circuit

Javorek's Abdominal Program # 3

1 Set on Each Circuit

Week 4 Day 3

Dumbbell Up on Toes Upright Row

20s Break between the sets

55%14	60%12	65%10	75%8	80%6	85%4

Dumbbell Pronated Curls

20s Break between the sets

55%12	60%12	65%10	70%8	75%8	80%6

Barbell Narrow Grip Upright Row

20s Break between the sets

65%12	70%10	70%10	75%8	65%12	75%8

Barbell Medium Grip Behind The Head Squat Push Press

30s Break between the sets

55%10	60%10	65%10	70%10	75%8	80%6

Dumbbell Alternate Leg Step Ups - Double Steps Count

30s Break between the sets

50%20+20	55%20+20	60%20+20	50%20+20
55%20+20	60%20+20		

Barbell Back Squat & Up on Toes

60s Break between the sets

60%12 70%10 65%10 75%8 70%10 80%6

Barbell Wave Squat(4 Wave + 1 Jump)
(4 Quarter Squat & Up on Toes +1 Quarter Squat Jump)

60s Break between the sets

40%40 45%40 50%40 55%40 60%35 65%30

Javorek's General Abdominal Program

30s Break between the sets

Ex.1-4 Ex 5-8 Ex 9-12 Ex.13-16 Ex. 17-20 Ex. 21-24

Up-Stairs Sprint - Minimum 22-24 Stairs (2 Flights)

30s Break between the sets

3 Length on Each Circuit

Week 5 Day 1
Javorek's Barbell Complex 3

60s Break between the sets

50%1 55%1 55%1 60%1 60%1 65%1

Barbell Front Squat

45s Break between the sets

50%10 55%10 60%10 65%10 70%8 75%6

Barbell Medium Grip Bench Press

40s Break between the sets

50%10 50%10 60%10 60%10 70%10 75%8

Parallel Bar Dips (With Waist Weight or Without)

60s Break between the sets

10%14 15%12 15%12 20%10 20%10 25%8
or 6 Sets X 14 Without Weight

on 6-8" Boxes Up & Down Plyo Push -Ups

60s Break between the sets

6 Sets X 8+8

Dumbbell Lateral Arm Raise

30s Break between the sets

40%14 45%12 50%12 55%10 50%10 65%10

Box Jump (The Height Must Be Individually Chosen)

30s Break between the sets

6 Sets X 10 Jumps
or 6 Sets X 10 Tuck Jump

Up-Stairs Sprint - Minimum 22-24 Stairs (2 Flights)

30s Break between the sets

3 Length on Each Circuit

Javorek's Half & Half Abdominal Program # 1
1 Set

Week 5 Day 2
Javorek's Dumbbell Program # 3:
Dumbbell Up on Toes Upright Row

30s Break between the sets

60%10 65%10 70%8 75%8 80%6 80%6

Dumbbell Raise To Armpit + From The Hip High Pull Snatch

30s Break between the sets

60%8 + 8	60%8 + 8	65%8 + 6	70%8 + 6
75%8 + 6	80%8 + 5		

Dumbbell Press + Push Press + Upright Row

40s Break between the sets

60%6+6+6	65%5+5+6	70%4+5+6	75%4+5+6
80%4+5+6	80%4+5+6		

Dumbbell Bent Over Row + Push Press

30s Break between the sets

65%8+6 65%8+6 70%8+6 80%6+5 90%5+3 90%5+3

Dumbbell Up on Toes Squat Push Press

40s Break between the sets

60%10 65%10 70%8 75%6 80%5 85%3

Dumbbell Bent Over Kick Back Triceps Curls

30s Break between the sets

40%14 50%12 55%12 60%10 65%10 70%8

Dumbbell Up on Toes Upright Row + Parallel Curls

30s Break between the sets

60%10+10 65%10+8 70%8+8 75%8+6 80%5+6 80%5+6

Dumbbell Regular(Supinated) Curls + Jump Push Press

40s Break between the sets

60%12+8 65%12+6 70%10+6 75%8+5 80%6+3 85%5+2

Dumbbell Press + Push Press + Squat Jump Push Press

40s Break between the sets

60%6+6+6	65%6+6+6	70%5+6+6	75%5+5+4
80%4+4+4	80%4+4+4		

Dumbbell Regular Curls X 10 + Upright Row X 8 + Press X 6 + Bent Over Row X 8 + Squat Push Press X 6

60s Break between the sets

70%1 75%1 75%1 75%10 75%1 75%1

Dumbbell Up on Toes Upright Row X 8 + Press X 6 + Regular Curls X 6 + Push Press X 6 + Upright Row X 8 + Squat Push Press X 6 + Squat Jump X 6 + Split Jump X 10

60s Break between the sets

70%1 75%1 75%1 75%10 75%1 75%1

Barbell Back Squat & Up on Toes

60s Break between the sets

60%10 70%10 65%10 75%6 85%5 90%2

Up-Stairs Sprint - Minimum 22-24 Stairs (2 Flights)

30s Break between the sets

3 Length on Each Circuit

Javorek's Medicine Ball Abdominal Program # 2

20s Break between the sets

1 Set on Each Circuit

Week 5 Day 3
Barbell Narrow Grip Upright Row

30s Break between the sets

60%10 70%10 75%8 80%6 85%6 85%5

Barbell Supinated (Regular) Curls

30s Break between the sets

50%12 60%10 70%8 80%6 80%6 85%5

Barbell Medium Grip Behind The Head Press

30s Break between the sets

50%10 60%10 65%10 70%10 75%8 80%6

Barbell Overhead Triceps Curls

40s Break between the sets

60%10 65%10 70%10 70%10 75%8 80%6

Dumbbell Walk Lunges With 6 From Hip High Pull Snatch on Each Step - Double Steps Count

40s Break between the sets

50%20+20	60%20+20	65%20+20	70%20+20
75%20+20	75%20+20		

Barbell Incline Bench Press

40s Break between the sets

65%10 70%10 75%8 75%8 80%6 85%4

Dumbbell Parallel Squat Push Press

40s Break between the sets

| 60%10 | 70%10 | 75%8 | 80%6 | 80%6 | 85%5 |

Barbell Front Squat

60s Break between the sets

| 60%10 | 65%10 | 70%8 | 75%6 | 80%5 | 85%3 |

Double Leg Up-Stairs Bounding - Minimum 22-24 Stairs (2 Flights)

30s Break between the sets

3 Length on Each Circuit

one Leg(Right) Up-Stairs Bounding - Minimum 22-24 Stairs (2 Flights)

30s Break between the sets

3 Length on Each Circuit

one Leg(Left) Up-Stairs Bounding - Minimum 22-24 Stairs (2 Flights)

30s Break between the sets

3 Length on Each Circuit

Up-Stairs Sprint - Minimum 22-24 Stairs (2 Flights)

30s Break between the sets

3 Length on Each Circuit

Javorek's Abdominal Program # 3

30s Break between the sets

1 Set on Each Circuit

Week 6 Day 1

Barbell Lying on Bench on Your Back Pull Over

40s Break between the sets

| 50%12 | 55%12 | 60%12 | 65%10 | 70%10 | 75%8 |

Barbell Supinated (Regular) Curls

30s Break between the sets

| 50%10 | 55%10 | 60%10 | 65%10 | 70%10 | 75%8 |

Barbell Medium Grip From Hip High Pull Snatch

40s Break between the sets

| 50%12 | 50%12 | 55%10 | 55%10 | 60%10 | 65%10 |

Dumbbell Lateral Arm Raise

30s Break between the sets

| 50%14 | 55%12 | 60%10 | 65%10 | 70%10 | 75%8 |

Barbell Overhead Triceps Curls

40s Break between the sets

| 50%12 | 55%12 | 60%12 | 65%10 | 70%10 | 75%8 |

Dumbbell Incline Bench Press

40s Break between the sets

| 60%12 | 65%12 | 70%10 | 70%10 | 75%8 | 75%8 |

Barbell Wave Squat(4 Wave + 1 Jump)

30s Break between the sets

| 60%40 | 65%40 | 70%35 | 70%35 | 75%30 | 75%30 |

Box Jump (The Height Must Be Individually Chosen)

30s Break between the sets

6 Sets X 12

Double Leg Up-Stairs Bounding - Minimum 22-24 Stairs (2 Flights)

30s Break between the sets

3 Length on Each Circuit

Run-Jump & Sprint - Minimum 22-24 Stairs (2 Flights)

40s Break between the sets

3 Length on Each Circuit

one Leg(Right) Up-Stairs Zig-Zag Bounding - Minimum 22-24 Stairs (2 Flights)

30s Break between the sets

3 Length on Each Circuit

one Leg(Left) Up-Stairs Zig-Zag Bounding - Minimum 22-24 Stairs (2 Flights)

30s Break between the sets

3 Length on Each Circuit

Up-Stairs Sprint - Minimum 22-24 Stairs (2 Flights)

60s Break between the sets

3 Length on Each Circuit

Javorek's General Abdominal Program

30s Break between the sets

| Ex.1-4 | Ex 5-8 | Ex 9-12 | Ex.13-16 | Ex. 17-20 | Ex. 21-24 |

Week 6 Day 2

Barbell Wide Grip Upright Row

40s Break between the sets

| 60%10 | 60%10 | 55%12 | 65%10 | 75%8 | 75%8 |

Dumbbell Pronated Curls

30s Break between the sets

| 50%10 | 55%10 | 60%10 | 65%10 | 70%10 | 80%6 |

Parallel Bar Dips (With Waist Weight or Without)

50s Break between the sets

| 15%14 | 15%12 | 20%12 | 25%10 | 25%10 | 30%8 |

or 6 Sets X 14 Without Weight

Barbell Lying on Bench on Your Back Pull Over

40s Break between the sets

| 45%14 | 50%12 | 55%10 | 60%10 | 65%10 | 75%8 |

on 6-8 Boxes Up & Down Plyo-Push Ups

60s Break between the sets

6 Sets X 8+8

Barbell Back Squat Jump

40s Break between the sets

| 50%8 | 55%8 | 60%6 | 65%5 | 70%3 | 50%8 | 75%3 |

Double Leg Up-Stairs Zig-Zag Bounding - Minimum 22-24 Stairs (2 Flights)

30s Break between the sets

3 Length on Each Circuit sets

one Leg (Right) Up-Stairs Bounding - Minimum 22-24 Stairs (2 Flights)

30s Break between the sets

3 Length on Each Circuit

one Leg (Left) Up-Stairs Bounding - Minimum 22-24 Stairs (2 Flights)

30s Break between the sets

3 Length on Each Circuit

Up-Stairs Sprint - Minimum 22-24 Stairs (2 Flights

30s Break between the sets

3 Length on Each Circuit5

Javorek's Half & Half Abdominal Program # 1
1 Set

Week 6 Day 3

Javorek's Barbell Complex 4

60s Break between the sets

| 50%1 | 60%1 | 70%1 | 60%1 | 65%1 | 70%1 |

Dumbbell Walk Lunges With 6 From Hip High Pull Snatch on Each Step - Double Steps Count

60s Break between the sets

| 50%20+20 | 60%20+20 7 | 0%20+20 | 75%20+20 |
| 70%20+20 | 75%20+20 | | |

Dumbbell Lateral Arm Raise

30s Break between the sets

| 60%12 | 60%12 | 70%12 | 75%10 | 80%8 | 80%8 |

High Bar Pronated Grip Behind The Head Pull Ups or Regular Chin-Ups Pull (With Weight or Without Weight)

60s Break between the sets

10%14	15%12	20%8	20%8	10%14	20%8

or 6 Sets X 10 Without Weight

Dumbbell Alternate Leg Step Ups - Double Steps Count

60s Break between the sets

50%14+14	60%14+14	65%14+14	70%14+14
70%12+12	75%12+12		

Barbell Back Squat & Up on Toes

60s Break between the sets

50%10	60%10	70%10	75%8	80%8	85%6

Box Jump (The Height Must Be Individually Chosen)

30s Break between the sets

6 Sets X 12

Double Leg Up-Stairs Bounding - Minimum 22-24 Stairs (2 Flights)

30s Break between the sets

3 Length on Each Circuit

Up-Stairs Sprint - Minimum 22-24 Stairs (2 Flights)

30s Break between the sets

3 Length on Each Circuit

Javorek's General Abdominal Program

Ex.1-4	Ex 5-8	Ex 9-12	Ex.13-16	Ex. 17-20	Ex. 21-24

Week 7 Day 1

Javorek's Dumbbell Complex 4

60s Break between the sets

55%1	60%1	65%1	65%1	70%1	75%1

Dumbbell Bent Over Row + "Kick Back " Triceps Curls

30s Break between the sets

60%12+10	60%12+10	70%12+8	75%10+8
80%8+6	80%8+6		

Dumbbell Walk Lunges With 6 From Hip High Pull Snatch on Each Step - Double Steps Count

45s Break between the sets

50%20+20	60%20+20	65%20+20	70%20+20
75%20+20	80%20+20		

Parallel Bar Dips (With Waist Weight or Without)

60s Break between the sets

25%10	25%10	30%10	30%10	35%10	40%10

6 Sets X 14 Without Weight

on 6-8 Boxes Up & Down Plyo-Push Ups

40s Break between the sets

6 Sets X 8+8

Barbell Front Squat

60s Break between the sets

50%10	60%10	65%10	70%10	65%10	75%8

Box Jump (The Height Must Be Individually Chosen)

40s Break between the sets

6 Sets X 12

one Leg(Right) Up-Stairs Bounding - Minimum 22-24 Stairs (2 Flights)

30s Break between the sets

3 Length on Each Circuit

one Leg(Left) Up-Stairs Bounding - Minimum 22-24 Stairs (2 Flights)

30s Break between the sets

3 Length on Each Circuit

Up-Stairs Sprint - Minimum 22-24 Stairs (2 Flights)

30s Break between the sets

3 Length on Each Circuit

Javorek's Abdominal Program # 3

30s Break between the sets

3   Sets

Week 7 Day 2

Javorek's General Fitness Dumbbell Conditioning Program:

Dumbbell Up on Toes Upright Row

30s Break between the sets

60%10	65%10	70%8	75%8	80%6	80%6

Dumbbell Raise To Armpit + From Hip High Pull Snatch

35s Break between the sets

60%8+8	60%8+8	65%8+6	70%8+6	75%8+6	80%8+5

Dumbbell Press + Push Press + High Pull Snatch

35s Break between the sets

60%6+6+6	65%5+5+6	70%4+5+6	75%4+5+6
80%4+5+6	80%4+5+6		

Dumbbell Bent Over Row + Squat Push Press

35s Break between the sets

65%8+8	65%8+8	70%8+6	80%8+6	90%6+3	90%6+3

Dumbbell High Pull Snatch

25s Break between the sets

65%10	70%8	75%6	80%5	85%3	90%2

Dumbbell Up on Toes Upright Row + Push Press

30s Break between the sets

60%10+8	65%10+8	70%8+6	75%6+6	70%8+6	75%6+

Dumbbell Parallel Curls + High Pull Snatch

30s Break between the sets

60%10+8	65%10+6	70%8+6	75%6+4	80%4+2	85%3+2

Dumbbell Push Press + Squat Jump Push Press

45s Break between the sets

60%8+6	65%8+6	65%8+6	70%8+4	75%6+4	75%6+4

Javorek's Dumbbell Complex 1

40s Break between the sets

55%1	60%1	60%1	—	—	—

Javorek's Dumbbell Complex 2

40s Break between the sets

—	—	—	45%1	50%1	50%1

Barbell Back Squat Jump

60s Break between the sets

60%10	70%10	65%6	75%8	80%6	80%6

Double Leg Up-Stairs Bounding - Minimum 22-24 Stairs (2 Flights)

30s Break between the sets

3 Length on Each Circuit

Double Leg Up-Stairs Zig-Zag Bounding - Minimum 22-24 Stairs (2 Flights)

60s Break between the sets

3 Length on Each Circuit

Run-Jump & Sprint - Minimum 22-24 Stairs (2 Flights)

30s Break between the sets

3 Length on Each Circuit

Javorek's General Abdominal Program

30s Break between the sets

1 Set

Week 7 Day 3

Barbell Lying on Bench on Your Back Pull Over

40s Break between the sets

65%10	75%10	80%8	75%8	85%6	85%6

Barbell Medium Grip Bench Press

60s Break between the sets

65%10	75%10	70%10	80%6	80%6	85%6

Barbell Supinated (Regular) Curls

40s Break between the sets

60%12	65%10	70%10	75%8	80%6	85%6

High Bar Pronated Grip Behind The Head Pull Ups or Regular Chin-Ups Pull (With Weight or Without Weight)

60s Break between the sets

10%14	15%12	20%8	20%8	10%14	20%8

or
6 Sets X 10 Without Weight

on 6-8 Boxes Up & Down Plyo-Push Ups

60s Break between the sets

6 Sets X 8+8

Barbell Wave Squat(4 Wave + 1 Jump)

45s Break between the sets

60%40	65%40	70%30	75%25	80%20	85%15

Box Jump (The Height Must Be Individually Chosen)

40s Break between the sets

6 Sets X 14

Up-Stairs Sprint - Minimum 22-24 Stairs (2 Flights)

30s Break between the sets

3 Length on Each Circuit

Javorek's Half & Half Abdominal Program # 1

30s Break between the sets

3 Sets

Week 8 Day 1

Barbell Narrow Grip Upright Row

30s Break between the sets

65%10	70%10	75%8	80%6	85%6	85%6

Barbell Overhead Triceps Curls

30s Break between the sets

60%12	65%10	70%10	75%8	75%8	80%6

Dumbbell Bent Over Row + Push Press

30s Break between the sets

60%10+10	65%10+10	70%10+10	75%8+8
80%6+6	85%5+5		

Barbell Supinated (Regular) Curls

25s Break between the sets

60%10	65%10	70%10	75%8	80%6	85%6

Dumbbell Up on Toes Upright Row + Parallel Curls

30s Break between the sets

60%10+10	65%10+10	70%10+10	75%8+8
80%6+6	85%5+5		

Barbell Wide Grip Upright Row

30s Break between the sets

55%12	65%10	75%8	70%10	80%6	75%8	85%5

on 6-8 Boxes Up & Down Plyo-Push Ups

60s Break between the sets

6 Sets X 8+8

Barbell Back Squat & Up on Toes

60s Break between the sets

65%10	70%10	75%8	80%6	70%10	85%3

Double Leg Up-Stairs Bounding - Minimum 22-24 Stairs (2 Flights)

30s Break between the sets

3 Length on Each Circuit

one Leg(Right) Up-Stairs Bounding - Minimum 22-24 Stairs (2 Flights)

30s Break between the sets

3 Length on Each Circuit

one Leg(Left) Up-Stairs Bounding - Minimum 22-24 Stairs (2 Flights)

30s Break between the sets

3 Length on Each Circuit

Up-Stairs Sprint - Minimum 22-24 Stairs (2 Flights)

30s Break between the sets

3 Length on Each Circuit

Javorek's Medicine Ball Abdominal Program # 2

30s Break between the sets

1 Set on Each Circuit

Week 8 Day 2

Dumbbell Lying on Back on Bench Fly

30s Break between the sets

50%14	55%12	60%12	70%10	75%10	85%5

Barbell Wide Grip Bent Over Row

30s Break between the sets

55%12	65%10	75%8	70%10	80%6	90%4

Dumbbell Walk Lunges With 6 From Hip High Pull Snatch on Each Step - Double Steps Count

40s Break between the sets

60%20+20	65%20+20	70%20+20	75%20+20
80%20+20	85%20+20	85%20+20	

Dumbbell Parallel Bench Press

40s Break between the sets

70%10	75%10	80%6	75%8	85%5	90%3

Javorek's Dumbbell Complex 3

60s Break between the sets

55%1	55%1	60%1	65%1	70%1	70%1

High Bar Pronated Grip Behind The Head Pull Ups or Regular Chin-Ups Pull (With Weight or Without Weight)

60s Break between the sets

10%14	20%12	25%8	30%8	10%14	30%8

or 6 Sets X 10 Without Weight

Dumbbell Incline Bench Press

45s Break between the sets

70%10	75%10	80%6	75%8	85%5	90%3	90%3

Javorek's Barbell Complex 4

60s Break between the sets

50%1	50%1	55%1	55%1	60%1	60%1	65%1

Barbell Back Squat & Up on Toes

50s Break between the sets

70%10	75%10	80%6	75%8	85%5	90%3	90%3

Up-Stairs Sprint - Minimum 22-24 Stairs (2 Flights)

15s Break between the sets between the sets

6 Sets of 3 Length

Javorek's Abdominal Program # 3

30s Break between the sets

6 Sets

Week 8 Day 3

Barbell Wide Grip Upright Row
30s Break between the sets

| 60%12 | 70%10 | 80%8 | 75%8 | 85%6 | 90%4, |

Barbell Front Squat
45s Break between the sets

| 55%10 | 65%10 | 75%8 | 70%10 | 80%6 | 85%6 |

Dumbbell Pronated Curls
40s Break between the sets

| 70%10 | 60%12 | 80%10 | 70%10 | 85%6 | 90%4 |

Barbell Wide Grip Bent Over Row
40s Break between the sets

| 60%14 | 65%12 | 70%12 | 75%10 | 80%6 | 90%4 |

Dumbbell Bent Over Row + "Kick Back " Triceps Curls
40s Break between the sets

| 60%14+10 | 70%12+10 | 65%12+8 | 75%10+8 |
| 80%8+6 | 90%4 +3 | | |

Dumbbell Alternate Leg Step Ups - Double Steps Count
60s Break between the sets

| 50%20+20 | 50%20+20 | 55%20+20 | 60%20+20 |
| 70%20+20 | 80%20+20 | | |

Javorek's Dumbbell Complex 3
45s Break between the sets

| 55%1 | 55%1 | 60%1 | 65%1 | 65%1 | 70%1 |

Dumbbell Lateral Arm Raise
30s Break between the sets

| 60%14 | 65%12 | 65%12 | 70%10 | 75%8 | 80%6 |

Barbell Back Squat Jump
45s Break between the sets

| 60%10 | 65%10 | 70%6 | 70%4 | 75%5 | 80%3 |

Barbell Wave Squat(4 Wave + 1 Jump)
40s Break between the sets

| 70%25 | 70%25 | 75%25 | 75%25 | 80%20 | 80%20 |

Box Jump (The Height Must Be Individually Chosen)
30s Break between the sets

6 Sets X 14 Jumps
or 6 Sets X 14 Tuck Jump

Up-Stairs Sprint - Minimum 22-24 Stairs (2 Flights)
30s Break between the sets

6 Sets of 3 Length

Javorek's General Abdominal Program
30s Break between the sets

1 Set

Week 9 Day 1

Barbell Narrow Grip Upright Row
40s Break between the sets

| 70%10 | 75%8 | 70%10 | 75%8 | 80%6 | 80%6 |

Barbell Medium Grip From Hip High Pull Snatch
40s Break between the sets

| 60%10 | 65%10 | 70%10 | 75%8 | 80%8 | 85%6 |

Barbell Incline Bench Press
40s Break between the sets

| 70%10 | 75%8 | 70%10 | 75%8 | 80%6 | 80%6 |

Barbell Medium Grip Behind The Head Press
40s Break between the sets

| 60%10 | 65%10 | 70%8 | 75%6 | 80%6 | 85%5 |

Dumbbell Walk Lunges With 6 From Hip High Pull Snatch on Each Step - Double Steps Count
40s Break between the sets

| 65%20+20 | 75%20+20 | 65%20+20 | 75%20+20 |
| 80%20+20 | 80%20+20 | | |

Barbell Medium Grip Bench Press
40s Break between the sets

| 50%14 | 70%12 | 60%12 | 80%6 | 70%10 | 85%5 |

Barbell Medium Grip Behind The Head Squat Push Press
40s Break between the sets

| 60%10 | 65%10 | 70%10 | 75%8 | 80%6 | 85%4 |

High Bar Pronated Grip Behind The Head Pull Ups or Regular Chin-Ups Pull (With Weight or Without Weight)
60s Break between the sets

| 20%10 | 20%10 | 20%10 | 25%10 | 25%8 | 30%6 |

or 6 Sets of 10

on 6-8 Boxes Up & Down Plyo-Push Ups
60s Break between the sets

6 Sets X 8+8

Dumbbell Overhead, From Parallel To Linear, Rotational Press
30s Break between the sets

| 60%12 | 70%12 | 60%12 | 80%6 | 70%10 | 80%6 |

Barbell Back Squat & Up on Toes
60s Break between the sets

| 50%14 | 70%8 | 65%12 | 80%6 | 70%10 | 85%5 |

Box Jump (The Height Must Be Individually Chosen)
60s Break between the sets

6 Sets X 10   Jumps
or 6 Sets X 10 Tuck Jump

Double Leg Up-Stairs Bounding - Minimum 22-24 Stairs (2 Flights)
30s Break between the sets

3 Length on Each Circuit

one Leg(Right) Up-Stairs Zig-Zag Bounding - Minimum 22-24 Stairs (2 Flights)
30s Break between the sets

3 Length on Each Circuit

one Leg(Left) Up-Stairs Zig-Zag Bounding - Minimum 22-24 Stairs (2 Flights)
30s Break between the sets

3 Length on Each Circuit

Up-Stairs Sprint - Minimum 22-24 Stairs (2 Flights)
30s Break between the sets

3 Length on Each Circuit

Javorek's Half & Half Abdominal Program # 1
30s Break between the sets

1 Set on Each Circuit

Week 9 Day 2

Javorek's Dumbbell Program # 2:

Dumbbell Up on Toes Upright Row
30s Break between the sets

| 60%10 | 65%10 | 70%8 | 75%8 | 80%6 | 80%6 |

Dumbbell Raise To Armpit + From Hip High Pull Snatch
30s Break between the sets

| 60%8+8 | 60%8+8 | 65%8+6 | 70%8+6 |
| 75%8+6 | 80%8+5 | | |

Dumbbell Up on Toes Parallel Press + Parallel Push Press + High Pull Snatch
35s Break between the sets

| 60%6+6+6 | 65%5+5+6 | 70%4+5+6 | 75%4+5+6 |
| 80%4+5+6 | 80%4+5+6 | | |

Dumbbell Bent Over Row + From Hip High Pull Snatch
35s Break between the sets

| 65%8+6 | 65%8+6 | 70%8+6 | 80%6+5 | 90%3+3 |

Dumbbell High Pull Snatch

					30s Break between the sets
65%10	70%8	75%6	80%5	85%3	90%2

Dumbbell Up on Toes Upright Rows + From Hip High Pull Snatch

					40s Break between the sets
60%10+6	65%10+6	70%8+6	75%6+4	70%8+6	75%6+4

Dumbbell Parallel Curls + High Pull Snatch

					40s Break between the sets
60%14+6	65%12+6	70%10+6	75%8+3	80%6+2	85%4+2

Dumbbell Parallel Push Press + Parallel Squat Jump Push Press

					40s Break between the sets
60%6+6	65%6+6	65%6+6	70%6+4	75%6+3	75%6+3

Javorek's Dumbbell Complex 3

		60s Break between the sets
50%1	60%1	

Javorek's Dumbbell Complex 4 60s Break between the sets
40%1 50%1

Barbell Back Squat & Up on Toes   60s Break between the sets
65%10   70%10   75%8   80%6   85%4

Up-Stairs Sprint - Minimum 22-24 Stairs (2 Flights)

30s Break between the sets

3 Length on Each Circuit

Javorek's Medicine Ball Abdominal Program # 2

30s Break between the sets

1 Set

Week 9 Day 3
Dumbbell Lying on Back on Bench Fly

				20s Break between the sets
60%14	70%12	80%8	80%8	

Dumbbell Pronated Curls

				30s Break between the sets
60%12	70%10	80%8	80%8	

Dumbbell Alternate Leg Lunges - Double Steps Count

			40s Break between the sets
70%14+14	75%12+12	80%12+12	80%10+10

Barbell Medium Grip From Hip High Pull Snatch

				40s Break between the sets
70%10	75%10	80%6	85%5	

Dumbbell Parallel Squat Push Press

				40s Break between the sets
65%10	75%10	85%4	85%5	

Dumbbell Walk Lunges With 6 From Hip High Pull Snatch on Each Step - Double Steps Count

			60s Break between the sets
70%20+20	75%18+18	80%16+16	80%16+16

Dumbbell Parallel Bench Press

				45s Break between the sets
60%12	70%10	80%8	90%3	

Dumbbell Alternate Leg Step Ups - Double Steps Count

			40s Break between the sets
70%16+16	75%14+14	80%12+12	85%10+10

Barbell Front Squat

				60s Break between the sets
65%10	70%8	75%6	80%5	

Javorek's Dumbbell Complex 3

				60s Break between the sets
60%1	65%1	70%1	70%1	

High Bar Pronated Grip Behind The Head Pull Ups or Regular Chin-Ups Pull (With Weight or Without Weight)

				60s Break between the sets
10%14	15%12	20%8	20%8	
or 4 Sets X 10 Without Weight				

Dumbbell Incline Bench Press

				40s Break between the sets
65%10	75%10	85%4	85%5	

Javorek's Dumbbell Complex IV

				60s Break between the sets
60%1	65%1	70%1	70%1	

Barbell Back Squat & Up on Toes

				60s Break between the sets
60%12	70%10	80%8	90%3	

Up-Stairs Sprint - Minimum 22-24 Stairs (2 Flights)

30s Break between the sets

4 Sets of 3 Length

Javorek's Abdominal Program # 3
1 Set

Week 10 Day 1
Dumbbell Up on Toes Upright Row

				30s Break between the sets
65%12	75%10	85%6	85%6	

Dumbbell Pronated Curls

				30s Break between the sets
65%12	75%8	80%6	85%4	

Barbell Incline Bench Press

				40s Break between the sets
70%10	80%6	75%8	85%5	

Barbell Wide Grip Bent Over Row

				30s Break between the sets
70%10	75%8	70%10	85%6	

Dumbbell Bent Over Row + "Kick Back " Triceps Curls

			30s Break between the sets
65%12 +10	75%8+8	80%6+6	80%6+6

Dumbbell Walk Lunges With 6 From Hip High Pull Snatch on Each Step - Double Steps Count

			40s Break between the sets
60%20+20	70%18+18	80%16+16	85%14+14

Barbell Medium Grip From Hip High Pull Snatch

				40s Break between the sets
60%10	70%10	80%6	85%6	

Barbell Medium Grip Behind The Head Press

				40s Break between the sets
60%10	70%10	75%8	80%6	

Barbell Medium Grip Behind The Head Squat Push Press

				40s Break between the sets
65%10	75%10	80%6	85%4	

Barbell Medium Grip Bench Press

				60s Break between the sets
70%8	75%6	80%8	85%6	

Dumbbell Alternate Leg Step Ups - Double Steps Count

			60s Break between the sets
65%14+14	75%12+12	80%10+10	85%10+10

Javorek's Dumbbell Complex IV

				60s Break between the sets
60%1	65%1	70%1	70%1	

Barbell Back Squat & Up on Toes

60s Break between the sets

65%10   80%6   70%10   85%12

Box Jump (The Height Must Be Individually Chosen)

60s Break between the sets

4 Sets X 12

Double Leg Up-Stairs Bounding - Minimum 22-24 Stairs (2 Flights)

15s Break between the sets

4 Sets of 3 Length

Up-Stairs Sprint - Minimum 22-24 Stairs (2 Flights)

15s Break between the sets

4 Sets of 3 Length

Javorek's Abdominal Program # 3
1 Set

Week 10 Day 2
Dumbbell Lying on Back on Bench Fly

30s Break between the sets

65%14   75%10   85%6   85%6

Barbell Supinated (Regular) Curls

30s Break between the sets

70%10   80%6   85%5   85%5

Dumbbell Alternate Leg Lunges - Double Steps Count

30s Break between the sets

70%20+20   75%18+18   75%18+18   80%14+14

Barbell Medium Grip From Hip High Pull Snatch

30s Break between the sets

75%8   80%6   55%8   85%5

Dumbbell Parallel Squat Push Press

30s Break between the sets

70%10   75%8   80%6   85%6

Dumbbell Walk Lunges With 6 From Hip High Pull Snatch on Each Step - Double Steps Count

40s Break between the sets

70%20+20   75%16+16   80%12+12   80%12+12

Barbell Lying on Bench on Your Back Pull Over

30s Break between the sets

65%12   70%10   75%10   80%6

Barbell Overhead Triceps Curls

30s Break between the sets

60%12   70%10   80%6   85%6

High Bar Pronated Grip Behind The Head Pull Ups or Regular Chin-Ups Pull (With Weight or Without Weight)

60s Break between the sets

10%14   15%12   20%8   20%8
or 4 Sets X 10 Without Weight

Javorek's Dumbbell Complex 3 60s Break between the sets
55%1   60%1   65%1 70%1

Dumbbell Incline Bench Press

45s Break between the sets

70%10   75%8   80%6   85%5

Javorek's Barbell Complex 4

60s Break between the sets

50%1   55%1   60%1   60%1

Barbell Back Squat Jump

50s Break between the sets

45%10   50%10   60%6   65%6

Double Leg Up-Stairs Zig-Zag Bounding - Minimum 22-24 Stairs (2 Flights)

15s Break between the sets

4 Sets of 3 Length

Up-Stairs Sprint - Minimum 22-24 Stairs (2 Flights)

15s Break between the sets

4 Sets of 3 Length

Javorek's Abdominal Program # 3
1 Set

Week 10 Day 3
Dumbbell Up on Toes Upright Row

30s Break between the sets

75%10   75%10   80%6   85%4

Dumbbell Lying on Back on Bench Fly

30s Break between the sets

70%10   75%10   80%6   85%6

Barbell Incline Bench Press

30s Break between the sets

75%10   80%8   85%6   90%3

Barbell Wide Grip Bent Over Row

30s Break between the sets

70%10   80%8   75%10   85%6

Dumbbell Bent Over Row + "Kick Back " Triceps Curls

30s Break between the sets

70%10+10   70%10+10   80%6+6   85%6+4

Dumbbell Walk Lunges With 6 From Hip High Pull Snatch on Each Step - Double Steps Count.

40s Break between the sets

70%20+20   75%18+18   80%16+16   80%16+16

Barbell Medium Grip From Hip High Pull Snatch

30s Break between the sets

60%12   70%10   80%6   85%6

Barbell Medium Grip Bench Press

50s Break between the sets

75%10   80%8   85%6   90%3

Barbell Medium Grip Behind The Head Press

40s Break between the sets

75%6   80%6   85%3   85%6

Barbell (Comfortable Width Grip) Behind The Head From Half Squat Press

50s Break between the sets

60%10   65%10   70%10   75%8

Dumbbell Alternate Leg Step Ups - Double Steps Count.

60s Break between the sets

70%20+20   75%18+18   80%16+16   80%14+14

Barbell Lying on Bench on Your Back Pull Over

30s Break between the sets

65%10   75%8   70%10   80%6

Barbell Medium Grip Behind The Head Squat Push Press

40s Break between the sets

70%10   75%8   80%6   85%6

Javorek's Dumbbell Complex 4

60s Break between the sets

55%1   60%1   60%1   70%1

Javorek's Barbell Complex 4

60s Break between the sets

55%1   60%1   60%1   70%1

Barbell Back Squat & Up on Toes

60s Break between the sets

70%10   55%12   80%4   85%5

Box Jump (The Height Must Be Individually Chosen)

4 Sets X 10 Jumps
or 4 Sets X 10 Tuck Jump

60s Break between the sets

Up-Stairs Sprint - Minimum 22-24 Stairs (2 Flights)

4 Sets of 3 Length

Javorek's Abdominal Program # 3

15s Break between the sets

4 Sets

15s Break between the sets

Week 11 Day 1

Dumbbell Up on Toes Upright Row

30s Break between the sets

70%12	80%8	85% 6	85%6

Barbell Wide Grip Upright Row

30s Break between the sets

65%10	75%10	85%6	85%6

Dumbbell Alternate Leg Lunges - Double Steps Count

60s Break between the sets

70%20+20	75%20+20	80%14+14	80%14+14

Barbell Supinated (Regular) Curls

30s Break between the sets

70%10	75%10	80%6	85%6

Barbell Medium Grip From Hip High Pull Snatch

30s Break between the sets

70%10	75%10	80%6	85%6

Dumbbell Walk Lunges With 6 From Hip High Pull Snatch on Each Step - Double Steps Count

40s Break between the sets

70%20+20	75%18+18	80%16+16	80%16+16

Dumbbell Parallel Squat Push Press

30s Break between the sets

70%10	80%8	90%4	90%4

Dumbbell Lying on Bench Pull Over

30s Break between the sets

70%10	70%10	80%6	80%6

High Bar Pronated Grip Behind The Head Pull Ups or Regular Chin-Ups Pull (With Weight or Without Weight)

60s Break between the sets

10%14	15%12	20%8	20%8
or 4 Sets X Without Weight			

Dumbbell Incline Bench Press

40s Break between the sets

70%12	80%6	85%4	85%4

Dumbbell Parallel Bench Press

40s Break between the sets

70%12	80%6	85%4	90%3

Javorek's Dumbbell Complex 3

60s Break between the sets

55%1	60%1	65%1	70%1

Javorek's Barbell Complex 3

60s Break between the sets

55%1	60%1	65%1	70%1

Barbell Wave Squat(4 Wave + 1 Jump)

60s Break between the sets

70%40	80%35	85%30	85%30

one Leg(Right) Up-Stairs Bounding - Minimum 22-24 Stairs (2 Flights)

15s Break between the sets

4 Sets of 3 Length

one Leg(Left) Up-Stairs Bounding - Minimum 22-24 Stairs (2 Flights)

15s Break between the sets

4 Sets of 3 Length

Up-Stairs Sprint - Minimum 22-24 Stairs (2 Flights)

15s Break between the sets

4 Sets of 3 Length

Javorek's Half & Half Abdominal Program # 1

30s Break between the sets

4 Sets

Week 11 Day 2

Dumbbell Lying on Back on Bench Fly

30s Break between the sets

70%12	75%10	80%6	80%6

Dumbbell Lying on Bench Pull Over

30s Break between the sets

65%12	65%12	75%8	80%6

Dumbbell Parallel Bench Press

30s Break between the sets

60%12	65%10	70%10	75%8

Parallel Bar Dips (With Waist Weight or Without)

60s Break between the sets

30%14	35%12	40%12	45%10
or 4 Sets X 14 Without Weight			

High Bar Pronated Grip Behind The Head Pull Ups or Regular Chin-Ups Pull (With Weight or Without Weight)

60s Break between the sets

10%10	15%100	20%8	20%8
or 4 Sets X 10 Without Weight			

Javorek's Dumbbell Complex 3

60s Break between the sets

55%1	60%1	65%1	70%1

Javorek's Barbell Complex 4

60s Break between the sets

55%1	60%1	65%1	70%1

Barbell Back Squat & Up on Toes

60s Break between the sets

70%12	75%8	80%3	80%5

Box Jump (The Height Must Be Individually Chosen)

60s Break between the sets

4 Sets X 10
or 4 Sets X 10 Tuck Jump

Up-Stairs Sprint - Minimum 22-24 Stairs (2 Flights)

30s Break between the sets

4 Sets of 3 Length

Javorek's Abdominal Program # 3

30s Break between the sets

4 Sets

Week 11 Day 3

Javorek's Dumbbell Program # 3:

Dumbbell Up on Toes Upright Row

40s Break between the sets

| 65%10 | 75%10 | 80%6 | 85%5 | 90%4 | 90%4 |

Dumbbell Raise To Armpit + From The Hip High Pull Snatch 40s Break between the sets

| 60%8+8 | 70%8+6 | 75%8+5 | 80%8+4 | 75%8+6 | 85%8+5 |

Dumbbell Press + Push Press + Upright Row

40s Break between the sets

| 70%6+6+6 | | 75%5+5+6 | 80%4+5+6 | 85%3+4+5 |
| 90%3+3+3 | | 90%3+3+3 | | |

Dumbbell Bent Over Row + Push Press

40s Break between the sets

| 65%8+6 | 65%8+6 | 70%8+6 | 80%6+5 | 90%5+3 | 90%5+3 |

Dumbbell Up on Toes Squat Push Press

50s Break between the sets

| 65%10 | 70%8 | 75%6 | 80%5 | 85%4 | 90%3 |

Dumbbell Bent Over+ Kick Back Triceps Curls

30s Break between the sets

| 70%10+10 | 75%10+8 | 80%8+6 | 80%6+4 |
| 90%4+4 | 90%4+4 | | |

Dumbbell Up on Toes Upright Row + Parallel Curls

30s Break between the sets

| 70%10+10 | 75%10+8 | 80%8+6 | 80%6+4 |
| 90%4+4 | 90%4+4 | | |

Dumbbell Regular(Supinated) Curls + Jump Push Press

40s Break between the sets

| 60%12+8 | 65%12+6 | 70%10+6 | 75%8+5 | 80%6+3 | 85%5+2 |

Dumbbell Press + Push Press + Squat Jump Push Press

40s Break between the sets

| 60%6+6+6 | | 65%6+6+6 | 65%6+6+6 | 70%5+6+6 |
| 75%5+5+4 | | 80%4+4+4 | | |

Dumbbell Regular Curls X 10 + Upright Row X 8 + Press X 6 + Bent Over Row X 8 + Squat Push Press X 6

60s Break between the sets

| 70%1 | 75%1 | 75%1 | 75%1 | 75%1 | 75%1 |

Dumbbell Up on Toes Upright Row X 8 + Press X 6 + Regular Curls X 6 + Push Press X 6 + Upright Row X 8 + Squat Push Press X 6 + Squat Jump X 6 + Split Jump X 10

60s Break between the sets

| 70%1 | 75%1 | 75%1 | 75%1 | 75%1 | 75%1 |

Barbell Back Squat & Up on Toes

60s Break between the sets

| 70%10 | 65%10 | 75%6 | 85%5 | 80%3 | 90%2 |

Double Leg Up-Stairs Zig-Zag Bounding - Minimum 22-24 Stairs (2 Flights)

30s Break between the sets

3 Length on Each Circuit

Up-Stairs Sprint - Minimum 22-24 Stairs (2 Flights)

30s Break between the sets

3 Length on Each Circuit

Javorek's General Abdominal Program

| Ex.1-4 | Ex 5-8 | Ex 9-12 | Ex.13-16 | Ex. 17-20 | Ex. 21-24 |

Week 12 Day 1

Dumbbell Up on Toes Upright Row

40s Break between the sets

| 75%10 | 80%8 | 90%3 | 90%3 |

Barbell Medium Grip Behind The Head Squat Push Press

40s Break between the sets

| 75%10 | 85%6 | 90%3 | 90%3 |

Dumbbell Bent Over Row + "Kick Back " Triceps Curls

30s Break between the sets

| 70%10+10 | 80%8+8 | 90%3+3 | 90%3+3 |

Barbell Incline Bench Press

40s Break between the sets

| 80%8 | 85% 5 | 85% 5 | 90%3 |

Barbell Front Squat

60s Break between the sets

| 70%10 | 80%6 | 90%3 | 90%3 |

High Bar Pronated Grip Behind The Head Pull Ups or Regular Chin-Ups Pull (With Weight or Without Weight)

60s Break between the sets

| 10%14 | 15%12 | 20%8 | 20%8 |

or 4 Sets X 10 Without Weight

Dumbbell Incline Bench Press

40s Break between the sets

| 75%10 | 80%8 | 90%3 | 90%3 |

Dumbbell Alternate Leg Step Ups - Double Steps Count

50s Break between the sets

| 70%20+20 | 75%16+16 | 80%14+14 | 85%12+12 |

Dumbbell Lateral Arm Raise

30s Break between the sets

| 70%10 | 80%8 | 90%5 | 90%3 |

Javorek's Barbell Complex 3

60s Break between the sets

| 60%1 | 65%1 | 70%1 | 70%1 |

Barbell Back Squat & Up on Toes

60s Break between the sets

70%10 80%8 90%3 90%3

Box Jump (The Height Must Be Individually Chosen)

60s Break between the sets

4 Sets X 10

or 4 Sets X 10 Tuck Jump

Double Leg Up-Stairs Bounding - Minimum 22-24 Stairs (2 Flights)

30s Break between the sets

4 Sets of 3 Length

Up-Stairs Sprint - Minimum 22-24 Stairs (2 Flights)

30s Break between the sets

4 Sets of 3 Length

Javorek's Half & Half Abdominal Program # 1

30s Break between the sets

4 Sets

Week 12 Day 2

Barbell Narrow Grip Upright Row 40s Break between the sets

70%8	80%6	85%5	85%5	90%3	90%3

Dumbbell Parallel Squat Push Press

40s Break between the sets

60%10	70%10	80%6	85%5	90%3	90%3

Dumbbell Press + Push Press + Squat Jump Push Press

45s Break between the sets

70%6+8+8	75%5+6+6	80%5+6+6	85%4+4+4
90%3+3+3	90%3+3+3		

Barbell Supinated (Regular) Curls

40s Break between the sets

70%10	75%8	80%4	85%6	90%3	95%4

Barbell Incline Bench Press

40s Break between the sets

70%8	80%6	85%5	85%5	90%3	90%3

High Bar Pronated Grip Behind The Head Pull Ups or Regular Chin-Ups Pull (With Weight or Without Weight)

60s Break between the sets

10%14	15%12	20%8	20%8	10%14	20%8

or 6 Sets X 10 Without Weight

Dumbbell Incline Bench Press

40s Break between the sets

70%8	80%6	85%5	85%5	90%3	90%3

Dumbbell Press + Push Press + Upright Row

60s Break between the sets

70%6+8+8	75%5+6+6	80%5+6+6	85%3+4+4
90%2+3+3	90%2+3+3		

Parallel Bar Dips (With Waist Weight or Without)

60s Break between the sets

55%12	60%12	70%10	55%12	65%12	70%8

or 6 Sets X 14

Javorek's Barbell Complex 3

60s Break between the sets

60%1	65%1	70%1	60%1	65%1	70%1

Barbell Back Squat & Up on Toes

60s Break between the sets

70%8	80%6	85%5	85%5	90%3	90%3

Double Leg Up-Stairs Bounding - Minimum 22-24 Stairs (2 Flights)

30s Break between the sets

3 Length on Each Circuit

Double Leg Up-Stairs Zig-Zag Bounding - Minimum 22-24 Stairs (2 Flights)

60s Break between the sets

6 Sets of 3 Length

Up-Stairs Sprint - Minimum 22-24 Stairs (2 Flights)

30s Break between the sets

6 Sets of 3 Length

Javorek's Abdominal Program # 3

Ex.1-4	Ex 5-8	Ex 9-12	Ex.13-16	Ex. 17-20	Ex. 21-24

Week 12 Day 3

Dumbbell Lying on Back on Bench Fly

40s Break between the sets

70%10	75%8	80%6	85%5	90%4	95%2

Dumbbell Parallel Squat Push Press

60s Break between the sets

60%10	70%10	80%6	85%5	90%3	95%2

Dumbbell Bent Over Row + "Kick Back " Triceps Curls

60s Break between the sets

70%10+10	75%10+10	80%8+8	85%6+4
90%4+3	95%2+2		

Barbell Lying on Bench on Your Back Pull Over

60s Break between the sets

60% 10	70%10	75%8	80%6	85%3	90%4

Barbell Medium Grip Bench Press

60s Break between the sets

60%12	80%6	70%10	90%3	80%8	95%2

Dumbbell Alternate Leg Step Ups - Double Steps Count

60s Break between the sets

70%20+20	75%18+18	80%16+16	85%12+12
90%10+10	90%10+10		

on 6-8" Boxes Up & Down Plyo Push - Ups

60s Break between the sets

6 Sets X 8+8

Javorek's Dumbbell Complex 3 60s Break between the sets

50%1	55%1	60%1	65%1	70%1	75%1

High Bar Pronated Grip Behind The Head Pull Ups or Regular Chin-Ups Pull (With Weight or Without Weight)

60s Break between the sets

10%14	15%12	20%8	20%8 10%14 20%8

or 6 Sets X 10 Without Weight

Barbell Back Squat & Up on Toes

60s Break between the set

60%10	70%10	80%6	85%4	90%1	90%2

Double Leg Up-Stairs Bounding - Minimum 22-24 Stairs (2 Flights)

30s Break between the sets

3 Length on Each Circuit

Up-Stairs Sprint - Minimum 22-24 Stairs (2 Flights) 30s Break between the sets

6 Sets of 3 Length

Javorek's Abdominal Program # 3

30s Break between the sets

3 Sets

General questions and answers:

A) Plyo-Push Ups: there are two variations

1- just the clapping push ups, when in the push up phase you separate your palms from the ground, (bouncing up) and clap your palms and continues the repetition

2- two very stable 10-12 inches boxes set wider than your shoulders: Start with your hands on the box - push up with an easy bounce and land between the boxes, perform the full push up and bounce back on the box. Perform the required repetition (6+6 for ex. Means that you perform six on the box + six on the floor!!!)

B) Exercise combination. For ex: Dumbbell Raise To Armpit x 8 + High Pull Snatch x 6, means you perform continuously 8 Raise to Armpit and continue with 6 High Pull Snatch

C) Complex exercises: perform in a continuous order as described without rest between the exercises. In case of Complex II and IV repeat from the beginning as many times described in the program.

D) Barbell behind The Head from half Squat or from Squat Press: get the start position, then press overhead followed by a leg extension. Reset the bar on your back and get back in the initial half squat or squat position. Repeat the same for each repetition.

Javorek's Conditioning - Heart Rate & Body Weight Chart

Day of Month :	1	2	3	4	5	6	7	8	9	10	11	12	13	14	15	16	17	18	19	20	21	22	23	24	25	26	27	28	29	30	31	Observation....
# Hours																																
Restless																																
Poor																																
Fair																																
Good																																
V.Good																																
Excell.																																

Javorek's Conditioning - Heart Rate & Body Weight Chart

Day of Month :	1	2	3	4	5	6	7	8	9	10	11	12	13	14	15	16	17	18	19	20	21	22	23	24	25	26	27	28	29	30	31	Observation...

| # Hours |
| Restless |
| Poor |
| Fair |
| Good |
| V.Good |
| Excell. |

Cycling Conditioning

157

Javorek's Conditioning - Heart Rate & Body Weight Chart

Day of Month :	1	2	3	4	5	6	7	8	9	10	11	12	13	14	15	16	17	18	19	20	21	22	23	24	25	26	27	28	29	30	31	Observation…

Hours
Restless
Poor
Fair
Good
V.Good
Excell.

Javorek's Conditioning - Heart Rate & Body Weight Chart

Day of Month :	1	2	3	4	5	6	7	8	9	10	11	12	13	14	15	16	17	18	19	20	21	22	23	24	25	26	27	28	29	30	31	Observation...

Hours
Restless
Poor
Fair
Good
V.Good
Excell.

Javorek's Conditioning - Heart Rate & Body Weight Chart

Day of Month:

	1	2	3	4	5	6	7	8	9	10	11	12	13	14	15	16	17	18	19	20	21	22	23	24	25	26	27	28	29	30	31	Observation….
H.Rate	x	x	x	x	x	x	x	x	x	x	x	x	x	x	x	x	x	x	x	x	x	x	x	x	x	x	x	x	x	x	x	
B.Weight	x	x	x	x	x	x	x	x	x	x	x	x	x	x	x	x	x	x	x	x	x	x	x	x	x	x	x	x	x	x	x	

Legend:
- **Heart Rate** — is an increasing tendency
- **Body Weight** — is an decreasing tendency
- = **OVERTRAINING OR ILLNESS**

	1	2	3	…	31	Observation….
# Hours						
Restless						
Poor						
Fair						
Good						
V.Good						
Excell.						

Javorek's "Challenger" Calisthenics Conditioning

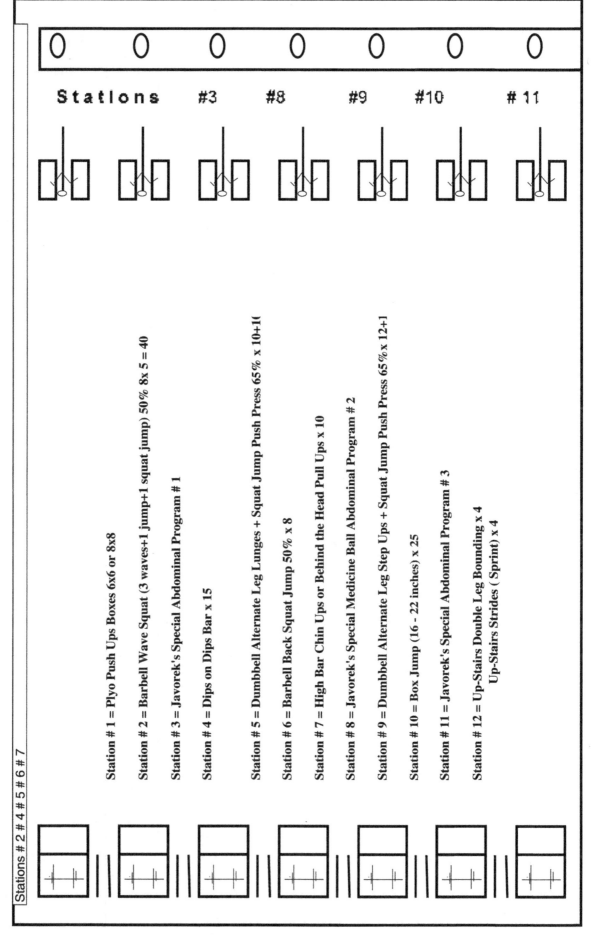

Stations #2 #4 #5 #6 #7

Stations   #3   #8   #9   #10   # 11

Station # 1 = Plyo Push Ups Boxes 6x6 or 8x8

Station # 2 = Barbell Wave Squat (3 waves+1 jump+1 squat jump) 50% 8x 5 = 40

Station # 3 = Javorek's Special Abdominal Program # 1

Station # 4 = Dips on Dips Bar x 15

Station # 5 = Dumbbell Alternate Leg Lunges + Squat Jump Push Press 65% x 10+10

Station # 6 = Barbell Back Squat Jump 50% x 8

Station # 7 = High Bar Chin Ups or Behind the Head Pull Ups x 10

Station # 8 = Javorek's Special Medicine Ball Abdominal Program # 2

Station # 9 = Dumbbell Alternate Leg Step Ups + Squat Jump Push Press 65% x 12+12

Station # 10 = Box Jump (16 - 22 inches) x 25

Station # 11 = Javorek's Special Abdominal Program # 3

Station # 12 = Up-Stairs Double Leg Bounding x 4
Up-Stairs Strides (Sprint) x 4

Daily Training Report

Date:_____

Nr.	Exercises	Set & Repetitions	Nr. Reps.	Nr. Sets	Load Volume	Average
1.						
2.						
3.						
4.						
5.						
6.						
7.						
8.						
9.						
10.						
	Total:					

Date:_____

Nr.	Exercises	Set & Repetitions	Nr. Reps.	Nr. Sets	Load Volume	Average
1.						
2.						
3.						
4.						
5.						
6.						
7.						
8.						
9.						
10.						
	Total:					

Charts

Weekly Cycle of Preparation

Year: **Month:** **Nr.** **Week:**

Monday	Tuesday	Wednesday	Thursday	Friday	Saturday	Sunday

Istvan "Steve" Javorek's Sport Videotapes & Programs

1. Javorek's Weightlifting & Dumbbell and Barbell Exercise techniques 3.35 minutes long DVD set. The exercises are demonstrated by Wesley Barnett, silver medalist at the 1997 World Weightlifting Championship, former multiple US national weightlifting champion and record holder and several performance athletes. These two DVDs provide a wide variety of Dumbbell and Barbell exercise techniques and plyometrics demonstration on Javorek's Conditioning Hill. This is an encyclopedia of my exercises with unique DUAL video angles so you can really learn the technique.

2. Javorek's Personalized "24 week year-round" weightlifting program (includes 12 week preparatory period + 12 week competition period+ Week of Competition (Peaking,) programs.

3. Javorek's Personalized "Four days a week" weightlifting program

4. Javorek's Personalized Six Week Mesocycle Conditioning #1

5. Javorek's Personalized Six Week Mesocycle Conditioning # 2

6. Javorek's Personalized "Big Fun" Off Season Conditioning.

7. Javorek's Personalized for Power Athletes - Football 12 weeks 6 times/week "Big Fun" program.

8. Javorek's Personalized for Power Athletes - Football 12 weeks 6 times/week "Big Fun" program.

9. Javorek's Personalized 12 Weeks General Fitness # 1 program

10. Javorek's Personalized 12 Weeks Body Building Fitness Program -

11. Javorek's Personalized 12 Weeks General Cardio-Vascular and Endurance Program

12. Javorek's Personalized 12 Weeks Introduction to Big Fun Program -

13. Javorek's Personalized Tremendous Pleasure -General Fitness Program

14. Javorek's Personalized 12 Weeks Dumbbell General Fitness # 2 Program

15. Javorek's Personalized 12 Weeks Dumbbell Body Building # 2 Program

16. Javorek's Personalized 12 Weeks Barbell Body Building # 1 Program

17. Javorek's Personalized Swimming Conditioning Program

18. Javorek's Personalized Boxing Conditioning Program

19. Javorek's Personalized Wrestling Conditioning Program

20. Javorek's Elite athletes General Abdominal program with pictures Poster size

21. Javorek's Dumbbell Complex # 1 and Complex # 2 Poster

22. Javorek's Barbell Complex # 1 and Complex # 2 Poster

23. Conditioning Personalized Programs for different sports (Baseball, Cross Country, Sprinters-Jumpers, Wrestling, Softball, Tennis, Throwers, Boxing, Swimming, Cycling Conditioning, etc.)

24. Javorek's Personalized Bodybuilders "Whoop Ass" program

25. Javorek's Personalized Football Players, Power Atheltes "Whoop Ass" program

E-mail ijavorek@istvanjavorek.com, ijavorek@gmail.com
My business web page: www.istvanjavorek.com